# A Prologue to Studies
*in the* Fourth Gospel

# A Prologue to Studies *in the* Fourth Gospel

Its Independency, Issues, and Interpretations

Riku P. Tuppurainen

WIPF & STOCK · Eugene, Oregon

A PROLOGUE TO STUDIES IN THE FOURTH GOSPEL
Its Independency, Issues, and Interpretations

Copyright © 2021 Riku P. Tuppurainen. All rights reserved. Except for brief quotations in critical publications or reviews, no part of this book may be reproduced in any manner without prior written permission from the publisher. Write: Permissions, Wipf and Stock Publishers, 199 W. 8th Ave., Suite 3, Eugene, OR 97401.

Wipf & Stock
An Imprint of Wipf and Stock Publishers
199 W. 8th Ave., Suite 3
Eugene, OR 97401

www.wipfandstock.com

PAPERBACK ISBN: 978-1-7252-7309-2
HARDCOVER ISBN: 978-1-7252-7310-8
EBOOK ISBN: 978-1-7252-7311-5

05/10/21

Scripture taken from the NEW AMERICAN STANDARD BIBLE®, Copyright © 1960, 1962, 1963, 1968, 1971, 1972, 1973, 1975, 1977, 1995 by The Lockman Foundation. Used by permission.

To *Richard Lemmer*†
my doctoral mentor at UNISA,
with gratitude to his encouragement and
contribution on my journey with the Fourth Gospel.

# Contents

*Preface* | ix
*Abbreviations* | xiii

**Part One: Independency of the Fourth Gospel** | 1

1. Logos and Divine Identity of Jesus | 3
2. Jesus and Jewish Feasts and Ceremonies | 19
   *Jesus's Platform for His Identity Claims*
3. Moses in the Fourth Gospel | 46
   *Jesus's Identity Compared and Contrasted*
4. Jesus's Miracles and Works as Signs for Jesus's Identity | 62
5. "I Am" Sayings as Jesus's Identity Markers | 77
6. Father-Son Relationship | 93
   *Sharing the Same Identity*
7. The Spirit as Paraklētos | 107
   *Jesus as a Model*

**Part Two: Issues in the Fourth Gospel** | 127

8. Authorship, Place and Date of Writing, and Audience | 129
9. Language, Style and Literary Devices | 156
10. "Anti-Judaism" and "Anti-Jewish" Language | 181
11. The Fourth Evangelist's Jesus | 198
12. The Fourth Gospel among First Three | 226
13. The Fourth Gospel and Revelation | 245
14. Chapter 21 | 262
    *An Annexure?*

**Part Three: Interpretations of the Fourth Gospel** | 285

    15    Questions Every Reader of the Fourth Gospel Faces | 287

    16    A Very Short History of Interpretation | 306

    17    The Fourth Gospel as a Window | 320

    18    The Fourth Gospel as Mirror and Ornamental Glass | 336

    19    The Fourth Gospel as Stained Class | 352
           *Text as Lived, Living, and Livable*

    *Bibliography* | 367

# Preface

THIS VOLUME HAS MATURED over two decades during which I have had the great privilege of teaching the Fourth Gospel (FG) in church, college, and seminary settings on four different continents. In each teaching context, students have commented that the FG is their favorite Gospel because it is different from the other three Gospels or because it is easy to understand. The FG is indeed different from the Synoptic Gospels, but arguments to back up that understanding have often been artificial. As for the second reason for the students' preference, it is not true that the FG is easy to understand. The claim that the FG is easy to understand is often based on individual statements taken out from their context. To read statements and stories as a part of the Fourth Evangelist's rhetorical presentation and its historical context requires more work than one perhaps expects. Thus, there is a need for a book that paints a big picture of the FG. This volume aims to do that by opening "windows" in readers' minds to see essential landscapes and horizons in the study of the FG which give a foundation and direction for further exploration.

This book is what the title suggests: A Prologue to Studies in the Fourth Gospel. The Prologue of the FG (John 1:1–18) has a distinct role in the Fourth Evangelist's presentation. It introduces the themes and gives perspective on how the readers should read the rest of the work. Similarly, this volume hopes to accomplish the same concerning studies in the FG. The book introduces selected unique perspectives, issues, and interpretations to help students of the FG get off from the ground before they learn to fly with it. In other words, it introduces the chosen topics and provides content and perspectives for students to advance in their studies. The topics that we have chosen include long-standing as well as newer conversations among Johannine scholars. Regardless of how long the chosen topics have been discussed in the scholarly world, casual readers might have overlooked them.

As the subtitle suggests, this volume concentrates on three areas. Part One focuses on the unique characteristics of the Fourth Gospel. I have titled that section FG's "independency." In this Part, unique features will be introduced related to the FG's exclusive Christology in general and to Jesus's identity in particular. The purpose is that students would be able to recognize the FG's uniqueness among the other Gospels and New Testament writings. In some sense, the title "Maverick Gospel," given to the FG by Robert Kysar, is suitable to the first part where unique Johannine terms like *logos* and paraclete are discussed among many other "maverick" elements. Part One also aims to argue for a certain kind of Christological approach to the FG that emphasizes the identification of Jesus as the divine savior. Part One does not discuss FG's "independency" from the other three canonical Gospels. That matter is introduced in Part Two, where various "issues" are considered. In short, the first section concentrates on certain unique characteristics in the FG that also argue for Jesus's identity and which are not found or which are not argued in similar fashion in the other New Testament writings—thus, the word "independency" is employed.

In Part Two, various issues in the FG that are discussed in Johannine scholarship are covered. These issues include authorship, place and date of writings, the FG's relation to the other NT writings, so-called anti-Judaism, and literary challenges, among other things. The aim is not to argue for specific positions in these issues, even though we will propose resolutions. The goal is to expose the FG's issues and introduce scholarly arguments for their solutions, which can be used as a launchpad for further studies.

Finally, but not least importantly, Part Three introduces various reading models applied to the FG. Hermeneutical approaches to the biblical narratives in general and the FG narrative in particular demand attention and explanation. Readers of this Gospel also face several challenges because of historical and literary questions and various hermeneutical approaches. The purpose is to offer an understanding of various approaches to how and for what the FG has been read in the past and present. This section may also help readers recognize their own hermeneutical paradigms or to form their own hermeneutical approach consciously.

I have had to be selective about which topics, issues, and hermeneutical approaches to include in this study. The choices have not been easy.

*Preface*

Perhaps the author of the FG experienced a similar difficulty as he also had to decide what to include in his account and what to leave out (John 20:30–31). The criteria for selecting the topics are based on my experience that these are the topics that help perhaps the most students, and which are continually, in some sense, "hot potatoes" in Johannine scholarship. The "Further Reading" suggestions at the end of each chapter are planned to provide readers of this volume with comfortable "targeted" suggestions to scholarly works for further learning.

My prayer is that readers would find this work informative and inspiring. I hope the book will stir curiosity and move the readers forward in their journey to discover the FG's transforming message expressed in the words of Thomas to the resurrected Christ, "My Lord and my God" (John 20:28).

**Riku P. Tuppurainen**
Vancouver, BC
December 20, 2020

# Abbreviations

## General Abbreviations

| | |
|---|---|
| ANE | Ancient Near East |
| ASV | American Standard Version |
| BBR*Sup* | *Bulletin for Biblical Research, Supplements* |
| BCE | Before Common Era |
| BETL | Bibliotheca Ephemeridum Theologicarum Lovaniensium |
| *BSac* | *Bibliotheca Sacra* |
| c. | circa |
| CBQMS | Catholic Biblical Quarterly Monograph Series |
| CE | Common Era |
| cf. | confer (compare or consult) |
| ch./chs. | chapter/chapters |
| ed(s). | editor(s); edition |
| e.g. | exempli gratia (for example) |
| EGGNT | Exegetical Guide to the Greek New Testament |
| ERV | English Revised Version |
| ESEC | Emory Studies in Early Christianity |
| esp. | especially |
| ESV | English Standard Version |
| et al. | et alii (and others) |
| etc. | et cetera (and the rest) |
| FE | Fourth Evangelist |
| FG | Fourth Gospel |
| Gr. | Greek |
| Heb. | Hebrew |
| ICC | International Critical Commentary |
| i.e. | id est (that is) |

| | | | |
|---|---|---|---|
| JEPTA | Journal of the European Pentecostal Theological Association | NICNT | New International Commentary on the New Testament |
| JBL | Journal of Biblical Literature | NIDNTT | New International Dictionary of New Testament Theology |
| JSNT | Journal for the Study of the New Testament | NIDOTTE | New International Dictionary of Old Testament Theology and Exegesis |
| JTS | Journal of Theological Studies | | |
| KJV | King James Version | NIV | New International Version |
| LB | Living Bible | NJB | New Jerusalem Bible |
| LNTS | Library of New Testament Studies | NRS | New Revised Standard Bible |
| ms/mss | manuscript/manuscripts | NT | New Testament |
| n./nn. | note/notes | NTL | New Testament Library |
| n.d. | no date | NTSer | New Testament Series |
| NA²⁷ | Novum Testamentum Graece, Nestle-Aland, 27th edition | NTSI | New Testament and the Scriptures of Israel |
| NASB | New American Standard Bible | OT | Old Testament |
| NCCS | New Covenant Commentary Series | PBTS | Paternoster Biblical and Theological Studies |
| Neot | Neotestamentica | PCNT | Paideia Commentaries on the New Testament |
| NET | New English Translation | | |

| | | | |
|---|---|---|---|
| PCS | Pentecostal Commentary Series | **Old Testament** | |
| | | Gen | Genesis |
| RBS | Resources for Biblical Study | Exod | Exodus |
| | | Lev | Leviticus |
| repr. | reprint | Num | Numbers |
| rev. | revised | Deut | Deuteronomy |
| SBT | Studies in Biblical Theology | 2 Sam | 2 Samuel |
| | | 1 Kgs | 1 Kings |
| SNTSNS | Society for New Testament Studies Monograph Series | Ezra | Ezra |
| | | Job | Job |
| *TDNT* | *Theological Dictionary of the New Testament* | Ps | Psalm |
| | | Isa | Isaiah |
| *TynBul* | *Tyndale Bulletin* | Jer | Jeremiah |
| | | Ezek | Ezekiel |
| UBS$^4$ | *The Greek New Testament*, United Bible Societies, 4th revised edition | Dan | Daniel |
| | | Joel | Joel |
| | | Amos | Amos |
| UBS$^5$ | *The Greek New Testament*, United Bible Societies, 5th revised edition | Jonah | Jonah |
| | | Hab | Habakuk |
| | | Zech | Zechariah |
| vol(s). | volume(s) | | |
| WBC | Word Biblical Commentary | | |
| WUNT | Wissenschaftliche Untersuchungen Zum Neuen Testament | | |

## New Testament

| | |
|---|---|
| Matt | Matthew |
| Mark | Mark |
| Luke | Luke |
| John | John |
| Acts | Acts |
| Rom | Romans |
| 2 Cor | 2 Corinthians |
| Eph | Ephesians |
| Phlm | Philemon |
| 1 Pet | 1 Peter |
| 1–3 John | 1–3 John |
| Rev | Revelation |

## Apocrypha

| | |
|---|---|
| 1–2 Macc | 1–2 Maccabees |

## Old Testament Pseudepigrapha

| | |
|---|---|
| T. Jud. | Testament of Judah |
| Apoc. Ab. | Apocalypse of Abraham |

## Other Jewish Writings

| | |
|---|---|
| 1QS | Rule of the Community |
| 1QM | War Scroll |
| 4QM | War Scroll (= 4QM$^{a-f}$ / 4Q490–496) |
| Ant. | Josephus, *Jewish Antiquities* |
| Q | Qumran |

## Other Christian Writings

| | |
|---|---|
| *Adv. Haer.* | Irenaeus, *Adversus Haereses (Against Heresies)* |
| *Hist. eccl.* | Eusebius, *Historia ecclesiastica (Ecclesiastical History)* |
| $\mathfrak{P}^{52}$ | Papyri 52 |
| $\mathfrak{P}^{66}$ | Papyri 66 |
| $\mathfrak{P}^{75}$ | Papyri 75 |
| $\mathfrak{P}^{90}$ | Papyri 90 |

## Other Ancient Literature

| | |
|---|---|
| *QG* | Philo, *Questions and Answers on Genesis* |

PART ONE

# Independency of the Fourth Gospel

CHAPTER 1

# Logos and Divine Identity of Jesus

"In the beginning was the Word"[1] is the surprising opening of the Fourth Gospel (FG). On the one hand, Jewish readers would have expected to read, "In the beginning was God," but instead of *ho theos* (God), the evangelist writes *ho logos* (the Word). On the other hand, Greco-Roman readers (Jews and Gentiles) who were familiar with Hellenistic philosophy and the writings of Philo may have also been surprised by the FG's opening statement. *Logos* for them was not the first cause but rather something that flows out from it.[2] Thus, the Fourth Evangelist's opening might have had a "shock" effect on the first readers, especially for those outside of Johannine community.

Today's readers may also marvel at the FG's opening. Several questions could be asked such as: To what end does the author use *ho logos*? Why does the author not use, for example, the title Christ or the name Jesus to refer the one who became flesh? What is the significance of *ho logos*? Does the author try to clarify something previously said in other Gospels, or is he aiming to give new information about God to his readers that is more appealing to his Hellenistic readers? Or, was this word simply the best available term to describe Jesus of Nazareth in his pre-existent state?[3] And if yes, why?

---

1. All Scripture quotations, unless otherwise indicated, are from New American Standard Bible (1995).

2. Evans, *Ancient Texts*, 170.

3. The reader needs to remind him/herself that Christian systematic theology did not exist at the time of writing. Phrases that are familiar to us today, for example, "the

## Preliminary Observations

Although many NT authors use the *ho logos* phrase, they use it mainly in its customary meaning of communication, referring to something that is said or written.[4] Its Christological usage is found only a few times in Johannine literature. It is employed in that special sense at the beginning of the Gospel in John 1:1 and 1:14, and in 1 John 1:1.[5] In a few other cases in Johannine literature, namely, in Revelation 19:13 and John 17:17, *ho logos* might also be understood Christologically, but this interpretation is a matter of dispute.

*Ho logos* in John 1:1 is translated into English by using its lexical meaning "word" with a capital "W" to convey its special reference to a divine being. Attempts to define its Christological meaning with another single English word is impossible. If one replaces it with "Jesus," it is not accurate since the name "Jesus" was given to the incarnated *ho logos*. Nor can one use the title "Christ" (Messiah) for the same reason. If we say that it refers to the second person of the Godhead, we are reading post-Johannine theology into Johannine text, a theology that was unknown to both the author and his readers. Thus, to grasp its meaning in the Prologue, we need to listen carefully to the Gospel itself and examine the contemporary philosophical-theological notion of *ho logos*.

In this chapter, we examine the backdrop for the Johannine technical use of *ho logos* in order to understand the Fourth Evangelist's conceptualization of *ho logos* and why he possibly employed this phrase. We conclude the chapter by looking at the relation of *ho logos* to the Gospel's presentation of Jesus's identity.

---

second person of the Holy Trinity," was not an option for the author.

4. The phrase *ho logos* in its special meaning, "the Word," occurs only in John 1:1, 14. (See also John 1:2–5 where third-person singular pronouns refer to *ho logos*.) It also occurs in the genitive (*tou logou*) in 1 John 1:1. In Rev 19:13, it is found in the phrase "*ho logos* of God" (cf. John 10:35). In both of these cases, it is arguable that logos is used in the same or similar sense than in John 1:1 and 1:14. In John 17:17, Jesus employs *ho logos*, which could be understood to be a reference to Jesus. Beyond these occurrences, it is very difficult to find any other passages where logos would be used in its technical sense.

5. In 1 John 1:1, *ho logos* is in the genitive, *tou logou*.

## Stoics and Philo of Alexandria: Logos as Hellenistic and Philosophical Concept

Pre-Johannine, first-century CE Hellenistic philosophy used the term *logos* as one of the many expressions to explain the beginning and existence of the universe. As early as sixth-century BCE, pre-Socratic Heraclitus, who had an influence in Ephesus, assigned the force behind the universe's order and course to "thought." His "thought" (i.e., *logos*) was not, however, a person or a divine being,[6] yet he referred to *logos* as an "eternal, omnipresent, and divine cause."[7]

Stoics, over two hundred years before Christ, took these ideas of Heraclitus and developed them further. For them *logos* was "the common law"—the law according to which every person should live in harmony with nature. Yet, *logos* was not passive but an active principle (guiding, controlling, directing) in the universe, which acts upon the passive principle, namely, the matter in the universe.[8] This kind of universalism took the Stoic notion of *logos* towards the idea of a pantheistic God "who penetrated all things."[9] Cleanthes (c. 330–231 BCE), a successor to the founder and head of the Stoic school, Zeno, presented similar ideas. In short, *logos* was used to explain the unseen force, principle, and action, which was believed to be behind the existence and order of the universe.

It is likely that the author of the FG knew these ideas, because (1) they were well established by the end of the first century CE, (2) some of them originated and likely circulated in Ephesus where the Fourth Evangelist most probably drafted his Gospel, and (3) because the evangelist's interest to introduce *ho logos* attached to cosmology and metaphysics. His usage of *logos* does not make him, however, a follower of Hellenistic philosophy. *Logos* in Hellenistic philosophy differs from *ho logos* as found in the Prologue. The most obvious differences are seen in these two points: (1) Johannine *ho logos* is personal, not a mere active principle; (2) Johannine *ho logos* is not pantheistic but monotheistic (see below). Yet, we cannot, nor is there a reason why we should rule out Hellenistic connotations of the FG's *logos*.

---

6. Heraclitus writes: "This world-order [*kosmos*], the same of all, no god nor man did create, but it ever was and is and will be: everliving fire, kindling in measures and being quenched in measures." Quoted in Graham, "Heraclitus," section 4.

7. Keener, *The Gospel of John*, 1:341.

8. Keener, *The Gospel of John*, 1:342.

9. Brown, *The Gospel According to John*, 1:520.

Another backdrop for *ho logos* is found in Philo of Alexandria's notion of *logos*. Philo was a Jewish philosopher who had adopted the Platonic philosophy of Forms and applied it to his Jewish-Hellenistic framework to persuade his Hellenistic contemporaries about the superior worldview seen in the Hebrew Scriptures by "interpreting the biblical stories (mostly those of the Pentateuch) in terms of Neoplatonism."[10] In his writings, Philo employed the word *logos* over 1200 times![11] According to Philo, *logos* was an agent of God that explains the creation and sustenance of the universe.[12] For Philo, *logos* was impossible to be fully grasped. *Logos* was a subordinate to God—God's firstborn—who functioned under him, but "above the powers through which God rules creation."[13] *Logos* was one who was created by God and is sometimes referred to as "God's archangel" or "eldest offspring" in Philo's writings. Philo explains: "Nothing mortal can be made in the likeness of the most High One and Father of the universe but (only) in that of the second God, who is his Word."[14]

Philo, like Hellenistic philosophies, connected *logos* to creation. But where other Hellenistic philosophies treated *logos* as an independent "force," Philo connected *logos* to the God of Hebrews. *Logos* for Philo was semi-divine, similar to personified Wisdom in Jewish thought. *Logos* was not mere "thought" or "mind" for Philo as it was for the Stoics. Yet, *logos* was not a person and never incarnated into the world in Philo's thought.

We do not know from where exactly Philo borrowed the term and the concept. He might have borrowed it from Hellenistic philosophy or Jewish traditions (e.g., Wisdom figure). Craig Evans suggests that Philo's *Logos* concept might have also grown up out of the synagogue setting in which Targumim and the concept of "*Memra*" (Aramaic word for "Word") developed.[15] Regardless of this unknown fact, we are confident that the Johannine community or the intended readership of the FG might have been aware of Philo's usage of that term and what he meant by it. Although Philo's writings and his theologizing are not in line with Christian theology, the early Christian community preserved Philo's writings, and

---

10. Evans, *Ancient Texts*, 168. Cf. Wolfson, "Philo Judaeus," 303–4. See also Hillar, "Philo of Alexandria."

11. Balfour, "Is John's Gospel Antisemitic," 224. See also Hengel, "The Prologue of the Gospel of John," 272.

12. See Dodd, *The Interpretation*, 276–77; Evans, *Ancient Texts*, 5.

13. Keener, *The Gospel of John*, 1:345.

14. QG 2.62, quoted from Evans, *Ancient Texts*, 170.

15. Evans, *Ancient Texts*, 170–71.

may, in some ways, have followed Philo's method of interpretation and theologizing. Therefore, it is not impossible that the Fourth Evangelist might have built on Philo's notions of *logos*. This was the common scholarly understanding until the end of the twentieth century.[16] The reason for this view is that Philo's *logos* shares more similarities with Johannine *ho logos* than with the Stoic's notion of *logos*. Philo reflected the Hebrew Scriptures, as did the Fourth Evangelist, and therefore resonates with the FG's presentation of *ho logos*.

Yet there are some significant differences between Philo's *logos* and the Fourth Evangelist's *ho logos* as well. First, *ho logos* in the Prologue becomes historical and immanent (John 1:14) whereas in Philo's writings *logos* remains impersonal and transcendent. Secondly, these authors' purpose of writing differs from each other. Philo aims to describe metaphysical reality behind the universe by employing this term, whereas the Fourth Evangelist's purpose was to reveal that *ho logos* is the life and light of humanity in both the physical and the spiritual sense, which is also manifested to humanity in his incarnation. The Fourth Evangelist further develops his theme and demonstrates how the incarnated *ho logos* is the only avenue to eternal life. *Logos* does not have such a role in Philo's writings.

It is reasonable to conclude at this point that the Fourth Evangelist used the Stoics' and Philo's *logos* concepts as intertexts. What we do not know is the exact source material he might have used. Despite this ambiguity, it is clear that the Fourth Evangelist neither used the *logos* concept in a vacuum, nor did he come up with that term and its cosmological connotations. Interestingly, even though he used the term differently than the Stoics and Philo, he did not argue against their notions of *logos*, but rather only gave a "corrective" and new content for the *logos*.

## Gnostic Ideas of Logos

Gnostic ideas of *logos* connect the concept not only to cosmological but also to soteriological categories. Some scholars (e.g., Richard Reitzenstein, Rudolf Bultmann, and Hans Conzelmann) have pointed out that the Prologue's *ho logos* is dependent on Mandaean Gnostic thinking. The background to this is found, according to Reitzenstein, in Near and Middle East religions that share a soteriological construction that is built on the same idea of a savior as is in the FG: a savior is the one who comes from

---

16. Keener, *The Gospel of John*, 1:343–44. Cf. Dodd, *Interpretation*, 276–77.

heaven and leads those who are in darkness to the kingdom of light.[17] Bultmann, among other history-of-religions scholars, re-worked these ideas and moved from mere Mandaean literature to the earlier first century Gnostic sources and compared their findings with Christian writings.

The Gnostic idea of *logos* included the view that God made a material world through his *logos*, and through this *logos*, humans can be delivered from the evil matter of a lower world to reach the higher world of God. This is possible if they follow the redeemer (*logos*), who deceives all demonic forces and can, therefore, free people from the bondage of matter.[18] Gnostic writing, such as *Gospel of Truth*, demonstrates these ideas.

Bultmann applied the Gnostic redeemer myth to Johannine Christology. He argues that "the Johannine redeemer is an entirely human person, Jesus of Nazareth, in whom the Logos . . . embodied."[19] This is a different interpretation of *ho logos* and Jesus of Nazareth to that held by most Johannine scholars and church tradition.

Gnostic ideas of *logos* are rejected as a backdrop to the FG's *logos* by most scholars for the following four reasons: (1) Gnosticism as a full-fledged movement and Gnostic (Mandaean) literature were not yet around at the time of "publication" of the FG; (2) it is more probable that Gnostic writers used FG's *ho logos* and other *logos* ideas rather than the other way around;[20] (3) the FG's *ho logos*, as well as his whole Gospel, leans more towards the OT writings, Philo's *Logos* concept, and/or early Christian views rather than to Gnostic (or Christian Gnostic) concepts (see below);[21] and (4) the Gnostic's *logos* did not become flesh like that of the Fourth Gospel's *ho logos*.

## Jewish Background for Logos: Genesis, Wisdom, and Torah

Today's scholarly opinion is that the prominent background for Johannine *ho logos* is derived from the OT writings and Jewish thinking.[22] (Yet, this is not to say that there are no scholarly views that hold other possible

---

17. McHugh, *A Critical and Exegetical Commentary*, 91.
18. See Brown, *The Gospel according to John*, 1:520.
19. Quoted in McHugh, *A Critical and Exegetical Commentary*, 92.
20. Cf. Keener, *The Gospel of John*, 1:340.
21. Schnackenburg, *The Gospel According to St. John*, 1:493.
22. Schnackenburg, *The Gospel According to St. John*, 1:481.

## Logos and Divine Identity of Jesus

backdrops for the Fourth Evangelist's *ho logos*.) We will outline two of these possibilities below, namely, Genesis and Wisdom/Torah.

The Gospel of John is sometimes called, quite adequately, the Second Genesis. Both, Genesis and the FG, tell the story of the "beginning" and "life" and how all of that is related to the eternal God. The striking similarity is found in the opening words of these books. Genesis opens with a statement, "In the beginning, God created the heavens and the earth"[23] (Gen 1:1), which is similar to John's opening statement (and theme), "In the beginning was the Word [*ho logos*].... All things came into being through Him" (John 1:1–3). The opening words in the FG are the very same Greek words used in the Septuagint (*en archē*; i.e., "In the beginning"). Uniformity of the opening phrases in Genesis and the FG hardly go unnoticed by anyone who is even moderately familiar with these Scriptures.

In Genesis (i.e., "In the beginning"), God spoke, and all things were created (cf. Gen 1:3, 6, 9, 11, 14, 20, 24).[24] The concept of "God's word" was, therefore, more than a mere verbal expression for Jews; "the word" spoken by God was understood as a powerful *action* that can create. The Aramaic Targum (the Aramaic translation of the Hebrew Scriptures) translates the Hebrew phrase "the Word of the LORD" sometimes as "God" and sometimes as "LORD," equating God's Word with the powerful God himself. Also, it needs to be noted that in a few places in the *Targum of the Minor Prophets*, "the Memra seems to take on the role of personality (cf. Amos 4:11; Hab 1:12). This could bear on the question of the relation of the Johannine Logos to the targumic Memra."[25] Moreover, the Aramaic word "word" (*memra*) carries the very idea of God's creative and powerful word. God's word as a powerful action may have contributed to the FG's usage of *ho logos*, for *ho logos* is identified as a powerful, acting being; indeed, he is a creator whom God (*theos*) sent to creation to act as savior (cf. Ps 107:20; Ezek 37:4–5; Isa 40:8).

In Hebrew Scriptures the phrase "word of YHWH" (Heb. *davar YHWH*) "is frequently used of God's communication with men, his self-revelation, especially through the prophets, to whom 'the word of the Lord came.'"[26] The "word of YHWH" phrase probably has its connotations

---

23. "In the beginning" (Heb. *berešit*) is the Hebrew name for the first book in the Tanakh.

24. Note that Wis 9:1–2 indicates that God created everything through his word and his wisdom.

25. Evans, *Ancient Texts*, 196.

26. Dodd, *The Interpretation*, 263.

with the FG's *ho logos* motif as it is not difficult to see the connection between these two. The idea of God's self-revelation through his word (*davar*) is related to the FG's *ho logos* who is the qualified revealer of God (cf. John 1:18). What is interesting here is that the "totality of God's self-revelation [for Jews] is denominated to [Torah] . . . , a term which is often parallel or virtually synonymous with [word of the Lord]."[27] It is also noticeable that "the Palestinian targums render Gn 1:1 as 'By wisdom God created . . . ' Rabbinic Torah speculation similarly portrayed the Law as interchangeable with 'the word of the Lord,' *i.e.*, as pre-existent . . . , and this too may well have had oral origins early enough for John to imbibe."[28] These observations connect the powerful and active word of God with the Jewish understanding of God's Wisdom/Torah.

The Jewish notion of Wisdom/Torah resonates closely to the Fourth Evangelist's *ho logos* and his Christology as a whole. The following list of attributes shows the similarities between Wisdom/Torah in Jewish literature and *ho logos* in the Prologue:[29]

| Wisdom/Torah | *ho logos* |
|---|---|
| Pre-existent | Pre-existent |
| Related to God in a unique way | Related to God the closest possible way |
| Played a significant role in the creation | Nothing is created without him |
| Eternal | Eternal |
| Related to life, light, and salvation | Is life, light, and the way for salvation |
| Appears in the world or among people | Became flesh and lived among people |
| Associated with truth | Is the truth |
| Associated with glory | Associated with glory |

Table 1.1

27. Dodd, *The Interpretation*, 263.
28. Balfour, "Is John's Gospel Antisemitic?" 225.
29. Keener, *The Gospel of John*, 1:352–55.

Despite similarities, which are hardly accidental, the Jewish notion of Wisdom/Torah does not equal the Johannine *ho logos*. What is clear, however, is that *ho logos* points towards Jewish understanding of God's Wisdom/Torah. It is quite obvious that Fourth Evangelist has purposefully used Jewish Wisdom/Torah concept to reveal God's Word, *ho logos*, who is revealed to be fulfilment of Torah. This clever presentation of *ho logos* creates a horizon of memory in the Jewish mind, which forces readers to go beyond the old concept of God's Wisdom/Torah. In short, what God's Wisdom/Torah was for Jews of the time in contemporary Jewish theology, and what it was not able to accomplish, is now fully revealed in *ho logos* for the entire world bringing fulfillment to the earlier promises. This is explicitly stated at the end of the Prologue where Torah is compared and contrasted with *ho logos* (John 1:17–18).[30] The FG points out that Torah, including grace and truth, is now fully revealed in *ho logos*. This fulfills God's promise that "law would go forth again, only this time from Zion rather than from Sinai (Isa 2:2–4)."[31] At that time, God would not write his law on stone tablets, but rather the hearts of his people (Jer 31:31–34; Ezek 36:27). That promise is fulfilled in *ho logos*.

## *Ho Logos* Defined in John 1

The *logos* concept that was related to creation/universe and metaphysics in Greek thought and Wisdom/Torah in Jewish thought, is now fully revealed as *ho logos* in the FG. Next, we will look into explicit *ho logos* statements to see how the Fourth Evangelist defines *ho logos*.

In the first phrase, *ho logos* is identified as the one who pre-existed before the beginning: "In the beginning was *ho logos*" (John 1:1a). In other words, before the beginning began *ho logos* already was. The Prologue presents *ho logos* from this point of view. The verse 14a assumes that the reader has grasped this as it proclaims that *ho logos* incarnated (became flesh) and lived among people. This theme is further demonstrated in the rest of the Gospel, for example, in Jesus's "I AM" sayings.

The second phrase reads, "*ho logos* was with (Gr. *pros*) God" (1:1b). A lexical Koine Greek meaning of *pros* (with the accusative) is "to" or "toward" ("to/toward the vicinity of").[32] *Pros* is also used in the sense of

---

30. Cf. Keener, *The Gospel of John*, 1:360–61.
31. Keener, *The Gospel of John*, 1:358.
32. Harris, *Prepositions and Theology*, 189.

"with," as in John 1:1b, and is so translated in most modern English translations.³³ Many scholars argue that *pros* carries here the idea of a close relationship that is not mere static but rather active communion. Murray Harris suggests a translation "fellowship" for *pros*.³⁴ William Hendriksen suggests that *pros* could read in this context: "face to face with."³⁵ This statement reveals not only a close and dynamic relationship between God and *ho logos*, but also that they are two distinct persons.

In the second and third phrases in the first verse (John 1:1b–1c), the word *theos* (g/God) is used first with and then without the definite article. It is important to notice that "[t]he function of the [Greek] article is not primarily to make something definite that would otherwise be indefinite."³⁶ Since the article in Greek is not used the same way as in English, one cannot translate "the God" when the definite article is used, and "a god" when the definite article is absent in the Greek text.³⁷ What then does the definite article before the word *theos* do and what does its absence mean in this context?

Verse 1b reads "and *ho logos* was with God" (Gr. *kai ho logos en pros ton theon*). Here the definite article (*ton*) is used before "God." The function of the definite article is to stress God as a person. Thus, *ho logos* was not with some kind of divine "thing" or "idea," but with a person, God, whom the Israelites have learned to know through various revelations, experiences, and the Scriptures. Also, Webster points out that the Greek "article seems to be used (1) when the Deity is spoken of in the Christian point of view, (2) when the First Person of the blessed Trinity is specially designed, unless it insertion is unnecessary by the addition of [*patēr* = father] or some distinctive epithet."³⁸ This is the case here as it speaks about God and *ho logos* in a Christian perspective and operates within the Father-Son arena.

In the third phrase, verse 1c, "and *ho logos* was God" (Gr. *kai theos en ho logos*), the definite article does not precede the word *theos*. This word order in the Greek text (i.e., first "God" and then "Word") and grammatical construction (i.e., use of the article before "Word" and its

---

33. Cf. NIV Mark 6:3; 14:49; 2 Cor 5:8; Phlm 13; 1 John 1:2
34. Harris, *Prepositions and Theology*, 190. See also the entire article, pp. 190–92.
35. Hendriksen, *The Gospel According to John*, 1:69.
36. Wallance, *Greek Grammar Beyond the Basics*, 209.
37. There is no indefinite article in Greek.
38. Dana and Mantey, *A Manual Grammar*, 140.

absence before "God") is a carefully designed grammatical construction. It is needed at least for the following reasons:

- This syntactical construction—God without the article, a verb "to be," and *ho logos*—makes "*ho logos*" to be subject (as it has a definite article) and "God" the predicate (as it stands without a definite article) even though in the Greek text God stands at the beginning of the phrase;[39]

- The word "God" at the beginning of the statement stands in this position for emphasis. In other words, it emphasizes that *ho logos* is nothing less than what God is;

- By using God without the article, the author is pointing out "divine essence" and "the essential attributes of Deity."[40] Thus this phrase does not say that one of the attributes of God was *ho logos* or that *ho logos* is the same person as God. Rather, it points out that *ho logos* has the same divine essence as God has, sharing the same divine identity.[41] This is to say that what God is, *ho logos* is. The identity of *ho logos* is further developed in the following verses where he is given essential attributes that only God has.

In verse 14, John connects *ho logos* with Jesus; *ho logos* became flesh, lived among people, and was the Father's unique One (cf. 1:18). Here the evangelist reveals who Jesus is, namely, that he is incarnated *ho logos*. All that *ho logos* is said to be, is what Jesus also is, but now in flesh, among the people and for all the people. As we have noticed already, *ho logos* is significantly different from Hellenistic or Jewish concepts, but he is similar enough to allude to both of these pre-understandings of the *logos* concept and to trigger the reader's interest for further explanation. Incarnated *ho logos* is God's ultimate revelation to explain who God is (1:18). This revelation is beyond the one communicated through Moses and Torah. Keener concludes:

> John's choice of the Logos to articulate his Christology was brilliant: no concept better articulated an entity that was both divine yet distinct from the Father. By this term, some Diaspora Jewish

---

39. See also, for example, John 1:6, 12, 13, 18; and especially John 1:49 where the King (not a king) as a predicative noun stands without Greek article. See also Balford, *A Step-by-Step Introduction*, 47.

40. Dana and Mantey, *A Manual Grammar*, 139–40.

41. Cf. Keener, *The Gospel of John*, 1:373.

writers had already connected Jewish conceptions of Wisdom and Torah with Hellenistic conceptions of divine and universal power. Finally, by using this term John could present Jesus as the epitome of what his community's opponents claimed to value: God's word revealed through Moses. Jesus was thus the supreme revelation of God; the Torah had gone forth from Zion.[42]

*Ho logos* phrase is connected to the early Church era as well. The good news that was the message of Jesus Christ, God's saving agent, who incarnated, died, and rose from the dead was referred to as "the word" by early Christians.[43] For example, in Acts 8:25 the "word of the Lord" and the "gospel" (good news) are used to describe the content of the early apostolic proclamation. In many places, simply "word" is used to describe the message that was preached as in Acts 2:41; 4:4, 29.

We conclude that the *ho logos* concept in the Prologue is the supreme example within Christian history of the communication of the gospel in terms which are related to the audience's pre-understandings and yet reveal new revelation to them. The author does not simply "copy and paste" previous meanings and connotations attached to *ho logos*, but rather builds on them, re-defining *ho logos* to give it fuller and throughout Christological meaning.[44] This is somewhat similar to what was taking place when Paul stood on Mars Hill and declared, "Therefore what you worship in ignorance, this I proclaim to you" (Acts 17:23). What Hellenists and Jews had partially discovered, the Fourth Evangelist reveals fully.

## Monotheism and Divine *ho Logos*

An obstacle that the Fourth Evangelist faced was the same as Jesus had faced: the leading Jews could not easily accept Jesus's identity as a divine Messiah. For them, YHWH is one and there is no other (cf. Isa 43:10). How, then, could the evangelist's Jewish audience accept Jesus as Messiah who is so clearly presented as divine and thus another to the Father? Below we argue that the evangelist presents *ho logos* such a way that does not violate "God is one" theology.

---

42. Keener, *The Gospel of John*, 363.
43. Brown, *The Gospel According to John*, 1:519.
44. Morris, *The Gospel According to John*, 108–10.

Jesus ministered in the context of Second Temple Judaism that ran from 515 BCE to 70 CE. Second Temple Judaism was utterly monotheistic.[45] Yet there are two views among scholars regarding Jewish monotheism. The first view is that the Second Temple Judaism was so strictly monotheistic that Jews could not include any other being as a divine besides YHWH. According to this understanding, some have reasoned that Jews could not have accepted Jesus as divine and equal with God. This is, in fact, evident in the Gospel narrative as (leading) Jews were ready to kill Jesus because they took Jesus's claims of his divine messianic identity as blasphemy. This was also the reason why (leading) Jews arrested Jesus and persuaded Roman authorities to execute him.

The second interpretation is built on the hypothesis that Second Temple monotheism must have been somewhat relaxed or flexible. This idea is based on the fact that Judaism accepted semi-divine beings. It is reasoned, therefore, that Jews could have possibly been lenient to accept a divine being, who had grown from their semi-divine status to divine. This idea relates to so-called Wisdom Christology; God's Wisdom (for some scholars pre-incarnate Christ) was personified in Scriptures like in Proverbs 8:22–31 and had also been given a semi-divine status in Judaism.[46] Therefore, Judaism was only half a step away from accepting *ho logos*, not only as pre-existent semi-divine being, but as a fully divine being. It is argued by some scholars that this happened in Christian circles where Jesus Nazareth became the Lord. These scholars suggest that the church created divine Jesus who is also presented as such in the NT. In other words, *ho logos* (Jesus Christ) was semi-divine (or human) who grew to be fully divine in Christian orthodox thought.[47] The same, therefore, could have happened in Jewish circles if this view and logic is accepted.

Assessing these two interpretations, we note that the latter interpretation requires a huge leap of faith without convincing evidence that such a move from semi-divine to the divine ever occurred in Jewish thought. Thus, it is very difficult to explain how Jewish monotheism could have

---

45. Routledge, *Old Testament Theology*, 94.

46. Routledge, *Old Testament Theology*, 220–21. Schnackenburg, *The Gospel According to St. John*, 1:485, notes that "*Memra de Adonai* (the word of the Lord) in the Aramaic translation of the Bible . . . has nothing to do with speculation on hypostasization, but merely a periphrasis for God, to avoid irreverence. It should also be recalled that personifications of God's wisdom—or spirit or word—are not really hypostasizations. Wisdom literature has still no inkling of the personal character of the Logos."

47. See Bauckham, *God Crucified*, 2–3, 5.

accepted that type of divine "evolution." Even though, it is arguable, the semi-divine concept existed in Second Temple Judaism (e.g., God's Wisdom, Word/Torah, principal angels), there is no indication that there would have been a theology in place which would have allowed that kind of evolution. Neither is there available any examples of such a development in Judaism.

Secondly, that kind of "detour" to explain Jesus's divinity would seem unfitting to the Fourth Evangelist's Christology. The Prologue gives divine status to *ho logos* right at the beginning. There are no hints of evolution or development in John's presentation of *ho logos*. His identity is claimed to be divine from eternity, never semi-divine.

The reality that Second Temple Judaism was strictly monotheistic and that the Fourth Evangelist operated still in this context in the end of the first century is more arguable and acceptable. How then could the divine *ho logos* ever been acceptable for Jews? To be able to draft an answer to this question, we need to understand our modern way of thinking about Jesus and how it differs from Jewish reasoning of who God is.

If *ho logos* and the divinity question are approached according to the early ecumenical church councils' Christology (cf. Nicaea 325 and Chalcedon 451), which leaned towards Greek rather than Jewish categories and which explained Jesus in terms of *his nature* rather than *his identity*,[48] we may not see any hope of how the FG's *ho logos* could fit Jewish monotheism. Jews did not think of God, however, in terms of his nature. They did not ask the question "what is God" but rather "who is God?"[49] The "nature of Christ" discussion was introduced to early Christian Christology because of heretics who held various distorted explanations of unity of Christ, his divinity, and his humanity. This demanded orthodox Christianity to defend the orthodox view of Christ with the vocabulary and philosophy of the day. But Jews viewed God in terms of his identity rather than in terms of his nature, and therefore, the question "who is God?" was the question to be answered.

The Fourth Evangelist seems to employ this same (who is *ho logos*/Jesus) approach. This becomes explicit, for example, in his presentation of who *ho logos* is. YHWH, for Jews, is eternal and the only one who creates. He is also distinguished as the God of Israel. The evangelist reveals *ho logos* as eternal, and as the one who has created everything that has

---

48. See Kärkkäinen, *Christology*, 72–78. See also Erickson, *The Word Become Flesh*, 41–86.

49. Bauckham, *God Crucified*, 78.

ever been created (John 1:1–3). Also, *ho logos* incarnated and came for Israel as well as for all the people (John 1:10–11). *Ho logos*, therefore, is presented as the one who shares the same identity with God. What God was, *ho logos* was. This way of looking at the questions of *ho logos* and his divinity opens a door for us to see how a Jewish audience could have accepted, as some did, *ho logos*'s (Jesus's) divine identity.[50] Because *ho logos* shares the same identity with the God of Israel, he belongs to God rather than man or a semi-divine body of beings. This view is strengthened, for example, by Jewish usage of *logos* (Aram. *memra*) as the circumlocution to the name of God, namely, YHWH.[51]

## Concluding Remarks

We conclude that John's *ho logos* was linked to the web of philosophical and theological ideas of the day, especially to the writings of Philo, the Hebrew Scriptures, and the Jewish notion of Torah/Wisdom. Yet it is not just a sum of all previous connotations attached to that term, but rather, it is a revelation of who *ho logos* is; he is a divine being, equal with God, who was manifested to mankind in flesh. Balford concludes: "John is not just unique; he is contrary to all previous Jewish developments. They offer circumlocutions for God and ultimately veil him: John's Logos fully reveals the Father by 'opening the way' to Him (1:18; cf. 14:6)."[52] In short, *ho logos* is not a mere great *IT* which mystifies YHWH into unknown eternity, existing beyond the creation, but rather he is eternal and equal with God the Father, who also became the ultimate revelation of God in the person Jesus of Nazareth. Thus, it is not an accident that the first chapter of the FG, after introducing *ho logos* incarnated, relates him to the Scriptures and the person of Jesus of Nazareth (cf. 1:45).

## Suggestions for Further Reading

Brown, Raymond E. *The Gospel According to John I-XII: A New Translation with Introduction and Commentary*. AB. New York: Doubleday, 1966. Pp. 519–24

---

50. See Bauckham, *God Crucified*, viii, 1–22, 25–28, 78.
51. Balfour, "Is John's Gospel Antisemitic?" 224–25.
52. Balfour, "Is John's Gospel Antisemitic?" 227.

Keener, Craig S. *The Gospel of John: A Commentary*. Peabody: Hendrickson, 2003. Pp. 341–63.

Morris, Leon. *The Gospel According to John*. Revised ed. NICNT. Grand Rapids: Eerdmans, 1995. Pp. 102–13.

Schnackenburg, Rudolf. "The Origin and Nature of the Johannine Concept of the Logos" in *The Gospel According to St John*, 1:481–93. New York: Seabury, 1980.

CHAPTER 2

# Jesus and Jewish Feasts and Ceremonies

*Jesus's Platform for His Identity Claims*

THE FOURTH EVANGELIST MENTIONS several Jewish feasts whereas the Synoptic authors mention only two: the Sabbath and Passover. Moreover, in the Synoptic Gospels the Passover is mentioned only in connection with Jesus's passion whereas in the FG several Passover feasts and other Jewish feasts and ceremonies are woven into narratives throughout the Gospel. The FG "sits" on the Jewish feasts. But what are the functions of these feasts in the FG?

It is doubtful that the feasts are used only as chronological markers of the story although they have sometimes been understood as such by casual readers and in some scholarly works.[1] For example, it is pointed out that because the FG mentions three Passovers (or even four if the unnamed feast in John 5:1 is also the Passover), Jesus's public ministry lasted roughly three years. But a chronological motif may not have been the reason why the evangelist includes feasts in his account.[2] His motif for inclusion is Christological rather than mere chronological. This does

---

1. Cf. Flebbe, "Feasts in John," 107, n2. At least one major work has appeared since Flebbe's comment on the lack of studies on Jewish feasts in the FG, namely, Wheaton, *The Role of Jewish Feasts*.

2. It is well argued that the Passover in John 2 is not a separate Passover but is actually the final Passover. Here the Evangelist has arranged his material thematically rather than chronologically. If this is the correct view, as it seems, the Synoptic Gospels' reference to the temple cleansing is chronologically accurate by placing it at the end of Jesus's ministry rather than at the beginning of it.

not mean that he does not pay attention to the chronology of the story. He does, but in his own style and for his own purpose.

Brian Johnson points out, "The frequency of the mention of the Jewish feast in John 5–12, and the associations made between these feasts and the teaching and action portrayed in connection with them, show intentionality in their presentation throughout John's Gospel."[3] The evangelist wrote rhetorically; that is, he wrote with a certain intention in mind which he also openly states at the end of the Gospel. He wrote to persuade his readers to accept that Jesus is Christ, the Son of God (John 20:30–31). Therefore, it is reasonable to think that feasts are purposefully chosen to support this purpose. The evangelist uses them for his rhetorical purposes to reveal Jesus's identity.[4]

The following list presents references to the Jewish feasts and ceremonies in the FG. The list does not include references to those verses where only the word "feast" is used, like in chapter 7 where it refers to the feast of Tabernacles and in chapter 11 where it refers to the Passover.

| Feast | Reference |
| --- | --- |
| Passover | 2:11, 23; 6:4; 11:55; 12:1; 13:1; 18:28, 39; 19:14 |
| Unnamed feast | 5:1 |
| Tabernacles | 7:2 |
| Dedication | 10:22 |
| Sabbath | 5:9, 10, 16, 18; 7:22, 23; 9:14, 16; 19:31 |
| Wedding | 2:1, 2 |
| Funeral | 11:31, 38 [tomb] |

Table 2.1

In the table below, these feasts are attached to narrative references. The purpose of this table is to demonstrate how a large portion of the FG

---

3. Johnson, "The Jewish Feast," 117–18.
4. Johnson, "The Jewish Feast," 118.

is embedded in the context of Jewish feasts and celebrations. Note that, in some cases, two feasts overlap with each other.

| Feast | Narrative Reference | Name Of The Narrative |
|---|---|---|
| Passover | 2:13–22 | Jesus clears the temple |
| Passover | 2:23—3:21 | Jesus and Nicodemus |
| Passover | 6:1–71 | Jesus, the bread of life |
| Passover | 11:55—12:50 | Jesus and pre-Easter events and the end of his public ministry |
| Passover | 13:1–32 | Jesus's last supper with his disciples |
| Passover | 13:33—17:26 | Jesus's farewell address to his eleven faithful disciples |
| Passover | 18:1—19:42 | Jesus's arrest, trial, and crucifixion |
| Unnamed Feast + Sabbath | 5:1–47 | Jesus heals a man at the pool of Bethesda |
| Tabernacles | 7:2-[7:53—8:11]—10:21 | Jesus teaching, arguing with the Jews, and healing a man born blind (including its aftermath) |
| Dedication | 10:22–39 | Jesus's teaching about the sheep and Shepherd |
| Sabbath | 5:1–47 (7:21–24) | Jesus heals at the pool of Bethesda |
| Sabbath | 9:11—10:21 | Jesus heals a man born blind (including its aftermath) |
| Wedding | 2:1–11 | Jesus changes water to wine |
| Funeral | 11:1–44 | Jesus raises Lazarus from the dead |

Table 2.2

It is striking that roughly seventy percent of the Gospel material is interwoven with various Jewish feasts. In the ensuing sections we outline the feasts' various features and how the Fourth Evangelist employs them to proclaim Jesus's divine identity.[5]

## Passover

A vast bulk of FG's narrative material takes place in the context of the final Passover, namely John 13:1—19:42. But other lengthy narratives in the book of signs (John 1:19—12:50) are also attached to the Passover.

The final Passover's events relate to OT prophecies and types which are now fulfilled in Jesus.[6] These fulfillments are employed by the evangelist as a part of Jesus's identity proclamation. But not only is the final Passover attached to Jesus's identity proclamation, several other Passovers, feasts, and statements which are strongly related to the Passover motif are mentioned throughout the narrative, directing readers towards Jesus's final Passover (i.e., Jesus's passion).[7] All these narratives and allusions to Passover contribute to the Gospel's goal to identify Jesus as God's Messiah, or in other words, to convince that God's Messiah is Jesus.

The Fourth Evangelist starts this as early as chapter 1 where John the Baptist proclaims that Jesus is the "Lamb of God" (John 1:29). Even though "Lamb of God" echoes several OT institutions and images, as D. A. Carson points out,[8] it is foremost linked to the Passover lamb. The Passover lamb was not an offering in the same fashion as, for example, the sin offerings were. The Passover lamb had a protective function, which Jesus's vicarious death also had in that he "takes away the sin of the world" (John 1:29). Moreover, Jesus's role as the Lamb of God has many links to the events during his passion.

In chapter 2, Jesus cleanses the temple at the Passover (John 2:13-22). Jesus's act of cleansing (John 2:14-17) and his following proclamation (John 2:19) are related to Passover. He is the new temple, the "place" of worship of YHWH. Through him, all have access to God. But that requires first his death and resurrection within three days. In chapter 3,

---

5. Cf. Wheaton, *The Role of Jewish Feasts*, 185.
6. Cf. Köstenberger, "John," 499–507.
7. Bruner, *The Gospel of John*, 1026–28.
8. Carson, *The Gospel According to John*, 149.

Jesus has a conversation with Nicodemus (John 2:2—3:15)[9] during the Passover feast. The conversation ends with reference to Moses and the nation's wilderness experience. Nicodemus was a competent conversation partner and knew that Jesus was referring to the nation's sin and the concomitant cure by the means of the bronze serpent. Now here was the God-given savior who is going to be lifted up at the Passover for a public view for salvation. In chapter 6, Jesus feeds over five thousand people in the context of the Passover feast (John 6:4). Jesus's miraculous act leads to his identity proclamation; he is the bread of life from heaven, and he is a true drink that gives life (John 6:35, 55). These words do not only relate to the miraculous work of Jesus at the beginning of chapter 6 but also to Israel's first Passover experience. At the first Passover, Israelites ate a meal prepared according to God-given instructions. As they obeyed those instructions, they were kept safe and led out (i.e., saved) from Egypt. Jesus points towards his passion as the up-coming Passover lamb (John 6:53–58), revealing his identity as the one who is the life-giving "Passover meal."[10] The first Passover was followed by the exodus. On the way to the promised land, God—not Moses—gave the people bread from heaven. Now in the new exodus, Jesus is the bread of life from heaven that is greater and better "food" than the "manna" because he ensures eternal life (John 6:27). These are Jesus's identity proclamations which are deeply embedded in the Passover feast.

The next Passover mentioned in the FG is Jesus's final one. Jesus's passion in the FG is placed as an antitype to the type of the Passover in the OT. Yet the evangelist makes but a few explicit statements of that relationship. He seems to write to the well informed (i.e., competitive) readers, expecting them to make these observations. But the few fulfillment quotations from the OT that are included are climaxes in the FG demonstrating how Jesus fulfills OT Scriptures.

The first OT fulfillment is recorded in John 19:24 where Psalm 22:18 is quoted, "They divided my outer garments among them, and for my clothing they cast lots." The Synoptic Gospels refer to Psalm 22 as well, but in different way. They record Jesus's cry from the cross, "My God, my God, why have you forsaken me?" (Matt 27:46; Mark 15:34), which is the first line in Psalm 22. This suggests that the evangelists saw this Psalm as important perhaps because it contains many prophetic statements now

---

9. John 3:16–21 is most likely the evangelist's commentary on the conversation recorded in 3:2–15.

10. Wheaton, *The Role of Jewish Feasts*, 88.

fulfilled in Jesus, such as the sufferer's thirst (Ps 22:15), pierced hands and feet (Ps 22:16), unbroken bones (Ps. 22:17), and finally, divided untorn garments (Ps. 22:18). The Fourth Evangelist quotes Psalm 22 only once out of these several options. But he must have had in mind the entire Psalm 22 and its fulfilment in Jesus's crucifixion in a similar way as it is arguably used by Jesus in the Synoptic Gospels. The Fourth Evangelist is alluding to Psalm 22:15 (cf. Ps 69:21) in John 19:28, when Jesus says, "I am thirsty." Also, it seems that his inclusion of Psalm 22:17 in John 19:36, and perhaps Psalm 22:16 in John 19:37 is intentional. These last two points concerning unbroken bones and piercing Jesus's side, however, are so central for the Fourth Evangelist that he quotes other OT passages to use them in their full rhetorical power.

Psalm 22 is taken as messianic by NT writers although it is not interpreted as such in Judaism.[11] In addition, the Fourth Evangelist may have had in mind more than the mere historical fact of untorn garments as fulfillment of Psalm 22:18. It may be seen also as a prophecy of the undivided Kingdom that God had promised to David (2 Sam 7:13).[12]

The next Scripture fulfillment is recorded in John 19:36. Exodus 12:46, "nor are you to break any bone of it" (cf. Num 9:12; Ps 34:20) is fulfilled in Jesus. The OT type, the Passover lamb whose bones were not broken, finds a greater and fuller meaning in the NT antitype Jesus, who is the Lamb of God crucified without a bone broken. During all the subsequent Passover lamb preparations and the Passover meal celebrations held after the initial Passover meal in Egypt, the Israelites also observed these OT instructions: the Passover lamb's bones were not broken. Therefore, the connection between the Passover lamb and Jesus is readily noticed. Köstenberg points out that "This [fulfilment] authenticates Jesus' claim of his messianic identity. . . . [A] powerful link is established between Jesus' sacrificial death and the Jewish Passover, which commemorated the deliverance of the Israelites from their bondage in Egypt."[13]

The final Scripture fulfilment is pointed out in the next verse in John 19:37. Zechariah 12:10, "They shall look on Him whom they pierced," which is only a small part of the entire verse in Zechariah 12:10, is fulfilled in Jesus. Therefore, not only this historical act of piercing is fulfilled but Zechariah's entire prophecy. Without going into a detailed study on

---

11. Köstenberger, "John," 502–1.
12. Daly-Denton, "The Psalms in John's Gospel," 132–33.
13. Köstenberger, "John," 503.

Zechariah's prophecy, we notice that "looking on Him" is a reference to YHWH in Zechariah. Therefore, this prophecy now fulfilled in Jesus is a proclamation of his divine identity. People are looking on God—that is, Jesus of Nazareth crucified. Also, they will bitterly weep (Zech 12:10) because they have literally killed (pierced) YHWH in his Son Jesus. The Fourth Evangelist's presentation differs from the theologizing of Zechariah's prophecy in Judaism.[14] His goal was to correct those views in Judaism in order to achieve his main purpose of writing his gospel, namely, to lead the readers to accept that Jesus is the Christ, the Son of God.

Some details of Jesus's passion emphasize Jesus's identity as the Lamb of God, but are not explicitly pointed out. For example, the timing of Jesus's death. Jesus was crucified approximately at the same time when Passover lambs were slaughtered on the day of preparation, Nissan 14. It is implicitly communicated that Jesus died at the time when the Passover lamb sacrifices ceased in the temple that afternoon before Nisan 14 was over.[15] According to our calendar, this would be Friday afternoon. Thus, the meal that Jesus ate with his disciples had to take place the day before and thus it could not be a Passover meal (John 13:1); there was no lamb on the table. Jesus was the paschal lamb slaughtered on the cross day later. The Passover meals in homes were celebrated on Nisan 15 evening, while Jesus was laying in the tomb. Jesus himself, therefore, is the Passover "meal" that needs to be eaten (cf. John 6:53–58). This timing as such indicates that Jesus replaces the Passover feast and slaughter of the Passover lamb with new and more complete meaning. His death on the cross is the antitype for the Passover commemoration and brings a fuller meaning to it: he is the deliverer that does not just bring freedom to Israel from her current physical/religious bondage, but instead, he is the deliverer who brings freedom to the whole world, freedom from the bondage of sin. As impossible as it was for Israel to get out from Egypt's bondage without divine intervention, so it is for the world to get out from the bondage of sin to the life eternal without divine intervention by Jesus, God's Lamb.

Finally, there are other type—antitypes, which can be reconstructed from the accounts of the first Passover and FG's narrative of Jesus's passion. These include the following:

---

14. Köstenberger, "John," 505.
15. Brown, *The Gospel According to John*, 2:933.

- First Passover lamb was sacrificed to bring "salvation" from the death of firstborn—Jesus was sacrificed to bring "salvation" from eternal death.
- First Passover lamb's death leads the nation of Israel to freedom from the bondage of Egypt—Jesus's death leads the whole world to freedom from the bondage of sin.
- First Passover led the nation of Israel to the exodus (from Egypt to the promised land)—Jesus's final Passover led people to the second exodus (from this life to eternal life).
- First Passover was celebrated to commemorate God's redemption of the nation of Israel—Jesus death was God's redemption of mankind.

In summary, the FG makes several connections between the first Passover and Jesus's passion during that feast. The most obvious and important single point that the Fourth Evangelist makes is that Jesus is the ultimate Passover lamb—the Lamb of God—who took the place of the lamb of the feast of Passover. Jesus brought a new and greater meaning to the Passover feast, namely, protection from God's wrath and release from the bondage of sin. If the first Passover Lamb brought redemption to the nation of Israel from the slavery of Egypt, the final Passover Lamb brought redemption to the entire world from the slavery of sin. Jesus is, therefore, the perfection of the Passover feast.[16]

## Unnamed Feast

We have an obvious problem with the unidentified feast (John 5:1) to demonstrate how Jesus's words and deeds are related to the feast's symbolism. Johannine scholarship has suggested that the feast could be Passover, Purim, Pentecost, Tabernacles, Rosh Hashanah (Jewish New Year/the Feast of Trumpets). It is noticeable that John names the feasts of Tabernacles (7:2) and Passover (6:4) as "the feast of the Jews." This same phrase introduces the scene in 5:1, but without any further information about the name of the feast, unlike chapters 6 and 7 where the name of the feast is spelled out elsewhere in the narratives. What makes the naming of the feast even more difficult is the textual variation in the text. Some early manuscripts include the article before the word "feast"

---

16. Cf. Matera, *New Testament Theology*, 268.

whereas some other manuscripts omit it.¹⁷ There is strong evidence that "feast" without the article is most likely the original, leaving the identification of the feast impasse to us.

There were three pilgrimage feasts in the Jewish religious calendar: Passover, Tabernacles, and Pentecost. If the unidentified feast is not the Passover or the Feast of Tabernacles, it could be Pentecost, for it is arguable that Jesus made these pilgrimages to Jerusalem as a "good Jew" was expected to do. In addition, Raymond E. Brown argues briefly for this option, pointing out that it "would explain the references to Moses in the discourse (v. 46–47); for, in history, the Feast of Weeks (Pentecost) was identified with the celebration of Moses's receiving the Law on Mount Sinai."¹⁸

The reason why the evangelist does not give the name of the feast is most likely rhetorical. He wanted to link Jesus's actions and following words to the Sabbath day rather than the feast. Jesus's miraculous healing act and the following proclamation are related to the Jewish notion of the Sabbath day observance. Therefore, the feast setting is, at this time, a mere historical marker giving an overall framework to the event.¹⁹ What is important for readers to know is that this took place in Jerusalem (5:1) where a large multitude of Jews were present because of the feast, and that it took place on the Sabbath day (5:9). Let us turn next to look at the narrative itself to see how it works to reveal Jesus's identity.

It was the Sabbath day when Jesus performed healing and when the healed man carried his bed. Readers are told this after the matter in v. 9 in order to create a drama between Jesus and the Jewish aristocrats.²⁰ This also emphasizes Jesus's action.²¹ In addition, the statement, "Now that day was the Sabbath," is a bridge between the event and its aftermath. It gives the proper framework to read both Jesus's actions and his debate with Jewish authorities.

The Jewish authorities are pointing their fingers not only at Jesus but also at the healed man. The healed man obeyed Jesus's command to get up and pick up his pallet and walk. That caused the Jews to point their

---

17. If there were a unanimous testimony in the mss that the original text included a definite article, it would be arguable that this feast was most likely the Passover or the Feast of Tabernacles. But due to the lack of such a testimony, we cannot draw this conclusion in any probability. See UBS⁵ *Greek New Testament* John 5:1 textual critical footnote.

18. Brown, *The Gospel according to John*, 1:206.

19. Carson, *The Gospel According to John*, 241.

20. See John 9:14 for the same pattern.

21. Burer, *Divine Sabbath Work*, 126.

fingers at the healed man. It would have been acceptable to carry a pallet with a lame person lying on it, as the works of passion (i.e., work with appropriate motivation) were occasionally allowed on the Sabbath. But in this case, the lame man was healed and did not need anyone to carry him; he himself was carrying his pallet according to Jesus's command. That was, however, contrary to the proper Jewish way to keep the Sabbath (cf. Mishnah, *Sabbath* 7:2)—yet it was not against OT teaching of the Sabbath rest.[22] The OT forbids customary work on the Sabbath, but "dominant rabbinic opinion had categorized the prohibition into thirty-nine classes of work, including taking or carrying anything from one domain to another."[23] In his case, the Jews' accusation against the healed man is not developed further after they found out that it was Jesus who was behind the instruction to "break" the Sabbath. Thus, it is Jesus, his actions (v. 16) and words (v. 17), that become the center of the dispute.

The evangelist indicates that Jesus was healing on the Sabbaths (John 5:16). Therefore, this "Sabbath healing" was not the first or the only time when Jesus had "broken" the Jewish Sabbath regulations. However, the frequency of the healings on the Sabbath is not the main question here. The main question is how healing and the Sabbath are revealed in relation to Jesus's role and identity.

The Jewish understanding of the Sabbath had developed throughout the centuries. The Sabbath observance formed one of the major tests to determine who took the God of Israel seriously. For example, some Gentiles who had become God-fearers adopted the Sabbath observance to demonstrate their devotedness. Many of the functions, which would have been permissible on the Sabbath according to the OT, were now denied. Rabbis formulated the Sabbath laws according to which one should live in order to please God. We could say that Jewish piety was demonstrated by correct behavior towards Sabbath observance. (i.e., to obey the scriptures). The one who did not keep the Sabbath was not pleasing God.

When this attitude regarding Sabbath is noted, it is little wonder why the Jews were questioning the healed man's action of carrying his mat and Jesus's action of healing on the Sabbath day. If one violated correct Sabbath behavior, one was violating not only the Sabbath law but was also rebelling against God. Jesus, however, corrects this when he says in v. 17, "My Father is working until now, and I am working" and again in v. 19, "the

---

22. Köstenberger, "John," 441.
23. Carson, *The Gospel According to John*, 244.

Son can do nothing of his own accord, but only what he sees the Father doing." These sayings imply that the Father works on the Sabbath. Jesus, as the Father's agent, also works and does the same things as his Father.

It was nothing new for the Jews that God was at work even on the Sabbath. According to the Jews' reasoning, God had to sustain the universe even on Saturday,[24] and God had to make each day anew including the Sabbath day.[25] In addition, God was understood to perform a number of perpetual activities on the Sabbath: (1) Jewish thinkers said that God exercised his power to judge even on the Sabbath; (2) Hellenistic Judaism held that God's creative power, and (3) ruling power were active also on the Sabbath. Jesus by his actions showed that he gives life, including eternal life, to an invalid man. This action and prerogative belonged only to God on the Sabbath day. Michael Burer summarizes this as follows:

> Jesus acts to heal the invalid man on the Sabbath. This is an example of the Father's divine Sabbath work of giving life, which Philo explains as the continually active creative power of God. The Son performs the same work by giving life through healing as well as giving eternal life, expressed through resurrection. Because the Father is the only one who can raise the dead, and Jesus makes this claim for himself, this passage is very nearly making a statement about the identity of Jesus in terms of actions restricted to the Father.[26]

What was new and incomprehensible for Jews was that Jesus reveals himself as God's agent and even calls God his Father. The evangelist summarizes this dilemma in v. 18, "the Jews were seeking all the more to kill him, because not only was he breaking the Sabbath, but he was even calling God his own Father, making himself equal with God." What follows is Jesus's long monologue where he explains his relationship with the Father and his own identity.

In short, the Sabbath day gives the proper context for Jesus to reveal his identity as equal with God in a much more emphatic manner than if this event had occurred on another day or even in a location other than Jerusalem. It seems reasonable to say that Jesus performed this miraculous act (1) to show his identity and that (2) he picked the Sabbath day in order to make his point very clear.

---

24. Cf. McGrath, *The Only True God*, 58.
25. Koester, *Symbolism in the Fourth Gospel*, 91.
26. Burer, *Divine Sabbath Work*, 133.

There is one more aspect that is related to the place of healing, namely, the Pool of Bethesda and Jesus's identity claim through this miraculous healing. The pool and its water were believed to have some extra-natural healing capacities as v. 7 and a gloss in 5:3b–4 point out. The site was also, in later times, a pagan sacred healing shrine to which some folklore traditions witness. If this is so, then Jesus's healing action is brought to compete with pagan gods and healing shrines. Jesus shows his superiority as a healer by not using the water of the pool that was central for healing cults.[27] He indeed revealed his divine identity also in that pagan context.

## The Feast of Tabernacles

The Feast Tabernacles (or Feast of Booths; Heb. *Sukkot*), one of the three pilgrimage feasts, was a harvest festival that centered on the celebration of God's provision during Israel's wilderness experience (Lev 23:43–43; Num 29:12–40; Deut 16:13–15). During the feast, people lived temporarily in booths to recall the journey from Egypt to the Promised Land. Festivities also included many offerings. It was marked by joy as a year's entire crop had been completely harvested. But as much as the feast was looking backwards, it was projecting the future blessings and hopes, which also were joyfully celebrated (Zech 9—14). Two public symbolic rituals were attached to the eschatological hope: (1) water drawing from the pool of Siloam, and (2) lighting the candles in the court of women.

George Beasley-Murray comments on Jesus's first recorded proclamation during the feast (John 7:37–39), which is also linked to the water drawing ritual, as follows: it is "an outstanding example of a characteristic of the Fourth Gospel, in that a saying or episode embodies memory or the great deeds of God in the past and anticipation of the saving acts of God in the future, both united in an affirmation of their fulfillment in Jesus in here and now."[28] In order to illustrate this, we will outline the major features of the water-drawing ritual.

The feast of Tabernacles was a seven-day long feast, which was extended by the following Sabbath making it an eight-day celebration.[29]

---

27. Keener, *The Gospel of John*, 1:638.
28. Beasley-Murray, *John*, 113.
29. It is a subject of dispute whether Jesus made his proclamation during the seventh day of the feast, which is officially the last day of the feast on which the

Early in the morning on each of the seven days, the priests walked from the temple to the pool of Siloam to draw water with a golden pitcher, and the water was brought to the temple in a joyful procession. Then the priests poured water onto the altar. While the water was carried to the temple, Psalms 113—118 were read/sang. During the reading of the opening words of Psalm 118, "Give thanks to the Lord," and again when the words, "O Lord save us!" from Psalm 118:25 were read, all male participants shouted, "Give thanks to the Lord!" This entire ritual was an extremely joyful occasion. The Mishnah even comments that "He who has not seen the joy of the water-drawing has not seen joy in his whole lifetime" (*Sukkah* 5:1).

Although the water drawing was related to prayer for rain in the coming year and thanksgiving for the past blessing when Israel had received water from the rock smitten by Moses, it was also related to the idea of future salvation as Isaiah 12:3 indicates: "you will joyously draw water from the springs of salvation." This feast was associated with an idea of the triumphant day of the YHWH described in Zechariah 9—14, the passage attached to the feast of Tabernacles. Among other things in this section of Zechariah, the idea in 14:8 stands out; here, Zechariah points toward the future blessing (salvation) when waters will flow from the city of Jerusalem to the east and the west forever (cf. Ezek 47:1–12; Joel 3:18). Thus, when Jesus stood up and cried out that he would give water to every thirsty person (John 7:37–38), he is proclaiming that the water-drawing ritual is fulfilled in him. He is in the temple (new temple, cf. John 2:21) and out of him will flow the waters of living water which will satisfy everyone who wants to drink.[30] The Evangelist clarifies this explaining that what in view was the "Spirit, whom those who believed in Him were to receive; for the Spirit was not yet given, because Jesus was not yet glorified" (John 7:39). Jesus's proclamation of the future blessing—availability of the Sprit—is further explained in John 14—16. In Jewish teaching, the water-drawing ritual was also related to the Holy

---

procession of the priests circled the altar seven times. Some scholars argue that it was on the eighth day, the day of solemn assembly of people when Jesus proclaimed himself as a source of water. See further comments from Brown, *The Gospel According to John*, 1:320.

30. See Beasley-Murray, *John*, 116–17, for further discussion about the word and idea of *koilia* (heart, belly or innermost being) in John 7:38. See also Bauckham, *The Testimony of the Beloved Disciple*, 280.

Spirit. Isaiah 12:3: "draw water from the springs of salvation" was interpreted to refer to the Spirit.[31]

While still in the temple, Jesus speaks again and pronounces that he is the light of the world (John 8:12).[32] This saying is linked to the second ritual, namely, lighting the candles in the court of the women. The water-drawing procession took place in the morning, and lighting the candles took place at night.[33] Four golden candlesticks were lit in the court of women. The light from the glow of the burning candles in the temple could be seen towards Jerusalem. This was a reminder of Israel's experience in the wilderness when a pillar of fire led the people at night (Exod 14:19–25). Secondly, it was an expression of hope for future light. Zechariah 14:7, the verse preceding the passage which predicts the living water flowing from Jerusalem, says, "For it will be a unique day which is known to the Lord, neither day nor night, but it will come about that at evening time there will be light." One cannot miss the relevant connection with the candlestick lighting ceremony. Jesus is the complete fulfilment of this as he is the light not only for Jews but also for the whole world.

Jesus's words "follow me" (8:12) also reminds us of the exodus and the pillar of fire that was followed as the nation sojourned in the wilderness at night (Exod 13:21, 22). Now not only the nation but the whole world should follow Jesus who is the light. The second exodus is at hand.

Jesus's statement triggered a long conversation between Jesus and the opposing Jews. That dialogue ends in a physically risky situation that leads Jesus to escape from the temple. While leaving, Jesus continues his teaching by providing an object lesson by healing a blind man (ch. 9). Jesus sent him to wash himself in the pool of Siloam—in the very same pool from which the water was drawn during the feast. At the end of that scene, the blind man is moved from darkness to light, which is used as a proof that Jesus's statements of his role are correct.[34] Jesus is God's agent who fulfills expectations attached to this Jewish ritual of the candlestick lighting ceremony.

---

31. *Sukkot* 5:55a; see Beasley-Murray, *John*, 117.

32. Note that it is the evangelist who is commenting and narrating in 7:39–52; 7:59—8:11 is not found in the oldest mss of the Gospel. Thus, Jesus's two sayings in 7:37b–38 and 8:12 occur in the same context and are perhaps addressed to the same audience.

33. Whether the lighting of the candlesticks took place every evening or whether they were lit once on the first night of the feast is not clear. What is clear, however, is that every evening there was a joyful celebration in the women's court under the light. See Beasley-Murray, *John*, 127; Brown, *The Gospel According to John*, 1:343–44.

34. Keener, *The Gospel of John*, 782. See also Wahlde, "The Pool of Siloam," 173.

## The Feast of the Dedication

The Feast of the Dedication (Hanukkah) in John 10:22–39 is the only observed Jewish feast mentioned in the FG that is not based on God's command. The feast itself was firmly established as a yearly celebration. It is recorded in 1 Macc 4:36–59 and 2 Macc 10:5–8. The celebration was a commemoration of the rededication of the cleansed temple and the altar rebuilt in 167 BCE under the leadership of Judas Maccabeus.

The feast's suitability for inclusion in the FG is argued in a variety of ways. First, some scholars think that it is included because of its historical significance. There is a link between Jesus's work as deliverer and the nation's celebration of its political (and religious) deliverance from Seleucid powers during which Antiochus IV (Ephiphanes) (215–163 BCE) ordered an image of Zeus to be erected to the temple and swine to be sacrificed on the altar.

Secondly, Hanukkah's inclusion can be argued by liturgical grounds. Lectionary readings around Hanukkah included the theme of sheep and shepherds. Also, a candle lighting ritual was part of the liturgy, which, according to some scholars, was perhaps the key ritual during the "Festival of Lights" (i.e., Hanukkah).[35] Obviously, Jesus speaks about sheep and shepherds in this context as well as about himself as the light of the world earlier in this chapter.

Thirdly, there is an argument that the name of the feast, Hanukkah, is included for the sake of narrative's chronology. The feasts in the FG are sometimes taken as chronological markers. For example, several mentions of Passover are interpreted to indicate how long Jesus's public ministry was before his crucifixion. In sum, because Hanukkah took place about two months after the feast of the Tabernacles, it is quite natural to think that the evangelist includes it at this time in his narrative to provide chronological flow.

Finally, the most recent argument for the inclusion of Hanukkah in the FG is because it includes the miraculous and therefore it fits with Jesus's miraculous works which point towards his identity.[36]

All these four views may carry meaningful reasons for Hanukkah's inclusion in the FG and its relation to Jesus's words during the feast. Even the chronological argument is somewhat valid; Hanukkah took place after Sukkot and thus describes the advancement in time in Jesus's public

---

35. *Ant.* 12.325
36. Dennert, "Hanukkah," 431–51.

ministry. There are, however, a few other indicators in that narrative that suggest more important reasons for the inclusion of this feast.

First, the Jews' opening question about Jesus's identity plainly informs the reader what is at the heart of the conversation (John 10:24).[37] Jesus's references to himself as a shepherd who looks after his sheep is fulfilment of the proclamation of God's promise to look after his own sheep himself (Ezek 34). This is an explicit statement about Jesus's identity as well; he is the one whom God himself has placed to look after his sheep.

It is noteworthy that John 10 is the chapter of the "Good Shepherd." Jesus's "sheep and the shepherd" talk extends from the beginning of the chapter until v. 30. It may escape the casual reader, however, that the context of the "sheep and shepherd" talk changes in v. 22. The point Jesus makes in this talk is that he is the Good Shepherd who takes care of the sheep and that there has not been such a shepherd prior to this. Previous "shepherds" have been thieves and robbers who have harmed the sheep. Therefore, this entire passage 10:1–30 is linked to Ezekiel 34, which is a prophecy spoken against Israel's shepherds and which indicates how God himself seeks the scattered sheep and takes care of them. What makes this significant is that the first half of Ezekiel 34 was read during the feast of the Tabernacles and the second half during the feast of the Dedication.[38] Thus the evangelist places Jesus's teaching about sheep and the Good Shepherd in these historical contexts and liturgical intertexts. His motivation to deal with the events that took place at these two feasts back to back in his literary presentation is found in the messianic passage Ezekiel 34.

In addition, because the shepherd was a "symbol for the Davidic king . . . the messianic implications of Jesus' claim to be the shepherd were apparent to the Jewish authorities."[39] So it is no wonder why Jesus continues his "sheep-shepherd" speech after the Jews asked him to state plainly if he was the Messiah (John 10:24) and after his own comment that the Jews do not believe his true identity although his works testify that he is Messiah (John 10:25). Jesus applies Ezekiel 34, where the Davidic king is a God-appointed shepherd, to himself; the Davidic king whose arrival the Jewish nation waited for has now arrived in Jesus.

---

37. Wheaton, *The Role of Jewish Feasts*, 159.
38. Aker, "John," 65.
39. Brown, *The Gospel According to John*, 1:406.

Jews were expecting the Messiah to be a national liberator, whereas Jesus's messiahship was more spiritual in nature, liberating the people from their sin.[40] Keener notices, "It is . . . strikingly ironic that the promised Messiah, Israel's deliverer, would face rejection at a festival commemorating a national deliverance."[41] Another pertinent aspect of Jesus's "sheep-shepherd" passage is that Jesus's audience are those who are supposed to act as the shepherd of the nation, but instead of giving this designation to them, Jesus goes to the other extreme—saying that they are not even his sheep (John 10:26–27).

The second way in which the feast of the Dedication is connected to Jesus is historical, namely, the theme of the dedication of the temple/altar. Festivities celebrated the rededication of the temple/altar, but at the same time, they brought to the minds of celebrants "the miraculous events associated with the dedication of the tabernacle and temple under Moses, Solomon, and Nehemiah."[42] As God consecrated the tabernacle/temple, displaying his presence/glory in the past, so some Jews continued to anticipate the day when the "Temple would again be dedicated in the likeness of its dedication in the days of Solomon."[43] This was now at hand in Jesus. Jesus says in John 10:36, "do you say of Him, whom the Father *sanctified* [*hēgiasen*] and sent into the world" (emphasis mine).

The Greek word used for "dedication" in John 10:22 is *egkainia*. This is the word that is used in the Septuagint for "dedication or consecration of the altar in the tabernacle in the Exodus (Num 7:10–11), in the Temple of Solomon (1 Kings 8:63), and in the Second Temple (Ezra 6:16)."[44] When Jesus refers his consecration in John 10:36 he uses the word *hagiazein*. This word is also used in the Septuagint for the consecration of the temple (Num 7:1), but not for the consecration of the altar where the verbal form *egkainia* is employed (*egkainizein*; Num 7:10–11). These two words (*hagiazein* and *egkainia*), although used in slightly different ways in the Septuagint, are synonyms; both describe the fact that the object is separated for God and his purposes.[45] Yet *hagiazein* is a more appropriate word to describe Jesus's concentration, for he offers himself as the

---

40. Brown, *The Gospel According to John*, 1:406.
41. Keener, *The Gospel of John*, 1:822.
42. Hoskins, *Jesus as the Fulfillment of the Temple*, 171.
43. Hoskins, *Jesus as the Fulfillment of the Temple*, 171.
44. Brown, *The Gospel According to John*, 1:402.
45. Brown, *The Gospel According to John*, 1:404.

sacrifice which is different from the inauguration of proper sacrifices in the temple/altar.[46] Now the Father consecrated his Son. This was "ratified by both his own claim (10:36) and his works (10:25, 32, 37–38)."[47] The point here is that it is possible to understand that Jesus fulfills the feast of the Dedication as he is the consecrated offering and a new temple, aspects that are attached to Jesus also elsewhere in the Gospel (e.g., John 2:13–22 and John 17:1, 4, 5, 19). God and the Son are glorified when Jesus is lifted up (John 17:1). Thus, the Jews' anticipation of the presence of God's glory in the temple is fulfilled in the new Temple, the Son of God, that is, in Jesus.

Finally, the recent study by Brian Dennert is worthy of mention. He argues that at this time Jesus is not claiming to be a "fulfillment" of the feast.[48] This is so perhaps because there is nothing to be fulfilled as the feast was not a God-given (i.e., OT) feast.[49] Instead, Jesus reveals his identity in an effective manner, in a way which relates closely to the feast.

Bennert makes an observation that "Jesus' works suits the festival of Hanukkah because of a tendency to associate Hanukkah with miracles."[50] 2 Maccabees refers to several miraculous events performed by God that led to the rededication of the altar and temple. "Since the book [2 Maccabees] seeks to promote observance of the feast, these miracles serve to prove the validity of Hanukkah."[51] That might be the reason why Jesus emphasizes his works (10:25, 32, 37–38) which are miraculous in that they came from God. Dennert concludes,

> The proposed connection between Hanukkah and miracles points to the discourse of John 10:22–39 operating as a defense of Jesus' identity as the Son of God rather than as an argument that Jesus "fulfills" or "replaces" Hanukkah. In effect, the discourse shows that, although "the Jews" recognize and celebrate Hanukkah because of miracles associated with the feast, they rejected Jesus in spite of his great miracles, which testify to his identity as the Messiah and the Son of God. Therefore, the

---

46. Cf. Bauckham, "Holiness of Jesus and His Disciples," 98–107.

47. Hoskins, *Jesus as the Fulfillment of the Temple*, 173.

48. We have argued above that Jesus fulfills some aspects of the feast. So, at this point, we do not fully agree with Dennert, but we do agree that the main point in this narrative is Jesus's identity proclamation. Cf. Wheaton, *The Role of Jewish Feasts*, 160–62.

49. Keener, *The Gospel of John*, 1:823.

50. Dennert, "Hanukkah," 432.

51. Dennert, "Hanukkah," 442.

members of the Johannine community are Jesus' sheep and have life, while the synagogue community, led by "the Jews," face judgment.[52]

## Sabbath

The Sabbath was an all-important and well-observed day by Jews. In the Hebrew Scriptures, the Sabbath is a sign of the covenant and holiness (Exod 31:12–17) that is related to God's rest on the seventh day after his creating activity (Gen 2:1–2). In Deuteronomy, the Sabbath is also attached to the idea of God's "definitive display of power and salvation on behalf of his people in the exodus from Egypt."[53] Thus the focus moves from creation to redemption, in other words, to "the creation of Israel as the people of God."[54] In Isaiah 56:1–8 (cf. Exod 20:8–11; Deut 5:12–15), the Sabbath is viewed as God's presence/salvation which is available for all. In Isaiah 66:23, it is linked to God's dealings in the future and thus his eschatological activity.[55] God will renew everything in the future, and the Sabbath is a sign or a down payment of this. From this brief overview, we see that God intended the Sabbath as a blessing and as a sign of his provision and holiness.

Over time, however, the nature of the Sabbath had changed from blessing to burden, from joyful weekly celebration to strict religious exercise. The Sabbath observance became a measuring stick for one's righteousness. Mishnah *Sabbath* 7:2, a well-known passage regarding the Sabbath's rest, reads the following:

> The generative categories of acts of labor [prohibited on the Sabbath] are forty less one: he who sows, ploughs, reaps, binds sheaves, threshes, winnows, selects [fit from unfit produce or crops], grinds, sifts, kneads, bakes; he who shears wool, washes it, beats it, dyes it; spins, weaves, makes two loops, weaves two threads, separates two threads; ties, unties, sews two stitches, tears in order to sew two stitches; he who traps a deer, slaughters it, flays it, salts it, cures its hid, scrapes it, and cuts it up; he who writes two letters, erases two letters in order to write two letters;

---

52. Dennert, "Hanukkah," 451.
53. Burer, *Divine Sabbath Work*, 40.
54. Burer, *Divine Sabbath Work*, 41.
55. Burer, *Divine Sabbath Work*, 48.

he who builds, tears down; he who puts out a fire, kindles a fire; he who hits with a hammer; he who transports an object from one domain to another—lo, these are the fourth generative acts of labor less one.[56]

There were only a few exceptions when Jews were allowed to work on the Sabbath. These exceptions were introduced after the horrible massacre of the Jews when they refused to defend themselves on the Sabbath against Antiochus IV's troops in 168–69 BCE (cf. 1 Macc 1:29–42). Now Jews could defend themselves and help a dying child on the Sabbath. The point is that the Sabbath was no longer a "sign of God's redemption of Israel and his sanctification of them. Instead, the Sabbath has become a requirement, the keeping of which will result in their salvation."[57]

Some Jewish texts indicate that God did not work on the Sabbath whereas some other texts confirm that he works to some extent on the Sabbath (cf. Ps 121). For example, Philo viewed God continuously creating and exercising his power to judge. There are also several passages elsewhere which imply that God is not in complete rest on the Sabbath.[58] Interestingly, even some Jewish texts reveal that not only God himself but also his agents/holy persons may carry out activities, which are not normally acceptable on the Sabbath, such as to execute duties in the Jerusalem temple.[59]

But how does the Sabbath relate to Jesus in the FG narratives? The FG begins the same way as the book of Genesis; both indicate that there was God/*Logos* before anything else and that God/*Logos* created everything; both accounts begin with the same words "in the beginning." Obviously, God's rest on the seventh day after his creative act and his later commandment to his people to keep the Sabbath were taken seriously. Jews withdrew themselves from all normal weekly business. But when Jesus did not do that (John 5:1–18; 9:1–41), he was accused of his actions. Jews viewed Jesus as a mere Israelite who needed to observe the Sabbath like everybody else in order to obey and please God and gain his favor. The evangelist, however, depicts Jesus as divine creator-*Logos* who shares the same identity with the Father. Therefore, Jesus may work even on the Sabbath imitating his Father who is also working. This is in line with

---

56. Adapted from Neusner, *The Mishnah*, 187–88.
57. Burer, *Divine Sabbath Work*, 95, 100; Yee, *Jewish Feasts*, 37–38.
58. Cf. Brown, *The Gospel According to John*, 1:216–17.
59. Burer, *Divine Sabbath Work*, 100–1.

some Rabbis' view that God "cannot rightly be charged with violating Sabbath law since the entire universe is his domain (Is. 6:3), and therefore he never carries anything outside it."[60] The Evangelist reveals Jesus as divine whose domain is the entire universe (cf. John 1:3, 10, 11; 8:12) and records Jesus's Sabbath works from that perspective.

The FG indicates that Jesus customarily healed the sick on the Sabbath (John 5:16). Yet the evangelist includes only two such healings in his account (John 5 and 9).[61] The literary pattern on both occasions is roughly the same: the healing takes place first, and afterwards it is stated that it was the Sabbath.

One of the evangelist's motives to include Jesus's Sabbath activity is eschatological. The Sabbath was a sign pointing toward the future times, namely restoration of life when there would be a complete rest. In both healing miracles, Jesus restores the life of the sick person giving him not only physical well-being but also eternal life. Burer points out that "In Jesus, God was acting now to fulfill the eschatological hope, and the Sabbath was a fitting day on which to do this."[62]

The second motif for Jesus's Sabbath healings in the FG is that they expose who Jesus is. The events in chapter 9 demonstrate the point. The scene opens with Jesus's disciples' question "who sinned, this man or his parents, that he would be born blind?" (John 9:2). This question reflects the Jewish notion of cause-effect thinking (cf. v. 34); there had to be sin that causes the blindness.[63] At the end of the narrative, it is Jesus whom the Jews judged as sinful (v. 24) based on the fact that he did this on the Sabbath. But the healed man came to a different conclusion about Jesus's identity saying, "If this man were not from God, He could do nothing" (v. 33). Sometime later, Jesus further reveals himself as "Son of Man" (v. 35b), which is a messianic title (cf. Dan 7:13–14). The formerly blind man understood the title as such, for he believed in Jesus and worshiped him (v. 38). In addition, at the end of the narrative, Jesus responds to the Pharisees' question about their blindness indicating that in their case sin causes their blindness (vv. 40–41). By this point in the healing narrative, Jesus has revealed his identity as the Son of Man. That identity is proved by his Sabbath healing and the testimony of the healed man. Yet

---

60. Carson, *The Gospel According to John*, 247. Cf. McGrath, *The Only True God*, 58.

61. The two healing miracles are similar to each other. See Malina and Rohrbaugh, *Social-Science Commentary*, 109.

62. Burer, *Divine Sabbath Work*, 111.

63. Köstenberger, "John," 460.

the Pharisees are identified as sinners, which is proven by their stubborn refusal to confess their spiritual blindness. The blind man was on the other side of the spectrum. "A review of later rabbinic literature reveals that the blind were categorized with the destitute and those incapable of being valid witnesses."[64] Yet, the healed blind man became a valid witness to Jesus's identity. The Pharisees who claimed to be God's witnesses were actually blind because of their sin, and therefore, not able to function as God's witnesses to the world.

It can be concluded that Jesus's purpose to heal on the Sabbath was to demonstrate his superiority. Jesus replaces Jews' understanding of Sabbath by his divine work which brings light/life, rest and restoration. It also reveals Jesus's divine identity as he is engaged in Sabbath work in the same fashion as the Father is.

## Jewish Wedding

The narrative in John 2:1–11 is difficult to reconstruct. As commentators have noted, several aspects of the story are elusive; for instance, what exactly is the significance of the chronology (the third day), Mary's request/command, Jesus' obscure answer to his mother, the Jewish purification rites, the six stone water jars, and the quality of wine? These topics among others has been discussed in scholarship, but the conclusions are less than uniform. We limit our study to the wedding context and Jesus's involvement in the central dilemma, a dilemma that ultimately reveals Jesus's identity.

It is significant that Jesus's first sign took place at a Jewish wedding (John 2:1–11). Yet the question follows: how does the sign relate to the wedding feast itself? Wine is not only served at weddings. Purification pots are found in every Jewish home. Water is not special either. Is the historical context just accidentally a wedding party? Is the Jewish ritual of purification more relevant background to Jesus's wine miracle than the wedding itself? Various suggestions of the primary symbolism of this narrative are found in commentaries; many of them are certainly valid observations. However, the primary point that the evangelist gives, we argue, is found from v. 11b where it says that by his miraculous act Jesus "manifested His glory, and His disciples believed in Him."

---

64. Brant, *John*, 153.

Keeping this in mind, we now take a closer look at the historical context of the wedding and of Jesus's involvement in the events during the wedding feast. We need to ignore many details of this narrative in order to keep our focus on the task.

Not only weddings as such but also elements like wine and joy were linked to messianic times. For Jews (as in all cultures), a wedding feast was a joyful celebration. Presence of wine was a part of the means to add joy to the occasion, for in "Jewish thought wine is a symbol of joy and celebration."[65] For this reason, we can understand why running out of wine was such an unfortunate situation. In addition, the wine was, at least partially, supplied by the wedding guests. Lack of wine might have been taken to indicate lack of friends, and this would definitely have been remembered long afterwards in the community. Whether or not Jesus and his disciples had provided such a gift (cf. Mary's comment in v. 3) is unknown, but at the end of the day, Jesus did both in quantity and quality. He restored the joy. Symbolically this may suggest that the old Jewish way has lost its joy, but that joy is restored in Jesus. Perhaps more significantly this situation and especially wine are linked to the messianic times that included the notion of a time when wine would flow in quantity (cf. Isa 25:6; Jer 31, especially vv. 12–13).[66] The fact that Jesus brings or restores joy at the wedding emphasizes that Jesus as Messiah brings joyful resolution in the midst of a hopeless crisis.

A wedding as such serves as an appropriate context in which Jesus's identity is revealed. In the OT, the wedding is a symbol of messianic days (Isa 54:4–8; 62:4–5). Jesus used wedding and banquet symbolism when referring to the kingdom of God (Matt 8:12; 22:1–14; Luke 22:16–18). The wedding motif is picked up again in Revelation (19:9).[67] Thus, when Jesus performs his first sign, revealing his glory during the wedding feast, that context supports Jesus's proclamation of the arrival of the messianic age. Restoration of joy and abundance of wine further support this. It is worth noting that the headwaiter's comment, "you have kept the good wine until now" (v. 10b), symbolically carries an idea of final days when there is quality and quantity of new wine.

Jesus's choice to use the stone waterpots instead of wineskins or other vessels which were now empty of wine is significant as well. As

---

65. Köstenberger, "John," 431.
66. Köstenberger, "John," 431.
67. Brown, *The Gospel According to John*, 1:104–5.

the evangelist points out, these waterpots were usually used for Jewish ritual purification (v. 6). Therefore, Jesus's act can be attached to purification. The old Jewish ways of purification, which were also much debated among Jews,[68] are not efficacious. Stone waterpots can be defiled and the purification ritual itself is not once for all. Jesus's act of using them, perhaps, is a hint that the purification that Jesus will provide is efficacious. If this is a valid observation, then Jesus's act points towards his passion (cf. vv. 4, 11, 19–22).

At the end of the day, Jesus's disciples believed in him, for he had now revealed his glory.[69] The Messiah who will restore the joy is also the one who has brought the final days into existence. His role, however, includes not only miraculous signs, but also passion, to which the concept of "glory" points.[70] However, we will not develop this idea further, for it is not our primary purpose at this time.

## Jewish Funerals

Jesus's final public sign prior to his crucifixion is found in the context of the funeral (John 11:1–44). Funerals were carefully observed occasions in Jewish culture. It was a duty for a Jew who was somehow related to the grieving family to visit and mourn with the family who had lost one of its members. In some cases, non-related mourners were invited to come as the number of mourners indicated the family honor[71]—the more mourners, the greater honor. The mourning (*shivah*) lasted seven days, during which friends visited the house of sorrow while neighbors provided food.[72] Therefore, it was Jesus's duty, as a friend of Lazarus, to go up to his funeral.

"People were normally expected to fulfill the symbolic contract implied in friendship by dropping everything and going immediately when summoned."[73] Jesus, however, did not act when he heard the news that Lazarus was seriously ill (John 11:6). Only after Jesus knew that Lazarus was dead, he called his disciples to go with him to Lazarus's home. The

---

68. Cf. Keener, *The Gospel of John*, 1:509–13.
69. Cf. Brant, *John*, 58–59.
70. See Keener, *The Gospel of John*, 1:515–16.
71. Brant, *John*, 174; Malina and Rohrbaugh, *Social-Science Commentary*, 199.
72. Keener, *Bible Background Commentary*, 292.
73. Malina and Rohrbaugh, *Social-Science Commentary*, 195.

reason for his delay can be seen in his purpose to demonstrate his role over the death (cf. John 11:4, 25–26, 43–44) and his identity (cf. John 11:41b–42). When Martha and Mary point out that Jesus arrived "too late" in order to help (John 11:21, 32), Jesus does not show any regrets about the fact that he did not arrive earlier.

Delayed arrival works also as a narrative design. It creates impasse—the situation in which, according to public opinion, even Jesus could not do anything (John 11:12, 21, 32, 37). But for Jesus, it was necessary to arrive "late" in order to reveal his role as resurrection and life. Thus, the sharp contrast between death-sorrow and resurrection-life is created. Jesus's demonstration of his role as the resurrection-life and reality of the life after physical death is so powerful that the narrative proceeds immediately to describe what kind of reaction it created among the Pharisees and chief priests in Jerusalem (John 11:47–53).

Jesus revealed his role over death by his "I AM" saying in vv. 25–26 prior to his demonstration of that role by raising Lazarus from the dead. Jesus's "I AM" saying is the result of the conversation between Martha and Jesus in vv. 21–24. There is a progression of thought in Jesus's sayings which Martha misunderstands. Her misunderstanding is taken care of when Jesus calls Lazarus out from the tomb. Martha's first statement, "Lord, if You had been here, my brother would not have died" (v. 21) indicates that nothing can be done any more. Thus, her second statement, "Even now I know that whatever you ask of God, God will give you" (v. 22) may not indicate Martha's hope or faith in Jesus that he could resurrect Lazarus at that point. Her indirect request has another meaning. Jo-Ann Brant notes, "Within the context of Jewish mourning, a typical petition would include request on behalf of the dead for forgiveness and inclusion in the book of life."[74] Therefore Jesus's response to Martha that Lazarus will rise again is understood by Martha not as an immediate possibility but as future eschatological hope of Lazarus's resurrection. Martha's "I know that he will rise again in the resurrection of the last day" is natural and according to the notion of Jewish soteriology and eschatology. But the reader who has read the "last chapter of the book" knows that this is not what Jesus meant. Jesus is clarifying his statement now with an "I AM" statement. The meaning of vv. 25–26 can be understood in the following way:

74. Brant, *John*, 174–75.

*Verse 25, First Line:*
Whoever believes in Jesus
Will, even when he [physically] dies,
[then, i.e., in the future physically re-] live
[i.e., will take part in Jesus' accomplished Resurrection of Life]

*Verse 26, Second Line:*
Whoever has [eternal] Life and believes in Jesus,
Will never [spiritually, definitely] die ["in sins"],
[i.e., one is freed from the eschatological damnation verdict, from "eternal" death].[75]

Martha's response to Jesus's "Do you believe this?" is "Yes," but the reader is still left with a feeling that Martha did not fully understand what Jesus meant. She shows, however, her willingness to accept Jesus's statement as she re-affirms her faith in Jesus by confessing her understanding of Jesus's identity as the Son of God.

Before the day is over, Jesus demonstrates that his "I AM" statement is true, for he calls Lazarus out from the tomb back to life. It needs to be kept in mind that Jesus's conversations with Martha and Mary were private and thus unknown to the mourners. Therefore, for the mourners, the full meaning of Jesus's revelation of himself is less readily available. They do hear, however, Jesus's prayer addressed to the Father which, as such, points out his relationship with the Father and his identity. For the reader, however, the private conversation is revealed. The reader is able to "feel" the full power of the narrative when Lazarus comes out from the tomb.

When Jesus requested the stone to be removed, Martha informs Jesus that Lazarus had been dead already for four days. This information is important for the point Jesus is making. Jews believed that "the soul stays near the grave for three days, hoping to be able to return to the body. But on the fourth day, it sees decomposition setting in and leaves it finally."[76] Therefore, by the time when Jesus arrived all hope for Lazarus's immediate resurrection had disappeared. Moreover, it would have been insulting for the grieving family and towards the dead if the tomb was opened as decomposition would have already started.[77] In spite of this, the stone was moved and only then Jesus cried out, "Lazarus come out!" (v. 43). Lazarus's resurrection was proof for Martha and Mary and the

---

75. Adopted from Bruner, *The Gospel of John*, 671.
76. Morris, *The Gospel According to John*, 485.
77. Brant, *John*, 176.

rest of the mourners that Jesus has the power to give life. Jews' attached the life-giving attribute only to God. Jesus revealed that he shares the same life-giving attribute with God and so proclaims his identity.

This event paves the road for Jesus's own death (cf. John 11:47–53)[78] and burial (cf. John 12:1–8). Jesus's first sign took place at the wedding and so began his way to the cross. His final public sign took place at the funeral, which hammered the last nail into his "coffin." Now his enemies made up their minds to get rid of Jesus (John 11:47–53).

## Concluding Remarks

There is ample evidence to conclude that the Fourth Evangelist uses the feasts as the platform for Jesus's identity proclamations. Jesus's actions and words replace, fulfill, or in other ways exceed Jewish rituals and their religious significances. For this reason, every reader of the FG should ask the following question while reading the feast narratives: why does Jesus say or do this right now during this feast or occasion? The Fourth Evangelist is a competent writer who did not write these things down by accident. He rhetorically communicates his points in order to persuade his readers to grasp his point, namely that Jesus shares the divine identity with the Father.

## Suggestions for Further Reading

Burge, Gary M. *Jesus and the Jewish Festivals: Uncover the Ancient Culture, Discover Hidden Meanings*. Grand Rapids: Zondervan, 2012.

Daise, Michael A. *Feasts in John: Jewish Festivals and Jesus' "Hour" in the Fourth Gospel*. WUNT 2.229. Mohr Siebeck: Tübingen, 2007.

Wheaton, Garry. *The Role of Jewish Feasts in John's Gospel*. SNTSMS 164. Cambridge: Cambridge University Press, 2015.

Yee, Gale. *Jewish Feasts and the Gospel of John*. Wilmington: Michael Glazier, 1989. Reprint, Eugene: Wipf and Stock, 2007.

---

78. Brown, *The Gospel According to John*, 1:428.

CHAPTER 3

# Moses in the Fourth Gospel

*Jesus's Identity Compared and Contrasted*

MOSES IS AN IMPORTANT character in the Hebrew Scriptures and the central figure for Judaism. Moses is the one through whom God gave the Law. In the FG, Moses/the Law define what is right and wrong for Jews. Jewish authorities referred to Moses in their arguments against heretical teachers and teaching (cf. John 9:28–29). Similarly, they used Moses against Jesus for they believed Jesus's deeds and proclamation were against Moses (cf. John 19:7).[1] In short, Moses was an authority and a very important source for orthodoxy and orthopraxy in Judaism.[2]

Moses's importance to the Fourth Evangelist's presentation of Jesus is demonstrated by several explicit and implicit references to him. Jesus, a Jew himself, often refers to Moses as well. Jesus's references and allusions to Moses are made, however, for a different *telos* than his opponents, who

---

1. Moses and the Law are used as parallel terms; when the Law is mentioned, it first refers to Moses who gave the Law. Moses is the one to whom God spoke; that is, God gave his Law to Moses (cf. John 9:29), and so we have the phrase "the law of Moses" (John 7:23). This is also demonstrated by the fact that Moses is spoken of as a giver of the Law (7:19), even in instances where the actual commandment was not communicated through Moses (7:22). See Harstine, *Moses as a Character*, 44.

2. Although the Fourth Evangelist probably wrote his Gospel outside of Judea-Galilee in the Hellenistic environment towards the end of the first century CE, its content (Moses motif included) indicates that the evangelist did not write a Hellenized Gospel. The FG can be best understood against a Jewish backdrop. Contra Rudolf Bultmann who argues that the FG is Hellenistic Gospel; see Rudolf Bultmann, *The Gospel of John*.

argued against Jesus by using Moses as their authority.³ In the FG, Jesus invokes Moses so that he may compare and contrast Moses and himself, thereby revealing his own identity (cf. John 1:17).

Although Moses/the Law of Moses is also mentioned several times in the Synoptic Gospels, Moses is used differently in the FG. Here, Moses is often used in the argumentative context where Jesus's identity or role is in view, whereas in the Synoptic Gospels he is not brought into such sharp argumentative discourses regarding Jesus's identity. In the Synoptic Gospels, Moses is mentioned with a few exception in narratives such as Jesus's circumcision (Luke 2:22), healing (Matt 8:4; Mark 1:44; Luke 5:14), the transfiguration (Matt 17:3–4; Mark 9:4–5; Luke 9:30, 33), as a reference to the Law in the discourses about divorces (Matt 19:7–8; Mar 10:3–4) and eschatology (Matt 22:24; Mark 12:19, 26; Luke 20:28, 37).⁴ Below we will sketch the role of Moses in the FG's narratives, giving special attention to its relation to Christology.⁵ But before looking into explicit references and allusions to Moses, we must outline how Moses was attached to messianic hope in Jewish, Samaritan, and Christian thought.

## Moses and Messiah in Jewish, Samaritan, and Early Christian Notions

The notion of Messiah varied in Judaism but was not without some uniformity. Moses's role and identity were related to the Messiah and messianic time. Judaism held a correspondence between Moses and the Messiah, and although the Rabbinic literature that points out these type-antitype similarities is dated later than Jesus's time, there is little doubt that these views were already circulating among Jews during the first century CE. The foundation for the view of the coming Messiah's similarities to Moses was the nation's exodus experience under Moses's leadership. Moses was the God-sent deliverer. This similarity was also exhibited in

---

3. All explicit references to Moses in the Fourth Gospel are found in the book of signs during Jesus's public ministry (3:14; 5:45, 46; 6:32; 7:19, 22, 23). See Culpepper, *Anatomy of the Fourth Gospel*, 105.

4. The exception is Matthew 23 where Moses is used similarly to the FG where Jesus speaks against the scribes and the Pharisees.

5. There are also other old covenant figures, such as John the Baptist, Abraham, and Jacob who have a role in the Gospel narrative. They are also used as a part of the argumentation to show Jesus's superiority. Cf. Coetzee, "The Gospel According to John," 53.

the Hebrew Scriptures even beyond the Pentateuch. Selective passages in the Prophets and Writings also gave rise to the view that the first and the last redeemers are similar in many ways. A striking text is found, for example, in the Midrash *Kohelet Rabbah* 1.9, and parallel passages, which states that the last redeemer (i.e., Messiah) will be like the first redeemer (i.e., Moses):

1. As Moses placed his wife and sons upon a donkey (Exod 4:20), so also the last redeemer will be seated on a donkey and ride on it (Zech 9:9);

2. Like Moses, the first redeemer brought down the manna (Exod 16:4), so also the second redeemer will bring down manna (Ps 72:16); and

3. As Moses opened the well, so too the last redeemer will provide water (Joel 4:18).[6]

The notion that the Messiah is also a deliverer like Moses was not out of place according to NT writers. Even Jesus alluded to this, for example, in John 3:14–15. Messiah Jesus was not, however, a deliverer in the same sense as Jews expected. Jesus came to deliver the nation (the whole world) from its sins (John 1:29). Jews' understanding of the concept of "deliverance" was attached to their theological construction, which was different from the person of Jesus and his role as a deliverer. This contributed to the rejection by the leading Jews of Jesus's claims of his identity as God-sent divine Messiah.

The Jews connected the promise about a coming prophet like Moses (Deut 18:18–19) to the messianic times.[7] The leading Jews separated the eschatological prophet figure from Messiah as a forerunner for Messiah (cf. John 1:21; 7:40–41). Even Jewish people generally seem to have this understanding as John 6:14–15 testifies; crowds, after witnessing Jesus's feeding miracle, concluded that Jesus must be the prophet who was

---

6. See *Midrash Rabbah* on Ecclesiastes 1.9. Quotation of this text is found, for example, in Brown, *The Spirit in the Writings of John*, 161.

7. There is also a valid argument that the "prophet-like-me" is realized in Jeremiah. The comparison of Jeremiah 1:7–9 and Deuteronomy 18:18 shows a close correspondence between these two. See Boismard, *Moses or Jesus*, 1–2. This does not, however, take away the fact that Jews were expecting Messiah to whom "prophet-like-me" is linked as John 1:21 demonstrates.

promised.[8] Some sources suggest that Moses himself may even appear again as the Messiah's forerunner.[9]

The Samaritans were expecting a teacher-Messiah who would be a promised prophet like Moses (Deut 18:15–19). The Samaritan woman verbalized this saying, "I know that Messiah is coming . . . when that One comes, He will declare [teach] all things to us" (John 4:25). Jesus agrees with her statement in the sense that he confirms that he is the expected Messiah. Some Samaritan sources indicate that there will be no prophet as great as Moses.[10] This is not, however, a contradiction that the Samaritans linked the prophet-like-Moses with some future eschatological prophet in messianic times. It is important to keep in mind that the Samaritans only accepted the Pentateuch as authoritative scripture on which they also based their eschatological views including the future coming prophet.[11]

Despite different emphases in Jewish and Samaritan thought, both these groups, one way or another, related the prophet-like-Moses-promise to messianic time. Thus, it is fair to say that the first-century Jews as well as Samaritans were expecting a Messiah who is linked to Moses and would thus perform similar deeds to Moses, yet perhaps even on greater scale (cf. John 7:31).

The early Christian notion regarding the Moses-Messiah connection can be seen in various NT passages. For example: (1) Moses was tested in the wilderness 40 years whereas Jesus was tested over 40 days and nights (Matt 4:2); (2) Moses had 70 elders—Jesus had 70 disciples (Luke 10:1); (3) Moses's face shone which can be compared Jesus's Transfiguration (Luke 9:28–36); (4) Moses and Jesus fasted 40 days (Matt 4:1–11); and (5) Stephen refers in his speech to Moses and Deuteronomy 18:15 (Acts 7:37; cf. 3:22).

As for the FG, it is noticeable that Deuteronomy 18:15–19 also stands in relation to Jesus and his messiahship. For example, Deuteronomy 18:16 refers to Israel's Horeb experience (cf. Deut 4:10–14) where God gave Moses the Law. This is compared and contrasted to Jesus, as incarnated *Logos*, through whom grace and truth were given (John 1:17).

---

8. As Deuteronomy 18:15–19 is the only text in the OT that announces the coming of a specific future prophet like Moses, people in John 6 must have referred to that text.

9. Glasson, *Moses in the Fourth Gospel*, 27.

10. Boismard, *Moses or Jesus*, 3–4.

11. Boismard, *Moses or Jesus*, 4.

At Horeb God spoke to Israel "face to face" (cf. Deut 4:10–11; 5:4), but even that was not a perfect revelation. It is Jesus who reveals the Father to people (John 1:18). Deuteronomy 18:18 points out that the promised prophet who speaks the words which God puts into his mouth is fulfilled in Jesus. Jesus repeatedly states that he speaks only the words that he hears from his Father (e.g., John 8:28; 12:49–50). For the Fourth Evangelist, Jesus is the "second Moses," yet greater than the "first Moses," but at the same time, Jesus does not play down Moses's role as God-given agent to his people in the past (cf. John 5:46).

In conclusion, we can say that there are several similarities between Moses and Jesus which were not missed by NT authors. The link between Moses and Messiah was well established in the early Christian thought. What makes this striking is that although this connection was also made between Moses and the coming Messiah in Judaism, Jewish authorities did not accept those similarities in Jesus's words and deeds. They missed Jesus's identity claims and his actions which validated those claims. What is also striking is that the FG shows how they did not just miss Jesus's identity, but they tried to demonstrate that there is no connection between Moses and Jesus stating, "We know that God has spoken to Moses, but as for this man [Jesus], we do not know where He is from" (John 9:29).

## Reading Moses in Two Different Ways

In the FG, Jesus's opponents and Jesus's readings of Moses are far apart from each other. Although Moses and the Law are part of both of their argumentations, the opponents and Jesus interpret them in different ways. For example, Jesus accused Jews that they do not believe Moses because they do not read Moses correctly, whereas Jews insisted that they are followers of Moses (John 5:46–47; 7:19; 9:28). Unbelieving Jews argued that Jesus's claims and deeds are not in line with Moses, which also implied that their views and actions were indeed according to the law of Moses. In short, their understanding of the requirements of the law of Moses made them conclude that Jesus should be put to death for blasphemy (John 18:31; 19:7).

On the other hand, the Fourth Evangelist repeatedly employs Moses, directly and indirectly, to argue for Jesus's identity. These arguments are almost always found on Jesus's lips. Jesus points out on several occasions how Moses and the law should be read such a way that demonstrates that

Moses wrote about him (cf. John 5:45–46). He also uses the OT texts, calling it "the law," to show how Jews' hostile actions toward him were predicted in the law (John 15:25).

Jesus's reading of Moses differed from that of the unbelieving Jews' reading, which in many cases created controversy, even hostility. Interpretation of the Scriptures (as it is today) was one of the central issues in these two opposing views that have not escaped the Fourth Evangelist's notice.

## References to Moses: Argumentation for Jesus's Identity

There are many references to Moses in the Gospel of John (1:17, 45; 3:14; 5:45, 46; 6:32; 7:19; 7:22, 23; [8:5];[12] 9:28, 29). The name "Moses" is used on several occasions in relation to Jesus. Moses is also implicitly referred to in various places where there is a reference to "the law." We will look at first explicit references to Moses before moving to texts which allude to him. We will do so under three headings: (1) Jesus of whom Moses wrote, (2) Jesus as the "Prophet" superior to Moses, and (3) Moses violation—Jesus violation.

### Jesus of Whom Moses Wrote

#### John 1:45

The second reference to Moses is found in John 1:45 (the first is in the Prologue v. 17), where Philip tells Nathanael "We have found Him of whom Moses in the Law and *also* the Prophets wrote—Jesus of Nazareth, the son of Joseph." This statement is a parallel to Andrew's statement in 1:41 although he does not make his point in the same words as Philip, "We have found the Messiah."[13] That brings forth a twofold statement regarding Jesus; it points out that Moses wrote about the coming Messiah and that this promise is now fulfilled in Jesus of Nazareth. Nathanael confirms this at the end of the narrative scene in 1:49.

---

12. The section 7:53—8:11 is not included in the earliest manuscripts and may not be the original part of the Gospel. See for textual critical argumentation, Comfort, *Early Manuscripts*, 115–16.

13. Keener, *The Gospel of John*, 1:482–83.

It is not impossible that the phrase "whom Moses . . . wrote" in the mind of Philip was a specific reference to the promised prophet-figure in Deuteronomy 18:15–19.[14] Francis Glasson points out that "[t]here can be little doubt that the way in which Christ is presented in the Forth Gospel is intended to indicate that he is the fulfillment of Deut. 18:15–19."[15] This would explain why John the Baptist denies the suggestion that he would be "the prophet" (John 1:21). He was neither the Christ nor the "Prophet-like-Moses" because both of these identifications were reserved for Jesus. Philip's statement in 1:45 is necessary to be noted and kept in mind while reading the rest of the FG as it identifies the promised Mosaic prophet with Jesus of Nazareth.[16] This identification is not recognized by Jesus's opponents but is used here and elsewhere in the FG as an argument for Jesus's identity.

### John 5:46

In John 5:46 Jesus declares to his opponents, "For if you believed Moses, you would believe Me, for he wrote about Me." Here Jesus is not only using Moses to prove his identity but also as one who is going to judge Jesus's opponents (v. 45). The Jews' misreading of Moses was the problem; they had set their hope on Moses but due to their interpretation of him, they missed the one of whom Moses wrote.

Earlier in the same narrative, the Pharisees accused the healed man about breaking the Sabbath law (John 5:10). Yet, it was Jesus who was the cause of the healed man's "wrong" action. Therefore Jesus, by his command to the sick man to pick up his pallet and walk (5:11), sets himself above the Pharisees' authority and interpretation of the Sabbath. Jesus also makes himself equal with God by demonstrating and proclaiming that he is imitating his Father who is working even on the Sabbath day (5:17–18).[17] Jesus is, therefore, standing in sharp contrast to the unbelieving Jews' understanding of Sabbath observance. For them, Jesus was

---

14. The phrase "Jesus of Nazareth" is exclusively a NT phrase not found in Moses or the Prophets. Thus, Moses did not write about "Jesus of Nazareth" but a God-sent-prophet like him who will function as a broker between God and his people. See also Matt 21:11 for the Synoptic Gospels' testimony of this view.

15. Glasson, *Moses in the Fourth Gospel*, 30.

16. See the purpose statement in John 20:30–31 to see how John 1:45 is in line with the overall purpose of this Gospel.

17. McGrath, *The Only True God*, 58.

violating the Sabbath command received through Moses. Jesus was, however, fulfilling his Father's task and revealing his own identity.

The Fourth Evangelist uses Moses as an authority who witnesses to Jesus and thus demonstrates continuum in God's revelation. This is one of the evangelist's rhetorical tools to persuade the Jews (and the entire readership) that Jesus is Christ who is sent by God.

## Jesus as the "Prophet" Superior to Moses

Jesus is presented as a prophet par excellence in the FG. He also is the fulfilment of the prophecy that there will be "the prophet like Moses," although that promise in Deuteronomy 18:18–19 is not explicitly quoted in the FG. Below, we will look at passages in which Jesus is presented as the prophet superior to Moses.

### John 1:17

The Fourth Evangelist introduces John the Baptist and Moses to his readers in the Prologue (John 1:1–18). Both their identities and roles are compared and contrasted with that of the incarnated *Logos*. They are vital agents of God, but they are not superior or even equal to *Logos*. Yet, in spite of their inferior identity in comparison to the incarnated *Logos*, they are not presented in negative terms. Moses's role is briefly but accurately stated in a way that every Jew could agree with; "the Law was given through Moses" (1:17a). Moses's role is then contrasted with the incarnated *Logos* through whom "grace and truth were realized" (1:17b). Moses and *Logos*, therefore, share some similarities in their roles. Both were (as John the Baptist was) agents (brokers) of God, but what they brought forth from God to mankind are different realities. Therefore, they were equal neither in their roles nor identities. *Logos*'s identity and role superseded that of Moses's identity and role. The realities (grace and truth), which incarnated *Logos* brings, are superior to the law, which was given to Moses to communicate. It is reasonable to say that through Moses God gave instruction about grace and truth (the Law), whereas Jesus fulfilled the law by being the very content of grace and truth (the atonement). Besides, Jesus's superiority is alluded to in the next verse where Jesus, incarnated *Logos*, is the one who knows God, whom no-one has ever seen intimately (1:18). This seems to be an allusion to Moses who saw God from behind (Exod 33:18–23). Jesus, however, is the one who has seen God in his full splendor and now explains (exegetes) him to the entire mankind.

## John 3:14

Jesus refers to Moses's agency in John 3:14, "As Moses lifted up the serpent in the wilderness, even so must the Son of Man be lifted up." Although Jesus does not make an explicit statement about his superiority over Moses and his mission as God's agent, it is implied. Just before this statement, Jesus has revealed that there is no one else who has gone up to heaven except the Son of God (v. 13).[18] By this statement, he refers to himself. This is surely a statement that claims Jesus's superiority over Moses. Also, Jesus is not merely God's agent to lift something up, but he is the Son of God who is going to be lifted up.[19] This can be read typologically. Moses's bronze serpent (Num 21:18) functions as a type and Jesus as its antitype (John 3:14; 19:37). Antitypes do not only function to make a link between the type and antitype but also to demonstrate superiority to their types. Thus, Jesus as God's agent to save is greater than the bronze serpent erected by Moses who saved Israelites' lives in the wilderness; Jesus's lifting up will bring salvation to the whole world. In other words, Moses's action pointed to a greater reality that was fulfilled in Jesus.

It is also noticeable that the Fourth Evangelist could have omitted Moses's name if only the historical act of erecting the bronze serpent for cure were pertinent.[20] The reason for the inclusion of Moses's name is important, however, to bring full rhetorical force to Jesus's proclamation. The context in which Moses erected the bronze serpent was a revolt against Moses (Num 16:13). Korah, Dathan, and Abiram "reproach him for having raised himself up as head above all the people . . . In other words, the opponents challenge the idea that Moses has received a special mission from God, they deny that he was sent by God."[21] Therefore, Jesus's reference to Moses as the one who erected the bronze serpent is significant as the Jews were opposing him as God-sent agent similar to the way that Moses's opponents in Numbers 16:13 opposed Moses's status.

---

18. Cf. Klink, *John*, 202.
19. Klink, *John*, 203.
20. Harstine, *Moses as a Character*, 53–57.
21. Boismard, *Moses or Jesus*, 15.

Yet Moses was God's agent who erected the bronze serpent for a public view for the purpose of healing. In the same way, Jesus as a God's agent was going to be lifted up for the healing and restoration of the world.

## John 6:32

Jesus again refers to Moses in his "bread of life" discourse in John 6:32. That discourse creates also a "greater than Moses" argument. Before that discourse, Jesus performed a miracle of feeding over five thousand people (vv. 1–14). This scenario ends with the statement of the crowd, "This is truly the Prophet who is to come into the world" (6:14b). This is an allusion to Moses who was used argumentatively in the previous chapter (John 5:39–47). Now in John 6:31, the crowd refers to the Scriptures and Moses, the one who gave them bread (manna) to eat in the wilderness during their forefathers wandering in the desert.[22] The context indicates that this statement is to show that the crowd knew Moses as a God-sent deliverer. After experiencing a similar miracle performed by Jesus, they concluded that Jesus had to be the prophet like Moses promised in the Law (v. 14). Yet, a little bit later, the crowd requests a sign from Jesus so that they can place their faith in him just as their forefathers (and currently the Jewish leaders) placed their faith in Moses (6:30). Jesus's response to this is twofold. First, he corrects their misunderstanding about who gave bread to their forefathers. It was not Moses but Jesus's Father (6:32). Secondly, he points out that he is the requested sign himself. He came down from heaven (6:33, 38). He is the bread of life. He will suffer to provide life (6:53–58). Whoever eats this bread shall receive eternal satisfaction (6:33, 35–40).

## John 6:14 and 7:40–41, 52

Three passages strongly suggest the application or the denial of the title, "the prophet" to Jesus, namely, John 6:14, 7:40–41, and 7:52. These passages are significant as they are referring to "the prophet like Moses," the eschatological prophet of Deuteronomy 18:18–19.

On the first occasion (6:14), Jesus fulfills the expectations of the people regarding "the prophet." The crowd concluded that "this is truly

---

22. Note that in the Jewish wisdom tradition "manna" and Torah are related; both of them are bread that gives life. See Barrett, *The Gospel According to St. John*, 293.

the Prophet who is to come into the world." As a result, they are ready to make him their king (v. 15). In John 7:40–41, after Jesus's proclamation at the feast of Tabernacles about offering the water that quenches the thirst permanently (vv. 36–37), some Jews conclude that Jesus must be "the prophet."[23] The reason for this conclusion seems to be based on the eschatological hope of the nation's salvation and the memory of how Moses provided water from the rock, now realized in Jesus.[24] Thus linking Jesus to Moses and the eschatological prophet should not become as a surprise. Finally, in John 7:52, Jewish leaders reject the idea that Jesus is fulfilment of the promise of the coming prophet-like-Moses. The argument is that no prophet comes from Galilee. The reader of the FG knows better because Jesus is the *Logos* whose origin is *pros ton theon* ("face to face with God") (John 1:1).

Marie-Émile Boismard has observed that in 11:27 Martha uses a structure similar to the confession as we have in 6:14 and 7:40. This time, however, Martha replaces the title "the prophet" with the title "Christ." Martha states, "You are the Christ, the Son of God, *even* He who comes into the world." The same takes place in 7:40–41 where these two statements: "This certainly is the Prophet" and "This is the Christ," are stated in immediate sequence in the text.[25] These three "the prophet" passages in chapters 6 and 7, therefore, seem to link these two titles together. They give readers the understanding that Jesus is "the prophet" promised in Deuteronomy.

### Moses Violation—Jesus Violation

Moses was a God-sent broker to bring Israel out from Egypt. The nation had to listen to Moses if they wished to listen to God. If they did not listen to Moses, they did not listen to God, and that always had negative consequences. Jesus's Jewish opponents thought that they were followers of Moses and thus were pleasing God. But Jesus pointed out that they were not following Moses because if they were, they would have listened to Jesus. Moses wrote about him (John 5:46), a God-sent broker, who has now arrived to explain the Father. But the Jews did not accept Jesus's status and identity and so dismissed his message as well. This made Moses

---

23. Tenney, *John*, 87.
24. Beasley-Murray, *John*, 117–18.
25. Boismard, *Moses or Jesus*, 6–10.

their accuser rather than their advocate. They violated Moses because they did not believe what he wrote (5:45–47). In short, that is tantamount to not heeding Moses during the exodus which would cause them to miss God and thus also the promised land.

Jesus uses Moses again in his argumentation in John 7:16–24 to uphold his action of healing a sick man at the pool of Bethesda (John 5:6–9). Jesus reminds the Jews that they occasionally had to break the Sabbath observance to practice Moses-given circumcision.[26] For this reason, they should not accuse Jesus of violating the Sabbath because his action brought life to that man. In this scenario, the reader gets the impression that Jesus's action of healing a man is greater than one receiving a circumcision on the eighth day. This is further demonstrated at the end of the chapter. The Pharisees complain that people do not know the law (7:49) but they are ready to violate the law themselves which is the intent of Nicodemus's remarks (7:50–52).

Jesus's argument is underpinned by another point. The law of Moses was given to protect life. Jesus provided life to the sick man on the Sabbath day. In this sense, Jesus is not breaking the law of Moses. However, Jesus's opponent Jews were seeking to kill him (7:19), that is, to violate the nature of the Law.[27] As they missed the nature of the Law, they missed Jesus as well. In short, Jesus demonstrates that he fulfills the Law by bringing life, whereas his accusers are violating the Law by their unrighteous judgments on Jesus (7:24).

A similar situation is found in 7:53—8:11,[28] which is a later insertion to early manuscript texts.[29] The scribes and Pharisees bring a test case before Jesus to see if he acts according to the Law—or better, their way of applying the Law in this particular case. Jesus's response to the scribes and the Pharisees demonstrates how the Law should be applied.

---

26. Jesus says that Moses gave circumcision although, as the text also points out, it was not from Moses but the Fathers (cf. Gen 17:10–12). Use of Moses's name may not only refer to the fact that the giving of circumcision is recorded in the law of Moses but also to bring rhetorical force to Jesus's argumentation. Cf. Matt 12:8–12 where Jesus defends his Sabbath work, *not* referring to Moses but to and the priests.

27. Klink, *John*, 368.

28. Perhaps the scribes' and Pharisees' attitude toward the law in 7:53—8:11 which is similar to 7:19–24 and Jesus's action and teaching in both these cases are the reasons why this section is placed in here.

29. See Comfort, *Early Manuscripts*, 115–16; Metzger, *A Textual Commentary*, 187–89.

The Law that brings judgment on the woman also brings judgment on those who accused her.

The last explicit references to Moses are found in John 9:28–29, where there is a conversation between the healed man and the Pharisees. As a response to the healed man's testimony and the question in 9:27, "You do not want to become His [Jesus's] disciples too, do you?" (which he was not yet; cf. vv. 35–38), the Pharisees responded that they were Moses's disciples, implying that they were *not* Jesus's disciples (vv. 28–29). This leads to the further dialogue which ends up with the excommunication of the healed man from the synagogue with the status "sinner" ascribed to him (v. 34, cf. vv. 22–23).

Here is an example of Johannine irony. The readers know better than the Pharisees in the narrative. Jesus speaks only the words he hears from the Father and performs acts he sees his Father does. Yet the Pharisees claimed to recognize Moses but missed Jesus who was greater than Moses. In this episode, Jesus's identity is contrasted to that of Moses. Jesus's opponents held Moses superior to Jesus. They thought that Jesus is not from God, whereas the healed man, using the Pharisees' own theological notions, argues the opposite (9:16, 29–33). The Pharisees dismiss Jesus as a sinner whereas the healed man worships Jesus as the Son of Man, that is, giving glory to God (9:24, 29, 35–38).

At the end of the chapter, the evangelist concludes that the Pharisees remained in spiritual darkness whereas the man who received his eyesight is now moved from physical and spiritual darkness to light. Thus, the Pharisees violate Moses (without even recognizing it) by casting the healed and spiritually enlightened man out of the synagogue community (i.e., Jewish community). This man had done nothing against Moses; he has just received healing from Jesus and accepted him as a new authority for spiritual light. In summary, it can be said that light was cast out so that darkness could stay in. Thus, by violating "Moses" the Pharisees also violated Jesus.

## Allusions to Moses and Jesus's Identity

In addition to the explicit references to Moses, there are various allusions to Moses in the FG. We will outline two of them to demonstrate how these allusions help readers grasp the Fourth Evangelist's agenda and how they are used to show identify Jesus's identity.[30] First, we take a look at Jesus's miraculous sign of changing water into wine, and then his role as the leader of the new exodus. These allusions show how the evangelist presents Jesus on a continuum from Moses to the agent of God superior to Moses.

## From First to Last Sign

In chapter two, the Fourth Evangelist records Jesus's first sign: turning water into wine. This event, as well as its manner of presentation have led to various interpretations and theories of how it fits the theology of the FG. Our purpose here is to see how it contributes to the Moses-Jesus motif. Glasson suggests that this incidence resonates with the very first plague in Egypt performed by Moses.[31] Through Moses water was turned into blood (Exod 7:17) as the first sign of a series of signs, so Jesus turned water into wine in Cana as his first messianic sign followed by other signs. Both of these signs, one in Egypt and one in Cana, inaugurated publicly the work of the God-sent deliverers, Moses and Jesus. The miraculous acts of Moses in Egypt (cf. Exod 8:23) and Jesus in Cana (John 2:11; cf. 4:54) are called signs which prove that these agents were sent by God.[32]

There is also a verbal similarity between these incidents. In Egypt, the water, which was turned to blood, was found in stone vessels. Similarly, Jesus uses stone water pots to provide plentiful wine. Jesus, although hidden away, points out that this is to reveal his identity as deliverer and to start his way to the cross. He does this by using "glory" language as a reference to his cross (2:11). In the same chapter (2:12–22), Jesus also cleanses the temple at the Passover so bringing his first sign together with his last sign, namely, his cross (2:13–22). One cannot miss the similarity to God's promise to Moses in Exodus 4:8 where he ensures that "If they will not believe you [Moses] or heed the witness of the *first sign*, they may believe the witness of the *last sign*" (emphasis mine).

---

30. See also other allusions to Moses in John 12:48–50; 8:28–29; 14:10 (cf. 7:16b–17); 17:8.

31. Glasson, *Moses in the Fourth Gospel*, 26. See also Boismard, *Moses or Jesus*, 55.

32. Boismard, *Moses or Jesus*, 56.

### Jesus as a Leader of the New Exodus

There are various connotations in the Fourth Evangelist's presentation of Jesus that resonate closely with Moses as the leader of the nation during the wilderness journey from Egypt to the promised land. Jesus is presented as such a leader in the "new exodus" that is from this world to the Father. Jesus's teaching in John 14:1–4 as well as the following response to Thomas's question about "the way" presents this the most explicitly. Jesus proclaims that "I am the way, and the truth, and the life; no one comes to the Father but through Me" (14:6).

The comparison of Moses and Jesus lead to several observations. In both cases, God sent his deliverer. Moses was sent for Israel, but Jesus was sent not only for Israel but for the entire world (1:29). Jesus is also greater than Moses; he is no mere man but eternal *Logos*, the Son of God (John 1:14). In both cases, the leader of the exodus performed signs to illustrate that this individual is indeed sent by God (see above). In Jesus's case, the greatest sign was when he was lifted up[33] as the lamb of God (John 1:29; 8:28). In both cases, the leader provides food and drink. Jesus, however, is himself the food from heaven that satisfies receivers eternally (John 6:51).

## Concluding Remarks

This chapter has not presented a comprehensive study on Moses in FG. Many allusions and themes, such as their farewell discourses, appointing their successors, the shepherd motif, glory and Sinai, and Jesus as Paraclete for the people have been left untouched. Enough evidence is given, however, to conclude that the Fourth Evangelist uses Moses extensively to reveal Jesus's role and identity to his readers. Jesus is an authoritative interpreter of Moses/the Law; he is a new Moses who leads people in the new exodus from spiritual darkness to light, from death to eternal life. Conversely, the Fourth Evangelist uses Moses as a prosecutor, rather than

---

33. "Lift up" is a typical language used in the Gospel of John to describe Jesus death on the cross. This phrase in 3:14–15 led the first reader (or hearers) to think a pole or standard, although it is not mentioned, on which the brass serpent was attached in the wilderness (Num 21:9). So "lift up" language elsewhere in this gospel may well be used by the author as an allusion to the Old Testament "pole" or "standard" as a reference to Numbers 21:9. As people were gathered around the brass serpent fastened on the standard, so people are called to gather around Jesus and his cross to receive healing (cf. John 12:32). See further Glasson, *Moses in the Fourth Gospel*, 36–37.

advocate, against those who did not accept Moses's testimony about Jesus and therefore missed Jesus as God-sent deliverer.

## Suggestions for Further Reading

Boismard, Marie-Émile. *Moses or Jesus: An Essays in Johannine Christology*. BETL 84a. Leuven: Leuven University Press, 1993.

Glasson, T. Francis. *Moses in the Fourth Gospel*. SBT. London: SCM, 1963.

Harstine, Stan. *Moses as a Character in the Fourth Gospel: A Study of Ancient Reading Techniques*. JNTSup 229, 2002. Pp. 40–78.

CHAPTER 4

# Jesus's Miracles and Works as Signs for Jesus's Identity

SEVERAL MIRACULOUS EVENTS ARE recorded in the FG which on some occasions are referred to as "signs."[1] Although Jesus's miracles are not always called signs, they are understood to be so based on the reason they are recorded. The evangelist is explicit about this in his purpose statement at the end of his account: "Therefore many other signs Jesus also performed . . . but these have been written so that you may believe that Jesus is the Christ, the Son of God . . ." (John 20:30–31). Jesus's miraculous deeds, therefore, carry a particular Christological slant. They are signs which speak to his identity.[2]

The word "sign" (Gr. *sēmeion*) is also used in the Synoptic Gospels. It is employed in the following two contexts:[3]

- Signs are used in eschatological contexts. For example, in Matthew 24:3 the disciples ask what the signs of Christ's return are and what the signs of the end times might be. Here eschatological "signs" are topics of discussion—they are not Jesus's performed signs as often is the case in the FG.

---

1. References to "sign" (Gr. *sēmeion*) is found from John 2:18; 4:54; 6:14, 30; 10:41; 12:18.

2. Cf. Anderson, *The Riddles of the Fourth Gospel*, 31.

3. Exceptions are found in Jesus's birth narrative where the baby lying in the manger is a sign for the shepherds (Luke 2:12), and Jesus's arrest narrative where Judas Iscariot's kiss is a sign to the Roman soldiers whom they have to arrest (26:48).

- Signs are also found in the Synoptic Gospels in the context where unbelievers are requesting a miracle from Jesus as proof of the credibility of his claims. For example, in Matthew 12:38–39 (cf. Mark 8:11–12; 11:29) the scribes and Pharisees wanted to see a miraculous sign from Jesus. Yet, there is no miraculous act of any kind. Instead, Jesus refers to the "sign of Jonah." In the FG there are two places where non-believers demand a sign from Jesus to believe him, namely, in John 2:18 and 6:30, which are not followed by the signs as the signs had preceded these questions already.[4]

Also, it is worth noticing that although the Synoptic Gospels contain more of Jesus's miraculous deeds than the FG, they are not spoken of as "signs." Besides, Raymond Brown reminds us that there is "difference in the circumstances accompanying the miracles" between the Synoptic Gospels and the FG. Even though the miracles themselves are very similar (and in some cases the same) in all the gospel narratives, Brown observes that the vivid coloring of the miracles has faded in the FG.[5]

One type of Jesus's miraculous deeds is missing entirely in the FG: exorcism. In the Synoptic Gospels, Jesus is depicted as the one who defeats the powers of Satan by performing an exorcism. But in the FG, Jesus demonstrates his power over Satan by his obedience to the Father, namely, by going to the cross. When he was lifted up, he glorified the Father and drew all people to himself. That is understood as the demonstration of his power over Satan (John 12:23–32). Jesus's miraculous deeds and works in the FG are attached to his claims of his identity rather than his power or authority like in the Synoptic Gospels.

## Meaning and Purpose of Signs

The meaning of the Greek word *sēmeion* is "sign" or "miracle."[6] It is used often to convey the idea of "miraculous sign" in the Gospels. The nature of signs is that they do not draw attention to themselves, but rather they point beyond themselves. In the case of Jesus's signs in the FG, they function as a part of Jesus's self-proclamation of his divine identity. A simple

---

4. Brown, *The Gospel According to John*, 1:527.
5. Brown, *The Gospel According to John*, 1:525.
6. For example, John 2:11 where *sēmeion* (in plural) occurs the first time in the Fourth Gospel, it is translated "signs" in ASV, ESV, NASU, NJB, NIV (2011) and "miracles" in KJV; it is translated as "miraculous signs" in LB, NET and NIV (1984).

analogy may help us here. If I wear a red hat, it is not a sign. But if it was told to someone who was tasked with meeting me at the airport that "the man who wears a red hat is the person whom you need to pick up," then my red hat becomes a sign, the sign of identification. The one sent to pick me up, however, does not pick up the sign (my red hat) but gives a ride to me as the person to whom the sign (the red hat) pointed. In the same way, John the Baptist testifies, he received a message from God that the one on whom the dove descended and remained is the one who baptizes in the Holy Spirit (John 1:33). The descending dove becomes a sign for the John the Baptist.

In the Septuagint (the first Greek OT translation), *sēmeion* is used also in this way. Signs point beyond the miraculous deed itself. God performed signs (*sēmeia*) through his chosen servants to reveal himself to his people. Graham Twelftree notes that the FG's "use of 'sign' is best understood in the light of the Septuagint, where the word is almost always used of God's showing himself to be the Almighty and Israel to be his chosen people through the miraculous events of the exodus (Deut. 26:8)."[7] Because of the Septuagint's usage of *sēmeion* and the FG's Jewish orientation, the meaningful intertexts for Jesus's miraculous signs are found in God's miraculous deeds in the OT rather than in other ANE literature. Especially the signs that were performed by God through Moses right before and during the exodus are noticeable. The series of signs in Egypt ends with the Passover when the blood on the doorposts functions as the sign to preserve the family from God's wrath (Exod 4:8; 12:13). Similarly, in the FG the series of signs lead to Jesus's final Passover, his death and resurrection, the greatest sign of all signs which ensures salvation for those who receive him.

Also, individual signs like Jesus's miraculous act of feeding more than five thousand people in a remote location in chapter 6 relates closely to Israel's exodus experience when God provided bread and meat in the middle of the wilderness. The feeding of over five thousand people with five loaves of bread and two fish is further used as the backdrop for Jesus's proclamation of his identity as the bread of life from heaven (cf. 6:35–58). It is worth noting that the connection between exodus/Moses and Jesus's act/proclamation was made by Jesus's audience, which Jesus uses to reveal his identity as the heavenly bread that satisfies for eternity.

---

7. Twelftree, "Exorcism in the Fourth Gospel and the Synoptics," 140.

It is interesting to note, however, that Jesus did not call his miraculous actions "signs." Rather he refers to them as "works"—works that the Father has given him to do (e.g., John 5:36; 9:4).[8] Jesus's vocabulary, however, is not playing down the evangelist's usage of the word "sign." In the OT, God's actions are referred to as his "works": God's creating activity is called "his work" (Gen 2:2), and God's salvific actions toward his people during their journey through the wilderness to the Promised Land are called God's "works." Brown points out that, "By the use of the term 'works' for his miracles Jesus was associating his ministry with the creation and the salvific works of his Father in the past."[9] Therefore, Jesus's "works" speak to his identity. As God (His Father) is creator and giver of life, so is he. As God has provided salvation in the past to his people, so is he providing salvation.

The author's purpose statement at the end of the Gospel (John 20:31) reveals the reason for the evangelist's inclusion of signs. They point towards Jesus's identity as Christ and the Son of God, namely, that expected Messiah is Jesus.[10] The purpose statement repeats what has already been said about signs at the time of the first recorded sign in John 2:11, "This beginning of *His* signs Jesus did in Cana of Galilee, and manifested His glory." "Jesus's glory" refers to his cross in the FG, and that is the very act of Jesus through which he makes his identity known as God's agent.[11] Since all signs in this Gospel carry rhetorical force to convince its readers about Jesus's identity as the only valid object of faith to have (eternal) life, the signs should be given adequate attention when the FG is read.

The evangelist also mentions that he did not include all the signs Jesus performed. He had to be selective which signs to include and which to exclude. He expresses this in these words: "many other signs Jesus also performed . . . these [signs] have been written so that . . ." (20:30–31). The Synoptic Gospels record more miracles than the FG.[12] What follows then is the question: Why did the author choose these signs and not the other ones of which he was also aware? We may not find the answer to

---

8. See O'Day, "Miracle Discourse," 186–87.

9. Brown, *The Gospel According to John*, 1:527.

10. Jensen, "John Is No Exception," 341–53, esp. 348–49.

11. O'Day, "Miracle Discourse," 182–83.

12. Brown notes that "some 200 of the 425 verses of Mark chs. i–x deal directly or indirectly with miracles, a statistic which means that almost one half of the Marcan narrative of the public ministry concerns the miraculous." Brown, *The Gospel According to John*, 1:525.

this question. Yet, we can confidently say that these signs were deliberately chosen and therefore readers should pay heed to them to grasp the evangelist's intention with his choice. These signs work rhetorically for his purposes, namely, to reveal Jesus's identity. They prove that Jesus, as the divine Messiah, is the one who brings God's salvation to the entire world (cf. John 20:30–31). Ben Witherington correctly notices that "[t]he goal is not to lead someone to faith in the power and possibility of miracles, but to lead them to faith in Christ."[13]

Jesus's audience for his signs included sometimes only his disciples (e.g., John 6:16–21) but other times his audience was public and included both his opponents and those who already trusted him (e.g., John 5:2–17). The signs did not bring always a positive outcome. They had a two-fold outcome: Some people trusted more in Jesus, whereas others (especially Jesus's opponents) grew in their dislike of Jesus. Those whose faith increased were willing to move towards what the signs signified. But in the other cases, the signs caused controversy between Jesus and his opponents and deepened their distrust in Jesus and his claims.[14] These reactions were caused by Jesus's signs which were performed to "back up" Jesus's proclamations about his identity.

## Miracles at the Time of Jesus and the Fourth Gospel

The Hebrew Scriptures were the source for Jewish living tradition. The authoritative Scriptures included also the Apocrypha writings from the intertestamental period onwards. The Greek translation of these writings is found in the Septuagint.[15] Further, many OT Pseudepigrapha[16] roughly from the sixth century BCE onwards were part of the Jewish "library." For example, a large number of Pseudepigrapha were found among the Dead Sea Scrolls at Qumran.[17] Also, Jewish oral law and scriptural com-

---

13. Witherington, *John's Wisdom*, 82. See also Brown, *The Gospel According to John*, 1:530–531; Keener, *The Gospel of John*, 1:276.

14. Cf. Anderson, *The Riddles of the Fourth Gospel*, 32.

15. Many Apocrypha writings are considered canonical in the Roman Catholic, Greek Orthodox, and Russian Orthodox churches, whereas only a few are canonical in Coptic Churches. The apocryphal books are considered extra-biblical (deuterocanonical) in the Protestant tradition. Evans, *Ancient Texts*, 9.

16. The word *pseudepigrapha* means "falsely superscribed." See Evans, *Ancient Texts*, 27–28.

17. For an introduction to Apocrypha and Pseudepigrapha, see Evans, *Ancient*

mentaries that began to appear in written form in Rabbinic literature, the Mishna (also called the Oral Torah) being the first one from the second century CE, were authoritative.[18]

Based on these writings, the Jews held that their God was a miracle-working God. This understanding was alive in the Diaspora and the following centuries as well when even some magical practices were found among rabbinic circles.[19] In some cases, miraculous activities were traced back to their heroes such as Abraham, who was later viewed to have a gift of healing.[20]

Jews, however, treated miracle workers in the pagan world with fear and detested them because the source of the "miracles" was not the God of Israel.[21] The FG's miraculous signs function within this framework. Jesus's miracles pointed toward the God of Israel, but Jesus's Jewish opponents disliked them as they introduced impasse to their notion of who Jesus was.[22] They could not match the miraculous signs and Jesus's identity proclamations. To disregard Jesus as Messiah and his miraculous deeds as God's work, they suggested that Jesus's power was from evil sources.[23] Jesus's opponents accused him of demon-possession (John 8:48).

The Fourth Evangelist wrote in the era when miracles and miracle stories were not unknown.[24] Miracles were uncommon yet not completely inexistent in Jewish circles at that time.[25] Yet, there was an expectation, at least in some Jewish circles, that miraculous signs would return at the messianic age.[26] This suggests that the evangelist's Jewish (Palestinian and Diaspora) audience hold God as the God of the miraculous. God who performed miracles holds an important place in their national identity because miracles demonstrated that *their* God's exists and is great in power, whose name *they* knew. The very existence of the nation is a work

---

Texts, 9–75. See also DeSilva, *Introducing the Apocrypha*, esp. 1–31.

18. Evans, *Ancient Texts*, 217.

19. Keener, *Miracles*, 1:59.

20. Keener, *The Gospel of John*, 255–56. See also Apoc. Ab., especially chs. 9—32 where Abraham is visiting in heaven.

21. Cf. Keener, *The Gospel of John*, 254.

22. Keener, *Miracles*, 1:58.

23. In the Synoptic Gospels, this is spelt out explicitly by Jesus's opponents. See Matt 10:25; 12:24, 27; Mark 3:22; Luke 11:15–19.

24. See Keener, *Acts*, 1:326.

25. Keener, *Miracles*, 1:59–60.

26. See Keener, *Acts*, 1:335.

of this God. For instance, God provided several miraculous answers to the nation during their wilderness journey providing all that was needed for his people to live and conquer the promised land.

## Source for Signs

Scholars have various views regarding the source that the Fourth Evangelist might have used for his sign narratives. Some scholars (e.g., Rudolf Bultmann, Robert Fortna, and Urban von Wahdle) believe that there was a literary sign-source that was used to form John's stories. Most of these scholars "agree that it included the seven miracle stories of John 2–11, which were presented as 'signs' of Jesus' messianic identity."[27] The problem with this view, however, is that there has been no discovery of such a literary source. Scholars who hold written source theory argue that written sources can be identified within the Gospel text and can be reconstructed from it.[28]

The most convincing source for the Fourth Evangelist's sign narratives is the evangelist himself and/or perhaps other eyewitnesses of those events. Certain misconceptions or pious views deny this as a possibility, believing instead that the evangelist was detached from the events and words of Jesus and therefore had to gather the material from various sources. We need to give more credit to the evangelist's own testimony about his eye-witness status.[29] The evangelist's purpose statement (John 20:30–31) claims that the disciples, most likely the author himself included, eye-witnessed these signs Jesus performed. This is a remarkable claim because it claims that the FG is based (at least mainly) on the primary source. This means that the sign narratives are reports of actual events. This is not to say that signs are written down without a certain theological point of view and for a certain Christological goal in mind. They are. We suggest that it is most natural to follow the Fourth Evangelist's lead and read the sign narratives as eyewitness stories written to persuade readers to accept Jesus's identity as Christ, the Son of God.

As for the conceptual backdrop, the Pentateuch functions well as an intertext for sign narratives. Keener notes that the Fourth Evangelist "develops his theme of signs especially from the term's use in the biblical

---

27. Thatcher, "Introduction," 3.
28. Thatcher, "Introduction," 4.
29. Cf. Bauckham, *Jesus and the Eyewitnesses*, 358–83.

exodus narratives."[30] Jews understood God's miraculous acts during the exodus as signs of God's presence and provision for "salvation." In the FG, Jesus, who takes his people to the Father (cf. John 14:1–3), demonstrates God's presence and provision of salvation also by performing signs.

## Traditional Seven Signs

The Johannine scholarship has often identified the following seven signs (as there are seven "I AM" saying with a predicate nominative):[31]

| Number | Sign Narrative | Reference |
|---|---|---|
| 1 | Changing of water into wine | 2:1–11 |
| 2 | Healing of the nobleman's son | 4:46–54 |
| 3 | Healing of the lame | 5:1–9 |
| 4 | Feeding of the five thousand | 6:1–14 |
| 5 | Walking on the water | 6:16–21 |
| 6 | Healing of the man born blind | 9:1–12 |
| 7 | Raising of Lazarus | 11:1–46 |

Table 4.1

These sign narratives include Jesus's revelation of his identity. It is recognizable at the general level, namely because God is miracle-working God and Jesus performs miraculous deeds as well because he does what his Father does. Thus, they become signs to demonstrate Jesus's identity with the Father. In addition, each miraculous sign is attached to Jesus's self-revelation of his identity. The following sketch shows some of the connections between each sign and Jesus's identity. This presentation is

---

30. Keener, *The Gospel of John*, 1:276.

31. Cf. Brown, *The Gospel According to John*, 1:525. The traditional seven signs are disputed in Johannine scholarship, however. Howard argues that the seventh sign, instead of Jesus's walking on the water, is the "great hour of Jesus' death." See Howard, "The Significance of Minor Characters," 64.

not comprehensive as we have discussed these passages elsewhere in this volume as well. The purpose of this sketch is to demonstrate that they include elements that support our thesis.

- Jesus changes water into wine: The ability to create was an attribute solely given to God. Here Jesus demonstrates that attribute by changing water into wine instantly and so displays his divine identity (cf. 2:11). There also is a symbolism that points towards Jesus's identity.[32] First, Jesus can be seen to be the "better wine" that was not available before now. The new and better covenant in his blood was about to be established. Secondly, Jesus is the new means of purification. The old Jewish ways of purification have not been effective, but Jesus brings the perfect way to be purified through his blood. This is symbolized by changing the water in the purification pots into wine.[33] The entire narrative points out that even though Jesus restores the wedding joy (perhaps symbolically referring to the joy of eternal life), for Jesus it meant a journey towards his death. Without Jesus's work of the cross and the following third-day resurrection, there is no "wedding joy," but because those events will take place that joy is found in him. It is not insignificant that the sign took place on the third day (2:1), "on a day, within the context of the early church, [which] cannot but evoke the resurrection."[34]

- Jesus heals the nobleman's son: Jesus's statement about "life" that he imparted and the exact hour (a seventh hour) speaks to Jesus's identity as the life-giver. The hour can be seen reflecting Jesus's hour of the cross and thus points toward his role as a savior. Also, the royal officer's faith in Jesus himself, rather than in his ability to perform a miracle, works as a model for others. Jesus is the proper object of faith even without miraculous signs because Jesus is the Son of God.[35]

- Jesus heals the lame man: Jesus's life-giving power goes beyond the popular belief in miraculous healing water (5:3–4, 7b).[36] The sick man is without anyone who could "work" for him, Jesus is working

---

32. See O'Day, "Miracle Discourse," 180–83.

33. Cf. Keener, *The Gospel of John*, 1:509–10; Leon Morris, *The Gospel According to John*, 160–61.

34. Brodie, *The Gospel According to John*, 172.

35. Cf. Howard, "The Significance of Minor Characters," 70.

36. Verses 3b and 4 are not found from the early mss but are added by a later copyist most likely to explain the popular belief attached to the water of Bethesda.

for him even though it is prohibited by the Jewish notion of keeping the Sabbath (5:7–9). After the miraculous sign, Jesus proclaims that he has the same prerogatives as the Father, namely authority to judge and give life even on the Sabbath (vv. 21–22).

- Jesus feeds the five thousand: This takes place in the context of the Passover. The aftermath relates to Israel's wilderness experience including Moses and manna. Jesus proclaims his identity is greater than Moses, he himself being the bread from the Heaven (the Father) that gives life.

- Jesus walks on the water: Here Jesus introduces himself with an "I AM" statement, which as such speaks to his divine identity. The act of walking on the water demonstrates his authority over the natural laws of the universe. He is the Lord of the creation. Also, it is a miracle that the boat reaches the destination in no time after Jesus was accepted into the boat (6:21). Jesus protects the life of his disciples who were in danger on the stormy sea of Galilee. This event points out symbolically that it is Jesus who will be the only entity who can provide his people with the final destination.

- Jesus heals the man born blind: Jesus performs this "sign" (or work) after his "I am the Light of the world" proclamation (8:12). He then moves on after healing the blind man to affirm his divine identity. The healed man, previously blind, has now greater spiritual insight than the Jews who set themselves to investigate the matter. The man confesses that this man (Jesus) has to be from God, whereas his hearers deny that possibility.

- Jesus raises Lazarus from the dead: Jesus's sign miracle comes here after Jesus's "I am the resurrection and the life" (11:25) identity proclamation. Also, the aftermath in Jerusalem among the Jewish leaders speaks especially to Jesus's role of the one who provides the salvation to the nation. This is done in the Johannine style of irony.

These seven signs are all in various ways related to Jesus's identity proclamation as the one who is the (eternal) life-giver. One should not concentrate only on the miraculous in these sign narratives but should also seek their significance in revealing Jesus's identity.

It is noticeable that the word "sign" (Gr. *sēmeion*) is employed in every of these seven "sign" narratives except one. It is used in the narratives of #1 (2:11); #2 (4:48, 54); #3 (6:2); #4 (6:2, 14, 26); #6 (9:16; 10:41); and

#7 (11:47); it is only omitted in narrative #5. Therefore, some scholars have questioned if the walking on the water is intended as a sign.[37] Yet the miraculous is connected to Jesus's identity proclamation even in this narrative although "sign" language is not used. Jesus reveals his identity by attaching the miraculous to his "I AM" proclamation, which is surrounded by two miraculous events, namely, Jesus's walking on the water and the boat's immediate arrival at its destination (6:19–21).

## Beyond Traditional Seven

Often readers of the FG focus only on the traditional seven signs which we have outlined above not considering other Jesus's deeds as signs. This view is perhaps motivated by the number "seven" rather than the testimony of the FG itself. We point to three other narratives which can be argued to be signs as well.

First, some scholars (e.g., C. H. Dodd) note and argue that Jesus's cleansing of the temple in John 2:13–22 is a sign. After Jesus had driven the animals and their sellers out of the temple and had made the following proclamation about "My Father's house," he was asked by Jews, "What sign do You show us as your authority for doing these things?" (2:18). Jews did not realize that what Jesus had just done was the sign. Jesus demonstrated his authority, and this was followed by his revelation of his identity as a new temple. However, everyone at that time missed this; later, his disciples recognized it (2:22).

This view is not, however, accepted unanimously in Johannine scholarship. Arguments include the following:

- The text itself seems to ignore this as a sign as it mentions a "first sign" referring to Jesus's miraculous act of turning water into wine (2:11) and a "second sign" referring to Jesus's healing miracle of a nobleman's son (4:54).
- There is no "miraculous" (i.e., supernatural) aspect in this event.
- This is similar event to the case in the Synoptic Gospels where Jesus's opponents requested the sign, to which Jesus did not respond by performing a miracle.

---

37. Howard, "The Significance of Minor Characters," 64.

Despite these arguments, it should be kept in mind that the cleansing of the temple is placed at the beginning of Jesus's public ministry in the FG to make a Christological point. Therefore, it is not counted as a second sign after Jesus's miraculous act of changing water into wine. Jesus's healing of the nobleman's son is the second sign in the chronology of the narrative. The event itself, as pointed out above, fits the sign motif of the FG.

Second, at the end of the FG (21:1–11), Peter and some other disciples went fishing but caught no fish. But Jesus appeared at the shore and gave them instructions on how to catch fish. After obeying Jesus's instructions, they made an enormous catch of large fish. Is this a miracle? Yes, it is. Does this function as a sign? It may.[38] It is not mentioned that it was a "sign," but that is not always the case with the traditional seven signs either (cf. John 6:16–21). When 21:1–11 is closely studied, we may conclude that this miraculous deed of Jesus has very similar characteristics to the other sign narratives in FG. Jesus performs a miracle to solve the obvious problem or dilemma. By doing so, Jesus demonstrates his authority. Here he shows his authority over human possibilities and skills. Notice that Jesus was giving instructions to "former" professional fishermen.

Jesus's miraculous deed also had a typical outcome of a sign: the disciples recognized that the performer of the miracle is Jesus, the Lord (21:7). As the narrative moves further there is an interesting commentary from the narrator in v. 12: "None of the disciples ventured to question Him, 'Who are You?' knowing that it was the Lord." This occasion takes place after Jesus's resurrection and therefore there is a newness in that situation to the disciples. That is perhaps reflected in the narrator's comment that they did not dare to ask the same question as the Jews had asked earlier in the Gospel, "Who are you?" (8:25). In the context of that question (Who are you?) in John 8:25, Jesus points out that those who questioned him regarding his identity will recognize that he is "I AM" when he is crucified (lifted up). Now the lifting up was behind him, that is the cross, and therefore the evangelist records that his own disciples did not dare to ask that question because they knew that he was not just "Jesus," but that he was the Lord (21:12). There is enough evidence to suggest that this narrative including an obvious miracle performed by

---

38. Contra Bauckham, *The Testimony of the Beloved Disciple*, 274.

Jesus functions as a sign. Through it, Jesus was recognized not only as Jesus but as the Lord.

Finally, Jesus's glorification (referring to Jesus's cross and resurrection in the FG) can be seen as the ultimate sign in the FG.[39] Whereas miracles (especially exorcism) in the Synoptic Gospels show Jesus's power to destroy Satan,[40] in the FG this is demonstrated not by Jesus's "signs" during his public ministry,[41] but by Jesus's going to the cross (12:31–32). Jesus's signs prior to his cross build up readers' understanding of his identity and role, which become a vital part of understanding the meaningfulness of his glorification.

Interestingly, the Gospels of Matthew and Luke refer to Jesus's cross as a sign of Jonah (Matt 12:39; 16:4; Luke 11:29–30). As Jonah was in the belly of the fish, so Jesus is going to be "in the belly of the earth" for three days and three nights. In the FG, not Jonah, but Moses and the bronze serpent function as a similar type-antitype relationship between the bronze serpent that Moses erected and Jesus himself (John 3:14–15).[42] Jesus's cross is therefore introduced in the context of former events which now is seen as greater fulfillment of those earlier signs. Jesus revealed his superior identity and role that was beyond the signs God provided among his people before his ultimate "sign" in Jesus and his cross.[43]

Jesus refers to his cross in the first half of the book, sometimes called the book of Signs (John 1:19—12:50),[44] using vocabulary such as "my hour" (2:4; 12:27), "lifted up" (3:14; 8:28; 12:32), and "glory" (5:44; 7:18; 8:50, 54). This vocabulary is symbolic and refers to the cross as a sign. "My hour" refers to Jesus's main purpose of his coming: he came to take away the sin of the world by suffering on the cross. "Lifted up" is not referring

---

39. Howard, "The Significance of Minor Characters," 64.

40. For example, Luke 8:26–39 and parallel passages.

41. Note that none of the situations in which Jesus performs a sign are caused by Satan. Even in chapter 9, when the disciples suggest that sin is behind the man's blindness, Jesus rejects it.

42. There are several other parallels between Moses as a leader of the nation in its exodus and Jesus (see below).

43. It is possible that John most likely was aware of other Gospel accounts. D. A. Carson calls the relationship between the Synoptic Gospels and the FG an "interlocking" relationship. This means, among other things, that John does not necessarily repeat everything that was already said in the Synoptic Gospels. If we can build on this understanding, Jesus's cross was understood as a sign prior to John's Gospel. See Carson, *The Gospel According to John*, 51–53.

44. Dodd, *The Interpretation of the Fourth Gospel*.

only to the fact that Jesus was to be lifted up by means of a wooden object (cross/crucifixion) which was the Roman method of execution. It also refers to the death of Jesus through which he was going to be lifted up back to the Father. In the book of Passion (chs. 13—20), Jesus refers to his cross and resurrection as "going back to the Father" (e.g., 16:5). Finally, "glory" is a concept that stands in contrast to the "shame" that the cross was expected to bring upon Jesus. From a divine and soteriological point of view, however, Jesus's cross is the ultimate presentation of God's glory; his goodness, presence, and involvement in his creation (*kosmos*) to make all people (*kosmos*) know his solution to the problem of sin. In short, the symbolical language that is employed to describe Jesus's suffering on the cross brings the idea of "sign" into Jesus's suffering. Jesus's cross is the ultimate sign of God and his love to humankind and is thus the purpose of Jesus's coming (cf. 3:16).

## Concluding Remarks

The miraculous acts of Jesus in the FG are signs that point beyond themselves. We have suggested that there are more than the traditional seven signs of Jesus in this Gospel. Also, we have argued that all signs function as a part of John's Christology, which we may call "sign-Christology." They are often used as a springboard to further Jesus's proclamation of his divine identity and his role as God's agent. As the author has been consciously selective in his selection of "signs," the reader needs to pay careful attention to them in order to read them with their full rhetorical and theological force.

Jesus refers to his signs as "works," which reminds us of YHWH's works in the Hebrew Scriptures. The works Jesus performed relate to everything that he saw and heard his Father was doing. In this regard, even the narratives, which do not include *sēmeion* language or miraculous acts, may function as a sign to reveal Jesus as a broker of the Father.[45] There are good reasons, therefore, to view Jesus's passion as the ultimate sign of Jesus's identity as Christ.

---

45. Note that there are many *sēmeioi*, like the covenant sign of circumcision, in the Septuagint. Jesus's works in John were similarly *sēmeioi* to the evangelist. By signs the evangelist persuades his readers to see beyond the signs to the reality to which they pointed.

## Suggestions for Further Reading

Brown, Raymond E. *The Gospel According to John*. AB. New York: Doubleday, 1966. Pp. 1:525–32.

Keener, Craig S. *The Gospel of John: A Commentary*. Peabody: Hendrickson, 2003. Pp. 1:251–79.

O'Day, Gail R. "Miracle Discourse and the Gospel of John." In *Miracle Discourse in the New Testament*, edited by Duane F. Watson, 175–88. Atlanta: Society of Biblical Literature, 2012.

CHAPTER 5

# "I Am" Sayings as Jesus's Identity Markers

A CHARACTERISTIC OF THE FG is its extensive usage of Jesus's "I AM" (*egō eimi*) sayings. It is found more than twenty times in this Gospel and thus much more frequently than in the Synoptic Gospels. In the FG, the *egō eimi* phrase is always, with one exception (9:9), spoken by Jesus.[1] The phrase can be understood as one's self-identification, but the way it is used in the FG suggests that it goes beyond its everyday meaning. That is the reason why we write the phrase with capital letters (I AM) when Jesus is the speaker. The Greek verb "to be" (*eimi*) in the first person singular carries the meaning "I am." To use *egō* ("I") makes it emphatic. It is not only its emphatic form but also Jesus's usage of it in various strategic places that makes it Christologically significant. Stanley Porter points out that "the 'I am' sayings are a major means by which the author structures an expansive messianic-christological revelation of who Jesus is in the Gospel itself."[2]

---

1. It is also found in negative form *egō ouk eimi ho christos* in John 1:20 as John the Baptist's response to the question "Who are you?" This form may not be a mere accident, as the motivation of the question is to find out if John the Baptist was indeed Messiah. (See below.)

2. Porter, *John, His Gospel, and Jesus*, 121–22.

## Sources for "I AM" Sayings

Current scholarly opinion regarding the background for Jesus's "I AM" sayings is relatively unified. But since there are variant views on the source for "I AM" sayings, we will outline them below.

### *Ancient Near East Writings*

The "I am" phrase was not unknown to religious writers in the Ancient Near East.[3] It is found, for example, in writings from India as well as in Mandean writings,[4] the Hermetic corpus,[5] Mithraic liturgy,[6] and in Egyptian magical papyrus.[7] Two observations need to be made regarding these "I am" sayings and their relation to the FG's *egō eimi* sayings. First, many of these above-mentioned bodies of writings are difficult to date. In some cases, such as Mandean writings, the text was drafted most likely after the FG.[8] It is somewhat difficult to build an argument without reasonable doubt that the Fourth Evangelist would have followed such concepts which were later found in Mandean writings. Secondly, in these writings "I am" is not used in the absolute sense (see below), but always with a predicative.[9] The FG, however, uses *egō eimi* frequently both in an absolute sense and with the predicative. Thus, we conclude that even though "I am" sayings can be found in these Hellenistic writings and the religious ANE texts, they are not very likely to have been used as a source by the Fourth Evangelist. Yet the phrase's occurrence in those writings with a predicative, when attached to the identification of gods, cannot be completely ignored as a possible backdrop for the FG's usage of *egō eimi*.[10] There is, however, another body of literature that offers much more obvious background for its usage in the FG, namely, the Hebrew Scriptures.

---

3. Burge, "'I Am' Sayings," 355.

4. Braumann, "I Am," *NIDNTT*, 2:278.

5. Harner, *The "I Am" of the Fourth Gospel*, 28.

6. Brown, *The Gospel According to John*, 1:535.

7. Bernard, *A Critical and Exegetical Commentary*, 1:cxix.

8. It is argued though that even though Mandean literature is dated late, its religious ideas were older and might have been contemporary to John and his community. See Bultmann, *The Gospel of John*, 7–9.

9. Porter, *John, His Gospel, and Jesus*, 123. There is only one occasion when *egō eimi* might have been used in its absolute sense. See Ball, *"I Am" in John's Gospel*, 24.

10. Cf. Bernard, *A Critical and Exegetical Commentary*, 1:cxix.

## Hebrew Writings and the Septuagint

The *egō eimi* phrase is found in the Greek translation of the Hebrew Scriptures, the Septuagint. The question is, however, which texts from these writings are the most probable background material for the Fourth Evangelist's usage of *egō eimi*?

It is often suggested that the FG's *egō eimi* comes from Exodus 3:14a where God reveals his name to Moses. This God's self-revelation is usually translated into English with "I AM WHO I AM" (NASB, NRS, ESV, NIV) or "I AM THAT/that I AM" (KJV, NET, ERV, ASV). These translations of Hebrew (*'ehyeh 'ašer 'ehyeh*) make God's answer to Moses's question, "Now they may say to me, 'What is His name?' What shall I say to them?" (Exod 3:13), sound somewhat offensive. Formal equivalent rendering of the Hebrew would read in English, "I am the one who is" or "I am he who is."[11]

In that grammatical construction, also reflected in the Septuagint translation of Hebrew (*egō eimi ho ōn*), the first "to be" verb is in the first-person singular (I am), and it identifies the speaker. The second "to be" verb is a third-person participle (is), and is the "name."[12] This is exactly how it is used in Exod 3:14b of Septuagint where God instructs Moses how to answer the Israelites, "*ho on* have sent me to you" (translation mine). In short, in Exodus 3:14a, *egō eimi* is not the name of YHWH, but instead, the participle *ho ōn* is the name that Moses was eager to know. Therefore, it is questionable that the FG's expression *egō eimi* as God's name (i.e., absolute usage of *egō eimi*) comes solely from Exodus 3:14. Jesus does not use participle *ho ōn* as his self-identification. To use it that way would be an awkward grammatical construction even though it is used so in the Septuagint in Exod. 3:14b.[13] But because several English translations translate the participle *ho ōn* with "I AM," many have concluded that Jesus's *egō eimi* in the FG comes from Exodus 3:14.[14] In other words, this conclusion is easy to make if only English translations are consulted.

Despite the grammatical mismatch, Exodus 3:14 cannot be completely ruled out as a source for *egō eimi* in the FG. It resonates especially

---

11. Schild, "On Exodus iii 4,'" 301; Brenton translates Exodus 3:14 the Septuagint Greek into English, "And God spoke to Moses, saying, I am THE BEING" See Brenton, *The Septuagint Version*, 73.

12. Schild, "On Exodus iii 14," 300–1; Büchsel, "εἰμί, ὁ ὤν," *TDNT*, 2:398.

13. Philo uses *ho ōn* frequently for a title of God. Harris, *Prologue and Gospel*, 131.

14. Harner, *"I Am" of the Fourth Gospel*, 17.

with *egō eimi* sayings with a predicative. Regarding the absolute *egō eimi* sayings, although the Greek form in the Septuagint (*egō eimi ho ōn*) does not fit the FG's absolute *egō eimi*, its content fits. God revealed himself to Moses as the one who is changeless and unique, as the one who is.[15] In the same way, theologically loaded absolute *egō eimi* sayings found several times in the FG (in John 8:58 for example) carry much of the same theological baggage as Exodus 3:14. Secondly, it has been noted that Exodus 3:14 may have been a source for the usage of the Hebrew phrase *'ani hu* (I am he) in second Isaiah[16] and perhaps in Deuteronomy as well.

The Hebrew phrase *'ani hu* (I am he)[17] as God's self-revelation is found in Deuteronomy and so-called Second Isaiah.[18] It is translated consistently with *egō eimi* in the Septuagint. The phrase *'ani 'ani hu*[19] occurs once in Deuteronomy (32:39), and five times in Isaiah (41:4; 43:10; 46:4; 48:12; 52:6) as God's self-revelation and name. In addition, the phrase *'anochi 'anochi hu* occurs twice in Isaiah (43:25; 51:12) and in both instances it is translated with double *egō eimi* (i.e., *egō eimi egō eimi*) in the Septuagint. On both occasions, the second *egō eimi* is understood as a divine name. In addition, the phrase *ani YHWH* (I am the LORD) found in Isaiah 45:18 is translated with *egō eimi* in the Septuagint, making *egō eimi* a shorthand expression of YHWH's name.[20] It is also important to note that mere *'ani* with a predicate, in some instances where God is in view, is rendered *egō eimi* in the Septuagint.

*Egō eimi*, the Greek translation of Hebrew *'ani hu* (see Deut 32:39; Isa 41:4; 43:10; 46:4; 48:12; 52:6) and *egō eimi egō eimi* translation of Hebrew *'anochi 'anochi hu* (see Isa 43:25; 51:12) are chosen by the Septuagint

---

15. Bernard, *A Critical and Exegetical Commentary*, 1:cxxi.

16. Harner, *"I Am" of the Fourth Gospel*, 17.

17. *'ani hu* is usually translated "I am He" where the verb "to be" is supplied. However, some scholars argue that "I am He" is not a correct translation of *'ani hu* as they argue that *hu* has only a force of copula. If so, *egō eimi* is a grammatically accurate translation of *'ani hu*. See Brown, *The Gospel According to John*, 1:536. See also Stauffer, *Jesus and His Story*, 177.

18. Second Isaiah includes chapters 40—54 in the book of Isaiah.

19. There are other occurrences of *'ani hu* in the Hebrew OT where God is not speaking and where it is not used as God's self-identification or his name. For example, in Daniel 4:20–22, Daniel addresses the king with *'ani hu*. This is also translated in the Septuagint with *egō eimi*. Thus, the formula itself is not a sacred one—its meaning needs to be drawn from the context. See Williams, "'I Am' or 'I Am He'?," 344. Cf. Harris, *Prologue and Gospel*, 131.

20. See also Isaiah 45:19 for a similar case.

translators when the speaker is God or God is in view and when it is associated with a divine self-manifestation.[21] Therefore, it is reasonable to think that OT writings, especially the Septuagint's usage of *egō eimi* as God's self-revelation and the name, are the intertexts for the Fourth Evangelist's usage of *egō eimi* phrase.

## 'ani hu in Judaism

The *'ani hu*, was utilized at least two ways in Jewish life.[22] It was understood not only as a self-identification ("I am that one"), but also as one of the divine names of YHWH.[23] Also, *'ani* alone was sometimes used as a reference to YHWH.[24] Rabbi Hillel said during the Feast of Tabernacles "If *'ani* is here, then all are here; if *'ani* is absent, who then is here?"[25] Hillel did not refer to himself but YHWH. As such *'ani hu* was used in worship services in synagogues and in the Jerusalem Temple. The *'ani hu* was also known to the members of the Qumran community, which is a significant piece of information if John the Baptist, who testified that he is no *'ani hu* (John 1:20), was at some level attached to that community.[26] The phrase as a reference to YHWH, however, is not found in the Apocrypha, Pseudepigrapha, or the Mishnah. But there are pieces of evidence that *'ani hu* was utilized as God's name during the Feast of Tabernacle as well as in the private liturgy during the eve of Passover Haggadah.[27] It is noticeable that Jesus used the *egō eimi* (*'ani hu*) for himself during both of these Jewish feasts (cf. John 8:59; 13:19). It would be difficult to imagine that Jesus's contemporary Jewish audience would have missed Jesus's

---

21. The Greek *egō eimi* is also employed in the Septuagint when a human is speaking. This is the case, for example, when Joseph reveals himself to his brothers in Egypt, "I am Joseph, the brother of yours" (Gen 45:4). Similar usage is found in the New Testament: in John 9:9, the man born blind uses the phrase as a self-identification.

22. See Williams, "'I Am' or 'I Am He'?"

23. Brown, *The Gospel According to John*, 1:537. See also Williams, "'I Am' or 'I Am He'?," 350.

24. Harner, "*I Am*," 18.

25. Sukkah 53a, in Epstein, *The Babylonian Talmud*, 253. Quoted in Harner, "*I Am*," 18.

26. Harner, "*I Am*" of the Fourth Gospel, 23.

27. Stauffer, *Jesus and His Story*, 190. See also Daube, *The New Testament and Rabbinic Judaism*, 325.

usage of *'ani hu* as a divine name. What was surprising for them was that Jesus applied it to himself.

The Hebrew Scriptures, Jewish notions of *'ani hu* and this phrase's usage during certain Jewish festivals are certainly part of the backdrop for Jesus's usage of *egō eimi* in the FG. Next, we will look to the Synoptic Gospels' usage of this phrase before examining it in more detail in the FG.

## Synoptic Gospels

*Egō eimi* sayings are also found on the lips of Jesus in the Synoptic Gospels, including absolute *egō eimi* sayings.[28] In one particular narrative, when Jesus walks on the water, *egō eimi* is used by two Synoptic evangelists as well as by the Fourth Evangelist (Matt 14:27; Mark 6:50; John 6:20).[29] Yet, there is a difference between the accounts in the Synoptic Gospels and the FG. In the Synoptic passages, the disciples do not know who is approaching them, but in the FG they know that it is Jesus. This suggests that John employs the *egō eimi* saying not as a mere self-identification, but as a proclamation of Jesus's identity as the one who has power over nature, indeed, the one who shares the same attributes with God. Yet, these *egō eimi* sayings, in the Synoptics and the FG, create connections between the Lord of the OT and Jesus, for they are alluding to Isaiah 41 in which both *'ani hu* and "fear not" phrases are present.[30]

At the trial before the high priest, Jesus uses *egō eimi* as self-identification (Mark 14:62; Luke 22:70; 24:39). It is definitely possible to read *egō eimi* here as a Christological statement and not mere self-identification. The Fourth Evangelist (John 4:26; 18:5, 6, 8), however, uses *egō eimi* in a similar way as well but adds more obvious Christological connotations to it. For example, in John 18:5–6, Jesus's supernatural power is manifested to indicate his authority.

There is an indication that in the Synoptic Gospels, Jesus was cognizant of the meaning of *egō eimi* as God's name. In the context where his disciples were asking about the destruction of the Jerusalem Temple, Jesus responded to them, "Many will come in My name, saying, 'I am

---

28. Matt 14:27; 22:32; 24:5; Mark 6:50; 13:6; 14:62; Luke 21:8; 22:70; 24:39.

29. This suggests that the saying goes back to Jesus, the source used by the Synoptic writers and John is the same, or the Fourth Evangelist follows here the Synoptic tradition.

30. Williams, "'I Am' or 'I Am He'?," 346.

[*egō eimi*] *He!*' and will mislead many" (Mark 13:6). In the NASB, the predicate 'he' is added, the correctness of which is a matter of dispute. It is notable that Jesus is speaking about "his name" and uses the *egō eimi* phrase in that context, suggesting that *egō eimi* is not a mere phrase of self-identification, but the divine name that cannot be applied to such a person who uses it. The parallel passage in Matthew 24:5 reads, "*egō eimi* the Christ" lends the meaning of one's self-identification as Messiah to *egō eimi* and diminishes the meaning of *egō eimi* as the name of God.[31]

There are two reasons why the Synoptic Gospels cannot be the *sole* source for Johannine *egō eimi*. First, the FG's usage of *egō eimi* is linked closely with Hebrew Scriptures' *'ani hu* and its usage in Judaism. It is, therefore, difficult to argue that the Fourth Evangelist copied it from the Synoptic Gospels. John's usage of the phrase cannot be accidentally embedded in the Hebrew Scriptures, the Septuagint usage, and Jewish notions of that phrase. That is not so obvious in the case of the Synoptic Gospels. Secondly, the Johannine *egō eimi* sayings are systematically used in a strategic way; they support the author's purpose to show Jesus's divine identity which is hardly the motif of the *egō eimi* sayings in the Synoptic Gospels even though in some cases it can be understood to carry Christological meaning as well.

We may conclude that if John was familiar with the Synoptic tradition, which we think he was, he uses the *egō eimi* phrase in a similar way to the Synoptic Evangelists, but employs it in its full rhetorical capacity to serve his Christological purposes to persuade that Jesus is the Lord of the Hebrew Scriptures.

## Johannine "I Am" Sayings Classified

There are various possibilities to classify Johannine *egō eimi* sayings. A three-class classification identifies *egō eimi* sayings (1) without a predicate nominative (absolute usage; I Am);[32] (2) with a predicate nominative (I Am the door);[33] and (3) with an implied predicate nominative (I Am he).[34] This classification is arguable. There is a problem with class num-

31. See Manson, *Jesus and the Christian*, 174–83.
32. John 8:24, 28, 58; 13:19.
33. John 6:35, 51; 8:12, 18, 23; 9:5; 10:7, 9, 11, 14; 11:25; 14:6; 15:1, 5.
34. John 4:26; 6:20; 18:5. Note that several English New Testament translations often imply "he" to *egō eimi* sayings which otherwise stand in the Greek text without a

ber three though. Scholars do not agree which *egō eimi* sayings without a predicate can be completed by adding the predicate "he."[35] Therefore, below *egō eimi* sayings are classified simply into two groups following their grammatical form as they appear in the Greek text:[36] (1) *egō eimi* with a predicate;[37] and (2) *egō eimi* without a predicate.[38] The second category of *egō eimi* sayings has, however, some variations which we will point out below. To classify *egō eimi* sayings into two categories is an appropriate starting point to begin to study their meaning and function in the FG.[39]

## Meaning and Purpose of "I Am" Sayings

We start with "I am" sayings with a predicate nominative, which are usually well recognized by readers. They are:

- I AM the bread of life (6:35);[40]
- I AM the Light of the world (8:12);
- I AM the door of the sheep (10:7);
- I AM the good shepherd (10:11);
- I AM the resurrection and the life (11:25);

---

predicative. Thus, for example, John 18:5 in ESV reads "I am he." This translation can be defended on some occasions like here, but still, it seems that it leads the modern reader to understand Jesus's words only as a mere self-identification without attaching any self-revelatory aspect of Jesus's divinity to them.

35. Cf. Porter, *John, His Gospel, and Jesus*, n128.

36. UBS[5]

37. Seven *egō eimi* sayings with a predicate are John 6:35; 8:12; 10:7, 11; 11:25; 14:6; 15:1. Some of these sayings are repeated.

38. John 4:46; 6:20; 8:18, 24, 28, 58; 13:19; 18:5, 6, 8 and in 9:9 where speaker is not Jesus.

39. A more advanced study of these categories may lead to other classifications as well. David Ball further divides the first category into three subdivisions: (1) "Those sayings combined with the definite article and a present participle [see 4:26 and 8:18]. (2) Those sayings, which are grammatically absolute and in which the words . . . [*egō eimi*] stand-alone [see 8:58; 6:20; 18:5, 8]. (3) Those sayings which are grammatically absolute and which stand in a *hoti* [that] clause to express future fulfillment [see 8:24, 28; 13:19]." Ball, *"I Am" in John's Gospel*, 168–69. Porter, *John, His Gospel, and Jesus*, argues also for three categories: (1) Absolute sayings, (2) locative sayings, and (3) sayings with a predicate.

40. Only the first reference to each I AM saying is given in this list. Note that NASB does not write "I am" in capital letters.

- I AM the way, the truth, and the life (14:6);
- I AM the true vine (15:1).

These Jesus's "I AM" sayings are not always directed to the same or even a similar audience. Occasionally Jesus's audience consists of his disciples or other sympathetic Jesus's followers, whereas on other occasions the audience is the public and at times even Jesus's opponents. As the content and the context of these sayings are further observed, it becomes clear that they are intended to carry significant Christological argument. They reveal Jesus's identity in relation to his role.[41] This means that these sayings are not on the same level with the statement, "I am a teacher," because other people who have the same profession can say the same. Jesus's "I AM" sayings with the predicate nominative would be inadequate to be heard from anybody else's lips other than the lips of a divine. For instance, when Jesus said, "I am the resurrection and the life" (John 11:25), he claimed to have attributes that belong only to God. Thus, the speaker does not only tell what he does but also who he is. In other words, he reveals his identity. In this case, Jesus called Lazarus to come out from the tomb alive which demonstrated his claim's truthfulness. Therefore, Jesus's usage of *egō eimi* instead of mere *eimi* is appropriate. First, it brings together Jesus's divinity with his role as "the resurrection and the life." Second, it points out that there is nobody else who can fulfill these roles other than the "I Am" (see below). It is obvious, then, that Jesus reveals his identity in relation to his role by these "I AM" sayings with a predicate nominative.

Some of these sayings Jesus spoke in the context where they related closely to Jewish life. For instance, Jesus's pronouncement "I am the bread of life" is attached not only to Jesus's feeding over five thousand people with two fish and five loaves of bread (John 6:1–13), but also to Moses and the manna miracle (John 6:30–33). This fits a typical Jewish interpretative principle "from lesser to greater." Moses was important as God's agent, but lesser than one who is present now, Jesus. Jesus is the bread of life from above that satisfies everyone.

Another example would be Jesus's "I am the Light of the world" proclamation at the feast of the Tabernacles (John 8:12). As the candlesticks were lit in the court of women, it was said that the whole city reflected the light that came from the temple. Jesus replaces the symbolic action of the feast by himself as he proclaims, "I am the Light of the world." Jesus reveals his role as a source of the light (i.e, life), the light not only for

---

41. Ball, "*I Am*," 174.

Jerusalem or for Jews but for the whole world. No wonder why it initiated a long argumentative and unfriendly conversation between opposing Jews and Jesus ending up with Jesus's absolute "I AM" proclamation (John 8:58–59).

Although there is no unanimity among Johannine scholars whether or not *egō eimi* sayings with a predicate function as Jesus's identity claims, it is well recognized in the Johannine scholarship that Jesus's absolute *egō eimi* sayings function as such claims. They are not mere self-identification in the sense "I am the one." They seem to be often, if not always, employed to point out Jesus's identity as divine.

On two occasions, the absolute "I AM" sayings' first person singular "I" is further defined with the usage of the definite article and the present participle (John 4:26; 8:18; cf. Exod 3:14). In the case when Jesus responds to the Samaritan woman with *egō eimi*, it is followed by his words "the one who is speaking to you" (John 4:26; translation mine). Sometimes it is argued that the participle functions as a predicate in these cases. This is, however, doubtful. If it were so, then John 4:26 would read "I am the one who speaks to you." This would be quite a pointless statement. Rather the participle should be taken as an apposition with the subject "I." Thus, Jesus's response to Samaritan woman's statement, "I know that Messiah is coming . . . when that One comes, He will declare all things to us" would read, "I AM, the one who is speaking to you" (translation mine).[42] This clarifies and further assures that Jesus is the Messiah (I AM), the very person who is speaking with the Samaritan woman.

In John 8:14–18, Jesus speaks about his and his Father's witness regarding his identity and role. In v. 18 he states, "I AM, who testifies about myself" (translation mine). In this occasion, as well as in John 4:26, Jesus's identity is at stake, and so Jesus uses the absolute *egō eimi* saying with an additional phrase ("the one who testifies about myself") to emphasize that the identity of *egō eimi* belongs to the present speaker. We conclude that these two "I AM" sayings, followed by the present participle with the definite article, are more than his self-identification "I am he." It is more probable that they also carry the idea of Jesus's self-revelation as divine Messiah (4:26) who is equal with the Father (8:18).

---

42. Note a coma after "I AM." NASB reads, "I who speak to you am *He*" taking the participle with the definite article as apposition but adding also the predicate "he" for smoother reading in English. See also NIV and ESV. John 8:18 is rendered in a similar way in NIV, ESV, and NASB.

The second sub-category of absolute *egō eimi* sayings is the one in which *egō eimi* is found in *hoti* (that) clauses (John 8:24, 28; 13:19). In these two chapters, Jesus's audiences are different; in chapter 8 the audience is unbelieving Jews whereas in chapter 13 the audience is Jesus's disciples. Although from a grammatical perspective these sayings are absolute, some argue that a predicate should be implied from the context. The question is, however, what is the right predicate? Again, we suggest that these sayings make the best sense and are more fitting to Johannine Christology when they are not extended (or limited for that matter) by adding predicates. Jesus's *egō eimi* statement in John 8:24b, "for unless you believe that I Am, you will die in your sins" (translation mine) is followed by the audience's question "who are you?" indicating that his listeners did not understand or could not believe Jesus's statement's meaning. The context of John 8:24, however, shows that *egō eimi* is the object of faith, and therefore, also the way to forgiveness and life (8:21, 23–24).

In John 8:28, Jesus first refers to his death and his title as "Son of Man" and then points out his identity by using *egō eimi*. It is the divine Son who can bring glory to the Father through the death of the cross. In John 13:19, we have a very similar occasion except Jesus's audience is now his disciples. Soon the disciples will believe that Jesus is *egō eimi*. Thus, even though we could supply the absolute *egō eimi* with a predicate, on these occasions it is difficult to argue convincingly for its appropriateness. We suggest that one should read these sayings as absolute even though it may cause an awkward reading in English. That way the statements receive proper attention as they point to Jesus's divine identity.

Finally, we look at the absolute *egō eimi* sayings that stand alone. The most obvious and undisputed absolute *egō eimi* saying is found in John 8:58. Here the statement, "Before Abraham was born, I am," points out Jesus's relation to Abraham as pre-existent. It also points out Jesus's divinity. This time it is also understood as such due to the Jews' desire to execute Jesus there and then. They were ready to execute Jesus—a new temple—at the temple mount using the stones, which were most likely debris from the temple construction. It is very likely that these Jews understood that Jesus applied the Hebrew *'ani hu* phrase from Isaiah as a name of God to himself. That is, Jesus made himself equal with God.

Other such sayings are found in John (6:20; 18:5, 6, 8). These absolute *egō eimi* proclamations for a casual reader may seem to be a mere "I am he" self-identification made by Jesus. Yet, in those contexts, there is some significant Christological intention. In the case of John 6:20, it is noticeable that John's account differs from that of the Synoptic Gospels, even though the same story, Jesus walking on the water, and his *egō eimi* response to his disciples are recorded. Catrin Williams comments:

> In the Synoptics, the disciples' initial fear stems from their suspicion that the figure whom they see is a ghost (cf. Mark 6:49; Matt. 14:26), but in FG they are afraid because they actually recognize Jesus as the one who approaches the boat across the sea (6:19). If *egō eimi* does not serve here as a statement of identity ("It is I, Jesus"), its purpose must be to explain the significance of Jesus' act of walking on water, for *egō eimi* is the vehicle whereby he makes himself manifested as the one exercising the power that the Hebrew Bible attributes to God alone (cf. Job 9:8; 38:16; Hab 3:15).[43]

The similarity in Jesus's *egō eimi* response to those who came to arrest him in John 18:5[44] appears, at first glance, like Jesus's self-identification, that is, that he is Jesus the Nazarene whom they came to arrest. But how should one understand the extraordinary consequence of that statement, namely, his arresters falling to the ground (18:6)? It seems that the *egō eimi* statement goes beyond Jesus's mere self-identification. At least two factors argue for this conclusion. First, the result of the pronouncement of *egō eimi* was that Jesus's opponents fell on the ground. Jesus's divine authority and power were demonstrated. This, in turn, suggests that Jesus could have walked away from the situation as he had done before in John 6:15. In addition, this fulfills the earlier promises that Jesus does not lose any of those whose the Father has given him (John 17:12), and that Jesus gives them life (6:39–40; 10:28). Secondly, *egō eimi* usage here brings the prediction of "Jesus's lifting up" vividly to the readers' mind from John chapter 8. Now in chapter 18, the reader is reminded that the prediction of Jesus's death as divine *egō eimi* is about to take place. Williams concludes his study on *egō eimi* sayings in John 18 as follows, "Indeed, Jesus' twofold pronouncement of *egō eimi* during his arrest serves as a powerful exemplification of the claims he has made with the aid of this expression in earlier Johannine narratives and discourses, for it encapsulates

---

43. Williams, "'I Am' or 'I Am He'?," 346.

44. John 18:6 and 8 are repetitions of John 18:5, yet it is at least interesting that here we find a cluster of *egō eimi* sayings which as such may suggest an authorial intention to emphasize this phrase and its significance.

Jesus' unique identity as the one in whom God is revealed and his saving promises are fulfilled."[45]

## Other Characters and "I Am" in John

There are two other characters in the FG, John the Baptist and the man born blind, who also use *egō eimi*. The question is: do they differ from Jesus's "I am" sayings, and if yes, how?

## John the Baptist

John the Baptist uses *egō eimi* in a negative construction, *egō ouk eimi* (I am not), in John 1:20.[46] This is his response to the question, "who are you?" asked by the Pharisees. Interestingly the question was not "Are you Christ?" John the Baptist's responds, "*egō ouk eimi ho christos*" (I am not Christ) (John 1:20). Is this anything more than a simple self-identification as "not Christ?" We need to note that as the narrative progresses and conversation between the Pharisees and John the Baptist moves on, John the Baptist does not use *egō eimi* anymore. When he denies that he is the Elijah or the prophet, he uses a less forceful negative construction than the *egō eimi* formula. This may suggest one of the following two things. First, *egō eimi* may be used here in order to make an emphatic statement that John the Baptist is *not* the Christ. Yet, if that would be the only reason of his *egō eimi* usage, one might wonder why he did not use the same utterance at other times when he denies the Pharisees' suggestions about his identity as Elijah and the prophet? Beside it is difficult to believe that the mere emphatic negative is the reason for the usage of the *egō eimi* phrase as the original discourse was most likely held in Aramaic. There is, therefore, a good reason to think that the Fourth Evangelist had a certain reason to employ *egō eimi* at the time when John the Baptist denied his identity as Christ.

Secondly, *egō eimi* might be used here to show the difference between John the Baptist and Jesus.[47] This differentiation is already forcefully revealed in the Prologue and continues throughout the first several chapters

---

45. Williams, "'I Am' or 'I Am He'?," 532.

46. See a similar statement by Pilate in John 18:35 where Pilate asks a rhetorical question, "I am not a Jew, am I?"

47. Cf. Porter, *John, His Gospel, and Jesus*, 128.

in the Gospel. If this is correct, *egō eimi* is a very proper phrase to be used in the negative form by John the Baptist as he reveals himself not as divine—not as Christ. This may suggest, then, that John the Baptist inserted the idea to his response that the coming Christ is the divine *egō eimi*.

## The Man Born Blind

In John 9, Jesus heals a man born blind as an aftermath to his "I am the Light of the world" statement (John 8:12). When people were wondering if the healed man was actually the one whom they used to know as a blind beggar, the man identifies himself as the one saying *egō eimi*. English translators render *egō eimi* in various ways like, "I am the one" (NASB), "I am he" (ASV), or "I am the man" (NIV). The translators have understood the *egō eimi* phrase as the speaker's self-identification and therefore add the predicate. Porter thinks that this is perhaps the best way to understand it, and one should not try to get it to fit the same or a similar category as Jesus's *egō eimi* sayings. He writes:

> One could plausibly argue that an "I am" statement on the lips of someone other than Jesus is not the same kind of statement as one uttered by Jesus because the context in which the statement is used is the decisive factor in determining its meaning. I believe that this is probably the best way to understand this statement—as not directly relevant to the Christology of John's Gospel.[48]

We may assume, however, that the healed man's *egō eimi* statement carries a weightier meaning than a mere everyday self-identification because *egō eimi* is otherwise a carefully designed Christological argument in the FG. It is worth noting that in chapter 8 Jesus employs *egō eimi* several times (vv. 12, 18, 24, 28, 58) as well as in chapter 10 (vv. 7, 9, 11, 14), but does not use it in chapter 9 although there would have been an ideal opportunity him to do so. In chapters 8 and 9, Jesus proclaims that he is the light of the world: in 8:12 Jesus uses *egō eimi*[49] in that statement but does not do so in 9:5.[50] It seems that the evangelist had purposefully reserved *egō eimi* for the man-born-blind-now-seeing in this time, for a man who was "an economic, social and religious outcast; living on the

---

48. Porter, *John, His Gospel, and Jesus*, 146.
49. *egō eimi ho phōs tou kosmou*
50. *phōs eimi tou kosmou*

periphery of society."⁵¹ He is the one in whom Jesus's "I am the Light of the world" (8:12) claim is manifested; one who was in darkness (blind) is now moved from darkness to light (seeing) provided by Jesus, that is, by *egō eimi*. He became a living testimony of the truth of Jesus's "*egō eimi* the Light of the world" statement. In this narrative, Jesus's opponents who thought that they were seeing (i.e., were in the light) were actually blind (i.e., in the darkness), and they stay in the darkness as they did not allow Jesus to illuminate their lives. Thomas Brodie notes that this human *egō eimi* in John 9:9 is often taken as the one which does not have anything to do with the "God-related" *egō eimi*. He states, "the immediate literary context of the man's very human *Egō eimi* is the increasingly clear divine *Egō eimi* of Jesus in chap. 8 (8:24, 28, 58). In other words, from a literary point of view, the man's *Egō eimi* is an echo of the divine *Egō eimi*."⁵²

Mikeal Parsons interprets this text narrative-critically, suggesting that this man becomes a "Johannine Model Disciple" who is "the locus of the revelation" as God's works are manifested in him. He is "a reliable witness even in the face of persecution" and is "sent by Jesus even as the Son was sent by the Father."⁵³ This may be a "pregnant" reading of the text but may also point toward the right direction. Not only the healing itself but also the healed man's *egō eimi* statement proves true Jesus's statement about his status as the light of the world. The healed man becomes a source of that divine presence (light) in a similar way as one who drinks the water given by Jesus and becomes the place from which that water flows (John 7:38–39). Therefore, the healed man is a character in the story, who brings honor to Jesus/God and shame to the Pharisees, thus placing him with Jesus and his group of disciples.⁵⁴ Thus, his *egō eimi* statement can be seen in relation to Jesus's *egō eimi* sayings and therefore fitting to the overall *egō eimi* motif of the FG.

## Concluding Remarks

In this chapter, we have demonstrated how important *egō eimi* sayings are for the Christology in the FG. Jesus's *egō eimi* sayings are used in two different ways: First, absolute *egō eimi* sayings are declarations of Jesus

---

51. Bennema, *Encountering Jesus*, 136.
52. Brodie, *The Gospel According to John*, 348.
53. Parsons, "A Neglected ΕΓΩ ΕΙΜΙ," 179. Note also that "Siloam" means "sent."
54. Cf. Porter, *John, His Gospel, and Jesus*, 147.

identity as a divine; Jesus who is equal to God the Father. Secondly, *egō eimi* sayings completed with the predicate nominative illuminate the role of the Son of God, especially concerning salvation.[55] Porter argues in his recent work that "'I am' sayings are a major means by which the author structures an expansive messianic-christological revelation of who Jesus is in the Gospel itself."[56] On those few occasions where *egō eimi* is uttered by John the Baptist (ch. 1) and the healed man (ch. 9), *egō eimi* stands in relation to the overall *egō eimi* motif in the FG, supporting their role as Jesus's identity claims.

## Suggestions for Further Reading

Ball, David Mark. *"I Am" in John's Gospel: Literary Function, Background, and Theological Implications.* JSNTSup 124. Sheffield: Sheffield Academic Press, 1996.

Dodd, C. H. *The Interpretation of the Fourth Gospel.* Cambridge: Cambridge University Press, 1953. Pp. 93–96, 349–50.

Porter, Stanley, E. *John, His Gospel, and Jesus: In Pursuit of the Johannine Voice.* Grand Rapids: Eerdmans, 2015. Pp. 120–48.

Williams, Cartin H. "'I Am' or 'I Am He'?: Self-Declaratory Pronouncements in the Fourth Gospel and Rabbinic Traditions." In *Jesus in Johannine Tradition*, edited by Robert T. Fortna and Tom Thatcher, 343–52. Louisville: Westminster John Knox, 2001.

---

55. Cf. Bauckham, *The Testimony of the Beloved Disciple*, 246.
56. Porter, *John, His Gospel, and Jesus*, 121–22, 147–48.

———— CHAPTER 6 ————

# Father-Son Relationship

*Sharing the Same Identity*

THE FATHER-SON RELATIONSHIP IS a motif used by the Fourth Evangelist to reach his rhetorical goal, which is to persuade his readers to accept the identification of the Messiah as Jesus.[1] The FG, although characterized as the Gospel of the Spirit, is also recognized as the Gospel of the Father and the Son.

In this chapter, we will look at how the Father-Son motif indicates Jesus's identity. This relationship is repeatedly presented in the FG in a variety of ways. Adesola Akala concludes that the Son-Father relationship is important to understand the FG's revelation of Jesus, which also "draws believers into that divine relationship, and in doing so, fulfils the purpose of the Fourth Gospel."[2] Rudolf Schnackenburg uses even stronger language claiming that "The 'Father-Son' relationship is the *key* to the understanding of Jesus as portrayed by the evangelist, and of his works and actions as interpreted by him" (italics mine).[3]

A quick look at how often the word "Father" (Gr. *patēr*) is used as the address of the heavenly Father in the FG in comparison to the Synoptic writers' use of the term illustrates its importance for the Fourth Evangelist:

---

1. Anderson, *The Riddles of the Fourth Gospel*, 29.
2. Akala, *The Son-Father Relationship*, 223.
3. Schnackenburg, *The Gospel According to St. John*, 2:172.

- Five times in Mark
- Twenty-one times in Luke
- Forty-two in Matthew
- 122 times in John[4]

The frequency with which "Father" is used by the Fourth Evangelist is overwhelming. However, not only its frequent usage but also the content of how the Father and the Son relationship is expressed in these passages carries much weight in Johannine Christology. This can be seen, for example, in explicit statements of that relationship like, "the Father who sent me" (5:37; 6:44, 57; 8:16, 18; 12:49),[5] "My Father is working . . . I Myself am working" (5:17), "the Father is in Me, and I in the Father" (John 10:38; 14:10–11), and "I and the Father are one" (10:30; cf. 17:11, 21). There is no room for misunderstandings: Jesus (the Son) has a close relationship with the Father.

## The Father, the Son and Jewish Monotheism

The Fourth Evangelist does not shy away from the proclamation of the Father-Son relationship although it is a key obstacle for the Jewish leaders' acceptance of Jesus as God's promised Messiah. The Second Temple Judaism was utterly monotheistic, yet in the Fourth Evangelist's account Jesus frequently emphasizes the Father-Son relationship and uses it to convince the readers about his identity and status. This issue has already been partially discussed in Chapter 1, where the *Logos* motif was under scrutiny. It is necessary, however, to discuss how Jewish notions of "God is one" and the FG's Father-Son motif work in meeting the evangelist's goal.

Jesus's divinity as such could have been blasphemous to Jews who held that God is one and that there is no other God. This was repeatedly confessed in the Shema, "Hear, O Israel! The LORD is our God, the LORD is one!" (Deut 6:4). Second Temple Judaism followed the same monotheistic beliefs. For those who accepted Jesus's messiahship and his divine identity, it meant a departure from Judaism as far as Jewish understanding of YHWH and monotheism was concerned.[6]

---

4. Wigram, *The Englishman's Greek Concordance*, 607–8.
5. John 5:37; 6:44, 57; 8:16, 18; 12:49
6. Köstenberger, *A Theology of John's Gospel and Letters*, 357–58.

Monotheism of the Second Temple Judaism was never relaxed to accept other divine beings beside one God. Although there was a notion of semi-divine beings such as angels, it cannot be argued that Jews believed that any such beings had the ability to transform into the fully divine. Thus, there is no reason to argue that the Fourth Evangelist tried to explain Jesus's divinity in terms of development to accommodate the Jewish notion of monotheism. There is also no textual support for this idea in the FG. Jesus is presented in a unique relationship with God/Father; he shares the same prerogatives as God right at the beginning of the Gospel (1:1–5). This kind of presentation of Christ is called "high Christology." In other words, the Fourth Evangelist does not start with the earthly man Jesus of Nazareth and then bring forth arguments that he is divine Christ equal with God. Readers cannot go further than the first verse in the Gospel without recognizing that "Jesus" (i.e., *Logos*) shared the unique relationship with God (John 1:1). That *Logos* became man rather than man became *Logos* (1:14). Therefore, in the incarnated *Logos*, God himself came to be with his people.

Richard Bauckham puts it this way, "Without contradiction or rejecting any of the existing features of Jewish monotheism, the Fourth Gospel, therefore, redefines Jewish monotheism as christological monotheism. Christological monotheism is a form of monotheism in which the relationship of Jesus the Son to this Father is integral to the definition of who the one true God is."[7] Taking this angle when reading the Gospel, one recognizes that as much as the evangelist tells Jesus's story and clarifies who he is, he also lets Jesus tell God's story thus revealing who God actually is (cf. John 1:18).[8]

---

7. Bauckham, "Monotheism and Christology in the Gospel of John," 165. For an opposing view, see McGrath, *The Only True God*, 55–70. McGrath argues that the reason for disagreement between Jesus and his opponent Jews was not that Jesus claimed to be equal with God, but rather whether or not Jesus was the God-sent agent. According to McGrath, Jesus claimed that he was sent by God and was thus God's agent (Messiah) whereas Jews in large did not accept that these things said about Jesus's role suited Jesus.

8. Köstenberger, *A Theology of John's Gospel and Letters*, 361.

## Father-Son Revelation and Jesus's Identity

The Father-Son passages are not equally spread over the FG even though they are found almost in every chapter.[9] The Father-Son passages are found in discourse material rather than narrative portions of the Gospel.

There are two major distinctive discourse contexts in which "Father" passages are found. They are found (1) in situations where Jesus is having an encounter with his opponent Jews, especially in chapters 5, 6, 8, and 10, and (2) in Jesus's Farewell Discourse to his faithful eleven disciples in chapters 14–17. Other Father-Son relationship texts are found in the Prologue and chapter three. The audience of the Father-Son passages includes both Jesus's faithful followers and his opponents.

Below we will study selected Father-Son passages in three categories: (1) Unity sayings, (2) "the one/Father who sent me" sayings, and (3) the obedient Son sayings. We have limited ourselves to the passages where "Father" language is used to keep this study reasonable in length, and on our main goal on learning how the "Father-Son" relationship is utilized by the Fourth Evangelist to argue for Jesus's identity.

## Father-Son Unity Statements

Unity between the Father and the Son is expressed in various ways in the FG.

- They are unified in their task. John 5:21 says, "For just as the Father raises the dead and gives them life, even so the Son also gives life to whom He wishes" (cf. 8:18).
- They have mutual knowledge of each other. John 10:15a, says, "even as the Father knows Me and I know the Father."
- They are equal in honor. John 5:23 says, "so that all will honor the Son even as they honor the Father. He who does not honor the Son does not honor the Father who sent Him."

---

9. It is good to recognize at this point that chapter and verse divisions were not done by the author of the Gospel, but they were added much later to make referencing easier. Thus clustering "Father" sayings become more obvious when chapters are ignored, and the test is examined as one long narrative.

Jesus also demonstrates their unity with twenty "my Father" statements.[10] The "my Father" phrase alone does not necessarily reveal unity but assumes it. Yet the context in which they are found demonstrates unity between the Son and the Father. For example, Jesus's "my Father" statement in John 5:17 was interpreted by his audience to refer to Jesus's unity and equality with God as they concluded, "He not only was breaking the Sabbath, but also was calling God His own Father, making Himself equal with God" (5:18; see also 6:40; 8:49, 54; 10:37).

Unity is perhaps most strongly expressed in John 10:30 where Jesus declares, "I and the Father are one."[11] Jesus expresses the same idea again a few verses later in 10:38 when he says, "the Father is in me and I am in the Father." The immediate literary context, before and after Jesus's declaration (John 10:30), indicates from where Jesus is coming to declare his unity with the Father. Jesus's sheep are given to him by the Father and they are secure in his hand (vv. 28–29a), and because the Father is greater than all, he can ensure that no sheep can be snatched from his hand (v. 29b). The Father and the Son are not the same person, but they are fully united in this purpose. Jesus's hand and the Father's hand are equally capable of providing security. Both have authority and power to keep their sheep safe.[12] The Father's hand and security of his sheep allude also to the Psalm 95:7 where God's people are the "sheep of his hand."

What follows is that Jesus's audience was ready to execute Jesus by stoning—the Jewish mode of execution for blasphemy (John 10:31). They verbally explained their motivation as well. They said that they intended this because of "blasphemy; and because You, being a man, make Yourself out *to be* God" (John 10:33). This reaction leaves little room for any other interpretation other than the Jews understood Jesus's statement in 10:30 to be a statement of his identity.

We have seen that the literary context before Jesus's declaration of his oneness with the Father directs readers to understand John 10:30 in terms of Jesus's and the Father's functional unity. But on the other hand, literary context after the declaration directs readers also to move further and deeper into the statement's meaning, namely, to understand it as Jesus's statement of his identity as equal with the Father.

10. John 5:15; 6:32, 40; 8:19 (twice), 49, 54; 10:18, 29, 37; 14:17, 20, 21, 23; 15:1, 8, 15, 23, 24; 20:17. Some mss include more "My Father" statements.

11. In John 14:10, we have a similar saying than in 10:30. Jesus addresses his opponents in John 10:30, whereas in John 14:10 he addresses his faithful disciples.

12. Cf. Brodie, *The Gospel According to John*, 376.

It is worth noticing that John 10:30 sounds somewhat similar to the Shema (Deut 6:4). It may indeed suggest more than mere functional unity between the Son and the Father. Grammatically we have here two persons, Jesus and the Father, who are kept separate by employing the word for "one" in the neuter (*hen*) rather the masculine (*heis*). Masculine *heis* would suggest that only one person is in view, but by use of *hen*, Jesus and the Father are kept separate. This is perfectly in line with other passages of the FG where the Son and the Father are two persons rather than just one (e.g., John 1:1–2).[13] These two persons relate to each other in such a way that the word "one" is appropriate to use. Therefore, Greek grammar in John 10:30 also suggests that Jesus is not merely speaking here of functional oneness. Jesus is not only a person who shares the same will with the Father, for example, what John the Baptist could have said. He points out that his unity with the Father goes deeper. D. A. Carson concludes saying that, "If instead Jesus' will is exhaustively one with this Father's will, some kind of metaphysical unity is presupposed, even if not articulated."[14] Paul Meyer does not speak of metaphysical unity but takes "oneness" here to refer to the unity that Jesus had from God as one who was sent by him. Mishnah summarizes the principle of "agency" (or *shaliach*) saying that: "The agent of a person is as the person himself."[15] Jesus's actions were not his but God's; Jesus's words were not his but God's; Jesus's authority was not his but received from God.

John 10:30 and its aftermath is linked to John 5:16–19. In John 5:17 Jesus speaks of his relationship with the Father in terms of performing the same things and at the same time (i.e., on the Sabbath day) as his Father, "My Father is working until now, and I Myself am working." Jewish theology argued that God was working all the time, even on the Sabbath.[16] In this light, it is understandable why the Jews looked for an opportunity to kill Jesus, for he was making himself equal with God (John 5:18). The same thing happens at the end of chapter 8, where the Father-Son relationship was the center of a heated conversation between Jesus and Jews. In the end, the Jews were ready to stone Jesus (John 8:59). This happens right after Jesus has employed an "I AM" saying in its absolute sense (see above) referring to himself by one of God's names. The

---

13. Newman and Nida, *A Translator's Handbook*, 341.
14. Carson, *The Gospel According to John*, 395.
15. Meyer, "The Presentation of God," 261.
16. McGrath, *The Only True God*, 58.

## Father-Son Relationship

Jews take this statement, although not verbalized but implied from the context, as Jesus's declaration of his equality with "I AM," that is God. Also, after Jesus's statement of his oneness with the Father in John 10:30, the Jews were ready to execute him.

The evangelist introduces the Father and the Son side by side already in the Prologue (cf. 1:1–5). In John 1:14, the glory of the Son is that of the glory of the Father. At the end of the Prologue, the evangelist states that "the only begotten God, who is in the bosom of the Father, He has explained *Him*" (John 1:18). These statements quite comprehensively convey the idea that the Father and the Son have a unity beyond the unity that can ever occur between a human person and the Father God. This is reflected in Jesus's statement after his resurrection when he says to Mary, "I ascend to My Father and your Father, and My God and your God" (John 20:17), thus keeping an appropriate distance between himself and his followers.

John 1:18 is quite a complex verse due to its variant readings and interpretation of those readings. Therefore, it requires comment. There are three variants which all use the word *monogenēs* ("only" or "unique").[17] I list them here in the order of most probable to less probable original reading: (1) *monogenēs* God; (2) *monogenēs* Son, and (3) *monogenēs*.[18] Even though many scholars think that the first option is a probable original reading,[19] it is interpreted in a variety of ways. NASB translates it, "the only begotten God," taking *monogenēs* as an adjective that modifies "God." This reading indicates strongly that the Son is indeed divine. NIV translates this differently but keeps its basic meaning the same. It reads, "God the One and Only." NET and NRSV do something different. They take the word "God" as in apposition to *monogenēs*. NET translates this, "the only one, himself God," and NRSV, "God the only Son." Thus, the meaning is this, "Only (begotten) Son, who is God himself." These translations (NET and NRSV) hold the view that *monogenēs* carries the idea of "only Son" itself. In other words, *monogenēs* was a noun and would not need to have

---

17. Some English translations translate this "only begotten." This is not the lexical meaning of the Greek word *monogenēs*. This translation was already introduced by Jerome, who translated the Vulgate and used the Latin word *unigenitus* in order to distance the translation from the Arian view, which was that Jesus was not begotten but made.

18. See Metzger, *A Textual Commentary*, 169–70; Brown, *The Gospel According to John*, 1:17.

19. For an opposite view, see McGrath, *The Only True God*, 64–67.

the word "son" to make up the meaning "only Son." This is actually how it is used in John 1:14.[20] For that reason, we can say that mere *monogenēs*, without adding "God" or "Son" would also make good sense. It also had to make a good sense to the first readers of the Gospel. It can be argued, however, that the evangelist, at the end of the Prologue, wants to envelop the Prologue by using a statement that is linked to the beginning of the Prologue (John 1:1).[21] God's agent's divine identity is therefore stated in the beginning and in the end of the Prologue employing an anarthrous "God."[22] Thus, "*monogenēs* God" as a probable original reading conveys the idea of the Son's (incarnated *Logos*'s) divine identity. He was with God before the beginning began. He was God. He, as an incarnated *Logos*, is divine God himself and revealed the Father to the world.

Let's take up one more Father-Son unity statement to demonstrate the Son-Father relationship. John 14:10a, "Do you not believe that I am in the Father, and the Father is in Me?" clearly suggests that relationship. Even the words that Jesus speaks are not his but the words of the Father (cf. 14:10b). This is a profound statement that is in line with Jesus's earlier teaching in this Gospel. In John 14:1–4, Jesus claims to prepare the place in the Father's house to be able to take the disciples there where he is, namely to a face-to-face relationship with the Father. When Thomas asks about the way there, Jesus points out that he is the way. This means that Jesus's going to the Father (his cross and resurrection) is the preparation that is needed so that the disciples can have that relationship with the Father that Jesus already had. Now in John 14:10, this is re-stated; Jesus is already in the Father and the Father in him. They are one, without any disunity or fraction. Therefore, Jesus can say in 14:7, "if you had known Me, you would have known My Father also."

This is quite different from what is happening in John 8:38. Here, Jesus refers to his Father and his opponents' father with the same word *patēr*. Although Jesus does not qualify the word, he refers to two different fathers, namely, "My Father" and "your father."[23] This tells much about Je-

---

20. There is a progression in *monogenēs* sayings in the Fourth Gospel from more obscure to more complete and more accurate. See John 1:14, 18; 3:16, 18.

21. Note that the Prologue's chiastic structure. See Neyrey, *The Gospel of John*, 39–41.

22. Anarthrous in Greek grammar means a subjective without the definite article.

23. There is variant reading which adds "my" and "your" before the word father and so clarifies whose father Jesus is talking about. This seems, however, to be an early scribal addition to shorter and more difficult reading. See Metzger, *A Textual Commentary*, 192.

sus and his opponents. Both their actions define what kind of father they have. In other words, because Jesus's and his opponents' actions are so far apart from each other and are different in nature, they are not "from" the same Father. That is why Jesus uses even his works as proof to tell not only who he is but also who his Father is (John 5:36). Also, although unbelieving Jews proclaim that God is their Father in chapter 8, Jesus denies this. If their Father were God, then they would believe in Jesus because this is the only way to know the Father.

## The Father Who Sent the Son

The phrase, "The One/Father/You who sent me," and other variations of this phrase occur around thirty times in the FG.[24] It is always spoken by Jesus except once at the beginning of the Gospel where John the Baptist pronounces these words (1:33; cf. 1:6). John the Baptist, however, does not use this phrase to refer to "Father" but to "God." This suggests that John the Baptist did not mean the same thing as Jesus when he uses the same statement.

Sending is always an act of purpose. This is obvious on all occasions where someone is sent in the FG. In John the Baptist's case, he was sent to preach about repentance and to baptize—to prepare the way for the Messiah to arrive. The priest and Levites were sent by the Pharisees to find out the identity of John the Baptist (John 1:19, 24). Jesus was sent by the Father for a purpose as well (cf. John 1:29; 3:16).

The phrase "the One/Father who sent me" is used as an epithet for God.[25] When it is used this way, it does not only tell about the one who was sent but also, the sender.[26] This was a part of Jesus's mission, namely, to explain who God is (cf. John 1:18). These statements caused disagreement, however, between Jesus and his opponents: Jesus's opponents did not accept Jesus's claims about his Father as his sending agent and thus his relationship with him. According to them, that identity did not belong to Jesus. Jesus, however, revealed that the Father is the one who is behind

---

24. "Father who sent me" is found in John 5:37; 6:44, 57; 8:16, 18; 12:49; 20:21. "He who sent me" and similar statements are found from in John 1:33 (John the Baptist); 4:34; 5:24; 6:38, 39; 7:16, 28, 33; 8:26, 29; 9:4; 12:44, 45; 13:20; 14:24; 15:21; 16:5. Jesus also addressed his Father in his prayers with "you who sent me" phrase. They are found in John 11:42; 17:8, 18, 21, 23, 25.

25. Meyer, "The Presentation of God," 262.

26. Meyer, "The Presentation of God," 265.

his appearance among them. Jesus is, therefore, satisfied that his disciples believed that the Father has sent him (John 17:8). This is a reminder that John's Gospel is rich in both Christology and *Theology*.

As we have already seen, the "sending" motif in the FG is connected to the Father-Son relation. This comes even clearer when the Jewish concept of agency (*shaliach*) and the first-century Mediterranean concept of brokerage are considered. The Jewish institution of agency (*shaliach*) is summarized in Mishnah *Berakot* 5:5 as, "the agent of a person is as the person himself."[27] This definition reveals that the one who is sent as an agent has the authority of the one who sent him. In this sense, he is, "equivalent to the person himself."[28] Many individuals in the OT were sent by God as envoy or emissary. Moses is a good example of such an individual. Moses brought instructions and gave godly leadership to the nation. If the nation listened to Moses, they were doing well; if not, the nation experienced negative consequences. Jews well understood that God sends his authorized agents to the nation from time to time, the ultimate one of them being his Messiah.

The brokerage model with patron-broker-client hierarchy was well established in the Mediterranean society during the first century CE. A broker was a representative (i.e., sent) of the patron before his clients. Clients had access to their patron only via the patron's broker. Characteristics of the broker were very similar to that in the *shaliach* model. A broker who had the authority from the patron had to represent the patron accurately and seek the patron's will. He stood between higher and lower orders. Clients, on the other hand, had to treat the broker the same way as they would have treated their patron. In short, the broker acted as a patron, but did not replace the patron.[29]

The Fourth Evangelist wrote in this socio-historical context. Jewish *shaliach* and Mediterranean brokerage models were well known. Furthermore, Jesus and his opponents must have been aware of these principles as they lived in that high-context society which means that the acceptable models of behavior were understood and thus practiced by the members of that society.[30] For this reason, we can assume, the evangelist did not

27. Meyer, "The Presentation of God," 261.
28. Keener, *The Gospel of John*, 1:313.
29. Brown, *Spirit in the Writings of John*, 28–30.
30. Malina and Rohrbaugh, *Social-Science Commentary*, 16. Malina and Rohrbaugh explain that "People in high-context societies presume a broadly shared, well-understood, or 'high,' knowledge of the context of anything referred to in conversation or in writing."

feel that the *shaliach*/brokerage model should be explained to his readers. He supposes that the recipients of his Gospel readily recognize the *shaliach*/brokerage features that are a part of the hermeneutical key to understand his Christological presentation.

To demonstrate this, we will give two examples of "who sent me" sayings. First, Jesus claims on several occasion that to know God (Father) is to know him. Jesus's words at the end of his public ministry in John 12:44–45 prove this point: "He who believes in Me, believes not in Me but in Him who sent Me. He who sees Me sees the One who sent Me." Another statement like this, but now in the negative form, is found in John 5:36–38. The words in v. 38 are especially forceful: "You (Jesus's opponents) do not have His (the Father's) word abiding in you, for you do not believe Him whom He sent." There is no detour. The only way to the Father is indeed through his broker, Jesus (cf. John 14:6).

Secondly, Jesus makes numerous statements regarding his accurate representation of the one who sent him. Jesus speaks about this in terms of doing his sender's will (e.g., John 4:34; 5:30; 6:38); to speak only what he hears from the one who has sent him (e.g., John 8:29; 14:24); and to perform the works what he has received from the Father who has sent him (e.g., John 5:30, 36). This fits the agency/brokerage models well.

In addition, there is one more of Jesus's statements that points towards his identity as a God's authentic agent. In John 16:5, Jesus reveals that he is going back to the one who sent him. This also speaks about the relationship that Jesus has with the Father. The question is, however, what kind of "going" Jesus is talking about. Here "going back" is not mere leaving (emphasizing one's absence), but it includes the cross, resurrection, and the ascension—in short, the glorification in Johannine language. Thus, going back to the Father for Jesus is to *complete the will of the one who sent him*. From the saying itself and its context, it is natural to read this to mean that Jesus is going to enter into the same realm to be with his Father where he was prior of his coming. Soon Jesus, God's agent/broker, will have finished his assignment successfully (cf. John 17:4).

## The Obedient Son

The phrase "the obedient Son" refers to those passages which point out how Jesus faithfully performs everything that the Father has given him. Jesus does and says only the things he receives from the Father (e.g., John

5:19–23, 30; 8:28; 12:49). These passages could be also viewed as part of the brokerage passages (see above), or as Rudolf Schnackenburg does, Father-as-giver passages.[31] The Father gives Jesus words to speak and works to do (e.g., John 5:17, 19, 36; 8:28, 38; 10:37). All that the Son received from the Father, he obediently did.

Here we see the same as we did while looking at "sending" passages, namely, that as much as these "the obedient Son" passages tell about Jesus, they also tell about God. This is the way that the evangelist presents the Father-Son relationship. It is "the Father who guarantees and endorses Jesus' revealing and saving activity on earth."[32] This means, therefore, that if one does not believe the Son, then one does not believe in or know God. It is only through the Son that one can truly know and worship God and have eternal life (cf. John 20:30–31).

The ultimate demonstration of Jesus's obedience to his Father is seen in Jesus's cross. In John 17:4, Jesus states, "I glorified You on the earth, having accomplished the work which You have given Me to do." This statement in aorist[33] is a part of Jesus's Farewell Discourse, his closing prayer before his death of the cross. Therefore, it functions as a summary of the past and a prediction of the future. The obedient Son had already set his course to face the cross, and for this reason, he considered the cross as an already faithfully completed task. In other words, this statement does not refer only to Jesus's signs and sayings during his public ministry (cf. John 5:36). He had come down to be the Lamb of God and provide forgiveness of sin (John 1:29), and that is what he is referring to in his final prayer.

## God as the Father of Others

In the FG, Jesus's relationship with the Father is a prominent motif. This motif in the FG is not limited to Jesus and his relationship with the Father; it extends to people and their relationship with the Father. We will take a brief look at that motif now.

---

31. Schnackenburg, *The Gospel According to John*, 2:175.
32. Schnackenburg, *The Gospel According to John*, 2:176.
33. Greek aorist is a tense. "The fundamental significance of the aorist is to denote action simply as occurring, without reference to its progress... It has no essential temporal significance... The aorist signifies nothing as to the completeness, but simply presents the action as attained." Dana and Mantey, *A Manual Grammar*, 193.

# Father-Son Relationship

Before looking into this particular topic, we briefly look at the passage where Jesus is saying something about his opponents' father. In John 8:38, Jesus refers to his Father and his opponents' father using the same word *patēr* (father) without qualifying the word. He refers to two different fathers, namely, "my" Father and "your" father.[34] This tells us about Jesus and his opponents' different patrons. Both their actions define what kind of father they have. In other words, because Jesus's and his opponents' actions are so far apart from each other and are different in nature, they are not "from" the same patron. That is one of the reasons why Jesus uses his works as proof to tell not only who he is but also who is his Father (John 5:36). Besides, although unbelieving Jews in chapter 8 proclaim that God is their father, Jesus denies this. If their father were God, then they would believe in Jesus because this is the only way to know the Father.

There are a few passages where Jesus reveals to his disciples something about their relationship with the Father. We outline two of them here, namely 14:2–3 and 20:17 (see also 4:23; 6:44; 16:23). Jesus in his Farewell Discourse reveals that he prepares the place for his disciples so that they would be where Jesus already is (John 14:2–3). The entire passage (John 14:1–4) has received much attention and led to various interpretations. One of the most common is that Jesus is going to prepare a heavenly place for us so that it would be ready when we die, a place in the Father's house. This is not, however, what Jesus is saying. Without a detailed argumentation, we only point out that Jesus is speaking here of being with the Father, not being "in the heaven." He prepares the way, by going to the cross, and for us to have a relationship with the Father, the relationship that Jesus already has with his Father (cf. 1:1; 17:5). So, he is the way, and there is no other way to the Father (John 14:6). We do not need to wait until we die to have that fellowship with the Father. It is available after Jesus's glorification (i.e., the cross).[35]

Finally, towards the end of the Gospel, Jesus's statement captures his earlier promise in 14:2–3. In John 20:17, Jesus reveals that his Father is also his followers' Father. The Father whom Jesus came to exegete (1:18) is now fully revealed through Jesus, through his death and resurrection. Now the Father's place is fully accessible. Yet, there is one major difference between the relationship of Jesus and his Father and his followers

---

34. Some English translations, like NASB, read "My Father" and "your Father." There is a variant later ms reading which includes "my" and "your" before the world father to clarify whose father Jesus is talking about. See Metzger, *A Textual Commentary*, 192.

35. Cf. Keener, *The Gospel of John*, 2:932–39.

and their Father. Jesus does not say to Mary, "I am returning to *our* Father and *our* God." Rather, Jesus distinguishes himself from his believing disciples when he says, "my Father—your Father; my God—your God." This suggests that Jesus's relationship with the Father-God is different from that of the disciples. Although the disciples believe in the Son (Jesus) and thus Father-God, they do not have the same identity with Jesus. Jesus as the Son of the Father is the one who shares the same divine identity with him. His disciples, however, are created human beings, and they will never share the identity with the Son.[36] As such people, Jesus sends them into the world to perform "Father-kind" works (cf. John 20:19–23).

## Concluding Remarks

As a summary for this chapter, we may suggest that in the FG Jews had two problems concerning the Father-Son relationship and Jesus's messiahship: (1) They did not accept the idea that a God-send-Messiah is divine (a problem of monotheism), and that (2) a man, Jesus of Nazareth, can be the God-sent Messiah (a problem of hermeneutics). If this is a correct conclusion, the Jews denied Jesus's messiahship on two levels: on the level of Jesus's divinity and the level of Jesus's humanity. That is the reason why the evangelist says that, although Jesus came to his own people, they did not accept him (John 1:11). Yet, the Fourth Evangelist includes various statements to indicate that Jesus shared the same divine identity with the Father. The Father-Son relationship, which is based on equality, authority, oneness, and unity was one of the indicators for such an identity.

## Suggestions for Further Reading

Akala, Adesola J. *The Son-Father Relationship and Christological Symbolism in the Gospel of John*. LTNS. London: Bloomsbury T&T Clark, 2014.

Schnackenburg, Rudolf. *The Gospel According to St. John*. New York: Seabury, 1980. Pp. 2:172–86.

36. Although in the Synoptic Gospels Jesus teaches his disciples to pray "Our Father," these words were meant to be words of his disciples, not his. Jesus said, "When *you* pray *you* say." In the same way in the FG, the Father-Son relationship is extended to include his disciples, but with that one major difference.

CHAPTER 7

# The Spirit as Paraklētos
## Jesus as a Model

THE FOURTH EVANGELIST IS the only NT author who uses the Greek word *paraklētos* (paraclete).[1] It occurs four times in the FG and once in the First Epistle of John. The five occurrences in Johannine literature are as follows:

- John 14:16: "I will ask the Father, and He will give you another *Paraklētos*."
- John 14:26: "But the *Paraklētos*, the Holy Spirit, whom the Father will send."
- John 15:26: "When the *Paraklētos* comes, whom I will send to you."
- John 16:7: "[I]t is to your advantage that I go away; for if I do not go away, the *Paraklētos* will not come to you."
- 1 John 2:1: "And if anyone sins, we have *Paraklētos* with the Father, Jesus Christ the righteous."[2]

---

1. The *Paraklētos* is also referred to as the paraclete in Johannine scholarship. A paraclete spelling is driven from Late Latin *paracletus* that comes from the Greek word *paraklētos*. We have chosen to use transliteration *paraklētos* of the Greek in this chapter. The name is written with capital *P* when Spirit-*Paraklētos*, Jesus, or glorified Christ is in view, but with lower case *p* when we refer to the mere word *paraklētos*.

2. In these references, the definite article "the" before "*Paraklētos*" is applied if the Greek (UBS⁵) text has a definite article.

In addition to these verses, the *Paraklētos* is referred to by the third-person masculine personal pronoun "he" (*ekeinos*) in John 14:26 and 16:8, 13.

Linguistically *paraklētos* is a verbal adjective with a passive sense used as a noun. As such, it means "called to one's side." Despite the absence of *paraklētos* in other NT books, its verbal form *parakaleō*[3] occurs often in the NT. The range of meanings of *parakaleō* is displayed in the NT translations, where its meaning alters according to the context in which it is found. NASB translates it, for example, with "to implore" (Luke 8:41), "to invite" (Acts 8:31), "to urge" (Rom 12:1), "to exhort" (1 Pet 5:1), "to comfort" (Matt 5:4; Eph 6:22), and "to appeal" (Phlm 9). These examples demonstrate that *parakaleō* is not used in a technical sense.

The noun *paraklētos* also has various connotations, and therefore, its translation into English with a single word presents a challenge. Some have suggested that *paraklētos* as a passive adjective is derived from its verbal meaning. Therefore, it should be understood as "one called alongside to help."[4] Although this can be argued linguistically, it does not capture the meaning of *Paraklētos* for the Fourth Evangelist. If the meaning "one called alongside to help" were accepted as the *sole* meaning for the *Paraklētos*, it would mislead the readers. This would reduce the *Paraklētos*'s role to a mere helping one which suggests that Jesus's disciples would be able to carry on after Jesus's physical absence by themselves, only needing "some" help from the *Paraklētos*. We argue that for the Fourth Evangelist the *Paraklētos* means more than a "helper." Since linguistic considerations alone cannot define its meaning, it is necessary to examine its background and the Fourth Evangelist's usage of it to comprehend its fuller meaning.

The verb *parakaleō* is not found in the Johannine literature at all. Its absence may indicate that the evangelist does not define *paraklētos* by its verbal form *parakaleō*. Many modern English NT translations, however, seem to follow that logic. For example, to translate the *Paraklētos* as "the comforter," because *parakaleō* mean "to comfort" in some NT contexts, is questionable.[5] The verb's absence from the FG may even suggest that the Fourth Evangelist intended to create some distinction between the verb *parakaleō* and noun *paraklētos*. This idea is, however, difficult to prove.

---

3. Several authors often use the first person singular of *parakalein*.

4. Brown, *Gospel According to John*, 2:1136.

5. *Paraklētos* includes the idea of "comforter," but it cannot be taken as *the* meaning of *paraklētos* in the FG.

English NT translations demonstrate the challenges of translating *paraklētos* into English. For example, in John 14:16 it is translated as "helper" (ESV), "comforter" (KJV), "advocate" (NET), and "counselor" (NIV). Also, it is suggested that "friend," "representative," "teacher/preacher," "intercessor/spokesman/mediator," and "supporter/sponsor" would be acceptable translations.[6]

Even though it is difficult to grasp the meaning of the *Paraklētos* in one word, he is described as the Spirit and compared to Jesus. The evangelist defines *paraklētos* as the Holy Spirit in John 14:26 and the Spirit of truth in 15:26 and 16:13. Also, Jesus's promise to give another (*allon*) *Paraklētos* implicitly refers to Jesus as the first *Paraklētos* (John 14:16), who was not mere helper, counselor, or comforter. In 1 John, this term is applied to the glorified Christ (1:2), and it can hardly be understood as a mere helper. We will return to some of these observations in the ensuing discussion.

One could ask, therefore, why should the meaning of *paraklētos* concern us any further if the term equals the Holy Spirit. In addition, why did the evangelist prefer this term above something else, or why he was not satisfied by using the more familiar phrase, "the Holy Spirit," when referring to the Spirit in Jesus's Farewell Discourse? What did the Fourth Evangelist intend to emphasize or convey by this term? We will perhaps never be able to address these questions satisfactorily. Yet, we aim to give some at least partial answers to these questions below.

At the outset, we assume that because *paraklētos* is used exclusively in Jesus's Farewell Discourse (John 13:33—17:26), its usage here may have specific significance for this historical moment. This term might convey the best connotations of Jesus's permanent presence through the Spirit in the lives of the disciples in the future. The disciples are troubled because of the news about Jesus's departure. By utilizing a new term for the Spirit, Jesus gains their attention as he ensures that their future is not only secure but also better than the previous situation because of the presence of the *Paraklētos*. The disciples will not be alone after Jesus's crucifixion, resurrection, and ascension. The *Paraklētos* is with them forever and will play a significant role in their future.

---

6. See Bennema, *The Power of Saving Wisdom*, 216; Harris, *John*, 260.

## Searching the Backdrop for the Paraklētos

Johannine scholars have long acknowledged that finding a single or detailed background for the *Paraklētos* concept in the FG is not satisfactory. Therefore, we aim to use broad brushstrokes to paint a backdrop for the Johannine *Paraklētos* against which its meaning can be best understood.

Although *paraklētos* is strictly a Johannine term, it was not new or unknown. The word was readily available to the evangelist. Also, its meaning, it can be assumed, must have been familiar to his first Greek speaking readers.[7] We will outline below several sources/concepts which might have functioned as intertexts and perhaps influenced the Fourth Evangelist's usage of that term. Our outline includes (1) early legal documents, (2) Philo of Alexandria, (3) Rabbinic literature, (4) the Septuagint, (5) angelology, (6) Merkabah mysticism, (7) Methurgeman, and (8) Qumran community's spirit of truth.

The word *paraklētos* is found in non-Johannine literature as early as the fourth century BCE. In these non-Jewish writings between the fourth century BCE and the third century CE, the term appears in legal contexts; however, it is not used in a juridical sense although it is found in forensic settings. It conveys the idea of "supporter" or "sponsor" or even "patron" rather than juridical view of "accuser" or "advocate."[8] Another observation is that in numerous non-Jewish juridical texts where the term *paraklētos* could have been used, it is missing. This indicates that the term did not convey strictly judicial meaning, at least in its primary sense. *Paraklētos* was in those texts someone who helps and supports the one who needed assistance of some kind.

Secondly, *paraklētos* is found in some Jewish sources. Philo of Alexandria uses the word *paraklētos* in his writings in its broad meaning of "someone called in to help another person."[9] Scholars, however, disagree whether he used the term in a legal sense or not. Philo uses the term in various other ways as well but mainly applies it to a concept of brokerage. A broker in the first-century Mediterranean world was one who stood between the patron and client. A broker made it possible for a client to receive benefits from one's patron.[10]

---

7. There is no Hebrew equivalent. Greek word *paraklētos* was transliterated into Hebrew.

8. Grayston, "The Meaning of PARAKLĒTOS," 67–82.

9. Grayston, "The Meaning of PARAKLĒTOS," 72.

10. For a detailed study on Spirit-*Parakletos* as a broker, see Brown. *Spirit in the*

Thirdly, we find the word *paraklētos* in Rabbinic literature. There is no Hebrew word equivalent to *paraklētos*, however. Therefore, Rabbis took the Greek word *paraklētos* and transliterated Greek letters into Hebrew letters. Hence, "there is no linguistic background for it in Hebrew or Aramaic."[11] The "loan" word *paraklētos* in these writings is used in the sense of "advocate" and is related to a judicial function. Garry Burge says that the loanword was "used to describe any heavenly defender of the righteous."[12] This is a weighty observation as the Spirit in the Pentateuch is, among other things, a defender of the nation of Israel. Thus, later Rabbinic usage of *paraklētos* and the Spirit in the OT overlap in their functions. It is also noteworthy that Rabbis used another Hebrew word that conveys a robust forensic meaning "accuser" (Gr. *katēgoros*; cf. Acts 23:35; 25:18; Rev 12:10). This word is not, however, employed by the Fourth Evangelist. This may indicate that he did not have in mind the mere forensic function of the Spirit as he chooses to employ the word *paraklētos* rather than *katēgoros*.[13]

Fourthly, the word *paraklētos* is not found in the Septuagint. Yet, the Septuagint employs the verb *parakaleō* and the noun *paraklēsis* often in the senses of "to comfort" and "comfort" respectively. Also, it is used in the present participle *ho parakalōn* (i.e., the one who comforts)[14] often in the first chapter of Lamentations. The participle *ho parakalōn* is also found in Isaiah 51:12 where the speaker is God. This verse is closely related to the FG because of its *egō eimi* usage. The verse begins with the phrase *egō eimi egō eimi ho parakalōn se* ("I, even I, am He who comforts you"). This statement is powerful, indicating that YHWH is the one who comforts. The Septuagint uses but only once the cognate *paraklētōr* (Job 16:2). There the word *paraklētōr* is used to describe Job's friends who were "helping" or "advising" Job. Again, the idea is not legal or forensic, but rather someone who comes near intending to comfort or help. The verb *parakaleō* is used in the Septuagint in the eschatological context (e.g., Isa 66:11, 13). It may not be an accident, therefore, that the Fourth Evangelist uses *Paraklētos* in the eschatological context in Jesus's Farewell Discourse.

---

*Writings of John.*

11. Bennema, *The Power of Saving Wisdom*, 216.
12. Burge, *The Anointed Community*, 14.
13. Grayston, "The Meaning of PARAKLĒTOS," 75–76.
14. *ho parakalōn* is found only thrice in the NT: Rom 12:8; 2 Cor 1:4; 7:6.

Fifthly, some scholars have seen Jewish angelology as a background of Johannine *Paraklētos*. In the OT, angels, often called "spirits," and especially the angel of the LORD, fulfil similar roles as the *Paraklētos* does in the FG such as announcing, defending, and helping. Also, the archangel Michael is seen as the intercessor model for the *Paraklētos*.[15]

Sixthly, there is a suggestion that Jewish mysticism and particularly Merkabah (or Chariot) mysticism,[16] as described in first-century Jewish and Christian writings and in the second-century Jewish *Hekhalot* literature in particular, would be a background for Johannine *Paraklētos*.[17] Merkabah mysticism is linked to Ezekiel 1, Isaiah 6, and Daniel 7. The basic tenet of this suggestion is that Jewish mysticism pointed towards gaining a position that leads one to enter before the throne of God. This kind of leading resonates with the FG as the *Paraklētos* guides the disciples. The statement that the Spirit-*Parkalētos* leads the disciples into all truth (John 16:13) "points to the Merkabah mystical visions in which the angels escort the mystic in the latter's heavenly ascent, guide him to see the glory of God and reveal all cosmological and heavenly secrets."[18]

Seventhly, there is an argument that the Methurgeman is the conceptual background for Johannine *Paraklētos*. The Methurgeman was an individual in a synagogue who "translated the scriptural readings into a targum as well as, later on, mediated the synagogal preaching."[19] Eskil Franck argues that the *Paraklētos*'s role cannot be traced from the word's literary meaning; his role is determined by what he does. He argues that when the functions of the *Paraklētos* are examined, they point towards his role as a teacher. The Methurgeman, in the synagogue, functioned as a kind of a teacher-mediator between the message/messenger and the people. Thus, the apparent similarities between these two justify this conclusion. Franck notices though that, "M[ethurgeman] was not of such importance that the G[ospel] of J[ohn] was built up around this figure."[20]

---

15. See further Brown, *Gospel According to John*, 2:1138; Betz, *Der Paraklet Fürsprecher*, 36–116.

16. Kanagaraj defines Merkabah mysticism as "seeing God in his kingly glory," and its goal as "to enter before the Throne of Glory." Kanagaraj, *"Mysticism" in the Gospel of John*, 56, 81.

17. Kanagaraj, *"Mysticism" in the Gospel of John*.

18. Kanagaraj, *"Mysticism" in the Gospel of John*, 253.

19. Franck, *Revelation Taught*, 132.

20. Franck, *Revelation Taught*, 144.

But he argues that the Methurgeman fits into the FG's framework, and that there is the organic relationship between these two.[21]

Finally, the Qumran community's pneumatology, especially its dualistic ideas and the usage of the phrase "spirit of truth" has caught the attention of Johannine scholarship. The *Paraklētos* is also identified as the Spirit of truth in John 14:7; 15:26; 16:13 (see also 1 John 4:6). This phrase is exclusively Johannine among NT authors.[22] The "spirit of truth" phrase is found in only a few Jewish writings such as the Dead Sea Scrolls. Although the same phraseology is used in the Dead Sea Scrolls and the FG, there are some differences between their conceptional pneumatology. Johannine *Paraklētos* is superior to all other spirits, whereas the Qumran "spirit of truth" is in the absolute dualistic position with the "spirit of deceit."

These suggestions for the Johannine Spirit-*Paraklētos* have received some attention and correctly so. Still, none can be pointed out as *sole* background for the Johannine usage of *Paraklētos*. Yet, the outline demonstrates that *paraklētos* itself is not new term either for the evangelist and or his first readers. It also is noticeable that the evangelist did not use it as it had been previously used. Daniel Stevick points out that "As he [the Fourth Evangelist] took over a word with a complex history and usage, he drew on some, but not all of its prior, largely secular meanings and his way of using the term stretched it to new significance. He asked his readers to grasp his word on the terms set by his usage."[23] Here the Fourth Evangelist seems to do to the word *Paraklētos* the same as he did to the word *Logos*. He takes the term circulated in the various writings and builds upon its previous connotations giving it a unique meaning and usage that work well for his rhetorical purpose.

## Ruach in the Old Testament

*Ruach* is a Hebrew word that has a wide range of meanings including "air in motion, blowing, wind, what is empty or transitory, spirit, [and] mind."[24]

---

21. Franck, *Revelation Taught*, 144.

22. The Spirit of truth occurs in John 14:17; 15:26; 16:13; and 1 John 4:6. It is noticeable that 1 John 4:6 compares the Spirit of truth and the spirit of falsehood bridging the Qumran idea of the Spirit of truth and the spirit of deceit.

23. Stevick, *Jesus and His Own*, 284.

24. Holladay, *A Concise Hebrew and Aramaic Lexicon*, 334.

These meanings describe *ruach* as an invisible entity. Because of this, in the OT, "the invisible essence of *ruach* is known primarily by its effect on the visible world, by which we can then attempt to perceive its essence."[25]

Theologically meaningful usage of *ruach* for this study is when it is used for the "Spirit of God," and the "Spirit of Lord."[26] In Israel's salvation history *ruach* of God/Lord is a life-force who "serves as an instrument that fulfills the divine purpose within history."[27] As such, *ruach* performs a variety of activities, which have similarities with the *Paraklētos*. Perhaps the most striking similarities between them is found in their roles towards God's people. This is noticeable in *ruach*'s activities as he defends and moves God's people, inspires prophetic utterances, gives the power that is greater than mere human strength, teaches and leads to knowledge and obedience to the Lord, and reveals the unknown.[28] This list of *ruach*'s functions is suitable to the Holy Spirit in the NT in general, but also the *Paraklētos* in particular.

## Defining the Paraklētos in the Fourth Gospel

The first time the word *paraklētos* is used in the FG (14:16), it is linked to Jesus. Jesus says, "Father . . . will give you another *Paraklētos*," referring himself as a *Paraklētos* as well.[29] This indicates that *paraklētos* is not a technical term reserved only for the Holy Spirit (cf. 2 John 2:1). Secondly, by means of this link between Jesus and the coming *Paraklētos*, the author makes it explicit that Jesus, whom the disciples knew, is the model for the coming *Paraklētos*, whom they did not yet know. Daniel Stevick points out, "When the Spirit is introduced as *another* paraclete (14:16), the expression suggests that the Spirit is Jesus' alter ego—that Jesus has been a 'paraclete' and the Spirit will be to Jesus' followers as he has been."[30] Thirdly, the opening verse reveals that, although Jesus as *Paraklētos* and the Spirit-*Paraklētos* are closely related, they are separate agents. Finally, the connection made between Jesus and *Paraklētos* further defines who

---

25. Van Pelt et al., "רוּחַ," NIDOTTE, 3:1073.

26. The phrase the "Holy Spirit" is found three times in the OT (Ps 51:11; Isa 63:10, 11).

27. Breck, *Spirit of Truth*, 12.

28. Breck, *Spirit of Truth*, 10–36.

29. Kärkkäinen, *Pneumatology*, 25.

30. Stevick, *Jesus and His Own*, 292.

Jesus is. What is said about the *Paraklētos* applies to Jesus as well. For example, the *Paraklētos* was coming down to the earth from the Father as Jesus had come. Also, after Jesus's going back to the Father, the disciples continue to learn about Jesus as the Spirit-*Paraklētos* who will speak what he hears from Jesus (John 16:14–15). This promise encourages the reader to read the rest of the *Paraklētos* passages with a Christological connotation in mind. A comparison between Jesus and the Spirit-*Paraklētos* reveals many similarities, which suggest that Jesus is a significant backdrop against which one should understand the *Paraklētos*. The following chart, adapted from Gary Burge,[31] demonstrates this.

| **Paraklētos** | | **Christ Jesus** |
|---|---|---|
| 14:16 | Given by the Father | 3:16 |
| 14:16–17 | with, in, by the disciple | 3:22; 13:33; 14:20 |
| 14:17 | not received by the world | 1:11; 5:53; 14:20 |
| 14:17 | not known by the world (only believers know him) | 8:19; 10:14; 16:3 |
| 14:17 | not seen be the world (only believers see him) | 14:19; 16:16–17 |
| 14:26 | sent by the Father | Cf. chs. 5, 7, 8, 12 |
| 14:26 | teaches | 7:14–15; 8:20; 19:19 |
| 15:26; 16:7, 13 | he comes (from the Father into the world) | 5:43; 16:28; 18:37 |
| 15:26 | gives testimony | 5:31ff.; 8:13ff.; 7:7 |
| 16:8 | convicts the world | Cf. 3:19–20; 9:41; 15:22 |
| 16:13 | speaks not of self but of what is heard | 7:17; 8:26ff.; 14:10 |
| 16:14 | glorifies the Sender (Jesus/Father) | 12:28; 17:1, 4 |

31. Burge, *The Anointed Community*, 141 (used by permission). See also Neyrey, *The Gospel of John*, 270; Brown, *The Gospel According to John*, 2:1140.

| Paraklētos | | Christ Jesus |
|---|---|---|
| 16:13ff. | reveals, discloses, proclaims | 4:25; (16:25) |
| 16:13 | leads into the fullness of truth | 14:6; 18:37 |
| 15:26; 14:17; 16:13 | is the Spirit of truth; Jesus is the Truth | 14:6 |
| 14:16 | a Paraclete | (14:16); 1 John 2:1 |

Table 7.1

Similarities between Jesus and the Spirit-*Paraklētos* are ample. These similarities cannot be accidental. It is reasonable to conclude that the evangelist must have deliberately inserted these similarities in the text to define the *Paraklētos*. Also, it is interesting that all the places where Jesus corresponds with *Paraklētos* are found in Jesus's Farewell Discourse or prior in the Gospel narrative. There are two implications to this. First, this helps a first-time reader to make the connection between Jesus and *Paraklētos*. Secondly, it endorses the paradigm shift that was going to take place after Jesus's glorification. What Jesus was for the disciples before his glorification, the *Paraklētos* is going to be (is) for Jesus's disciples after that.[32] The paradigm shift points out that the *Paraklētos* is an eschatological figure.[33] The Spirit in general, and the *Paraklētos* in particular, belong to the eschatological framework.

After the initial statement about the *Paraklētos* in John 14:16, the Fourth Evangelist does not identify the *Paraklētos* with Jesus again. Instead, he defines the *Paraklētos* as the Holy Spirit (14:26) and the Spirit of truth (14:17; 15:26; 16:13). The *Paraklētos* is placed in apposition to these titles. The reference to the *Paraklētos* first as another like Jesus, together with further defining him as the Holy Spirit and the Spirit of truth, helps readers identify who the *Paraklētos* is. Yet, we can assume that the *Paraklētos* does not equal fully with either of them; every term has its connotations that work in the context of the use.[34]

32. See Tuppurainen, "Jesus, the Spirit, and the Church," 42–56.
33. Cf. Burge, *The Anointed Community*, 30–31.
34. Louw and Nida note that "The first principle of semantic analysis of lexical items is that there are 'no synonyms,' in the sense that no two lexical items ever have

## The Spirit as Paraklētos

The *Paraklētos* as the Holy Spirit links him to other Spirit passages in the FG and the author's community's experience of the Spirit and the OT references to God's *ruach*. In the FG, the phrase "the Holy Spirit" (Gr. *to pneuma to hagion*) is found only in John 14:26. Yet, the Fourth Evangelist refers to the Spirit in different ways several times elsewhere.[35] We are not able to engage with every Spirit passage in this study. We point out only two passages and outline how they might have helped the first readers to understand the *Paraklētos*.

The phrase "Holy Spirit" (without definite articles) is found in 1:33[36] and 20:22. In both of these cases, the Spirit has two important functions. Firstly, the Spirit inaugurates the ministry of Jesus (1:33) and the disciples (20:22). The ministries assigned to these brokers were to be performed in the presence of the Spirit. Secondly, John the Baptist points out that the Spirit's coming on Jesus was an identity marker. When the Spirit came on Jesus, he recognized that Jesus was the Son of God. In the case of the disciples in 20:22, the Spirit's coming on the disciples is similar as an identity marker authorizing them to go to the world as Jesus's representatives. Moreover, in John 1:33 John the Baptist points out that it is this Jesus who will baptize in the Holy Spirit. Therefore, it is reasonable to assume that some of these references to the Spirit have been in the first readers' minds when the *Paraklētos* was brought to apposition with the Holy Spirit in John 16:26.

It is difficult to prove if the FG's first readers were able to make cross-references to other Christian writings, which were to be a part of the NT Canon. We may assume that this was very unlikely yet not impossible in some degree. Yet, Burge's conclusion that "the Johannine community was a vital, pneumatic community"[37] is well-argued and convincing. Thus at least those readers who were familiar with the Christian community had testified to the Spirit's presence among the community. Therefore, their understanding of the *Paraklētos* as the Holy Spirit was a likely helpful definition. The privilege to use other NT writings to understand the

---

completely the same meanings in all of the contexts in which they might occur." Louw and Nida, *Greek-English Lexicon of the New Testament*, 1:xv. See also pages xvi–xx.

35. As "the Spirit" in 1:32, 33; 3:6, 8, 34; 6:63; 7:39; as "Spirit" in 3:5, 6; 4:23, 24; 6:63; 7:39; as "Holy Spirit" (i.e., without definite articles) in 1:33; 20:22; as "the Spirit of (the) truth" in 14:17; 15:26; 16:13.

36. In 1:33, Spirit is mentioned twice: The Spirit (*to pneuma*) and Holy Spirit (*pneuma hagion*) in the dative.

37. Burge, *The Anointed Community*, 45.

*Paraklētos* belongs to later readers. Yet, we need to keep in mind that the *Paraklētos* is a solely Johannine term not used by others. Therefore, we need to be cautious not to read other NT Spirit texts into that of the FG's presentation of the *Paraklētos*.

The OT was a literary context within which the disciples constructed their understanding of the *Paraklētos* as the Holy Spirit. They did not have any of the NT writings available. Neither did they live in the early Christian community—it was still to be formed. They had to rely only on their previous sources of knowledge of the Holy Spirit. In the OT, God's *ruach* functions towards the people of God. *Ruach* also has a central role in creating life (cf. Gen 1). Yet, the phrase "Holy Spirit" occurs only twice in the OT, namely, in Psalm 51:11 and Isaiah 63:10. David prays in Psalm 51 that God would not take away his Holy Spirit from him after he had sinned. This request is argued to mean either one of the following two things. David may have prayed that God's presence would not be lifted from his life as it has happened in the case of King Saul. Or, David may have prayed that he could keep his life. If God's *ruach* is taken away, he would simply die.[38] In both cases, the consequences would have been severe. In other words, the Holy Spirit's presence was necessary for David to function as God's representative, as a king, for the nation. In Isaiah 63:10, we find a similar situation. Here people caused God's Holy Spirit to grieve, with the result that God turned away from them. The least we can say based on these two examples is that the disciples (and the readers) might have understood that the Holy Spirit as the *Paraklētos* is necessary for them to keep on living and performing deeds of Jesus in this world (cf. John 14:12).

The Fourth Evangelist repeatedly brings together the *Paraklētos* with the phrase "the Spirit of truth." Connecting these terms speaks about his intention to emphasize this identification of the *Paraklētos*. The question is, however, how the Spirit of truth should be understood. In Johannine scholarship, there are two views on how *to pneuma tēs alētheias* should be understood, namely, as the Spirit of Truth (capital T) or as the Spirit of truth (lower case t). Godet holds that "truth" refers to the fact that the Spirit communicates the truth. In other words, the Spirit is neither the truth nor possesses the truth. "The teaching of the Spirit . . . causes the divine truth to enter into the soul; it gives to it a full reality within us by making us have experience of it; it alone makes the

---

38. See Levison, *Filled with the Spirit*, 26–33.

world a truth for us."³⁹ This takes "truth" as descriptive of what the Spirit does. Yet, the phrase is also understood as a name; thus, the Spirit of Truth. The evangelist is clearly making this point: The *Paraklētos* is the one who communicates the truth. And if so, it implies that other agents who might claim to bring the truth of God to the post-resurrection world are not God's agents for truth.

The references to the Spirit of truth might be deliberate not only to define the *Paraklētos* but also the Spirit. Other NT authors do not use this phrase. It is found in the Dead Sea Scrolls and the Testament of the Twelve Patriarchs.⁴⁰ In the Dead Sea Scrolls the phrase is applied in the context of absolute dualism that relates more closely to the Persian concept of opposing spirits rather than the OT *ruach* of God having power over all other spirits. Here the evangelist might have a corrective purpose in mind to show that the Spirit of truth is something else than what the Qumran community holds. At least, the evangelist points out that this Spirit that is known also as the *Paraklētos* stands for the truth. The Spirit of truth is God's agent who accurately presents God and his message (cf. John 16:14–15). Breck points out that "Throughout the Old Testament truth signifies, among other things, moral knowledge which is acquired by hearing the Word of God uttered by the Spirit through the mouth of the prophet. The Spirit may be described as a 'Spirit of Truth' insofar as it proclaims the true Word of the Lord."⁴¹

The Twelve Patriarchs (T. Jud.) depicts the Spirit of truth as an independent angelic figure having a prophetic function.⁴² The Fourth Evangelist does not share this understanding of the Spirit as he emphasizes that the *Paraklētos* as the Spirit of truth is not independent, but dependent on the one who sends him (cf. John 15:26; 16:7, 14–15). As we have seen a few times already, it is the Fourth Evangelist's style to pick up terminology known to his readers (i.e., *logos* and *paraklētos*), but he did not choose to use it in the previously known sense. Instead, he re-defines them, making them work for his rhetorical purposes.

The final reference to the *Paraklētos* in 16:7 stands on its own. In other words, it is connected neither to Jesus nor the Spirit. By now, the

---

39. Godet, *Commentary on the Gospel of John*, 2:279.
40. Forestell, "Jesus and the Paraclete," 176.
41. Breck, *The Spirit of Truth*, 141.
42. Tuppurainen, "The Role(s) of the Spirit-Paraclete," 137.

reader has adequate knowledge about whom the author is speaking when he refers to the *Paraklētos*.

The *Paraklētos* is referred to thrice by a personal pronoun (John 14:26; 16:8, 13). The personal pronoun is the third-person singular masculine "he" (*ekeinos*). Sometimes the Greek grammar and syntax in these verses are misunderstood. For example, although NASB renders Greek correctly in 16:13a, "But when He [*ekeinos*], the Spirit of truth, comes, He will guide you into all the truth," readers easily take masculine personal pronoun "he" (*ekeinos*) to refer to neuter "the Spirit of truth." This reading is then used for an argument that the Fourth Evangelist, breaking the rules of Greek grammar, uses the masculine pronoun for neuter "Spirit" to indicate that the Spirit is not mere a thing (it), power, or force, but a person (he). More careful reading, however, shows that personal pronoun "he" refers not to the neuter Spirit, but the masculine *Paraklētos*.[43] Thus, the personal masculine pronoun "he" in 16:13a refers to masculine *Paraklētos*, who is mentioned back in 16:7 and who is also referred in v. 8 with the personal masculine pronoun *ekeinos*. We find the same situation in John 14:26, where the personal pronoun *ekeinos* refers to the *Paraklētos* rather than the Spirit. It reads, "But the . . . [*Paraklētos*], the Spirit of truth, whom the Father will send in my name, He [*ekeinos*] will teach you . . ." This is not to say that the Holy Spirit (or the Spirit of truth) is merely an impersonal (it), force or power. One cannot, however, build an argument of personification of the Spirit based on the gender of the word that is used to describe the Spirit. The neuter "Spirit" does not mean that the Holy Spirit is mere "it." Grammatical gender does not mean that feminine and masculine nouns always refer to feminine or masculine persons and that neuter words would refer to impersonal things.[44] It is still worth noticing that the FG's use of the masculine noun for the Spirit, however, is unique in the NT.

The Fourth Evangelist lists various tasks the *Paraklētos* will perform. His deeds assist readers in understanding who the *Paraklētos* is. The explicit statements regarding his functions range from reminding about Jesus's teachings to disclosing the future, and from his permanent staying with the disciples to his witnessing and convincing/exposing activity to the world. These various kinds of works propose that the *Paraklētos* does not have limited functionality, as if he would do only partially the work

---

43. See Wallace, *Greek Grammar Beyond the Basics*, 331–32.
44. Mounce, *Basics of Biblical Greek*, 24.

of the Spirit. Instead, he is assigned to the tasks that belong to the total range of the Spirit's works.

## The Role of the Paraklētos

The *Paraklētos*'s role, like Jesus's role, fits the first-century Mediterranean brokerage model and Jewish *shaliach* model as a "broker." There are many features in that model (see above), but here especially the following two need to be kept in mind. First, the broker's unique role was to stand between the patron and client as the gateway. Secondly, the broker was sent in the name of the patron. The FG's Jesus explicitly presents himself as the Father's broker who is a gateway for people to the Father's presence (cf. John 14:1-6). Jesus, as the broker, speaks the Father's words and performs the Father's deeds. Examples of that are numerous in the FG, as we have already noticed (see above). For instance, at the end of his public ministry Jesus (once again) proclaims whose ministry he has been doing, "For I did not speak on My own initiative, but the Father Himself who sent Me has given Me a commandment *as to* what to say and what to speak" (John 12:49).

Also, the *Paraklētos* was about to be sent as the agent for Jesus's clients, the disciples (14:26; 15:26). In OT times, God had sent many agents like Moses, Joshua, Samuel, Amos, and Jeremiah. Thus, the concept of a God-sent-agent who brings forth things from God was well known not only to the Fourth Evangelist but also to all who were aware of the Hebrew Scriptures. The *Paraklētos* shares some of the same characteristics of the broker; he is sent by the Patron (Father/Jesus) to his clients (disciples) to accomplish the Patron's work.[45] Jesus explains in his Farewell Discourse how the *Paraklētos* will function as a broker between Jesus and his people. He will (1) stay with them (14:16; 16:7); (2) teach and remind them about Jesus's teachings (14:26; 16:13); (3) testify (15:26); and (4) expose/convict[46] the world concerning sin, righteousness, and judgment (16:8). The *Paraklētos*'s role is to be *the* gateway between the Patron and his clients.

---

45. For a detailed study on Spirit-*Parakletos* as a broker see Brown, *Spirit in the Writings of John*.

46. John 16:8-11 has been impasse for interpreters. One of the difficulties in that passage is how the verb *elegxō* and its object *kosmos* should be understood. See Carson, "The Function of the Paraclete," 547-66; Bennema, *The Power of Saving Wisdom*, 234-42; Tuppurainen, "The Whole World or Not Quite," 165-84.

All *Paraklētos* passages in the FG are found in Jesus's Farewell Discourse. The Farewell Speech is its own genre (text-type) that has specific characteristics including but not limited to the following: (1) the speaker is the one who is going to die soon; (2) the speaker gives an overview of the past and predicts what is going to happen after his departure; (3) there is some kind of encouragement given to those who are left behind including some exhortations; and finally, (4) the speech usually ends up with a prayer and blessing.[47]

Jesus's speech in John 13:33—17:26 includes all these elements of the farewell-speech genre. Jesus announces his going back to the Father, which does not mean that he is going to be deceased, but that he is going to the Father via death and resurrection. His disciples did not understand this at the time of Jesus's announcement about his departure. Jesus reveals how things are going to be after his departure. The disciples are going to have a difficult time in the world (cf. John 15:18—16:4a), but Jesus has overcome the world and gives the disciples his peace (John 14:27; 16:33). Jesus also encourages his disciples in a variety of ways, especially by promising the *Paraklētos* (John 14:16–18).

Jesus's promise of the *Paraklētos*'s coming encourages the disciples. It persuades the disciples to understand Jesus's departure as a benefit rather than a disaster (cf. John 16:6–7). The verb "be profitable" (Gk. *sympherein*) that is used in here (16:7) is found in only two other places in the FG (11:50; 18:14), always concerning Jesus's death and its profitability for others.[48] The *Paraklētos*'s presence in them will be such a great benefit that Jesus's physical presence, which would have meant the absence of his death and resurrection, would not have matched what is about to come. But because the disciples were soon going to see Jesus arrested, judged, and executed, the promises of the *Paraklētos* were needed to bring hope for them. How much of that was realized by the disciples at that time, however, remains questionable.

The role of the *Paraklētos* is mainly related to the future, the time of Jesus's physical absence. The disciples and all the future followers of Jesus benefit from his presence.[49] There are a variety of roles that the *Paraklētos* has when he comes. Some of these roles can readily be noticed by looking at explicit statements of what the *Paraklētos* does:

---

47. For a more detailed explanation, see Brown, *The Gospel According to John*, 1:597–601.

48. Cf. Berg, "Pneumatology," 197 n10.

49. Cf. Burge, *The Anointed Community*, 33–35.

## The Spirit as Paraklētos

he teaches, witnesses to Jesus, exposes truth, reveals the future, and discloses Jesus's words.

It is often missed that the significant role of the Spirit-*Paraklētos* is not, however, found in his "doings" that are explicitly listed in the Farewell Discourse or the role which is driven from the semantics of the word "*paraklētos*." His most significant role, we argue, is found by looking at the entire picture that Jesus paints in his Farewell Discourse. Jesus's going back to the Father by means of the death of the cross could have easily caused the group of disciples to dissolve. The current leader, Jesus, was about to depart. Moreover, Judas Iscariot had already left the group, giving a negative model for the group to deal with. There was, therefore, the danger that the rest of the disciples would scatter under the pressure of the Jews (cf. John 20:19) and would never form the post-resurrection community of believers. Therefore, the role of the *Paraklētos* is to be a new leader of the group of disciples. His presence ensured that the loyal disciples, including the future disciples, would not dissolve. On the contrary, the *Parakelētos* enables them to stay as a believing community and to not only preserve the boundary between them and the world but also to function soteriologically in the world.

Another point of importance is that Jesus's Farewell Discourse (thus his *Paraklētos* sayings) is addressed to his eleven loyal disciples.[50] When Judas Iscariot had departed, Jesus turned to his remaining disciples, saying, "Children," and so began his speech (13:33). Judas's departure likely gives Jesus the desired opportunity to present his farewell address as it contains material (teaching and promises), which would not have been fitting to Judas Iscariot as a traitor. Jesus's teaching, like the promises of the Spirit-*Paraklētos*, was only for his followers. Jesus's address to his loyal disciples, together with the content of his final prayer (John 17), which includes a prayer for his current and future disciples, indicates that the *Paraklētos* is for the entire body of believers.[51] Thus, the role of the Spirit-*Paraklētos* is not limited to eleven faithful disciples but is extended to all faithful disciples. To compare this to that of Jesus's coming, we note that Jesus's coming was not limited either by the historical context of his coming as he came for to take away the sin of the world (John 1:29; cf. John 20:19–23).

---

50. For more information of the socio-cultural concept of "loyalty," see Malina and Rohrbaugh, *Social-Science Commentary*, 228.

51. Cf. Kim, "The Paraclete," 255–70.

The *Paraklētos* will come when Jesus goes. He is, therefore, in some sense, Jesus's successor. Yet, the pneumatic community of believers, after Jesus's glorification and Spirit-*Paraklētos*'s coming, is *the* successor of the earthly Jesus (cf. John 20:19–23). The disciples will function as brokers between the sender (Jesus) and the client (the world) in the presence of the Spirit. The disciples, as such Spirit-people, have authority received from the glorified Jesus, their Patron.[52] Therefore, the *Paraklētos*'s presence also gives a new identity to the community of believers and its individual members. They are the channels through whom God communicates to the rest of the world. As the disciples go about as Jesus's brokers, the *Paraklētos* will teach, guide, reveal the things to come, and remind the disciples.

The *Paraklētos*'s coming also functions as an attestation that Jesus has gone back to the Father. If Jesus's work of the cross had not been satisfactorily completed and thus Jesus had not gone back to the Father, then the *Paraklētos* would not have come. By his coming, the disciples were sure that Jesus had indeed gone back to the Father, and now they had access to him through the permanent presence of the *Paraklētos* (cf. John 14:16–17; 16:14–15).

Although the roles of the *Paraklētos* are mainly related to Jesus's disciples, his role also extends to include the entire world. Jesus mentions in 16:8 that the *Paraklētos* "will convict the world concerning sin and righteousness and judgement." In John 16:8–11, the *Paraklētos* is found in the forensic context. Yet, the more detailed examination of his role in this passage shows that it is not mainly judicial but rather soteriological.[53] The *Paraklētos*'s role is towards all humankind to make it recognize and know sin, righteousness, and judgment. All these elements are necessary so that one may realize his/her need to repent and receive the grace that is found in Christ Jesus glorified.

We started asking questions such as: why did the Fourth Evangelist[54] choose the word *paraklētos*? And: why did he not only use "the Holy

---

52. Note that the brokerage model is only a backdrop that helps readers of the FG to grasp the roles of the sent ones such as Jesus, the *Paraklētos*, and the disciples (church). Therefore, we recognize several patron-broker-client chains in the FG such as the Father-the Son-the world; Jesus/Father-the *Paraklētos*-the disciples; and Jesus-the disciples-the world.

53. Bennema, *The Power of Saving Wisdom*, 234–42.

54. It is possible that the Fourth Evangelist received this word from Jesus (or Jesus tradition). Yet, the question still remains: "Why did the tradition of Jesus or Jesus himself use this term instead of the other?"

Spirit" terminology? To answer the latter question, it must have been the Fourth Evangelist's deliberate choice to employ various terms for the Spirit and not to use much "Holy Spirit" terminology.[55] To answer the former question comprehensively is equally difficult.[56] Yet, this study has shown that the evangelist strategically choose the term *paraklētos* for the Spirit, which is fitting for the Farewell Discourse and its forensic context. The disciples are informed that their leader is going to depart from them. Therefore, the word *paraklētos* is suitable as it conveys the idea of "coming alongside." Also, the forensic context supports the Fourth Evangelist's choice of this word. It was used in extra-Johannine literature in the forensic settings as well, although not necessarily in the meaning of a legal advocate. The Fourth Evangelist uses the *Paraklētos* in such a way that goes, however, beyond these previous connotations of the word.

Although the evangelist re-defines *paraklētos* as the Holy Spirit/Spirit of Truth, his role is related to connotations of previous (extrabiblical) usages of that word. In other words, the Fourth Evangelist uses the term's background for his purposes but does not limit himself by its previous meaning. The main point is that, in the *Paraklētos*, the disciples have a permanent presence of the Son and the Father (cf. John 14:18; 16:14–15). He remains in and with disciples offering help, assistance, divine presence, and access to the glorified Jesus and the Father (cf. brokerage model). All this leads us to identify the *Paraklētos* as a new leader of the believing community of disciples who gives them a new identity as the people of God.

## Concluding Remarks

The *Paraklētos* is a unique term for the Spirit, exclusively and distinctively used by the Fourth Evangelist. The evangelist has chosen the word *paraklētos* not just for aesthetic but rather rhetorical purposes. Using this term in the Farewell Discourse and forensic contexts, the author demonstrates his skills to use a term that was applied previously to someone who also had a role in the forensic context. The Fourth Evangelist, however, used it in a much "wider" sense. The *Paraklētos*, as the Holy Spirit

---

55. "Holy Spirit" phrase is used only thrice in the FG (1:33 and 20:22 without articles, and 14:26 with two articles). The word "Spirit" alone as the reference to God's Spirit is employed more often (see 1:32, 33; 3:5, 6, 8, 34; 6:63; 7:39).

56. Köstenberger, *A Theology of John*, 396.

(of truth), has the identity and role beyond previous connotations of the word *paraklētos*. The *Paraklētos*'s central role is to be the leader-broker to the community of the loyal disciples. The disciples continued to have Jesus's presence, even after his return to the Father, through the *Paraklētos*. His presence gives the disciples a new identity which differentiates them from the rest of the world. Yet, the role of the *Paraklētos* is not a mere boundary keeper between the disciples and the world. He also has a soteriological goal enabling the disciples to penetrate into the unbelieving world and make new disciples.

We have also seen that the *Paraklētos* is related to Jesus and his identity. What is said about Jesus applies to the *Paraklētos* as well. When Jesus said that he would send another *Paraklētos*, he compares himself with the coming Spirit, implicitly referring to his identity. The *Paraklētos* is the broker, sent from the Father, who works in the name of the sender. The Johannine community was a Christocentric pneumatic community of believers.[57]

## Suggestions for Further Reading

Bennema, Cornelis. *The Power of Saving Wisdom: An Investigation of Spirit and Wisdom in Relation to the Soteriology of the Fourth Gospel*. WUNT 148. Tübingen: Mohr Siebeck, 2002. Pp. 213–48.

Brown, Tricia Gates. *Spirit in the Writings of John: Johannine Pneumatology in Social-scientific Perspective*. JSNTSup. London: T&T Clark International, 2003.

Burge, Gary M. *The Anointed Community: The Holy Spirit in the Johannine Tradition*. Grand Rapids: Eerdmans, 1987. Pp. 1–45; 137–43; 203–4.

---

57. Cf. Burge, *The Anointed Community*, 45.

PART TWO

# Issues in the Fourth Gospel

CHAPTER 8

# Authorship, Place and Date of Writing, and Audience

THE AUTHORSHIP QUESTIONS, PLACE and date of writing, and intended audience are connected. Nevertheless, in order to provide a more accessible presentation and reading, these issues are discussed separately. This discussion, however, is not easy. Margaret Davies says, "[W]e do not know with certainty when, where and by whom the Fourth Gospel was written. No reliable external information exists, and the Gospel itself does not tell us."[1] For this reason, in this chapter, we work cautiously with theories and suggested conclusions.

We may categorize the suggestions for the author, date, and place of composition as follows. The first suggestion is that the FG was written before the destruction of the Jerusalem Temple in 70 CE in Palestine by the first-generation Jesus's disciple. The second suggestion is that it was written after the Jerusalem Temple's destruction by the first-generation disciple/believer (or community) outside of Palestine. The third proposed theory is that the FG was written much later during the first half of the second century outside of Palestine. In this case, the author must be a second-generation believer or a believing community. The chart below presents these theories:

---

1. Davies, *Rhetoric and Reference*, 68.

| | | | |
|---|---|---|---|
| **Date of Writing** | First Century before 70 | First Century after 70 | Second Century |
| **Place of Writing** | Jewish Palestine | Outside of Palestine | Outside of Palestine |
| **Author** | Jesus's disciple | Jesus's disciple and/or his community | Second generation believer or believing community |

Table 8.1

Table 8.1 is obviously a simplification of the matter. Nevertheless, it presents the major components of this debate that are the focus of this chapter.

## The Author

A quick overview of scholarly literature reveals that the question of authorship of the FG is far from a settled matter. Scholarly suggestions regarding the authorship remain hypothetical at best.[2] The traditional view of the apostle John's authorship, including Westcott's well-known argument for his authorship (see below), was challenged in the nineteenth century as a result of historical skepticism. The most common rival theories for authorship include: John the Elder, a disciple of the apostle John, the Beloved Disciple (whoever that individual or community might be), or unknown Johannine community leader(s).[3]

Nevertheless, not only the identity of the "author" but also the question of possible redactors or editors who were involved in the production of the FG are challenges when we discuss this topic. Oscar Cullmann's questions, which reflect a historical-critical approach to Johannine studies, substantiate this aspect of the dilemma.

> Of which author are we speaking? Of the author of the original Gospel? Of the final redactor? Of intermediary redactors? Of the author of a particularly important source? Of a man revered in the Johannine circle who could have been regarded by tradition as

---

2. Cf. Culpepper, *John, the Son of Zebedee*.
3. Harris, *John*, 3–4.

the author of the Gospel, because his testimony stood behind the real author, although he himself had not composed the Gospel?[4]

Due to the uncertainty, it has become common practice to refer to Gospel of John as "the Fourth Gospel." The FG is a neutral name without any claims of its authorship, but at the same time, a deviation of the early superscription "Gospel According to John" (Gr. *euangelion kata iōannēn*).[5] The authorship question is not as difficult with the Synoptic Gospels as it is with the FG. Scholars usually refer to them by the traditionally accepted name of their authors, that is, Gospel of Matthew, Mark, and Luke, although on a scholarly level their authorship has sometimes also been brought into question.[6]

Below we will discuss the authorship by studying the internal textual hints and then outlining the external evidence for the authorship. Finally, some contemporary suggestions for the theories of the authorship of John are summarized. The conclusion of this study is left to the end of the chapter after we have also considered the date and place of writing as well as the question of the intended readership.

## Internal Textual Evidence for the Authorship

Lack of internal testimony of the authorship is not the problem of the FG alone. Other New Testament writings share the same problem. A part of the reason for the anonymity of the Gospels is that "ancient Jews had not developed a concept of authorship as ownership."[7] Authorial ownership is a more Greek than Jewish idea. The lack of internal evidence does not suggest that the FG is pseudepigraphy, which was a typical and acceptable literary practice at the time.[8] The FG does not fulfil the characteristics of pseudepigraphic writing. It does not claim to be authored by someone who is a well-known person.[9] The lack of the text's self-identification of the author leads us first to examine internal evidence for the qualifications of its author and, thereafter, to consider his identity.

---

4. Cullmann, *The Johannine Circle*, 64.
5. McHugh, *John 1-4*, 1-3.
6. Cf. Michaels, *John*, xv.
7. Casey, *Is John's Gospel True?*, 140.
8. Pseudepigraphic means that the literary work was falsely named as authored by a known person.
9. Cf. Keener, *Gospel of John*, 1:89.

*Author's Qualifications*

The text suggests that the author was an eyewitness to the events he records. If so, the author had to be a first-generation believer who wrote before the turn of the century. A few "we" passages and "he" passages speak for the eyewitness authorship. "We" passages are found in John 1:14–16; 3:10–13; 21:24 (cf. 1 John 1:1–5; 4:11–16; 3 John 9–12). We start off by making a few observations regarding the very last "we" passage (21:24). It can function as internal or external evidence for the eyewitness testimony (see below chapter 14). Here is the syntactical outline of that verse:

> This is the disciple
> > *the one who is testifying* about these things
> > and
> > *the one who wrote* these things,
> and
> we know
> > that his witness is true.[10]

Several observations should be made. First, the two phrases in italics are active participles (the former present; the latter aorist) in Greek, and therefore, they read most naturally as parallel subject participles. Hence, the disciple is the one who is witnessing and who also wrote. An alternative interpretation is that the person in question is testifying of these things and is the one who caused others to write these things down. Even though the latter reading is possible grammatically, it would require one to move from subject participle (the one who testifies) to causative participle (cause to write), which is doubtful and not a natural way to read these active participles in this context. This reading seems to be influenced by the view that this statement is a later addition.

Secondly, the disciple in question is the Beloved Disciple (cf. John 21:20–23), but it is not clear who "we" are? First-person plural pronouns and verbs can be used the following three ways in ancient Greek:[11]

1. The first-person plural can be used to indicate that an author is with his/her readers forming one group. In other words, the author is saying, "I and you."

---

10. The translation is mine. I have kept the word order the same as in Greek UBS[4] Greek text. The bold italics are there just to draw attention to the points I am commenting on below.

11. Bauckham, *Jesus and the Eyewitnesses*, 371–72.

2. "We" can be used to indicate a difference between an author's group and his/her reader's group. In other words, an author's group distinguishes itself from others.

3. The first person plural, "we" was used in ancient Greek to replace the first person singular "I." This practice is meant to give "added force to the self-reference" and is called "a plural of majesty or a plural of authority."[12]

Bauckham convincingly argues that, in all these cases, Johannine usage of "we" indicates the "authoritative testimony."[13] He says that the author "uses the first person plural ('we know') because this is Johannine idiom when solemnly claiming the authority of testimony . . . [H]e uses the first person singular ('I suppose') [John 21:25] as the natural way to address his readers when it is no longer a matter of solemn testimony."[14] Yet, it needs to be noticed that in 1:16 "we" does not have the same meaning as in 1:14. In 1:16, "we" refers to all Christians who benefit from grace and truth that are revealed through Christ. Also, in 1:14a, it seems that "we" is the authoritative testimony of the author, whereas "among us" in 1:14b refers to humanity in general.[15]

The "he" passage indicates that the author is an eyewitness in 19:35: "And he who has seen has testified, and his testimony is true; and he knows that he is telling the truth, so that you also may believe." This statement functions the same way as John 21:14. Bauckham notes that "[t]he emphatic 'he' (*ekeinos*) . . . functions to provide 'augmented empowerment' for the testimonial claim, just as the first person plural does in 21:24."[16] By these emphatic eyewitness testimonies, the author, however, is not only presenting arguments about his status but the status of the story. This account is trustworthy.

Other qualities of the author include knowledge of Jewish customs, history, and Palestinian geography. There are several passages that indicate that the author knew Jewish life, feasts, and many rituals related to those feasts, as well as their religious beliefs. Many of these are discussed in more detail in Chapter 2, so they are not repeated here. Regarding

12. Bauckham, *Jesus and the Eyewitnesses*, 372.
13. Bauckham, *Jesus and the Eyewitnesses*, 370.
14. Bauckham, *Jesus and the Eyewitnesses*, 380. See also Jackson, "Ancient Self-Referential Conventions," 8.
15. Bauckham, *Jesus and the Eyewitnesses*, 381.
16. Bauckham, *Jesus and the Eyewitnesses*, 380.

Jewish history, detailed information about the erection of the Second Temple is presented (2:20), the dichotomy between Jews and Samaritans is explicitly pointed out (4:9), and information about high priest hierarchy is given (11:49; 18:13). The evidence of the author's knowledge of Palestinian geography is explicit. There are many locations mentioned by name, and their description is accurate, for example, the Sheep Gate/Bethesda (5:1–2); Gabbatha (19:13); the Pool of Siloam (9:7); and the book of Kidron (18:1). These qualifications point towards the conclusion, that the author was indeed an eyewitness, who was one of Jesus's contemporaries from the region in which Jesus ministered.

## Author's Identity

Although the text does not name the author, the Gospel gives the authorship to the Beloved Disciple. In John 13:23–26, the Beloved Disciple is present at the Last Supper; in 19:25–27, he is at Jesus's cross; in 20:1–10, he visits the empty tomb of Jesus; in 21:1–14, he is at the sea of Galilee and meets with the resurrected Jesus; and in 21:20, the Beloved Disciple is with Jesus and Peter. Later in 21:24, the Beloved Disciple is referred as the one who testified and wrote these things down.

The problem is to know who that Beloved Disciple was. It is challenging, if not impossible based on the internal evidence, to decide to whom the title goes. Our purpose here is not to engage in that debate. Instead, we only introduce the most convincing arguments of various views for the identity of the Beloved Disciple.

Several individuals have been suggested as the "Beloved Disciple": Lazarus, the apostle John, Thomas, John Mark, Matthias, and the apostle Paul. Internal evidence for Lazarus's authorship is based on John 11, where Lazarus is referred to as "he whom You [Jesus] love" (John 11:3). The strength of this theory is that this passage explicitly connects Lazarus with Jesus as beloved. It is also suggested that Lazarus might fit better at the scene in John 18:15–16 when a disciple and Peter enter the high priest's house. Lazarus, who was from Bethany, might have had access to the high priest's house more readily than Galilean disciples.[17] He might have also been with Jesus's disciples at the last supper as the Fourth Evangelist frames the group saying, "His own" rather than "His disciples" (John

---

17. Keener, *The Gospel of John*, 1:86.

13:1). Besides, it is not difficult to imagine how much Lazarus would have loved his master, especially after experiencing Jesus's resurrecting power.

The other option, namely, that the apostle John is the Beloved Disciple seems to have some internal textual support, but not without some challenges. The text does not identify him as the apostle John, but it seems to suggest it. If we give any weight to the facts that (1) every other member of the inner circle of disciples is mentioned by name in the Gospel except John, and (2) that ancient writers had a tendency to keep their identity secret, as well as the possibility that (3) the author does not want to draw any attention to himself as a person, it is not impossible to argue that the apostle John is the Beloved Disciple.

It is also possible, yet not agreed by all scholars, that the unnamed disciple is the same as the Beloved Disciple. The unnamed disciple is mentioned in John 1:35-40; 18:15-16; 20:3-4; and 21:21. The argument that the unnamed disciple is the Beloved Disciple is based on the observation that the unnamed disciple is sometimes mentioned in the same literary context where the Beloved Disciple is mentioned, perhaps hinting at the identity of the unnamed disciple.[18]

The FG indicates that the author was an eyewitness to the events that he recorded, and therefore, he must have been close to Jesus, perhaps one of his disciples (John 13:23). Also, it is pointed out that Jesus's giving of his mother to the Beloved Disciple's care works as an internal evidence to identify him as the apostle John, as some have argued that Mary was John's aunt.[19] We also note, although only tentatively, that since John the Baptist is mentioned by the name several times, the apostle John might have deliberately kept himself anonymous so as not to create any confusion. These readings of internal evidence argue for the Beloved Disciple's identity as the apostle John, the author.

A disciple of Jesus, Thomas, who is often and perhaps unfairly referred to as "doubter," also fits the description of Beloved Disciple. Keener notes that "the best specific candidate besides John son of Zebedee would be Thomas."[20] Thomas is a devoted disciple who was ready to die with Jesus, his master, and also encourages other disciples to do the same (John 11:16). Although a little bit later, on the day of Jesus's resurrection, Thomas doubts the other disciples' testimony about the resurrected

---

18. See John 20:2-3; 21:20-24.
19. See further Culpepper, *John, the Son of Zebedee*, 74.
20. Keener, *The Gospel of John*, 1:86.

Jesus. His fearless choice not to join with them behind the locked doors demonstrates his devoutness to Jesus. As earlier (cf. John 11:16), also in this occasion, Thomas demonstrates that he is not afraid to face possible martyrdom in the hands of the Jews. He is ready to die as his master had died. This reading of Thomas suggests as close a relationship with Jesus as the Beloved Disciple enjoyed. Also, the Beloved Disciple's identity as Thomas might be made by connecting Jesus's "wounds" with the Beloved Disciple in 19:34–35 and with Thomas in 20:25.

John Mark was not one of the twelve disciples. In the Gospel of Mark 14:51–52, he followed Jesus after he was arrested. He was present but fled naked from the garden. The FG does not mention him. The supporting internal evidence is that he was from Jerusalem. Therefore, he knew Judea and Jerusalem well, the places where the majority of the events took place. He might have had the best chance to have access to the high priest's house that night, especially if he was a cousin of Barnabas, who was a Levite. Also, Mark seems to have had contact with Peter (Acts 12:12; 1 Pet 5:13) as the Beloved Disciple had in the FG.[21] It is also argued that the last supper might have taken place in his mother's house, and therefore, John Mark had a place of honor next to Jesus at the supper.[22]

The view that John the Elder was the author is quite strong in early Christian tradition.[23] Primarily Papias's and Eusebius's comments are used as an argument for this view. Nevertheless, there is very little internal evidence in the FG or other Johannine writings which would argue one way or another about his identity as the Beloved Disciple. The second and third epistles of John give authorship to John the Elder, but whether that is the same person or a different person from the Fourth Evangelist and the Beloved Disciple continues to be an unsettled matter. Bauckham says, "It seems plausible that John the Elder was so called not primarily in order to distinguish him from other Johns . . . , but because of his longevity."[24] This observation may be used to argue that John the Elder was the same as the apostle John. Nevertheless, this cannot be proved beyond doubt.

---

21. Cf. Brown, *The Gospel According to John*, 1:xcv–xcvi.
22. Culpepper, *John, the Son of Zebedee*, 77–79.
23. Cf. Keener, *The Gospel of John*, 1:95–98.
24. Bauckham, *Jesus and the Eyewitnesses*, 422.

Matthias is the apostle who was chosen to replace Judas Iscariot (Acts 1:15–26). Biblical evidence for his identity as the Beloved Disciple rests on the testimony of Acts. He was an individual who was an eyewitness to the significant events from Jesus's baptism until his resurrection. It is also argued that the Beloved Disciple has symbolic significance. Accordingly, Judas Iscariot symbolizes Judaism whereas Matthias symbolizes the church.[25]

Many modern studies of the internal evidence conclude that we can only be certain that we are uncertain who wrote the FG. Alan Culpepper puts it this way: the search for the author "illustrates the fact that *something* could be said in favor of the identification of almost any New Testament character as the Beloved Disciple. In all cases, the evidence is neither conclusive nor persuasive."[26]

## External Testimony about the Authorship

Before giving a few of the most critical external pieces of evidence for the authorship, we point out a few general observations. First, in antiquity, eyewitness stories were preferred in historical and biographical writings. Eyewitnesses were needed if one wished to produce an authoritative account of the past.[27] Secondly, the early external writings, like the earliest apostolic fathers, could have mentioned the apostle John as the author of this Gospel, but they fail to do so. Martin Hengel argues that for *Ignatius of Antioch* (c. 110 CE), the FG's "author was not yet an apostolic authority."[28] It is further reasoned that perhaps Gnostic groups came to use the FG, and therefore references to it might have been avoided. Alternatively, it is also argued that the nature of Ignatius's writing was exhortative in nature, and therefore he drew from Paul and Jesus's ethical teaching rather than the more Christological text of the FG.[29] Gnostic reasons might have also caused Polycarp to remain silent about the FG in his writings. Still, the fact that Polycarp was a disciple of the apostle John has caused scholars to question Polycarp's silence. Thirdly, during the second half of the second century, the church fathers readily attributed the FG to the apostle John.

25. Culpepper, *John, the Son of Zebedee*, 79.
26. Culpepper, *John, the Son of Zebedee*, 79.
27. Keener, *Christobiography*, 402.
28. Hengel, *The Johannine Question*, 14.
29. Cf. Blomberg, *The Historical Reliability of John's Gospel*, 23.

Finally, it is not until the fourth century CE that some ambiguity appears.[30] Nevertheless, it is also necessary to keep in mind that the FG was given the title *euangelion kata iōannēn* (the Gospel According to John) as early as the second or early third century as witnessed by the papyruses P[66] and P[75].[31] Traditionally, John (perhaps the apostle) is attached to the authorship/authority of this account due to his eyewitness testimony.[32]

Several external statements attribute the authorship to the apostle John. The most important comes from Irenaeus (130–202 CE) who describes the composition of each Gospel account around 180 CE. Irenaeus says, "Afterwards, John, the disciple of our Lord, who also had leaned upon his breast, did himself publish a Gospel during his residence at Ephesus in Asia."[33] This statement reveals the name John and defines which John is in question, namely, Jesus's disciple.[34] It is reasoned that Irenaeus received this information from Polycarp (d. 156 CE), who was most likely the apostle John's partner in ministry towards the end of the first century.[35] Polycarp (69–155 CE) himself, however, does not make specific comments on apostle John in relation to the FG, as mentioned above.[36]

The Muratorian Canon, the list of authoritative books by the late second century, written in Latin and contemporaneous with Irenaeus, suggests that John is the author or at least the key figure under whose name this Gospel account was written. It reads the following:

> The fourth book of the Gospel is that of John, one of the disciples. In response to the exhortation of his fellow disciples and bishops he said: "Fast ye with me for three days, and then let us tell each other whatever shall be revealed to each one." The same night it was revealed to Andrew, who was one of the apostles that it was John who should relate in his own name what they collectively remembered. And so to the faith of believers there is no discord, even though different selections are given from the facts in the individual books of the Gospels, because in all of them, under the one guiding Spirit, all the things relative to his

---

30. Blomberg, *The Historical Reliability of John's Gospel*, 25.
31. McHugh, *John 1–4*, 1.
32. Cf. Keener, *Christobiography*, 402–3.
33. *Adv. Haer.* 3.1.1.
34. See Anderson, *The Riddles of the Fourth Gospel*, 153–55.
35. A new argument for Papias's knowledge of the FG is presented by O'Connell, "A Note on Papias's Knowledge," 793–94.
36. Hengel, *The Johannine Question*, 15.

nativity, passion, resurrection, conversation with his disciples, and his twofold advent, the first in his humiliation rising from contempt, which took place and the second in the glory of royal power, which is yet to come, have been declared. What marvel is it then if John adduces so consistently in his epistles these several things, saying in person: "what we have seen with our eyes, and heard with our ears, and our hands have handled, those things we have written." For thus he professes to be not only an eye-witness but also a hearer and narrator of all the wonderful things of the Lord, in their order.[37]

Apostolic father, *Papias of Hierapolis* (c. 70–163 CE), differentiates John the apostle (a son of Zebedee, one of the twelve) from John the Elder. Martin Hengel notes that John the Elder "was also a disciple of the Lord, but is separated from the first group of seven disciples and is not mentioned in the synoptic lists of disciples."[38] Papias wrote, according to Eusebius, somewhere between 125–35 CE. "And if anyone chanced to come who had actually been a follower of the elders, I would enquire as to the discourses of the elders, what Andrew or what Peter said, or what Philip, or what Thomas or James, or what John or Matthew or any other of the Lord's disciples; and the things which Aristion and John the elder, the disciples of the Lord, say."[39]

However, it is questionable whether there were two Johns, the apostle and the Elder. Although the tradition of two Johns was alive by the time of Eusebius, "the reliability of Eusebius's interpretation of Papias, a source nearly two centuries before him, is open to question."[40]

Also, Tertullian (c. 155–240 CE) ascribes the FG to the apostle John in his *Against Marcion IV*. The list of external pieces of evidence goes further, including names like Clement of Alexandria (late second century) and Origen (the first half of the third century).

So, the apostle John's authorship was not doubted before the fourth century. Eusebius of Caesarea (c. 260–339 CE) was a Christian scholar who was interested in Christian canon. He refers to "John" in his *Ecclesiastical History*, but in such a way that may confuse the identity of John between the son of Zebedee (an apostle) and John the Elder. Prior to

---

37. Quoted from Hendriksen, *The Gospel According to John*, 1:23.
38. Hengel, *The Johannine Question*, 17.
39. Quoted from Carson, *The Gospel According to John*, 69.
40. Keener, *The Gospel of John*, 1:96.

Eusebius's writings, there was unity among the church that the author of this Gospel was the apostle John.

At this point, we may summarize that, whereas the earliest external evidence is silent about the FG and its author, the second century church fathers hold that John the apostle is the author. Later on, in the church father tradition, interpretation of earlier tradition led to the emergence of other views. Eusebius introduced the notion, perhaps erroneously, of two Johns, holding that John the Elder was the author. There is no church father tradition that would testify for any other individual to be the author of the FG. Also, second or early third-century papyruses $P^{66}$ and $P^{75}$ contain the superscription *Euangelion kata Iōannēn*. Although the title does not include the definition of which John is in view, it is assumed that this John is the one whom "everybody knows." Thus, the well-fitting suggestion for his identity is the apostle John, even though we cannot be sure about that. The Beloved Disciple was not an option to be included in the inscription for the early copies.

## Contemporary Scholarly Suggestions for the Authorship: An Outline

This section is needed because our presentation of internal and external pieces of evidence for the authorship of the FG is limited and cannot give the full picture of the depth and difficulty of the authorship question. The following outline of modern scholarly suggestions is meant to assist students of the FG to delve deeper into the dilemma. The Johannine scholars chosen to be part of our outline are well known, and their works are helpful for all students of this Gospel.

The Johannine scholarship's suggestions for the authorship of the FG can be categorized many ways. We have chosen to divide it into two groups to keep the matter as simple as possible. These two groups are (1) scholars who argue for a single author who wrote the Gospel, and (2) scholars, who argue for a group or several people being responsible for its composition. The second view often includes the idea of development.

## Single Author

In his *The Johannine Question*, Martin Hengel asks which John is the author of the FG.[41] He argues that its authorship is closely related to the Elder who was a teacher of "a school" and who also wrote all three epistles attributed to John. This John is not the same as the apostle John. In addition to this conclusion, Hengel believes that the Gospel developed over a long period of time "in parallel to the development of the teaching of the school."[42]

C. H. Dodd, Rudolf Schnackenburg, D. A. Carson, and Richard Bauckham argue that an individual, not a community, is behind the text. However, they do not agree on how much of the individual author's work is independent from the contribution of other individuals or editorial bodies. Dodd thinks that the writer was a "powerful and independent mind."[43] He calls him the "Fourth Evangelist" without saying who that individual might have been.[44] Schnackenburg is more cautious, saying that the author was probably a spokesman and theologian who had first-hand access to the Johannine tradition. However, he was not the apostle John, the son of Zebedee. For him, the Gospel's apostolicity is a much more important matter than the name of the person who wrote the account.[45] Carson claims that the individual behind the text is the evangelist John, the apostle, the son of Zebedee, who had churches around him which played some kind of a part of the composition of the Gospel.[46] Despite naming the author so specifically, Carson claims that his view of the authorship makes very little difference in the interpretation of the Gospel of John.

Richard Bauckham argues that the Beloved Disciple is the author, but that he was not one of the twelve disciples. He thinks that it makes much more sense if he was "a disciple resident in Jerusalem, who hosted Jesus and his disciples for the Last Supper and took the mother of Jesus in his Jerusalem home (19:27)."[47] The value of the fact that the author was outside of the twelve, Bauckham argues, is that then we indeed

---

41. Hengel, *The Johannine Question*, 7.
42. Hengel, *The Johannine Question*, 102.
43. Dodd, *The Interpretation of the Fourth Gospel*, 6.
44. See also Dodd, *Historical Tradition in the Fourth Gospel*, 10–14.
45. Schnackenburg, *The Gospel According to St. John*, 1:102.
46. Carson, *The Gospel According to John*, 75.
47. Bauckham, *The Testimony of the Beloved Disciple*, 15.

have the voice and witness to Jesus outside of the immediate circle of Jesus's disciples.[48]

George R. Beasley-Murray thinks that the apostle John can be the author if the external evidence we have on hand is correct. External testimony, however, cannot prove that this John was the apostle John or the same John who wrote the Apocalypse. The Beloved Disciple, Beasley-Murray argues, is a historical figure. However, he is not the author or an eyewitness; he is someone who belongs to the Johannine church but is not well known outside of it. Thus, the author could not be one of the twelve disciples. He concludes that the Gospel was derived from a Johannine school whose master interpreter is the author who is not known but is referred to as Beloved Disciple.[49]

Craig S. Keener and Craig L. Blomberg emphasize the question of historical reliability of the FG's account while discussing its author and draw much from Westcott's century-old arguments.[50] Keener hesitates to give a concrete "written in the stone" answer but favors the view that the author is John the son of Zebedee. He notices that internal and external evidence best supports that conclusion, but John "undoubtedly used a scribe or scribes, probably members of his own circle of disciples, who may have exercised some liberty."[51] Despite this possible liberty and some editing, Keener, as well as Blomberg, thinks that we can make a strong case for Johannine authorship and thus also for the historical reliability of Jesus's story.

## Several Composers and Stages

Rudolf Bultmann maintains that the "author" of the FG is an unknown individual who created the figure of the Beloved Disciple. The only thing we know about him, Bultmann argues, is that he was not an eyewitness. He further argues that Beloved Disciple, not the same as the unnamed disciple,[52] is a literary figure who represents an ideal disciple and only

---

48. Bauckham, *The Testimony of the Beloved Disciple*, 16.

49. Beasley-Murray, *John*, lxvi–lxxiii.

50. Blomberg, *The Historical Reliability of John's Gospel*, 22–41. Keener, *The Gospel of John*, 1:81–139.

51. Keener, *The Gospel of John*, 1:115.

52. Bultmann, *The Gospel of John*, 483.

later, by the ecclesial redactor, is personified as the author in chapter 21.[53] Also, Bultmann believes that, for the community which edited the Gospel, the Beloved Disciple was an authoritative figure who was placed side by side with Peter. The ecclesiastical redactor's theological and ideological agendas become the focus in the historical-critical study of the authorship. An example of the redactor's theological agenda, so it is argued, was to insert the community's orthodox view of the sacraments in the text. Warren Carter summarizes Bultmann's view as follows.

> The earlier version of the gospel, according to Bultmann, emphasized faith and obedience and had misgivings about baptism and the Eucharist. It recognized that Jesus was baptized (3:22) but omitted the institution of the Last Supper . . . the ecclesiastical redactor sought to overcome this reluctance by giving greater prominence to the sacraments and integrating them into the gospel.[54]

As far as the source theory goes, Bultmann argues that the redactor has used two main sources: (1) sign source (stories), and (2) saying source. The sign source springs from oral Jesus tradition whereas the saying source is developed from a Gnostic saying source.[55] This author/source theory argues the FG's independency from the Synoptic tradition.

In his *The Johannine Circle*, Oscar Cullmann argues that the FG was developed over a period having various stages of composition. According to Cullmann, the Johannine circle grew up from heterodox marginal Judaism, which later had a close relation to the John the Baptist movement. Cullmann summarizes, "We thus arrive at the following line, moving back in time: Johannine community—special Hellenist group in the early community in Jerusalem—Johannine circle of disciples—disciples of the Baptist—heterodox marginal Judaism."[56]

Marie-Émile Boismard has developed a four-stage development of the FG. The first draft was written soon after Jesus, around 50 CE, including the narrative covering John the Baptist to Jesus's resurrection. Another writer, probably John the Elder, picked up the work and wrote his first edition of the Gospel as well as the Johannine epistles around 60 CE. This version shows some opposition to the Jews as the

---

53. Bultmann, *The Gospel of John*, 11, 483–84.
54. Carter, *John*, 156–57.
55. Thatcher, "Introduction," 4.
56. Cullmann, *The Johannine Circle*, 87.

circumstances of the community changed. There is also the second edition by the same editor around 90 CE. This time the order of the gospel narrative was changed to much what we know today. This time the language also changed from Aramaic to Greek. The final edition of the FG includes the third redactor, an unknown individual from Ephesus, who was a part of the "Johannine school."[57]

Raymond E. Brown serves as an example of a scholar who has altered his own view. He once held the view that the apostle John was the author but later argued that the FG is the production of editorial bodies, not an individual mind. He has formed a hypothetical five-stage theory of composition, albeit proposing a key individual who greatly influenced the composition of the text (see below). That individual must have been a Palestinian Jew, a disciple of John the Baptist called the Beloved Disciple, and the hero of the community.[58]

## Westcott's Proposal

Before we leave this section, it is worthwhile to outline B. F. Westcott's theory of authorship, to which Johannine scholars often refer when tackling with authorship question. His conclusion is still common and stands as a possible solution for the dilemma. It is favored by several scholars such as F. F. Bruce, D. A. Carson, Leon Morris, Craig Keener, and Craig Blomberg, although in a more recent nuanced way. Westcott's argument employs the method of limitation by narrowing down the possible options for authorship and finally arriving at the conclusion that the author is John the son of Zebedee, the apostle and a Palestinian Jew. Here it is presented in point format:[59]

- *The author of the Fourth Gospel was a Jew*: "The whole narrative shews that the author was a Jew. He is familiar with Jewish opinions and customs, his composition is impressed with Jewish characteristics, he is penetrated with the spirit of the Jewish dispensation. His special knowledge, his literary style, his religious faith, all point to the same conclusion."[60]

---

57. Brown, *The Community of the Beloved Disciple*, 178–79.
58. Brown, *The Community of the Beloved Disciple*, 31.
59. Westcott, *The Gospel According to St. John*, v–xxv.
60. Westcott, *The Gospel According to St. John*, v–iv.

- *The author of the Fourth Gospel was a Jew of Palestine:* "It is inconceivable that a Gentile, living at a distance from the scene of religious and political controversy which he paints, could have realised, as the Evangelist had done, with vivid and unerring accuracy the relations of parties and interests which ceased to exist after the fall of Jerusalem; that he could have marked distinctly the part which the hierarchical class—the unnamed Sadducees—took in the crisis of the Passion; that he could have caught the real points at issue between true and false Judaism, which in their first from had passed away when the Christian society was firmly established: that he could have portrayed the growth and conflict of opinion as to the national hopes of the Messiah side by side with the progress of the Lord's ministry."[61]

- *The author of the Fourth Gospel was an eye-witness of what he describes:* "His narrative is marked by minute details of persons, and time, and number, and place and manner, which cannot but have come from a direct experience. And to these must be added various notes of fact, so to speak, which seem to have no special significance where they stand, though they become intelligible when referred to the impression originally made upon the memory of the Evangelist."[62]

- *The author of the Fourth Gospel was an Apostle:* "A further examination of the narrative shews that the eye-witness was also an apostle. This follows almost necessarily from the character of the scenes which he describes, evidently as has been shewn from his own knowledge, the call of the first disciples (i. 19–34), the journey through Samaria (iv.), the feeding of the five thousand (vi.), the successive visits to Jerusalem (vii. ix. xi.), the Passion, the appearances after Resurrection. But the fact is further indicated by the intimate acquaintance which he exhibits with the feelings of 'the disciples.'"[63]

- *The author of the Fourth Gospel was the Apostle John:* "If the writer of the fourth Gospel was an apostle, does the narrative indicate any special apostle as the writer? In the Epilogue (xxi. 24) the authorship of the book is assigned . . . to the disciple whom Jesus loved . . . This

---

61. Westcott, *The Gospel According to St. John*, x–xi.
62. Westcott, *The Gospel According to St. John*, xviii.
63. Westcott, *The Gospel According to St. John*, xx.

disciple appears under the same title twice in the narrative of the Passion xiii. 23, xix. 26), as well as twice after wards (xxi. 7, 20), and once in connexion with St Peter under a title closely resembling it . . . He is known to the high-priest (xviii. 15), and stands in very close relationship with St Peter (xiii. 24, xx. 2, xxi. 7; comp. xviii. 15; Acts iii)."[64]

## Summary on Contemporary Theories

The overview of contemporary theories about the FG's authorship demonstrates that it is far from a settled matter. The recent scholarship has suggested various possibilities for the author but has not been able to come up with convincing arguments. However, the new theories have cast doubt on the once accepted view that the Beloved Disciple, identified as the apostle John and the son of Zebedee, is the author. At the same time, it is noticeable that the Beloved Disciple, whomever that person might have been, is understood to be related one way or another to the composition of the account. There are still convincing conservative voices that suggest that the apostle John, son of Zebedee, is the author of the FG. However, some others theorize that he is an authority or idealized disciple behind the text, or that he was the primary source for the text even though his penning/dictate may have gone through some scribal/community's editing or process of redaction.

We have not engaged counterarguments for any of the outlined arguments or theories. Further study is left for readers. The list of suggested further reading includes works that bring different views into this discussion. We can promise a wild ride for those who would engage with this question on a deeper level.

## Date and Place of the Writings

There are three distinctive views for the date of the FG. First, Leon Morris, together with A. T. Olmstead, W. F. Albright, V. Burch, and C. C. Tarelli, hold that the FG was written before the Jerusalem Temple was destroyed. Morris concludes, "[T]here is nothing that demands a date later than AD

---

64. Westcott, *The Gospel According to St. John*, xx–xxi.

70."⁶⁵ This view is supported, for example, by the view that the "atmosphere" in the FG is very Palestinian, including a primitive portrayal of Jesus with titles like Rabbi/teacher. Perhaps, the most robust support for an early date is that the Gospel does not mention the destruction of the temple but tells the Gospel story as if the temple was still standing.

Secondly, a once popular view states that the FG was written during the first half of the second century CE or even later. Scholars who hold this view include O. Holtzmann, T. Keim, E. Schwartz, and F. C. Baur. The late date theory is supported by observation that the FG is not mentioned in the earliest Christian writings and may also lack early recognition. Also, it is argued that Johannine theology, especially its Christology, is advanced in comparison to other NT writings, that it had to go through a longer period of development.

Finally, the most common view, which also enjoys the church tradition's support, is that the FG was composed towards the end of the first century.⁶⁶ It is not an insignificant piece of support that the earliest manuscript of the NT, $P^{52}$—which contains a small portion of the FG (18:31–34, 37–38)—is dated c. 100–125 CE, or perhaps even earlier during the time of Trajan 98–117.⁶⁷ The date of $P^{52}$ suggests that it was copied soon after the original Gospel was written. Hence, the discovery of $P^{52}$ argues against a late date of composition.

Internal supports for this theory include the suggestion that the FG fits well post-temple era (contra Morris). Destruction of the Jerusalem Temple is hinted in chapter 2 where Jesus is the new temple and way to the Father who wants people who worship him "in spirit and truth" (John 4:23). Jews still feeling the trauma of the temple⁶⁸ destruction and not having a unifying center among themselves are now offered unifying

---

65. Morris, *Studies in the Gospel of John*, 291.

66. Eusebius, *Ecclesiastical History* III, xxiii, 1, 6; V, viii, 4: xxiv, 4; Clement of Alexandria, *Who Is the Rich Man That Shall Be Saved?* XLII, ii. Also, Origen and Tertullian held the late first-century date.

67. See Comfort, *Early Manuscripts & Modern Translations*, 55–56. The $P^{52}$'s early date is challenged, however. The new suggestion is 25–50 years later, that is, 150–75 CE. Nevertheless, it is a very early papyrus. See Culpepper, *John, the Son of Zebedee*, 108. Other significant early papyrus include $P^{22}$, $P^{75}$, $P^{66}$, and $P^{90}$. Papyrus Egerton 2 is also significant. Blomberg says that it "is a composite fragmentary narrative of stories about Jesus that quotes or alludes to several passages from John and the Synoptics and probably dates to the mid-second century." Blomberg, *The Historical Reliability of John's Gospel*, 42.

68. Motyer, *Your Father the Devil?*, 77–79.

unity that is possible among disciples of Jesus. The unity, which the disciples have, demonstrates the fact that Jesus came from the Father (cf. John 17:20–21). Also, after the destruction of the Jerusalem Temple, various Jewish sub-groups disappeared, which seems to be reflected in the FG. Jesus's opponents are mainly called *Ioudaioi* (Jews or Judeans), rather than categorizing them in Jewish sects like in the Synoptic Gospels.[69] Scholars who cautiously prefer the late first-century date include Raymond E. Brown, Craig S. Keener, Jey J. Kanagaraj, Craig L. Blomberg, D. A. Carson, and Edward W. Klink III to mention but only a few.

As for a place of writing, it is not a surprise that several theories are offered. They include Palestine, Transjordan, Alexandria in Egypt, Antioch in Syria, and Asia Minor/Ephesus. We comment briefly on each of these suggestions.

Palestine is suggested by the scholars who prefer a very early date of composition or who theorize that there have been many versions of the FG, the first one(s) being completed closer in time and space to the events and to the first Christian community. The support for the Palestinian origin is based on the author's eyewitness role, the Qumran community's proximity, and Semitic and Aramaic aspects of the language in the FG.

Transjordan theory also requires an early date of composition. The argument here is that since the FG has a polemic tone towards John the Baptist and his disciples, its location fits the area where John the Baptist mainly resided and where his followers were present. This view has not received much scholarly support.

Alexandria in Egypt is offered to be a place of composition as well. This view is based on the finding of a very early NT manuscript $P^{52}$ discovered in Egypt in 1920 (published in 1934). Besides, the FG is sometimes linked to the allegorical method of interpretation that was characteristic in Alexandria and was adopted by early Christian interpreters Clement and Origen. We also find early Gnosticism in Egypt. Therefore, if the FG is viewed to resonate with Gnostic ideas (or counter ideas), this observation can support the Alexandrian hypothesis.

Antioch in Syria is a common suggestion for the place of the composition. These scholars hold that *Odes of Solomon*, classified as the OT pseudepigrapha by Craig Evans, from the late first or early second century, serves as an argument for this theory. In the most recent research, the *Odes of Solomon* has shown pieces of evidence to be early Christian

---

69. The FG does not record the narratives where, for example, Herodians and Sadducees are mentioned.

## Authorship, Place and Date of Writing, and Audience 149

writing. Evans notes, "Dualism, the hypostatic and mediatorial role of the Word, and the concept of salvation are similar to the ideas in the Fourth Gospel."[70] Other arguments include the observation that the early church father Ignatius, the bishop of Antioch, shares some similarities of language with that of the FG.[71] Peter, who receives a somewhat unique treatment in the FG, was highly respected in Antioch. Also, the first orthodox commentary on the FG was written in Antioch by Theophilus.[72]

Ephesus in Asia Minor as the place of writings is supported by many early external testimonies. Those pieces of evidence include Eusebius *Hist. Eccl.* 3.39.3.; Irenaeus *Adv. Haer.* 2.22.5; 3.1.1–2;[73] Montanists; and Clement of Alexandria and his *Who is the Rich Man That Shall Be Saved?* XLII. Also, if we can argue that the same person pens the book of Revelation, then there is a clear Asia Minor connection that supports this view. Montanists, who were an influence not far from Ephesus in Phrygia, made use of the FG. Acts 19:1–7 testifies that in that area, there was also a John the Baptist "sect." The FG includes John the Baptist in his narrative in a way that can be understood as "corrective." In other words, the FG presents a portrait of him which keeps him as God's servant who even gave up his disciples so that they could become Jesus's disciples (John 1:35–37). If this reconstruction is correct, it supports the Ephesus hypothesis. The majority of the Johannine scholars hold this view as there is no more robust evidence available for any other theories for the place of composition.

## Audience

Who were the intended readers? It is necessary to make a distinction between the first possible readers and the intended readership. The author of the FG must have had a specific readership in mind to whom he wrote the Gospel account. Literary works are always written a particular readership in mind. However, the text might be read by someone who is not among the author's intended readers. In the case of the FG, the first readers were most likely included in the group of the evangelist's intended

70. Evans, *Ancient Texts*, 60.
71. Morris, *The Gospel According to John*, 54.
72. Morris, *The Gospel According to John*, 54–55.
73. *Adv. Haer.* 3.1.1 reads, "Afterwards, John, the disciple of the Lord, who also had learned upon His breast, did himself publish a Gospel during his residence at Ephesus in Asia."

readership, but later readership naturally incorporated a broader readership than the author considered. It is doubtful that the evangelist had in mind, for example, readership beyond his generation. This fact, however, does not exclude the FG's meaningfulness for other readers, including modern readers. However, modern readers are in a better position to understand the FG if they have a rough idea of the audience to whom it was first written.

The question of the intended readership is another issue in the Johannine scholarship that has generated many studies with various conclusions. The views of the intended readership have changed throughout history. To simplify our outline, we ask only two questions: First, was the FG written with Jews or Gentiles in mind? Secondly, was it written for unbelievers or believers? In other words, was it written to evangelize or to encourage?

## The Gospel for Gentiles or Jews?

It was once firmly believed that the Fourth Evangelist wrote a Hellenistic Gospel. Therefore, it was believed that the primary readership was Gentiles. The view that the FG is Hellenistic is supported by the Prologue's usage of the concepts and terms that are linked to the Hellenistic world. For example, the term *logos* and its involvement in the universe was read as an indication of Hellenism. Also, the FG's above-below, spirit-flesh, eternal-natural, and other binary pairs point towards Platonic philosophy of forms. Brown notes, "These contrasts may be compared to a popular form of Platonism where there is a real world invisible and eternal, contrasted with the world of appearances here below."[74] Some NT scholars have also found similarities between the FG and *Corpus Hermetica*, writings produced in Egypt during the second and third century CE.

The FG, as the writing for Gentiles, is also argued on account of anti-Jewish language and Jesus-superior-to-Moses motif. One can ask the question: How can the author, most likely a Jew himself, tell a Jewish Messiah story and address Jews so harshly? Also, one may build an argument that the evangelist elevates Jesus over Moses with one purpose in mind, namely, to demonstrate that those old Jewish ways are invalid.

The theories that John wrote to Gentiles who were familiar with Hellenistic categories were brought into question when the Dead Sea

---

74. Brown, *The Gospel According to St. John*, 1:lvii.

Scrolls at Qumran were discovered in 1947. The focus changed from Hellenistic to Jewish categories. The same textual evidence used to argue for the Gentile audience was now used to argue for the Jewish audience.

The distinction between Gentile and Jews, however, is not so sharp. We have to bear in mind that the FG was published in the world where the Hellenistic influence was evident. Brown notes, "In raising the question of Greek influence on John, we must make an important distinction. There was a strong Hellenistic element already present in the Judaism of NT times, both in Palestine and Alexandria. Therefore, if John was dependent on contemporary Judaism, there was inevitably a Hellenistic influence on Johannine thought."[75] This fact was evident even in the Qumran community, which identified itself as an eschatological and orthodox Jewish sect. Thus, Hellenistic tones in the FG do not provide evidence to call it a Hellenistic Gospel written exclusively for a Gentile audience.

In Part One, we have shown various ways that the FG contains a tsunami of Jewish elements, and that those elements were employed for rhetorical purposes to persuade the readership to believe that Messiah is found in Jesus. Due to the nature of these arguments, they point towards the Jewishness of the FG and, therefore, also support the view that the evangelist had in mind a Jewish audience.

The *Torah* also relates to our question of the intended readers.[76] The keyword of Judaism was *the Torah*. The Septuagint systematically translated it as *nomos*. The Fourth Evangelist uses *nomos* the way the Septuagint uses it. "[I]t never strays away from the Jewish into the Greek field of meaning."[77] This is evidence that the evangelist was embedded in Judaism and did not break away from its fundamental concept. Nevertheless, not only the way the evangelist uses *nomos*, but also his presentation of Jesus's actions and words concerning Jewish understanding of *nomos* and its explanations in the Talmud supports the conclusion that Judaism is the backdrop against what the FG can be understood the best. Also, the evangelist's usage of *Logos* brings the Torah and Jesus onto the same page. The *Torah* was life and light for Jews as the *Logos* is the life and light. The *Torah* is called the son of God, as the *Logos* is.[78] The *Torah*

---

75. Brown, *The Gospel According to St. John*, 1:lvi.
76. Dodd, *The Interpretation of the Fourth Gospel*, 74–96.
77. Dodd, *The Interpretation of the Fourth Gospel*, 76.
78. Dodd, *The Interpretation of the Fourth Gospel*, 86.

makes men sons of God, so does the *Logos* make men sons of God. For these reasons, it is difficult to think that the evangelist would have had only or mainly a Gentile audience in mind while writing.[79] We do not exclude Gentile readers among the first readers (or hearers) who were, we assume, a part of the Johannine community. As far as Jewish audience is concerned, we still have the second question to be answered: was the intended Jewish audience within the Johannine church (believers) or outside of it (unbelievers)?

## Gospel for Believers or Unbelievers?

We start by quoting Paul Anderson, "John's statement of purpose in 20:31 ('these things are written that you might *believe*') is the clearest explicit statement of literary intentionality anywhere in the Bible, but what does 'believing' really mean? While the end result is clear, that believers have life in Jesus' name, controversy has revolved around what is meant by the verb *believe*."[80]

There is the textual variant regarding the verb "believe" in John 20:31 and 19:35. Some mss read *pisteuēte*, which is present active subjunctive that would translate into English, "you may continue to believe." The active subjunctive reading suggests that the author is encouraging believers to keep already established faith. In this case, the purpose is pastoral encouragement, directed to members of the believing community. The variant reading, *pisteusēte*, which is aorist active subjunctive, would translate into English, "you may believe." The aorist active reading would suggest that the author had an evangelistic aim in mind hoping that those who were not a part of the believing community would become its members. UBS[5] Greek New Testament gives both readings in the text. The following is what Bruce M. Metzger, on behalf of the editorial committee of that text says.

> Both [*pisteuēte*] and [*pisteusēte*] have notable early support. The aorist tense, strictly interpreted, suggests that the Fourth Gospel was addressed to non-Christians so that they might come

---

79. It is interesting that already before the DSS were discovered in 1947, which turned scholars' eyes back to the FG's Jewishness, "In 1924 Israel Abrahams, a rabbinics scholar at Cambridge and an orthodox Jew, addressed stunning news to the university's theological society: 'To us Jews, the Fourth Gospel is the most Jewish of the four!'" Burge, *Interpreting the Gospel of John*, 20.

80. Anderson, *The Riddles of the Fourth Gospel*, 29.

to believe that Jesus is the Messiah; the present tense suggests that the writer aimed to strengthen the faith of those who already believe ("that you may continue to believe"). In view of the difficulty of choosing between the readings by assessing the supposed purpose of the evangelist (assuming that he used the tenses of the subjective strictly), the Committee considered it preferable to represent both readings by enclosing [sigma, i.e., *pisteu[s]ēte*] with square brackets.[81]

In his *"Mysticism" in the Gospel of John*, Jey Kanagaraj concludes that neither reading of "believe" in 19:35 and 20:31 carries a major criterion for deciding whether the evangelist's audience was intended to be believers or unbelievers.[82] He notes that the evangelist uses present subjective (*pisteuēte*) in John 6:29 while addressing unbelievers. He also uses aorist subjunctive (*pisteusēte*) in John 6:30 and 11:42 to refer to the unbelieving crowds. Further, present subjunctive (*hina pisteuē*) in John 17:21 refers to the world, but aorist subjunctive (*pisteusēte*) in John 11:40 refers to Martha and in John 9:36 to the healed blind man who has put some trust in Jesus.

For this reason, Kanagaraj convincingly argues that "John's purpose should be understood in the light of the whole Gospel and in its historical context rather than on the basis of one Greek word used at the end."[83] The dilemma still remains since the content of the FG does not give away the intended readership. For this reason, Anderson concludes,

> Might we have two main purposes of the Johannine Gospel instead of only one? Especially if some parts of John were added to an earlier edition (such as 1:1–18, chaps. 6, 15–17, and 21, and 19:34–35, etc.), the purposes of earlier and later editions of John might indeed have been different. The first edition seems to be apologetic—leading people to believe in Jesus as the Jewish Messiah/Christ; the latter material seems to call for solidarity with Jesus and his community in the face of later hardship. So, in response to whether John's rhetorical thrust is apologetic or pastoral, the answer may well be "Yes."[84]

We would offer a slightly different view. We agree with Kanagaraj that the one word at the end of the Gospel account ("believe"), which has

---

81. Metzger, *A Textual Commentary*, 219–20.
82. Kanagaraj, *"Mysticism" in the Gospel of John*, 55.
83. Kanagaraj, *John*, 204.
84. Anderson, *The Riddles of the Fourth Gospel*, 87.

two variant readings supported by early mss, cannot exclusively function as a base to resolve the question of the intended readership. Instead, we must take the entire Gospel into account. We also agree that historical context needs to be considered as well. Regarding the historical context, we understand that the Gospel was not read in the first place in the contexts where the purpose was to evangelize. What would that context have been? The synagogue? Hardly. The synagogue and the church had most likely separated from each other by the time of this Gospel. The evidence to this is often found in the Jewish Synagogue closing prayer's twelfth benediction, "Let the Nazarenes and Minim be destroyed in a moment," and, "let them be blotted out of the book of life and not be inscribed with the righteous."[85] Passages in John 15:18—16:4a suggest a similar conclusion. Neither is it believable that the FG was read in other Gentile or Jewish contexts for unbelievers, like public squares. Paul did not do that either; he did not read the scriptures in public spaces. Nevertheless, he used the scriptures by appropriately quoting or alluding to them from memory. This leads us to suggest that the FG was intended to be read within the Johannine or a larger believing community. In other words, it had a pastoral purpose.[86]

We further suggest that the FG's persuasion is not just to encourage believers to stay in faithful to Christ Jesus, but also to urge the community to evangelize. They were the people of the Spirit to whom resurrected Christ gave the task of being his witness (cf. John 16:7–11; 17:13–21; 20:19–23). Perhaps later, the Gospel text itself became a tool and means to evangelize unbelievers, which also is reflected by early variant readings including the variant reading of "believe" in 19:35 and 20:31. It has to bear in one's mind that theories of first and second editions of the FG (cf. Anderson and others) remain hypothetical and lack the evidence since proto-FG versions are not found. However, we do have evidence that the scribal pen introduced variant readings, which may reflect the FG's shifted or added usage to persuade believers to continue in faith and also call people into the faith. Hence, we think that the intended readership was the believing community, perhaps mainly Jewish or familiarized with Jewish concepts. However, the evangelist's intention was not to help the believing community to keep boundaries closed (i.e., to ensure only doctrinal purity), but instead he wrote this to equip the community to

---

85. See Evans, "Evidence of Conflict."
86. Cf. Thatcher, *Why John Wrote a Gospel*.

penetrate the unbelieving world.[87] The evangelist's concern is the entire world's well-being (cf. John 1:29), which was the reason of the Jesus's coming and glorification.

## Concluding Remarks

At the end of this chapter, we find ourselves back to square one. We have informed ourselves of many hypotheses for authorship, the date and place of writing, and the intended audience. Yet, we cannot conclude with certainty which one of the theories in each category would be the best. We suggest that the still long-standing traditional view that the apostle of John wrote this account and/or was attached to its content as an authoritative individual, and that it was produced (or finished) in Ephesus towards the end of the first century CE.

We have also tackled the question of intended readership. Our view is that it was written for the believing community to preserve the view of Jesus as divine Messiah and, therefore, to encourage believers. However, the perlocutionary act of the FG seems to encourage the community and its members to be witnesses about this Christ in the hostile unbelieving world. This is perhaps the reason why scribes very early in the history of copying the FG introduced variant readings that reflect this usage of the text. This hypothesis calls for further research.

## Suggestions for Further Reading

Bauckham, Richard. *Jesus and the Eyewitnesses Testimony: The Gospel as Eyewitness Testimony*. Grand Rapids: Eerdmans, 2006. Pp. 358–508.

Blomberg, Craig L. *Historical Reliability of John's Gospel: Issues & Commentary*. Downers Grove: InterVarsity, 2001. Pp. 1–44, 61–63.

Culpepper, R. Alan. *John, the Son of Zebedee: The Life of a Legend*. Edinburgh: T&T Clark, 2000.

Keener, Craig S. *The Gospel of John: A Commentary*. Peabody: Hendrickson, 2003, Pp. 1:81–115, 140–49.

---

87. Cf. Witherington, *John's Wisdom*, 11.

CHAPTER 9

# Language, Style and Literary Devices

It is easy to recognize that the Fourth Evangelist's language and style of writing differ from that of the Synoptic Evangelists. There are several suggestions for these differences. First, the Fourth Evangelist wrote in Greek which was not his first language. This can be the case. The problem, however, is that we do not know for certainty who wrote the FG and what was the process of its composition.

Secondly, it is proposed that the entire Gospel (Burney, Torrey), or some pre-texts of it, was written in Aramaic (Black, Boismard) and then translated into Greek. The translated text, therefore, mirrors the FG's Semitism. The same phenomenon is seen in the Greek translation of the Hebrew OT, the Septuagint, used by early Christians.[1] The theory that FG was written in Aramaic, however, has not received much attention. One of the problems is that we do not have Aramaic autograph or manuscripts to support this.

Thirdly, there is a belief that the Fourth Evangelist's different presentation is due to the questions that were asked by the believing community and by community in large. Life situations influence the content, language, and style of writing, but its extent on the FG's presentation is difficult to determine.

Finally, it is argued, especially by those working socio-scientifically, that the Fourth Evangelist's language is so-called anti-language. Anti-language relexicalizes words, meaning that words do not convey necessarily

---

1. Brown, *The Gospel According to John*, 1:cxxix–cxxx.

their obvious everyday meaning but rather the meaning that the antisociety has given to them (e.g., life means "eternal life"). On other occasions, the anti-language may cause overlexicalization (different words are used to refer to the same thing). When the FG uses terms like the Spirit, the Holy Spirit, the Spirit of truth, and the Paraclete for the same thing, that can be called overlexicalization.[2] If the anti-language theory is correct, it may have influenced to its vocabulary that is at the same time limited and "plentiful." Nevertheless, it is difficult to think that all linguistic differences would have been caused by anti-language.

We may not find a satisfying answer to why the FG's language is so unique. We simply do not have enough evidence to form solid conclusions. Even if we had better information about the author, his language skills, and his community, it would not alone provide a satisfactory answer to our question of why the FG has distinctive vocabulary and style. Therefore, in this chapter, we pay historical questions less attention and use the space to study the evangelist's language, style, and literary devices.

## Characteristics of the Fourth Gospel's Vocabulary

The Fourth Evangelist's vocabulary can be characterized as simple, limited, and repetitious. Merrill C. Tenney observes that "Out of seventy-five terms that are used most frequently in John, not more than thirty-five occurs so often that they are important; and the number may be reduced even more if [Greek word] roots rather than words are counted, and if some synonyms are regarded as being exact."[3] This phenomenon cannot be explained only by referring the author's possibly limited Greek language skills. The reason is because some of the repeated terms have profound connotations, and in some cases words are used as pregnant theological words with significant importance (e.g., *Logos* and *Paraklētos*).

Simple, limited, and repetitive language is found throughout the FG. The illustration below of the first five verses of the Prologue demonstrates this. All words that are used more than once are in bold and placed in columns.

---

2. Cf. Malina and Rohrbaugh, *Social-Science Commentary*, 4–9.
3. Tenney, *John*, 303.

| | | | | |
|---|---|---|---|---|
| **In the beginning** | (was) | the **Word**, | was | |
| And | | the **Word** | was | with |
|     God, | | | | |
| And | | the **Word** | was | |
|     God. | | | | |
| He | | | was | |
| **in the beginning** | | | | with |
|     God. | | | | |
| **All things** | | | were | |
|     **made** through | **him**, | | | |
| and without | **him** | | was not | |
| any thing | | | | |
|     **made** that | | | was | |
|     **made**. | | | | |
| In | **him** | | was | life, |
| and the | | | | life |
| | | | was | |
| the | **light** of men. | | | |
| The | **light** shines in | the **darkness**, | | |
| and | | the **darkness** has not overcome it.[4] | | |

Table 9.1

This demonstration would be more precise if we had used Greek text, but above the English (ESV) text articulates the point: the evangelist repetitively uses a limited number of different words. Also, some ideas are repeated.

Verse 1 shares similarities with Hebrew poetry (cf. Psalms) in which rhythm is based on repetition. Here the first line is followed with the second and third lines which develop the idea of the first line.

| | |
|---|---|
| First line: | In the beginning was the Word, and |
| Second line: | the Word was with God, and |
| Third line: | the Word was God. |

---

4. For more detailed presentation of Greek vocabulary in the Prologue, see Hengel, "The Prologue of the Gospel of John," 293–94.

Repetition is also present in v. 3, where the same statement is made twice, first positively and then negatively.

The reason for repetitive language in the Prologue is, at least partially, caused by the Prologue's genre.[5] Nevertheless, that does not explain why the evangelist uses repetitive language elsewhere in his narrative. For example, frequent "amen, amen" formula catches attention. More importantly, key terms are repeated several times for emphasis. In Greek, the NT word "to believe" occurs ninety-eight times; "know/understand" eighty-four times; "to see" sixty-seven times; "to hear" fifty-nine times; "to know" fifty-seven times. Also, keywords like "life" occur thirty-six times; "glory" and "to glorify" forty-two times; "to receive" forty-nine times; "to remain" forty times.[6]

Limited and repetitive language presents readers with a hermeneutical challenge. The evangelist's usage of limited vocabulary inevitably creates a situation where he uses the same words in different senses. Therefore, readers need to look at the historical, literary, and theological context to determine the meanings of words. An example of this is the word "Jews." Greek word *Iuodaioi* (plural) cannot always simply be translated "Jews." This word has different connotations in different contexts (see below). Another example is the word "*logos*." This word reminds us that a word may be used in a pregnant manner, and therefore, its theological meaning and historical richness may not be grasped by a mere casual reading of the text. In short, the vocabulary may be limited and simple, but it does not mean that the text is readily understood.

The Fourth Evangelist's vocabulary is also independent from the Synoptic Gospels. Although all the Gospel's are stories of Jesus, there is limited literary agreement between the Synoptic Gospels and the FG. As pointed out, the verb "believe" (*pisteuō*) is the most common word in the FG occurring ninety-eight times. This word is also used by the Synoptic authors, but much less frequently: in Matthew eleven times, in Mark fifteen times, and in Luke nine times. It is also noticeable that the noun "faith" (*pistis*) occurs in the Synoptic Gospels roughly as often as the verb "believe" but does not occur at all in the FG. Similarly, the verb "see" (*horaō*) is often used in the FG, whereas only a few times in each Synoptic Gospel. The

---

5. It was once a widespread view that it was a later addition to the FG because of its unique style. Its addition to the original text, however, cannot be approved. Cf. Brant, *John*, 23–24.

6. Bennema, *The Power of Saving Wisdom*, 262–63. Bennema notices that all these words are part of the evangelist's soteriological language.

Fourth Evangelist does not use words "prayer" (*proseuchē*) and "to pray" (*proseuchomai*) which are quite common in the Synoptic Gospels.

Nevertheless, it is not only how often the FG or Synoptic Gospels use certain words, but also how those words are used that singles out the FG. For example, not only the fact that the author of the FG uses the word "water" (*hydōr*) much more than the Synoptic authors, but also that he uses it to convey a symbolic meaning. The Synoptic writers use the word only in its ordinary sense.

At this point, a word of caution is due. The difference between the FG and the Synoptic Gospels does not prove (or disprove) the Fourth Evangelist's independency from the Synoptic tradition. However, it demonstrates that the author of the FG leans toward his own (other) traditions outside of the Synoptic Gospels and their sources and that if he knew them, he deliberately wrote his Gospel account differently that is fully integrated to his style of communicating the *bios* of Jesus.[7]

## Characteristics of the Fourth Gospel's Literary Presentation

### Symbolic Language

The Fourth Evangelist's language includes symbolism. The FG's symbolism is related not only to the everyday life of the first century Palestine, but also to the OT, the Jewish world, and some Hellenistic categories.[8] It is necessary to understand that symbolic language does not take away the historicity of the Gospel narrative.[9] Nevertheless, even historical characters and events are used symbolically, beyond their historical value, to bring forth theological-spiritual truths. For example, the six stone pots that Jesus used at the wedding for his first sign may not have been mentioned only as historical fact with regard to their availability. The Fourth Evangelist might have mentioned them because Jesus's use of them signifies that old Jewish ways of purification have come to an end as Messiah has arrived. Messiah Jesus now offers a new and effective way of purification. Also, some scholars (e.g., John Painter and Dorothy A. Lee)

---

7. Carson, *The Gospel According to John*, 51.

8. Cf. Du Rand, "The Gospel According to John," 12–14. See also Koester, *Symbolism in the Fourth Gospel*, 15–24.

9. Koester, *Symbolism in the Fourth Gospel*, 7.

argue that not only images, people, or events, but also entire narratives have "symbolic" significance.[10]

The reader is required to a make connection between a symbolical word (image) and a referent. Craig Koester defines a symbol as, "something that stands for something else," and, "an image, an action, or a person that is understood to have transcendent significance."[11] This can only be recognized when the symbolic language is read in its historical-symbolical context.

One of the challenges for today's readers is that we must determine which images, events, and persons the author uses symbolically and which ones the author uses in a regular (e.g., physical) sense. For example, it would be a mistake to read "water" each time symbolically. The other misreading would be to take "water" to mean physical water without any symbolical significance. Sometimes even the narrative characters misunderstand Jesus's symbolic language. For example, Jesus uses word *anōthen* ("again" and "above") symbolically to describe how one enters the kingdom of God. Nicodemus, not grasping a symbolic meaning of *anōthen* thinks that one has to be born again in the fashion of physical birth.[12]

The words that are often used symbolically include *light, water, bread, darkness,* and *life*. Light is used symbolically in a variety of ways. It refers to Jesus (*Logos*), who is the source of life and the life that can stand before God (e.g., John 1:8–9; 3:20–21). Water (also used in the phrase "living water") is used for Spirit, perhaps emphasizing the cleansing aspect of the Spirit in soteriological contexts (e.g., John 4:10–14). Bread is used by Jesus to refer to himself as life and life nourishment. Without heavenly food, no-one can have spiritual life (e.g., John 6:41). Darkness indicates spiritual darkness, life without God, the life that is associated with Satan (e.g., 3:19; 12:46). Life (sometimes in the phrase "eternal life")

---

10. See Lee, *The Symbolic Narratives*, who argues that the following stories fall into her definition of "Symbolic Narrative": (1) the story of Nicodemus, (2) the Samaritan woman, (3) healing at the pool, (4) feeding the five thousand, (5) healing of the man born blind, and (6) raising of Lazarus.

11. Koester, *Symbolism in the Fourth Gospel*, 4.

12. Nicodemus is an excellent example of how necessary it is for readers to understand the world of the FG narrative. Nicodemus's response to Jesus may not be just a simple misunderstanding even though the face value of the narrative may so suggest. His rejection of Jesus's suggestion of a need to be born again/above is more than misunderstanding here. It is his rhetorical strategy to ignore who Jesus is. See Whitenton, "The Dissembler of John 3," 141–58, esp. 151–53.

is often used in the sense of life with God what carries on beyond the earthly life (e.g., John 5:24).

Sometimes symbolical usage of words (images) are indicated in the text. Jesus's "I AM" sayings are metaphors. When Jesus said, "I am the light of the world," the reader naturally understands the word "light" symbolically. Jesus is the light symbolically and is not replacing the sun. When there is a mismatch between the word and what it describes, then symbolic usage of the word can be expected. On some other occasions, it is more difficult to recognize symbolic language usage, particularly when the word (image) also refers to physical reality. This is the case when the spiritual reality is described by the word "night." Light and darkness are prominent symbolical concepts in the FG. Therefore, one needs to pay close attention to the terms that suggest light-darkness dualism.[13] When the evangelist employs the word "night," a word associated with darkness, the reader should examine if the author wanted to convey also symbolic meaning and not only the time of the day. There are two instances where "night" may carry the idea of spiritual darkness.

(1) Nicodemus came to Jesus by night (John 3:2). Whether or not Nicodemus accepted Jesus as God's Messiah at the end of this conversation, there are a few indicators that argue for the idea that "night" also carries the symbolical meaning of spiritual darkness. Nicodemus's responses to Jesus demonstrate that he is in the "darkness;" he does not have an understanding of what Jesus was talking about, or he deliberately ignores Jesus's self identity claims.[14] Nicodemus also speaks using "we" language, which suggests that he represents others who live in spiritual darkness as well. It is noticeable that Jesus makes a reference to light and darkness at the end of the narrative saying, "men loved the darkness rather than the Light . . . For everyone who does evil hates the Light, and does not come to the Light" (John 3:19–20). Nicodemus and those whom he represents remain in darkness. It is still night for them.

(2) Judas Iscariot left Jesus and the rest of the disciples at night while they were at the last supper (John 13:30). The evangelist, almost in passing, adds "and it was night," which is not be necessary to support the narrative's plot, unless it was designed to carry a symbolical meaning

---

13. Koester, *Symbolism in the Fourth Gospel*, 141.

14. Michael Whitenton has argued that Nicodemus's response to Jesus may not be just a simple misunderstanding even though the face value of the narrative may suggest it. Instead, "misunderstanding" is his rhetorical strategy to ignore who Jesus is. Whitenton, "The Dissembler of John 3," 141–58, 151–53.

of spiritual darkness. Judas had been with the Light (Jesus) but now separates himself from the Light and thus inevitably enters the darkness. Judas's deeds later in the narrative demonstrate this further. These two examples demonstrate that words may carry symbolical meaning which is not readily available for readers.

A word used symbolically does not necessarily always convey the same symbolical meaning. Context is the key to determine the meaning of the words. The word *water* is a good example. In the first chapter, John the Baptist mentioned water concerning his role and task, even though the evangelist omits the narrative of Jesus's baptism event. In the second chapter, Jesus turns water into wine that points towards a new source of purification. Jesus refers to water as an element of birth from above in chapter 3. Jesus promises living water, that is, life in the Spirit, to the Samaritan woman in chapter 4. Water in the pool of Bethesda plays a part of the healing narrative in chapter 5. Jesus walks on water in chapter 6. In chapter 7, Jesus proclaims that "rivers of living water" will flow from one's innermost being if one drinks from him, referring to the Spirit. In each one of these occurrences, readers need to read "water" in its context—not overlooking rhetorical intentions and theological context. We cannot do a comprehensive study on the usage of the word "water" here, but we will do a brief study on it in the discourse between Jesus and Nicodemus (John 3:1–15) to substantiate our point further.

Water is mentioned only once in the entire discourse between Jesus and Nicodemus: "unless one is born of water and the Spirit, he cannot enter into the kingdom of God" (3:5). It seems that "water" is used symbolically, but what it symbolizes is not explicitly stated in the text. Commentators have offered a few suggestions. First, it is suggested that "water" here refers to natural birth. An unborn baby in the mother's womb is surrounded by water, and thus "water" here points out this physiological reality. This reading would mean that one must be born first into this world before he/she can experience spiritual birth through the Spirit. This is hardly a justifiable reading although Jesus goes on to say in v. 6, that "which is born of the flesh is flesh, and that which is born of the Spirit is spirit," and this seems to support this particular interpretation of "water." However, the transition from "water" to "flesh" imagery is not smooth nor is the train of the logic of this reading convincing.

Furthermore, "water" imagery with natural begetting in Jewish literature is rare, whereas "blood" imagery would have been much more suitable.[15]

The second suggestion is that "water" refers symbolically to the Torah (the Scriptures). If "water" equals with the Scriptures, then the meaning is that Nicodemus must apply Scriptures plus accept the Spirit's work to be born from above. To follow this logic, Nicodemus was missing only the Spirit part. This reading is not supported anywhere in the narrative context, however, and therefore does not add value to the conversation.

The third proposal is that "water" refers to baptism. Koester notes that "the Fourth Gospel closely connects baptism and the activity of the Spirit without fully elaborating the relationship."[16] Nicodemus had to know John the Baptist and his water dipping activity, including his message of repentance. He also knew Jewish proselyte baptism that was required when a Gentile converted to Judaism. John the Baptist is also mentioned in the same chapter, strengthening the connection between "water" and baptism. Nevertheless, to think that Jesus elevates John the Baptist's baptism to a prerequisite to entering the kingdom is unthinkable as elsewhere in this Gospel his activity is made subordinate to that of Jesus's activity and role. It has been pointed out, however, that water baptism (whether John the Baptism's, proselyte, or even Christian baptism) is linked to the idea of confession and repentance. So, Jesus might mean that although entering into the kingdom of God is the Spirit's work, there is a part that Nicodemus has to play, namely, he must repent.

Finally, "water" here may refer to the Spirit and especially his purification activity. It is noticeable that Jesus does not repeat the word "water" later when he refers to new birth in the Spirit (cf. John 3:6, 8). This reading emphasizes that Jesus is speaking only about one thing, namely, entering/seeing the kingdom of God that requires one to "be born again/above" by the Spirit. This is fitting to the OT, especially Ezekiel 36:25–27 where water and Spirit of God are mentioned working together to revive the people. In other words, Jesus is using "water" imagery to bring the testimony of the Scriptures about the promises of a new era when the people of God, through the cleansing by the Spirit, enter the eschatological life of the Spirit.[17] Nicodemus surely knew the OT scriptures and could have made this connection as well.

---

15. Keener, *The Gospel of John*, 1:547.

16. Koester, *Symbolism in the Fourth Gospel*, 185.

17. Keener, *The Gospel of John*, 1:550; Köstenberger, *A Theology of John's Gospel and Letters*, 163.

## Dualistic Language

The symbolic language of the FG is also dualistic. Here we see two types of dualism, vertical and horizontal, with vertical dualism being more prevalent. Vertical dualism compares worlds "above" and "below," whereas horizontal dualism contrasts members of these worlds.

Dualism is expressed with various word pairs which project opposites. Paul Anderson lists the following posing word pairs: "light/darkness, life/death, disciples/the world, believe/unbelief, hearing/not hearing, seeing/not seeing, knowing/not knowing, day/night, true/false, right/wrong, saved/lost, Israelites/Jerusalemites, the Judeans (believing)/the Judeans (unbelieving), of divine origin/of creature origin, God or the Father/Satan (or the devil or the evil one of the ruler of this world)."[18] However, vertical dualism in the FG does not place opposing realities on the same level of power. In other words, they are not equal and constant struggle with each other. Things that are from above are superior to things that are from below. Light is more robust than darkness; truth stands forever, whereas falsehood is already condemned; love is from eternal God, whereas hatred is from the devil.[19] This nuance is well presented in chapter 8, where Jesus contrasts the opposing Jews and himself using vertical dualism: "You are from below, I am from above; you are of this world, I am not of this world" (8:23).

Dualistic language in the FG is often compared to the Qumran community's writings and dualistic ideas expressed in them, especially in those writings which express the community's own theology.[20] At the outset, we need to note that even though the Fourth Evangelist and the Qumran community include dualism and share the same dualistic vocabulary (e.g., light/darkness), it may not necessarily mean a direct connection between these two. Richard Bauckham gives several arguments why the FG's light/darkness dualism fits better to the OT and Second Temple Jewish thought than the Qumran's Rule of the Community (1QS) and the War Scroll (1QM, 4QM).[21] First, light and darkness in Qumran texts are attached to terminology like Prince of Lights—Angel of Darkness; the spirit of

---

18. Anderson, *The Riddles of the Fourth Gospel*, 36.

19. Cf. Charlesworth, "A Critical Comparison," 89–96.

20. Charlesworth, "A Critical Comparison," 76; Bauckham, *The Testimony of the Beloved Disciple*, 125.

21. Bauckham, *The Testimony of the Beloved Disciple*, 125–36. The following points are adopted from Bauckham.

truth—the spirit of deceit; the sons of light—the sons of darkness; the paths of light—the paths of darkness. However, "the sons of light" is utilized by the Fourth Evangelist only once concerning light/darkness imagery (John 12:36). This is a noticeable point because other NT writers, namely Luke and Paul, use the same phrase just once. Yet, it is not argued that Luke or Paul "borrow" the phrase from the Qumran community as is the case with the Fourth Evangelist. Secondly, the terminology which the Fourth Evangelist uses concerning light/darkness, like the "true light" and "light of the world," are not found in the Qumran scrolls. Thirdly, the manner in which light/darkness imagery functions in Qumran thought is entirely absent in the FG's presentation. For example, whereas the light and the darkness are two equal spirits for the Qumran community, they do not appear as such in the FG.[22] Fourth, the FG's light that is superior and overtakes the darkness (cf. John 1:5) is a foreign idea for Qumran texts. Finally, the FG brings Christological and soteriological dimensions to "light," whereas light and darkness in Qumran texts are portrayed as cosmic hierarchies of good and evil.[23] These points can be used to argue that Qumran writings were not a direct and perhaps not even an indirect source for the Fourth Evangelist. Instead, OT texts and Second Temple Jewish literature are closer to the FG's light/darkness dualism than the Qumran's writings. Bauckham concludes that "the dominant picture of light and darkness in the Fourth Gospel results from a creative exegetical fusion of Jewish speculation about the primordial light of the first day of creation and messianic interpretation of the prophecies of eschatological light."[24]

## Double Meanings

Perhaps the most puzzling literary features in the FG is that some texts carry possible "double" meaning. Play on words is an everyday phenomenon in our daily communication. It was also a typical rhetorical device in antiquity. What is interesting, though, is that pervasive use of play on words is not found in the NT except in the FG.[25] There are words,

---

22. Charlesworth notes that the Rule (1QS) states that God is the creator of everything, including the "Spirit of Darkness," and therefore, it has never fallen from an original state of purity. See Charlesworth, "A Critical Comparison," 79, 81.

23. Charlesworth, "A Critical Comparison," 83–87.

24. Bauckham, *Testimony of Beloved Disciple*, 134.

25. Hamid-Khani, *Revelation and Concealment of Christ*, 46.

passages, and statements that can be understood in two different ways because their theological or literary context does not strictly limit their meaning to only one possible reading but allow the reader to understand the text in two different ways. Double meanings are sometimes created by specific words that have a range of meanings, and the context wherein they occur supports that not only one, but perhaps two of those meanings can be argued to be present at once. This feature is related to the socio-scientific concept of anti-language, which means that the words are given other meanings, usually meanings that are not their ordinary meanings, by the anti-society.

Double-meaning words cause a hermeneutical challenge for readers. First, the concept of "double meaning" challenges traditional historical-grammatical interpretation which argues that the text can only have one intended meaning. Second, who has the authority to determine which text has double meaning and which text has only one meaning? Therefore, we must exercise much caution in this area.

We can categorize double meanings into the two following groups. First, the words or phrases that have one ordinary meaning but may have a double meaning in their context. Saeed Hamid-Khani calls these "conceptual *amphibologia*."[26] Second are the words or phrases which have double reference. These kinds of words, Hamid-Khani, calls "lexical *amphibologia*."

Conceptual *amphibologia* is created by a word or phrase that has one meaning but is used in the context where it may refer to not one but two things. For example, the phrase "his own" in John 1:11 may refer to Jews or to humanity or both. It is easy to grasp the meaning of the phrase, but when one asks to whom "his own" refers, we begin to see that there is probably a double reference.[27] This is also seen when a word, phrase, or sentence has so-called earthly meaning and spiritual/theological meaning. An example of this is found in the FG's opening statements (John 1:3–4). Following the *Textus Receptus* text and its punctuation, 1:4 reads, "In Him was life, and the life was the light of men." The question here is, what is the "light of men?" Does the author mean "life" generally (i.e., creation), or does he refer to "spiritual/eternal life" (i.e., redemption)? A reader may argue that "life" refers to creation as the previous verse speaks about creation.[28] Nevertheless, another reader may take the following verse (as well

---

26. *Amphibologia* comes from Greek *amphi*, "on both sides," *bolos*, "a throw," and *logos*, "word." Hamid-Khani, *Revelation and Concealment of Christ*, 46 n63.

27. Hamid-Khani, *Revelation and Concealment of Christ*, 52–53.

28. For more detail, see Brown, *The Gospel According to John*, 26.

as overall content of the Gospel) to refer to spiritual reality, arguing that "light of men" refers to redemption rather than physical creation.

Some scholars have found an answer to this dilemma in "double meaning" reading. D. A. Carson comments that "it is quite possible that John, subtle writer that he is, wants his readers to see in the Word both the light of creation and the light of the redemption the Word brings in his incarnation."[29] Similarly, Beasley-Murray argues that "the Logos is Mediator not only in the act of creation, but in its continuance. Hence *zoe* (life) and *phos* (light) include the life and light which come to man in *both* creation *and* new creation."[30] Although this matter is debatable, the Fourth Evangelist might have intended to his readers to grasp the double meaning here which points towards the comprehensive meaning: The *Logos* (eternal and incarnated) is light of man in every sense, physical and spiritual.

The phrase "lifting up." (8:28; 12:32) is also a conceptual *amphibologia*. The Fourth Evangelist uses this phrase to describe Jesus's death on the cross. Such a way of dying was shameful for Jews. Nevertheless, in the FG, Jesus's death on the cross is exaltation and, therefore, in sharp contrast with the socio-cultural concept of shame. Jesus's death was not something that brought shame to Jesus and his patron, but rather honor and glory. In this case, like many other places where a word is used in double meaning, a misunderstanding occurs. The Jews, whom Jesus was addressing in chapters 8 and 12, understood the meaning of "lifting up" inadequately only as a physical act. Its "fuller" meaning as a reference to Jesus's exaltation was dismissed. Jesus exalted his Father, and his Father exalted Jesus when "lifting up" took place.

The third example of double meaning is Jesus's last word *tetelestai* (It is finished) from the cross (John 19:30). The occasion when Jesus said this, just prior to his last breath, can be understood as a statement indicating the end of life. In the Fourth Evangelist's theological agenda, it means Jesus's completion of the task for which he came. Therefore, it does not refer to death, but rather to life that is now available through Jesus's work of the cross.

Double meaning words also create misunderstandings, like when Jesus uses the words "living water" in a sense other than the everyday meaning of running water. Another example of this is found in John chapter 2,

---

29. Carson, *The Gospel According to John*, 120.
30. Beasley-Murray, *John*, 11.

where Jesus refers to temple destruction and re-building. The characters did not understand that Jesus was referring to his body. Their misunderstanding is, however, explained to the readers by the narrator.

The second category of double meanings is lexical *amphibologia*, where a single word has two or more meanings. Hamid-Khani notes that "The amphibological [double meaning] figure encapsulates two dimensions of the same thought in a situation where the author does not wish to force an either/or choice."[31] We give two examples of possible double meaning words. First, the word *anōthen* (John 3:3, 7) that Jesus uses while addressing Nicodemus. This word means "above" as well as "again." Nicodemus took this word in the sense of "again," as it is seen in his response (3:4) to Jesus's initial *anōthen* statement (3:3). However, Jesus did not refer only to a sequential meaning "again." Instead, he also meant "above" in a spiritual sense. Entering God's kingdom required the Spirit's involvement. The birth into God's kingdom is characterized by both of these ideas which *anōthen* conveys, namely, "again" and "above."

The second example is the verb *elegxō* that occurs a few times in the FG (3:20; 8:46; 16:8). It has various lexical meanings and two distinctive nuances, namely, "to expose" and "to convict." It has been a struggle to decide what is meant each time when *elegxō* is used, especially in John 16:8. Is the Paraclete exposing to the world sin, righteousness, and sin, or is he convincing (i.e., judging) the world in these three areas? Alternatively, should one accept the verb's double meaning in this case? It is possible, according to Hamid-Khani, to read *elegxō* without making a choice between these two meanings.[32]

## Misunderstandings

Misunderstandings, a skilled author's literary device, are a common feature in the FG.[33] The FG's narratives where misunderstanding occurs are comparable with the Synoptic Gospel's parables. Yet D. A. Carson warns

---

31. Hamid-Khani, *Revelation and Concealment of Christ*, 47.

32. Hamid-Khani, *Revelation and Concealment of Christ*, 47. See also Bennema, *The Power of Saving Wisdom*, 236–42.

33. For a comprehensive chart of misunderstandings in John, see Carson, "Understanding Misunderstandings," 91.

us that if one treats misunderstandings in the FG as a *mere* literary device of the author, one misunderstands misunderstandings![34]

Characters in the FG often misunderstand Jesus's teaching. Why did the Fourth Evangelist include them, and why did Jesus communicate in such a way? There are two ways to approach these misunderstandings. The first approach is that Jesus intentionally spoke in such a way that his listeners would not understand him and thus would stay outside of his group.[35] In his work on this subject (*Rätsel und Missverständnis*), H. Leroy argues that misunderstandings based on double-meaning words, function as a unique riddle in the middle of dialogues. "Such riddles, he says, use words in two ways, a general meaning for 'outsiders' and a special meaning for 'insiders.'"[36] However, this view is contrary to the evangelist's purpose statement (John 20:30–31) that includes all people (readers), not only the in-group of Johannine circle. Also, it should be noticed that, although the narrative characters sometimes misunderstand Jesus's words, the readers of the FG understand them.

The other way to understand misunderstandings is to take them as a rhetorical device. When misunderstanding occurs, it allows Jesus or the narrator to clarify the point further. Here is an example from John 4:10–14:

| | |
|---|---|
| *Statement:* | "If you knew the gift of God, and who it is who says to you, 'Give me a drink,' you would have asked Him, and He would have given you living water." |
| *Misunderstanding:* | "Sir, You have nothing to draw with and the well is deep; where then do You get that living water?" |
| *Clarification:* | "Everyone who drinks of this water will thirst again; but whoever drinks of the water that I will give him shall never thirst; but the water that I will give him will become in him a well of water springing up to eternal life." |

---

34. Carson, "Understanding Misunderstandings," 59–60.
35. Cf. Neyrey, *The Gospel of John*, 13–14.
36. Carson, "Understanding Misunderstandings," 61.

Clarification does not always mean that the character in the narrative fully grasps what is communicated. In the example above, the Samaritan woman was taken further in the conversation by this clarification, although she did not fully grasp its full meaning. Her better understanding of this takes place later in the narrative. However, her understanding is not explicitly stated. Nevertheless, it is quite clear that Jesus is not speaking about well water vs. running water (e.g., water in the river). Instead, he is using a living water analogy symbolically to convey the spiritual reality.

Also, Carson argues that misunderstandings have a role beyond mere functioning as a literary device. He agrees with C. K. Barrett that "misunderstandings in John are not merely some literary trick by a writer given to [Johannine] irony, 'but represent in miniature the total reaction of Judaism to Christ.'"[37] The evangelist wrote his Gospel with his rhetorical style following historical realities regarding Jews' rejection of Jesus. Thus, misunderstandings, in his narrative mirrors that reality.

Jesus's disciples, on the other hand, although they did not understand everything that Jesus said in the first place, understood the meaning of his teaching (and events) after his resurrection (cf. John 2:22). Therefore, readers of the FG have better access to the understanding of Jesus's sayings and deeds. The Gospel was not written to confuse or keep outsiders ignorant but to persuade and encourage them to believe. In other words, the aim was not to create misunderstanding but understanding. Thus, misunderstandings in the FG as a rhetorical technique can be argued to function in such a way that they help readers to accept and agree with narrative characters who understand and accept Jesus rather than with those who repeatedly misunderstand Jesus and thus disregard him.[38]

## Irony

Irony occurs when a "distinction can be made between the words used and the implication: the words used are on one level, the implication on an ostensibly higher level. In the story the speaker does not realize what he is saying, but the reader of the gospel is challenged to reach the higher level and identify with the implication."[39] The irony is often found in the

---

37. Carson, "Understanding Misunderstandings," 79.
38. Carter, *John*, 116.
39. Du Rand, "The Gospel According to John," 11.

sayings of those who do not trust Jesus and his words. Those characters think that they "know" who Jesus is, but miss the mark. For example, the Jews say, "Is not this Jesus, the son of Joseph, whose father and mother we know? How does He now say 'I have come down out of heaven'?" (John 6:42). The readers know, however, that this statement is false, creating an irony.[40] The same also happens at the grand level in the FG. The Jewish nation was waiting for Messiah to arrive (cf. John 1:19–28), but they missed him and even executed him (cf. John 18–19).

Irony is a powerful rhetorical tool that appeals not only to the readers' intellect but also to their emotions. This is how the Fourth Evangelist uses irony. Readers who notice irony move closer to narrative characters who accept the truth and distance themselves from those who are guilty of irony and therefore miss the mark. This happens because of emotional coldness towards those who miss the true meaning of gospel's revelation. In other words, readers do not want to be identified with those upon whom irony brings ridicule. Carter explains that "irony engages the gospel's readers. It functions positively to delight and secure the audience's insight, emphasizing central aspects of the gospel's worldview and inviting the audience to share this perspective, which is contrary to false understandings of Jesus."[41]

In John 11:47–50, the Jewish elite evaluates the nation's situation after they heard the news about Jesus raising Lazarus from the dead.[42] They imagine what is going to happen if they let Jesus go free. They were afraid that people might turn to Jesus in the hope that he would free the nation from Roman bondage. However, that might backfire on the nation.

Caiaphas, the high priest, sketched the plan to eliminate Jesus for the benefit of the nation (v. 48). He claims that one man (Jesus) needs to be executed for the nation (v. 59). The suggestion is based on an "if not—then" argument: If they do not do anything (1) everyone will believe in Jesus (rather than current Jewish leadership), (2) the Romans will take away the temple rights, and (3) the Romans will take over the nation.

Caiaphas is portrayed as a skilled but cruel political leader who was walking a tight rope between the Romans and the Jews. Jesus's popularity was a threat not only in terms of Judaism and its notions of God

---

40. Cf. Culpepper, "Reading Johannine Irony," 195–99.

41. Carter, *John*, 119. See also p. 120.

42. For an outline of other narratives where irony occurs in the FG, see Carter, *John*, 118–22.

but also in terms of nation's politics and Caiaphas's personal interest.[43] Thus, his suggestion to kill Jesus would solve these problems. Peace can be retained if people's "faith" is put on Jewish leaders rather than Jesus. Then the temple and nation can continue to exercise its cult under gained (limited) freedom.

The irony is found at various levels in this episode. First, the chief priests and the Pharisees were fearful that soon all people would believe in Jesus. Jesus came for that very purpose, not only that Jews but also Gentiles would believe in him (cf. John 1:29). Jesus also said in 12:32 that his "lifting up" (i.e., cross) draws all men to him. The evangelist's purpose of writing was also the same: "you may believe that Jesus is the Christ" (John 20:31). To kill Jesus (11:50, 53), therefore, was fulfilling God's purposes so that all people could come to him (12:32). Jesus's execution did not quench peoples' faith in him. However, the one who gives life, as he had just demonstrated by raising Lazarus from death, was condemned to die.

Second, when we read the FG after 70 CE events, the statement that the Romans will take away "our place" (i.e., the temple) if Jesus was not eliminated becomes ironic. Jews worked hard to get Roman authorities to execute Jesus (cf. John 2:19), and yet Romans came and destroyed the temple.[44]

Third, it was also said that the Romans would come and take the nation. They came in 68–70 CE, although the Jewish elite acted according to the high priest's suggestion. The irony is that the readers are more informed and know more than the high priest did at that time.

Fourthly, there is irony in the phrase "You know nothing at all" (11:49). In retrospect, this becomes an ironic statement. The priests did not know anything; the high priest Caiaphas does not know even that much. His solution to the problem demonstrates his complete ignorance of God's agenda for redemption. He misses the mark, yet he is also accurate in a sense so that the evangelist points out that he, as the high priest, "prophesied" without knowing it. However, the prophecy had an entirely different meaning than what the high priest had intended with his words. Jesus died for the nation to save both the nation and the world.

---

43. Keener, *The Gospel of John*, 1:853.
44. See Keener, *The Gospel of John*, 2:855.

## Discourses

A prominent difference between the Synoptic Gospels and that of the FG is the Fourth Evangelist's use of discourses whereas the Synoptic writers record Jesus's teaching in his parables. Jesus and various characters engage in conversation in the FG, creating the main bulk of the entire Gospel narrative and Jesus's teaching. Sometimes discourses contain lengthy teaching sections, like in Jesus's Farewell Speech (John 13:33—17:26), but most of the time, discourse comprises fast-moving dialogue between the characters (e.g., John 4:7–26). These discourses (like parables in the Synoptic Gospels) capture the readers' attention and engage them to be part of the discourse—if not participants in the discourse, active listeners of the discourse.

For today's readers, discourses do not make for easy reading. Perhaps one of the most significant challenges is the sociological gap(s) between characters in the story and the reader. Characters, as well as the author and his first audience, were living in a high-context society. Thus, much essential socio-cultural data were omitted because it was matter-of-fact knowledge for people living in that world.

There is also another difficulty. Discourses can be so abrupt that it is difficult to catch their flow. What easily happens in those times is that the reader fills the blanks. The problem is that "filling" material, if not carefully done, may color the entire discourse with the colors that were not originally used. Occasional abruptness reminds us that perhaps the original discourse was longer. However, the author edited discourses for his purposes. Therefore, it is necessary to read them carefully to grasp the intended meaning of the author.

The following is a list of the discourses where Jesus engaged with one or more of named characters.[45] We have limited these discourses only to those where Jesus speaks at least twice to the character(s) and where arguably a conversation is taking place. We give the reference (which includes also opening and closing narrative portions of the given discourse but does not include the narrator's comments on the discourse), the names (or other identification) of the character(s), and the topic.

---

45. Note that sometimes all characters are not named. For example, in 1:51, Jesus responds to Nathanael, but shifts from the second person singular to second person plural, including other people. Where were these others? If they were there with Nathanael, we do not know the others by name except Philip, and perhaps Peter and Andrew who are mentioned earlier in the narrative. However, the plural "you" may also relate to a people group whom Nathanael was representing.

# Language, Style and Literary Devices

| Reference | Character(s) | Topic |
|---|---|---|
| 1:35–42 | Unnamed disciple, Andrew, Peter | First disciples |
| 1:43–51 | Philip and Nathanael | True Israelite |
| 2:1–10 | Mary, servants | Water into vine |
| 2:13–20 | Merchandisers | Cleansing the temple |
| 3:1–15 | Nicodemus | The new birth |
| 4:7–30 | The Samaritan woman | Jesus reveals himself to Samaritans |
| 4:31–38 | The disciples | True food |
| 4:46–50 | A nobleman | Healing the nobleman's son |
| 5:2–9a | Man ill for thirty-eight years | Healing a man |
| 5:9b–47 | The Jews | Jesus reveals himself to Jews |
| 6:1 13, 26 58 | Philip and other disciples | Bread: physical & spiritual food |
| 6:60–70 | The disciples | Following Jesus |
| 7:2–8 | Jesus's brothers | Going to Jerusalem |
| 7:14–29 | Jews in Jerusalem Temple | The source of Jesus's teaching |
| [7:53—8:11] | Jews and the adulterous woman | Sin no more |
| 8:12–59 | The Jews | Jesus's identity |
| 9:1–5 | The disciples | Question of the course of the sickness |
| 9:35–18 | The healed man and Pharisees | Jesus's identity/deity as the good shepherd at the time of the Feast of Tabernacles |

| Reference | Character(s) | Topic |
| --- | --- | --- |
| 10:24–39 | The Jews | Jesus's deity at the Feast of the Dedication |
| 11:1–16 | The disciples | Going up to Bethany |
| 11:17–44 | Martha and Mary | Raising Lazarus from the dead |
| 12:1–8 | Judas Iscariot | Mary anoints Jesus |
| 12:20–36 | The disciples and crowds | Greeks and Jesus's death |
| 13:5–32 | The disciples | The last supper |
| 13:33—16:33 | Jesus's eleven faithful disciples | The Farewell discourse |
| 18:1–11 | Roman cohort and Peter | Jesus's arrest |
| 18:19–24 | The high priest | Jesus questioned before the high priest |
| 18:33–38 | Pilate | Jesus questioned before Pilate |
| 20:11–17 | Mary | Resurrected Jesus appears to Mary |
| 20:19–29 | Thomas | Jesus's resurrection appearance to his disciples |
| 21:4–13 | The disciples | Jesus at the sore of the sea of Galilee |
| 21:15–23 | Peter | Do you love me? |

**Table 9.2**

This table demonstrates that stories in the FG that are framed as discourses. The events are not just narrated, but characters are actively involved in making a story conversational. This style invites readers to participate as active listeners and respondents. Sometimes bystanders break into the conversation as well. For example, in John 9:40, the Pharisees are active listeners of the conversation between Jesus and the healed man. As such, they cannot remain silent but ask the question to find out how they relate to the theological/spiritual truth Jesus is revealing to the healed man. In the discourse, the lines that characters say steer the narrative-discourse toward its theological and spiritual meaning.

Discourses also help readers learn who Jesus is during these encounters with various kinds of characters like Jews, Samaritans, men, women, sick, healthy, poor and rich, and his disciples to mention but a few. Beyond this, the discourses shed light on how the reader should respond to Jesus.[46] Characters are usually divided into two groups: main characters and minor characters. For example, Alan Culpepper lists John the Baptist, Jesus's mother, Nicodemus, the Samaritan woman, the royal official, the lame man, the brothers of Jesus, the blind man, Mary, Martha, and Lazarus as well as Pilate and Mary Magdalene as minor characters.[47] Although Jesus is the main character, readers need to notice the significant role minor characters play. Even a character who appears in a discourse once or very briefly, may "advance the plot, highlights aspects of Jesus' significance, and disclose God's life-giving purposes."[48]

Tom Thatcher has observed that riddles are frequent in Jesus's discourses in the FG. Riddles are intentionally ambiguous sayings, which demand time from listeners to solve them and which are understood only by those who share the same systems of logic as the speaker.[49] For example, Jesus's saying in John 9:41—10:5 is a riddle. Jesus's listeners (the Pharisees) did not get the meaning of Jesus's words. That caused them to think about what the message might be but they could not figure it out. Jesus then steps in and explains it for them (10:7–18).

There are discourses in which Jesus does not take part. For example, John the Baptist and his disciples have a dialogue in Jesus's absence in John 3:22–36. Despite this, the discourse is also rhetorical, supporting the overall purpose of the Gospel. The FG is filled with discourses that require adequate attention on many levels as they contribute to the plot development, the rhetoric of the gospel narrative, revelation of Jesus's role and identity, and the evangelist's overall theological/spiritual purposes.

---

46. For more about character, studies see Bennema, *Encountering Jesus*.

47. Culpepper, *Anatomy of the Fourth Gospel*, 132–44.

48. Carter, *John*, 67.

49. Thatcher, "The Riddles of Jesus," 267. See also Anderson, *The Riddles of the Fourth Gospel*.

No one has yet, as far as we know, offered a credible theory why the Fourth Evangelist chose to include discourses rather than parables into his account (if this was even a choice he had to make). One suggestion is that the location (Judea rather than Galilee) of the events (and perhaps the location of the intended readership) influenced its literary presentation. It is imaginable that Jews in Judea, especially in Jerusalem, were people of intellectual conversation. If the first readers were in Ephesus, a significant city of learning, discourses rather than parables make much sense. This suggestion, however, remains only a hypothetical at its best.

## Old Testament Quotations and Allusions

Based on UBS[4], the FG has sixteen OT quotations, whereas Matthew has thirty-two quotations from the OT. Regarding allusions, Glenn Balfour gives the following statistics:

> As a bare minimum, John has 69 Old Testament and seven purely extra-canonical allusions in as many verses. By comparison, Matthew has 155 Old Testament allusions in 165 verses and 8 purely extra-canonical allusions in 8 verses; Mark has 53 Old Testament allusions in 55 verses and one purely extra-canonical allusion in a single verse; and Luke has 150 Old Testament allusions in 159 verses and 7 purely extra-canonical illusions in 9 verses.[50]

At some point in the past, especially before Qumran Scrolls' discovery, the lack of the OT quotations was believed to reflect the fact that the FG was a Hellenistic Gospel and was, in other words, less Jewish than the Synoptic Gospels were. However, this understanding has been challenged, and today, scholarship holds that the FG is much more Jewish than previously thought.[51]

Although there are fewer OT quotations in the FG than in the Synoptic Gospels, there are several allusions to events and themes found in the OT. For this reason, it is argued that themes in the FG find their foundation in the OT. Here again are a few examples. There are commandments of love in John, but not direct quotations like in the Synoptic Gospels (cf. Mark 12:30–31, 33; and parallel passages). However, the command in

---

50. Balfour, "Is John's Gospel Antisemitic?," 218.

51. See, for example, Davies, "Reflections," 43–64. See also Borgen, "The Gospel of John and Hellenism."

Leviticus 19:18 is a reference point in John 13:34-35 where Jesus gives a "new commandment of love" to his disciples, and in 15:12-13 where he similarly instructs them to love each other as he has loved them. Also, there are references to Moses, Law, manna, water, bronze serpent, shepherd, and vine, which are embedded in OT themes, but yet, are not quoted verbatim. Rather, these are allusions to the OT without further explanation, assuming that the readers will make the connection between them. Above we looked into Jesus's "I AM" sayings which are coming from the OT without attributing any OT reference to them. A reader gets the feeling that either the author is referring to these from memory, relying on oral tradition, or that the author's intended audience was well versed in OT themes. This literary "tactic" brings the heuristic aspect to reading as the reader discovers the connection between the FG and OT.

Besides the OT quotation is not always precisely a quotation of any OT text. A well-known example is found in John 7:38b, where Jesus uses the introductory phrase, "as the Scripture has said," making his listeners wait for a verbatim quotation. This is not, however, the case as what follows, "From his innermost being will flow rivers of living water," is not found in the OT. This practice tells us something about the hermeneutical principles at that time. The "quotation" is a combination of few OT passages, referring to the OT revelation in a bigger scale rather than a mere particular text.

Menken finds four passages that closely resonate with these quotations.[52] They are the Septuagint text of Psalms 104:41; 77:16, 20; 114:8; Isaiah 48:21; and Zechariah 14:8. All of these texts have some overlapping with their wording, ideas, and/or usages with John 7:37b-38. Psalm 77:16, 20 is the closest literary resemblance whereas Psalm 114:8 and Zechariah 14:8 were connected with the occasion (the Feast of Tabernacles) where Jesus said these words.

Thus, the evangelist is not confused as he gives "Scripture" status to the quotation which is not found from the Scriptures. He is confident in combining various OT passages and wording the "quotation" to fit his purposes in the best possible way. Menken concludes that "Jesus is presented as the new rock in the wilderness, which is also the new temple, from which life-giving water will flow after his death."[53] This is an allusion to a more significant OT motif that appeals to the audience's memory horizon. Jesus, once again, connects his role to the Scriptures as the one who fulfills them.

52. Menken, *Old Testament Quotations*, 187-203.
53. Menken, *Old Testament Quotations*, 203.

## Concluding Remarks

This chapter has demonstrated that although the FG's vocabulary and language can be described as simple, it is still rich and complex. Readers are required to slow down when reading to give the evangelist's language chance to speak with "its own terms" that are foreign and not readily available to us. This calls readers to tackle hermeneutical questions on how to read (see Part Three below). The FG requires its readers to be aware of the horizon of living texts (esp. OT) of the first readers. The text evokes many conceptual, theological, and historical connections that are used rhetorically (persuasively) to reach the purpose of the Gospel.

Secondly, we sketched various literary devices that the Fourth Evangelist employs, which may not be easily grasped by today's readers. Readers should not only recognize misunderstandings, double meanings, irony, symbolism to list but a few but also how they are employed to advance the plot and purpose of the writing. To grasp these literary devices, readers need to enter the context of the narrative world that inevitably involves the author's historical context. Finally, the discourses, a big bulk of the FG's material, are essential components for the Gospel's persuasion. They should not be read only as isolated discourses. Instead, we must read discourses in the context of the entire Gospel to see their contribution to the Gospel's purpose.

## Suggestions for Further Reading

Koester, Craig R. *Symbolism in the Fourth Gospel: Meaning, Mystery, Community*. 2nd ed. Minneapolis: Fortress, 2003. Pp. 1–32; 141–206.

Carter, Warren. *John: Storyteller, Interpreter, Evangelist*. Peabody: Hendrickson, 2006. Pp. 107–28.

CHAPTER 10

# "Anti-Judaism" and "Anti-Jewish" Language

IN THE PREVIOUS CHAPTER, we looked at the language of the FG. However, that study did not deal with a somewhat troubling "language" issue, namely, the Fourth Evangelist's negative language towards the Jews that has been labeled as "anti-Jewish."[1] What is meant by "anti-Jewish language" is that when the evangelist addresses *oi Ioudaioi*, it is often used to suggest some kind of negativism towards Jews. One may ask the question for a reason: Why does an otherwise markedly Jewish Gospel employ language that is seemingly against Jews?[2] At the end of this chapter, we will offer suggestions what might have influenced the evangelist's usage of "anti-Jewish" language.

"Anti-Jewish" language in the FG is one thing, but another question is how "anti-Judaism" entered this Gospel. The answers have been offered on three levels: "(1) the level of the interpreter(s) (*intentio lectoris*); (2) the level of the text (*sensus textus*); and (3) the level of the author (*intentio auctoris*)."[3] On the level of *intentio lectoris*, the blame for making the FG

---

1. The words "anti-Jewish" (and related terms) are placed in quotation marks, indicating that this is not the best label to describe the FG's language and attitude towards the Jews. However, this terminology is still used because it is common in Johannine scholarship, and it characterizes the apparent issue in the FG.

2. John Ashton, *Understanding the Fourth Gospel*, 109; see also de Boer, "The Depiction of 'the Jews,'" 141; Lieu, "Anti-Judaism," 181.

3. Bieringer et al., "Wrestling with Johannine Anti-Judaism," 5. The following paragraph is also based on Bieringer et al., 5–8.

181

"anti-Jewish" is laid on the interpreters. Negative interpretations occur at least for the following two reasons. First, several individual negative comments towards Jews may lead interpreters to suggest that "anti-Judaism" is the tone of the entire Gospel. Secondly, interpreters may read their own contemporary views into the text. In that case, the interpreters may not listen to the text in its ancient context. Rather, they read according to stereotypes, concluding that "*Ioudaioi*" in the FG means "Jews" in general. On the level of *sensus textus*, the onus of making the FG "anti-Jewish" is not in the intended meaning of the author, but the text that is freed from authorial intent. In other words, the author is released from the guilt of being "anti-Jewish," but the text is not. On the level of *intentio auctoris*, the guilt rests on the author. *Intentio auctoris* is the most common view which holds that evangelist had "anti-Jewish" attitudes towards Jews.

At the outset, we need to point out that viewing the FG as "anti-Jewish," (sometimes suggested to be even "anti-Semitic") is problematic for many reasons. First, the FG does not depict only Jews in a negative light.[4] For example, Jesus declares to the Samaritan woman that salvation is from the Jews (John 4:22). Secondly, Judaism was not homogenous as a religion. Even though some Jewish sects ceased to exist after the Jewish war 70 CE, Judaism did not become homogenous.[5] Thirdly, the FG does not place the Jewish feast in a negative light. This implies that observance of the feast as such was not wrong. How could this be since most feasts mentioned in the FG were established by God! Fourthly, the evangelist's purpose of writing (i.e., "that you may believe") does not rule out a people group or individuals. The FG is clear that Jesus was the Lamb of God for the entire world. Fifthly, there were Jews who genuinely placed their faith in Jesus, including Jesus's disciples. For these reasons, we have to approach this issue with an open mind and a balanced view of Jews in the FG.

## Demonstration of "Anti-Jewish" Language in the Fourth Gospel

The FG includes several passages where Jesus and his followers are juxtaposed with "Jews" who oppose them.[6] Suppose these individual

---

4. See Keener, *The Gospel of John*, 1:217, for a list of passages where the evangelist portrays Jews.

5. Sheridan, "Issues in the Translation of οἱ Ἰουδαῖοι," 671 n1.

6. See John 5:16–18; 7:1, 11–13; 8:48, 52, 57; 9:18, 22; 10:31, 33; 11:8; 18:31–38;

## "Anti-Judaism" and "Anti-Jewish" Language 183

"anti-Jewish" passages are emphasized. In that case, it is not difficult to conclude that Gospel's attitude is negative towards Jews in general and the Jewish elite in particular (cf. *intentio lectoris*). Below we will use chapter 8, an exemplary narrative to demonstrate "anti-Jewish" language.

In chapter 8, Jesus has a long discourse with Jews. This encounter is launched by Jesus's "I am the Light of the world" proclamation (8:12). The initial critique of Jesus's proclamation was made by the Pharisees (v. 13). However, it is noticeable that as the narrative progresses, it is no longer just the Pharisees but the Jews too (v. 22) who are opposing Jesus. As the conversation develops, it becomes an increasingly heated argumentation in which the Jews' attitude towards Jesus moves from initial critique (v. 13) to attempted execution (v. 59). Along the way, Jesus and the narrator make several statements, which can be categorized as "anti-Jewish." Here is the summary of these statements:

- Jesus knows from where he came and where he is going, but the Jews do not know any of that (v. 14);
- The Jews judge according to the flesh, but Jesus is not judging anyone (v. 15);
- Jesus refers to the law as "your law," which the Jews did not apply to Jesus's and Father's testimony (vv. 17–18);
- The Jews know neither Jesus nor the Father (v. 19; cf. vv. 43, 55);
- The Jews will die in their sins (unless . . . ) (vv. 21, 24);
- Where Jesus goes, the Jews cannot come (v. 21);
- The Jews misunderstand Jesus's statement about his going (v. 22)
- Jesus is from above whereas the Jews are from below (v. 23);
- The Jews are from this world; Jesus is not from this world (v. 23);
- The Jews have not grasped Jesus's identity even though Jesus has revealed it to them "from the beginning" (v. 25);
- Jesus has many things to judge concerning the Jews (v. 26);
- The Jews will realize who Jesus is "too late," i.e., after his crucifixion (v. 28);
- Jesus's Father is God, whereas the Jews' father is the devil (8:38, 44);

---

19:7, 12–14, 38; 20:19, where Jews are presented as Jesus's adversaries.

- For some "believing Jews," Jesus gives further instruction pointing out that if they "truly were his disciples" then they would continue in his words and then they would know the truth (vv. 31–32);
- The Jews, even those called "believing Jews" had to get still free (vv. 32–33);
- The Jews are slaves of sin, but Jesus can make them free (vv. 34–36);
- The Jews seek to kill Jesus because they do not have room for Jesus's words in them (v. 37);
- The Jews do things they hear from (their) father, whereas Jesus speaks the things which he has seen with his Father (v. 38);[7]
- Jews are not doing the deeds of Abraham whom they claim to be their father (vv. 39–40);
- The Jews do not love Jesus because God is not their father (v. 42);
- The Jews are from their father the devil whose desires they are fulfilling (v. 44);
- Since the Jews are following lies of their father, they do not accept Jesus who speaks truth (vv. 46–47, cf. v. 55);
- The Jews dishonor Jesus calling him demon-possessed; Jesus honors his Father (vv. 48–49);
- Jesus is not seeking his glory—it is implied that Jews seek their glory (vv. 50, 54).

These points demonstrate "anti-Jewish" language not only in chapter 8 but also in the FG as a whole. Similar sayings are found in various places throughout the Gospel: the Jews do not know; they miss the Father, Moses, and the Law, as they miss Jesus; they think more about themselves than what they should, and so forth. Besides, irony is often found in the passages where "anti-Jewish" language is present. For instance, in John 8:22, the Jews are guessing what it means when Jesus says, "where I am going, you cannot come." They do not have a clue that they will be catalysts in the death of Jesus. Jesus is not going to kill himself, but they will with the help of their "enemies," namely, the Roman authorities.

---

7. There are early Greek mss which omit "my" and "your" possessive pronouns, and yet, some early mss includes them. UBS[4] Greek New Testament apparatus suggests that the most certain original reading is without "my" and "your" possessive pronouns. Nevertheless, personal pronouns can be implied from the literary context. See John 8:41, "your father," and John 8:19, "My father."

It is clear, that at this point, the FG requires careful reading. How should readers understand "the Jews" (*oi Ioudaioi*) in the FG? The question is, therefore, the referentiality of the word "Jews."[8] Bieringer, Pollefeyt, and Vandecasteele-Vanneuville note that even very early in the church's history, the FG's "anti-Judaism" was caused by interpreting *Ioudaioi* as a general reference to Jews. The understanding of *Ioudaioi* as "Jews" caused anti-Judaism to enter, not only the FG, but also begs the question as to how *Ioudaioi* was understood in other canonical Gospels.[9] However, recent interpretation endeavor to correct that view by offering various solutions to how "anti-Jewish" language should be understood to avoid "anti-Jewish" notions.

## Suggestions How to Read "Anti-Jewish" Language

Below, we will outline several suggestions to solve the "anti-Jewish" language in the FG. These suggestions vary greatly. Some argue that *oi Ioudaioi* refers to a small group of people, like Jewish aristocrats, whereas some read the symbolic meaning. We do not have space to engage with the counterarguments to these theories. However, we will suggest reasons for the evangelist's "anti-Jewish" language at the end of this chapter.

### "Jews" as Judeans

In their socio-scientific reading of the FG, Bruce J. Malina and Richard L. Rohrbaugh suggest that "Jews" means "Judeans." They observe that modern readers think that "Jews" in the FG relates to "Jews" or "Jewishness" as we know the terms today. However, they argue that taking the term to refer to the entire people group is a misconception and an anachronistic reading. They begin with the observation that modern English translations, such as NRSV, which translates *Ioudaioi* as "Jews," (e.g., in 1:19 ". . . when the Jews sent priests and Levites"), convey wrong connotations to the reader. They point out that modern readers "will think John makes

---

8. John Ashton also asks two other important questions, namely, "what role or function did they [Jews] fulfill," and "why the evangelist regards them with such hostility." Ashton, *Studying John*, 36. We limit ourselves to the present question.

9. Bieringer et al., "Wrestling with Johannine Anti-Judaism," 7.

reference to those persons whom readers today know from their experience to be Jews."[10]

Malina and Rohrbaugh believe that all sixty-nine times when the word *Ioudaioi* appears in the text, it refers to the first century "Judeans."[11] Charlesworth agrees with this and suggests that the Greek word should be taken "whenever possible, as 'some Judean leaders.'"[12] Judeans (*Ioudaioi*) are, therefore, a people group within the Israelites. "The correlatives of Judean in John are 'Galilean' and 'Perean.'"[13] They observe further that given the prominent role of the Judeans in John's Gospel, usually as opponents of Jesus, is a critical translation correction. The term *Ioudaios* (Judean), used either as a substantive or an adjective appears seventy times in John's Gospel. It is used only five times in Matthew, six times in Mark, and five times in Luke. The striking contrast between the FG and the Synoptic Gospels makes understanding the term critically important.[14]

## "Jews" as Jewish Leaders/Pharisees

D. Moody Smith moves beyond the "Judean" reading of "Jews." He suggests that *Ioudaioi* is mainly referencing Jewish leaders (similar to Charlesworth) and not Judeans generally.[15] He observes that the Pharisees were authoritative Jews among other Jewish groups during Jesus's time and were Jesus's opponents as well. Smith finds support for his reading in John 9:22 where "Jews" use their authority to evict believers from the Synagogues, whereas in John 12:42 they are named the Pharisees. The Pharisees use authority and oppose Jesus also in the Synoptic Gospels. Where the difference is in that "In the synoptics the Pharisees are . . . a group within Judaism, whereas in *John* they sometimes seem to be identical with Judaism, or at least with its essence." Thus, the evangelist reflecting the historical situation presents the Pharisees (= Jewish leaders) who

---

10. Malina and Rohrbaugh, *Social-Science Commentary*, 44.

11. Meeks also thinks that the term *Ioudaioi* had a mainly geographical meaning and thus could be translated "Judeans." Meeks, "'Am I a Jew?'" See also Ashton, *Studying John*, 37–39; Ashton, *Understanding the Fourth Gospel*, 60–78. Ashton presents a criticism on this view as well as the symbolic view of "Jews."

12. Charlesworth, "The Gospel of John," 247.

13. Malina and Rohrbaugh, *Social-Science Commentary*, 44–45.

14. Malina and Rohrbaugh, *Social-Science Commentary*, 45.

15. Smith, "Judaism and the Gospel of John," 82.

are identified as Jesus's enemies by the term *Ioudaioi*.[16] This same suggestion is made by Urban C. von Wahlde and Mark W. G. Stibbe.[17]

Smith also points out that the evangelist, who wrote after 70 CE, drew from contemporary Rabbinic Judaism that was tailored after Pharisaism.[18] The Johannine community lived in that context that continued to oppose Christianity, for example, by modifying the Twelfth Benediction by the addition of the word *notzrim* (Nazareans). This Christian-opponent Jewish leadership is then referred to in the FG as *Ioudaioi*. This reading removes the accusation that the FG is being "anti-Jewish" (and even "anti-Judean") as the term "Jews" is not understood to refer to all Jewish people or to Judeans.

## "Jews" as "anti-Johannine" Christianity

Henk Jan de Jonge interprets the "anti-Jewish" language symbolically. He suggests that the FG should be read as a double-deck story which is not only reporting the historical Jesus-story but also the story of the Johannine community. The idea of a two-story narrative reading is not new as it was popularized to Johannine scholarship already in the 1960s by J. Louis Martyn.[19] De Jonge thinks that the author is not only reflecting the historical situation of Jesus when Jews were Jesus's opponents, but rather, the historical situation of the evangelist. He contrasts the situation of the evangelist and his community with the historical situation of Jesus and his opponents. This framework allows de Jonge to argue that the Fourth Evangelist wrote a polemic Gospel that "was targeted against contemporary Christians who refused to accept the Johannine group's particular Christological understanding."[20] In other words, the battle is not between Jesus and Jews but between two Christian communities, namely the Johannine community and others. De Jonge specifies that the main problem between the Johannine community and the others was its distinctive Christology. In sum, de Jonge offers the solution suggesting that "in one single passage, 'the Jews' can refer to the characters in the biographical story of Jesus and, at the same time, represent a group of non-Johannine

16. Smith, "Judaism," 81.
17. See Sheridan, "Issues in the Translation," 676.
18. Smith, "Judaism," 84, 87.
19. Martyn, *History and Theology in the Fourth Gospel*.
20. De Jonge, "'The Jews' in the Gospel of John," 121.

Christians with whom the author is engaged in a dispute."[21] In a somewhat similar way, Rudolf Bultmann holds the view that the "Jews" have historical connotations and are thus, for the Fourth Evangelist, also the representatives of unbelief.[22]

## Extended Explanation of "Jews"

In his publication, *Your Father the Devil?*, Stephen Motyer argues that the polemic language used by the Fourth Evangelist was "normal" in the first-century context and that it is somewhat "mild" language when compared to other Greco-Roman or Jewish polemic standards.[23] However, this is, according to Motyer, not enough to explain such strong language. Therefore, he further argues that although not employing the genre of the OT prophets, the FG should be read "against the *prophetic* background." In short, the evangelist is not merely condemning "Jews." Instead, he is calling them to turn towards God, which included his Christ Jesus. Motyer applies this understanding to chapter 8 and concludes, "The polemic of John 8 serves not merely to denounce but more particularly to *warn*, to *persuade*, in fact to *prompt its own negation*."[24]

Secondly, Motyer notes that the Fourth Evangelist writes to Jews who were still experiencing the trauma of the destruction of the Jerusalem Temple, and this affected their identity.[25] Therefore, Motyer thinks that the Fourth Evangelist's commitment to rebuild Israel is the correct slant to be taken when reading the FG. The evangelist's suggestion on how to rebuild and heal the nation, however, differs from Jewish views, and this has caused the clashes between the "Jews" and Jesus's followers. In Motyer's own words, the evangelist is warning his readers, "Don't put faith in the failed formula, the illusory promise that the Torah life-style can still bring freedom!"[26] The answer is found in Jesus, not in re-building the Jerusalem Temple. The only way to move forward is not based on future restoration, but today's reality found in Jesus, the Messiah.[27]

---

21. De Jonge, "'The Jews' in the Gospel of John," 125.
22. Bultmann, *The Gospel of John*, 86.
23. Cf. Motyer, *Your Father the Devil?*, 35–104.
24. Motyer, *Your Father the Devil?*, 211–12.
25. Motyer, *Your Father the Devil?*, 212; see also p. 77.
26. Motyer, *Your Father the Devil?*, 214.
27. Motyer, *Your Father the Devil?*, 214.

Motyer urges readers to give attention to "first voice," which means that readers should pay attention to the historical context in which the evangelist and his community found themselves.[28] To help the modern reader implement the historical context in the understanding of "Jews," Motyer, using dynamic equivalence translation principles, suggests that the best way to do this is to use extended translations. He translates John 5:18, for example, "For this reason, *these Jews, passionate about legal observance*, sought all the more to kill him." Another example, John 9:22, could be translated, "His parents said this because they were afraid of *the more hard-line Jews in the synagogue leadership*. For *these Jews* had determined that anyone who confessed Jesus as Christ should be expelled from the synagogue."[29]

## "Jews" as 'Jews'

Ruth Sheridan has critiqued Motyer's attempt saying that "The focus on a 'hardline' stance and on a convocation of established synagogue leadership sounds more like 90s C.E. than 20–30 C.E."[30] In addition, she points out that Motyer's reading of "these Jews" in John 9:22 when the Greek reads *oi Ioudaioi*, as well as Motyer's other particularizations of *oi Ioudaioi*, "take a significant and unwarranted liberty with the Greek."[31] Sheridan has argued that since we have only the text to work with, the best option we have is to translate *oi Ioudaioi* "'Jews' rather than seeking to create qualifying clauses around the term to specify a distinct group of Jews with whom the author meant to dialogue."[32] She also says that placing "the Jews" in quotation marks "is also ideal in many settings, as it implies that not all 'Jews' in the narrative are bothered by the Gospel text, even if it does also imply something about their putative historical identity in the 90s C.E."[33] However, this view has also been criticized by some Johannine scholars.[34]

28. Motyer, "Bridging the Gap," 148.
29. Motyer, "Bridging the Gap," 153.
30. Sheridan, "Issues in the Translation," 681.
31. Sheridan, "Issues in the Translation," 682.
32. Sheridan, "Issues in the Translation," 694.

33. Sheridan, "Issues in the Translation," 695. See also Pippin, "'For Fear of the Jews,'" 91–92.

34. See, for example, Reinhartz, "'Jews' and Jews in the Fourth Gospel," 227.

Herman Ridderbos notes that the term "Jews" was increasingly replacing the term "Israelite" when a person belonging to the nation of Israel was referred to. In his own words, "Whereas 'Israel' was still the people's self-designation, "Jew" was generally used by non-Jews for Jews, and Jews in the diaspora gradually adopted this designation."[35] It is reasonable to think that the Fourth Evangelist adopted this usage of the word "Jew" that did not have a negative connotation attached to it.

## "Jews" as Later Additions to the Text

J. C. O'Neill's solution is related to *sensus textus* as edited text. He argues that "the words *the Jews* in John's Gospel are pointless additions to the narratives."[36] He finds two arguments for his thesis. First, he thinks that the words "the Jews" are not intrinsic to the story. In other words, the story makes good sense without specific reference to "Jews." He has observed that, when those words are found in the narrative, they occur without any narrative explanation.[37] When the Synoptic Gospels are contrasted to the FG, it is noticeable that their accounts are much more specific about who Jesus's opponents are in the narratives of controversy. "The Synoptic Gospels almost always specify who Jesus' opponents are, using terms like Pharisees, Sadducees, Herodians, High Priests, Elders, Scribes and the like."[38] We need to keep in mind that if the FG was written after the destruction of the Jerusalem Temple 70 CE, many Jewish sects had ceased to exist. This historical situation might have influenced the Fourth Evangelist's vocabulary. Therefore, the more general address "Jews" was used to describe Jesus's Jewish opponents.

O'Neill's second argument is based on textual tradition, which, according to him, shows that the words "the Jews" are later additions; he simply states, "the better manuscripts do not have them."[39] Thus we can think of the words as glosses. According to O'Neill, the pronouns "their" and "your" with reference to Jews are also glosses. This argument is backed up with an observation from the historical development of Jewish-Christian relations. O'Neill points out that what "we know of the

---

35. Ridderbos, *The Gospel of John*, 62.
36. O'Neill, "*The Jews* in the Fourth Gospel," 58.
37. O'Neill, "*The Jews* in the Fourth Gospel," 63.
38. O'Neill, "*The Jews* in the Fourth Gospel," 72.
39. O'Neill, "*The Jews* in the Fourth Gospel," 59.

history of the church would lead us to suppose that anti-Jewish feelings would grow rather than diminish. The synagogue expelled Christians, and Christians became more and more of Gentile origin, liable to share the anti-Jewish sentiments of their compatriots."[40] In sum, O'Neill thinks that anti-Jewish trends in the FG are "probably based on a series of unfortunate late scribal corruptions."[41]

## Towards a Solution to "Anti-Jewish" Language

The outline above of various suggestions for solutions how to read the words *oi Ioudaioi* demonstrate the need for a careful reading of the evangelist's so-called anti-Jewish language. To grasp the FG's presentation of Jews, one needs to tackle several aspects such as *sitz im leben* of Jews, the evangelist, and the community, as well as theology, the purpose of writing, and the rhetoric used.

We suggest that the so-called anti-Jewish language is found in the FG for several reasons. Our presentation of these reason is divided into four sections: (1) theological reasons, (2) historical reasons (i.e., pre- and post-70 CE Jewish life), (3) needs for Jewish-Christian's self-identification, and (4) rhetorical reasons. We hope to be able to show even partially that "anti-Jewish" language does not function as mere polemic against Jews.

### Theological Reasons

On the narrative level, negativism against Jews is specifically directed to Jews who were Jesus-Messiah opponents.[42] First of all, that was a spiritual and Christological issue (cf. John 8:24), but also one which truthfully reflected the historical situation (cf. John 19:15); Jesus's own people (cf. John 1:11) did not receive him but rather opposed him. Historical-religious background indicates that a significant part of the Jewish community and especially the majority of Jewish leaders did not share Jesus's claims about himself. Throughout the narrative the Jewish elite is reported to oppose Jesus's claims and deeds, which pointed toward his divine identity and role, as they did not fit the Jewish elite's notion of Messiah. At the end of the day, Jesus was executed as a heretical religious leader by the Romans

---

40. O'Neill, "*The Jews* in the Fourth Gospel," 73.
41. O'Neill, "*The Jews* in the Fourth Gospel," 74.
42. Cf. Sandmel, *Anti-Semitism in the New Testament?*, 102.

according to the Jewish religious leaders' request.[43] This theological reality is carried on into the FG (e.g., John 19:14–15).[44]

Therefore, it would be an unfortunate misinterpretation to read the FG as anti-Semitic work as was the tendency at times in the past.[45] The author of the FG did not write against the Jewish nation or even Judaism as such. His negativism was focused on those who did not accept Jesus's identity as the divine broker of the Father. This negativism of Jesus can be demonstrated, for example, by what he said about Judas Iscariot in 6:70, "Did I Myself not choose you, the twelve, and *yet* one of you is a devil." Judas is not called here "a Jew" but is given the same description than "Jews" received from Jesus in 8:44; both "Jews" and Judas (a Jew) opposed God's ways.[46]

## Historical Reasons

The anti-Jewish language is also a reflection of the historical setting of the time of writing.[47] After the destruction of the temple 70 CE, Judaism changed in many ways concerning its worship, divisions/sects, and political influence. In particular, the Jews' self-identity was severely damaged, and they experienced what Motyer calls trauma.[48] This crisis caused Judaism to refigure itself.

In the process of re-organizing Judaism, Jamnian Judaism (Rabbinic Judaism) developed. The "new normal" *sitz im leben* without the possibility to carry out the sacrificial practices was drastically different from previous temple-centered Judaism. Jamnian Judaism, in the long run, was the catalyst for a more uniform Jewish religion. One of the reasons for a more uniform Judaism was that many Jewish sects like the Essenes and the Sadducees ceased functioning after the first Jewish rebellion against

---

43. Dunn, "The Embarrassment of History," 43; Cf. Collins, "Speaking of the Jews," 175.

44. Cf. Reinhartz, "'Jews' and Jews in the Fourth Gospel," 220.

45. Cf. Balfour, "Is John's Gospel Antisemitic?," 5–19.

46. Lieu, "Anti-Judaism the Jews," 179.

47. The circumstances during the writing of the FG do not approve that one should read it as a two-level drama, mainly telling the story of the community. Instead, this is to acknowledge that contemporary questions and life setting influenced the evangelist's presentation. Cf. Thompson, *John*, 203.

48. Motyer, *Your Father the Devil?*, 77.

Rome.[49] Jamnian Judaism also resisted all divisions within Judaism and acted against other groups, including Christians.[50]

One practical way to condemn deviations from Jamnian Judaims was the re-formulation of the Twelfth of the *Shemoneh Esreh*, probably between 85–90 CE.[51] This benediction that the synagogue congregation prayed together condemned sectarians (*minim*) within Judaism and Nazarenes (*notzrim*, i.e., Christians) in order to strengthen Judaism and the unity of Jews.[52] Christians experienced pressure especially in Asia, the region where John wrote, not only from Romans (cf. Book of Revelation) but also from Jews.[53]

Thus, the Fourth Evangelist's negative tone is a reflection of the past *and* perhaps also the contemporary context in which Jews carried out negative actions towards Jesus's followers (cf. John 15:18—16:3). Nevertheless, the critical issue seems not to be Judaism per se, but lack of belief in, and even rebellion against, Jesus as Messiah.

## Church's Self-Identification

While Christians and Christian communities experienced pressure from outside, they continued to build up their own distinctive identity. They distanced themselves from old Jewish ways of life and theology, but they did not distance themselves from the Hebrew Scriptures. This situation may be another factor for the Fourth Evangelist's anti-Jewish language. Christian self-identification moved in two directions. Christian communities had to define not only who they were in relation to society but also who they were in relation to other religious communities and Judaism in particular. They had to answer questions like what is the role of the

---

49. Davies, "Reflections," 48–52.; Cf. Dunn, "The Embarrassment of History," 46; Balfour, "Is John's Gospel Antisemitic?," 26.

50. See Balfour, "Is John's Gospel Antisemitic?" 30–31.

51. Davies, "Reflections," 50; Smith, "Judaism and the Gospel of John," 85. Note that the date is only suggestive since there is no definite evidence of when *notzrim* was added to the benediction. There are suggestions that it was added no earlier than the fourth century. Also, there are arguments that *minim* was to address all Jewish sectarians. See Van der Horst, "The Birkat ha-minim in recent research."

52. Smith, "Judaism and the Gospel of John," 85; Cf. Van der Horst, "The Birkat H-Minim in Recent Research," 115, 124.

53 Cf. Johnson, *Discipleship on the Edge*, 69.

Law to them, and who are the people of God. Both Christian and Jewish communities played a part in this process.

Before 70 CE, at the beginning of Christianity, "Jesus and the earliest Christian congregations were, in effect, part of . . . ongoing debate over what it meant to be a Jew, what was involved in being Israel."[54] Thus, the question of identification at that time was mainly an "in-house" issue.

Glenn Balford builds an argument on James Dunn's inference that early believers of Jesus Messiah during the late Second Temple identified themselves as "Israel" (or "Israelites") rather than "Jews" so distancing themselves from "Jews." The FG uses "Jews" when appropriate to make that distinction between those who believed and who did not believe in Jesus as Messiah. Therefore, Balfour suggests that Jesus was "king of Israel" (John 1:49; 12:13) for insiders, but "king of Jews" (John 18:33, 39; 19:3, 19, 21) for outsiders.[55]

After 70 CE, when factionalism within Judaism was disrupted, "we can see only two substantive contenders for the heritage of Second Temple Judaism beginning to emerge from the pre-70 factionalism—Christianity and rabbinic Judaism."[56] This development suggests that when the FG was written, Christianity was ideologically separated from rabbinic Judaism and sociologically separated from the synagogue.[57] From the Jews' point of view, Christianity was now considered more a threat from outside rather than from inside Judaism.[58] Thus, the content of the dichotomy between Jesus and Jews in the Gospel was not only a matter of belief and unbelief. It also was rooted in the concept of the "people of God." Jews identified themselves as people of God and expected others to accept their religious life and ideology. Nevertheless, the FG presents a different message to Jews (cf. John 3:3; 8:31–47); to be included in the "people of God,"

---

54. Dunn, "The Embarrassment of History," 45.

55. Balfour, "Is John's Gospel Antisemitic?," 309. Cf. Porter, *John, His Gospel, and Jesus*, 150. Porter points out that the issue in the FG is not race or region but religion.

56. Dunn, "The Embarrassment of History," 46. This development was not, however, an event that happened at once after the first Jewish war. Judaism, as well as Christianity, kept on developing, including the sharper division between the two over a period of time. Some scholars are convinced that the complete separation between them did not happen before the *Bar Kokhba* revolt in 132–35 CE.

57. Cf. Culpepper, "Anti-Judaism," 78; see also Aker, "John," 92; Meeks, "Breaking Away," 98.

58. Cf. Meeks, *In Search of the Early Christians*, 120. See also Culpepper, "Anti-Judaism," 63; Reinhartz, "'Jews' and Jews," 225.

one must accept God's broker, Jesus. There is no other way one can come to the Father and enter his kingdom (cf. John 3:3; 14:6).

Christian self-identification in the FG is centered around Christology, which dominates the Gospel.[59] The evangelist's Christology remained the most significant problem and obstacle to Jews.[60] We argue that his aim was not to rule out Jews from salvation but to persuade them to come to salvation by accepting Jesus as Messiah. This message would have also been a solution to their post 70 CE trauma. This view brings us to the consideration of yet another reason for the FG's anti-Jewish language, namely the evangelist's rhetorical goals.

## Rhetorical Goal

The Fourth Evangelist's narrative is a persuasive communication that Jesus is the Son of God and Messiah (cf. John 20:30–31). His persuasive style has partly to do with his overall purpose to present Christ in the OT prophetical manner like Hosea, Isaiah, Jeremiah or Ezekiel did in their persuasion.[61] His approach is fitting for Jews, even though there is evidence that the Johannine church and the synagogue experienced a sharp divorce sometime earlier. The evangelist's OT prophetic type language suggests that he does not only blame Jews but instead, he urges them to trust Jesus as Messiah. The evangelist is explicit in his goal; he wants Jews to experience what they are longing for, namely, closeness with God and times of blessing/salvation.[62]

There is evidence that the Fourth Evangelist makes rhetorical choices regarding his language while addressing his unbelieving Jewish audience. He identifies the Pharisees as Jews and then identifies Jews as the world, so indicating their status in relation to God. The move from Pharisees to the Jews is explicit in chapters 3 and 8. Nicodemus, a Pharisee, represents Jews in chapter 3, and Sadducees lead a long and sharp conversation between Jews and Jesus in chapter 8. When the narrative develops in chapter 8, Jesus is not referring to Jews any

---

59. Cf. Culpepper, "Anti-Judaism in the Fourth Gospel," 69; Smith, *The Theology of the Gospel of John*, 51.

60. Cf. Collins, "Powers in Heaven," 9.

61. Motyer, *Your Father the Devil?*, 212; Helyer, *The Witness of Jesus, Paul and John*, 325.

62. Dunn, "The Embarrassment of History," 52; See also Dowell, "Why John Rewrote the Synoptics," 454.

longer as his opponents, but rather the "world" has taken that role (cf. John 15:18—16:4). Therefore, in the FG, the Pharisees do not enjoy a special status among Jews, for they are integrated into "Jews." In the same way, the Jews are not given a special status, but they are integrated into the "world" as Jesus's opponent. This, however, is not an utterly negative picture. The Fourth Evangelist is emphatic that Jesus came for the world—for all who are lost, including Jews. Jews, in the FG, have, therefore, a place in God's salvation plan.

## Concluding Remarks

This chapter has sketched reasons why FG's language is identified as "anti-Jewish." We have also outlined several recent proposals on how scholars have tried to solve the issue. Those views include valuable observations, yet they all have some difficulties or shortcomings. The final part of this chapter outlined suggestions for why the Fourth Evangelist has used "anti-Jewish" language. The outlined points demonstrate that the Fourth Evangelist was not "anti-Jewish." Instead, these points help today's readers recognize the evangelist's truthfulness to historical and theological realities, the historical setting in which he wrote, and his goal to persuade all people, the Jews included, to recognize that Jesus is the Son of God, the Christ, in whom one should put one's trust.

What is necessary is that the evangelist's usage of *oi Ioudaioi* is evaluated case by case.[63] It would be a mistake to interpret *oi Ioudaioi* always the same way. For example, if *oi Ioudaioi* is always taken to refer to the Jewish elite then Jesus's statement that the salvation is from Jews (4:22) would create an impasse. We cannot attribute it consistently to Judeans since, on some occasions, *oi Ioudaioi* refers to Galilean Jews (e.g., 4:22, 18:20). Nevertheless, we should perhaps remain faithful to the Greek text and not explain the meaning of *oi Ioudaioi* in the English translation of the FG. Also, as Balfour reminds us, the discussion of "anti-Judaism" in the FG should go beyond a mere study of the phrase, *oi Ioudaioi*. He has demonstrated that the overall presentation of the Fourth Evangelist, and especially his usage of the OT, substantiates that

---

63. Cf. Barrett, "John and Judaism," 245; Charlesworth, "The Gospel of John," 249–56; Dunn, "The Embarrassment of History," 55; Tomson, "'Jews' in the Gospel of John," 198.

he is Jewish rather than anti-Jewish/Semitic, and thus the FG should be read within that Jewish setting.[64]

## Suggestions for Further Reading

Ashton, John. *Studying John: Approaches to the Fourth Gospel*. Oxford: Clarendon, 1994. Pp. 36–70.

Smith, D. Moody. *The Fourth Gospel in Four Dimensions: Judaism and Jesus, the Gospels and Scripture*. South Carolina: University of South Carolina Press, 2008. Pp. 3–46.

Thompson, Marianne Meye. *John: A Commentary*. NTL. Louisville: Westminster John Knox, 2015. Pp. 199–204.

---

64. Balfour, "Is John's Gospel Antisemitic?," 217.

CHAPTER 11

# The Fourth Evangelist's Jesus

ONE OF THE MOST loved television shows in our family has recently been "The Portrait Artist of the Year." In that show, various artists, professional and amateurs, paint portraits of well-known individuals. In each episode, the judges choose the winner. We, who are not portrait artists, are astonished to see which portrait contains qualities that rank it above other portraits. It is not only the likeness, that is, how well the portrait imitates the person, but also other qualities like color, style, excitement, technique and light that win an artist the trophy. Painting a portrait of someone is a suitable analogy to writing a biography of a person.[1]

The four Gospels are not merely historical accounts of the protagonist, Jesus (i.e., "portraying" him merely in his historical likeness). The Gospel authors used portrait techniques available within the framework of the literary genre they chose to employ. Using the flexible ancient biography genre,[2] they were allowed to exercise a good deal of freedom in their portrait of Jesus.[3]

We have four portrait artists (i.e., evangelists) who have painted a portrait of Jesus. A significant challenge for them was that the "model" was not "sitting" in front of them. Instead, they had to rely on memory and other sources. Each of their final work is different not only because of their memory and sources, but also because of the author's distinctive

---

1. Cf. Loader, *Jesus in John's Gospel*.

2. Burridge, "The Gospels and Acts," 507–8, 530. Burridge argues that Gospels as biographies are also rhetorical writings.

3. Cf. Keener, *Christobiography*.

style and emphasis. We are not going to rank them to find a winner, however. That would be a pointless exercise. With regard to the FG, our interest lies in what kind of portrait of Jesus the Fourth Evangelist wants his readers to "see" in his work: how he presents Jesus. However, we do not try to evaluate how closely his portrait represents the likeness of historical Jesus. Various judges (i.e., readers) throughout history have engaged in that evaluation. Some have argued that the FG's presentation does not correspond to the likeness of the historical protagonist (e.g., Bultmann), whereas others argue quite the opposite (e.g., Blomberg).[4]

## Jesus on the Journey

The Fourth Evangelist depicts Jesus on a journey. The journey, which is simultaneously earthly and heavenly, is extraordinary. The narration of Jesus's earthly journey, which includes his disciples, moves from the Jordan river via the cross to the sea of Galilee. The heavenly journey, which is accompanied by the Father and the Spirit, is from the Father to the earth and, via the cross, back to the Father. During his earthly journey, Jesus meets different kinds of people and people groups ranging from sympathetic to hostile. His heavenly journey is marked by his close relationship with the Father (cf. John 1:18). The earthly journey takes Jesus around Jewish Palestine and Samaria, including Jerusalem, where he attends several Jewish feasts. Jesus's heavenly journey as an obedient Son is in contrast to Israel's unfaithful wilderness experience.

Jesus (*Logos*) is revealed as the one who has always been face to face with the Father. However, now he has become flesh to reveal the Father (1:18). Jesus frequently refers to his coming with the phrase "the one who sent me" and other similar expressions. He articulates his oneness with the Father on several occasions in a variety of ways.[5] These testimonies indicate that Jesus is journeying with his Father doing his Father's business. Jesus is the divine *Logos*—the only God-sent agent/broker—and as such, he is journeying towards the cross, which is not his destination but rather the turning point in his journey.

The evangelist communicates Jesus's cross, the turning point, in heuristic ways. Jesus refers to his body as a temple which would be re-built in

---

4. Cf. Bultmann, *Jesus and the Word*, 12; Blomberg, *The Historical Reliability of John's Gospel*, 41.

5. Cf. Bauckham, "Monotheism and Christology," 163–65.

three days (ch. 2); he is lifted up like the serpent (ch. 3, cf. ch. 8); the living water that he offers implies and requires the cross (chs. 4, 7); the death of the cross is spoken in term of glorification (ch. 17); and he is going back to the Father which includes the cross and resurrection (chs. 13, 16). Each expression conveys different characteristics of his cross to his listeners. The evangelist's expressions do not resonate with the earthly point of view, namely, a shameful death by Roman hands. Instead, Jesus's death on the cross is viewed as an honorable moment that glorifies the Father and the Son, the moment that launches Jesus's journey back to the Father.

We can conclude that the FG depicts the Jesus-event as a journey, and that its zenith is the cross—not the cross of the shame but the cross of honor and glory. Jesus was sent for a purpose; he lived for that purpose and went back to the Father with that purpose fulfilled. The Fourth Evangelist records neither Jesus's incarnation event nor his physical departure from the earth. In this regard, the Synoptic writers are more explicit. Instead, John ends his account, and thus Jesus's journey, with Jesus's charge to his disciples to go and start their journey with the purpose and task that Jesus had given them (John 20:19–23; 21:15–23).

## The Fourth Evangelist's Jesus Portrait Contrasted with the Synoptic Gospels

Each Gospel writer presents Jesus in his own way, emphasizing certain theological aspects which differ from other evangelists' presentations of Jesus.

1. In Matthew, Jesus is the Son of David and heir of the messianic throne.
2. In Mark, Jesus is the Servant of God, fulfilling the will of the Father.
3. In Luke, Jesus is the Son of Man who is fully human performing God's will.
4. In the FG, Jesus is the Son of God who is the fully divine "I Am."

Although the above evaluation is an oversimplification and therefore can be argued as not entirely accurate, it reveals that each evangelist's portrait is different. These slants are already evident in the opening paragraphs of each Gospel.

1. Gospel of Matthew: "The record of the genealogy of Jesus the Messiah, the son of David, the son of Abraham: Abraham was the father of Isaac, Isaac the father of Jacob, and Jacob the father of Judah and his brothers."
2. Gospel of Mark: "The beginning of the gospel of Jesus Christ, the Son of God. As it is written in Isaiah the prophet: "Behold, I send My messenger ahead of You, who will prepare Your way; the voice of one crying in the wilderness, 'make ready the way of the Lord, make His paths straight.'"
3. Gospel of Luke: "Inasmuch as many have undertaken to compile an account of the things accomplished among us, just as they were handed down to us by those who from the beginning were eyewitnesses and servants of the word, it seemed fitting for me as well, having investigated everything carefully from the beginning, to write *it* out for you in consecutive order, most excellent Theophilus; so that you may know the exact truth about the things you have been taught."
4. Fourth Gospel: "In the beginning was the Word, and the Word was with God, and the Word was God. He was in the beginning with God. All things came into being through Him, and apart from Him nothing came into being that has come into being."

The FG begins in a distinctively different way than the Synoptic Gospels. The Synoptic accounts begin with Jesus's birth story (Matthew and Luke) or his public ministry (Mark), that is, relating the narrative to Jesus's earthly life. The Fourth Evangelist starts from above, the time before the creation (John 1:1). Whereas the Synoptic evangelists paint their portrait of Jesus from below towards the heaven (human to divine), the Fourth Evangelist begins from above and comes down to the earth (divine to human). The Synoptics' different portrait does not support the view that the Synoptic Evangelists only emphasize Jesus's humanity (cf. Matt. 1:23), or that the Fourth Evangelist only emphasizes Jesus's divinity (cf. John 1:14). Both of these aspects are present in every Gospel account.

In the case of the FG, the evangelist is not trying to correct one or several heretical notions of Jesus's nature (e.g., his divinity or humanity), but instead concentrates on present arguments which include both his divinity and humanity. His focus is to persuade his readers to accept Jesus of Nazareth as God's divine Messiah.⁶ A growing tendency among Johannine scholars is to give more credit to the FG's historicity and its accurate presentation of the Jesus of history than previously acknowledged. Some have even suggested that the FG might be more reliable source for the historical Jesus than Mark's Gospel which Matthew and Luke followed.⁷

All the Gospels link Jesus to the OT one way or another. This link was necessary for the evangelists to show that Jesus of Nazareth is the one about whom the Scriptures speak. Matthew starts with Jesus's genealogy, specifically referring to David's and Abraham's line (Matt. 1:1–17); Mark starts with Old Testament prophecy regarding Jesus (Mark. 1:1–3); and Luke begins with fulfilment narratives, namely with birth stories of John the Baptist and Jesus (Luke 1:5—2:20). However, the FG's opening is in alignment with the creation story of Genesis: In the beginning, God created—In the beginning was the Word.

The FG's portrait of Jesus can also be further examined by comparing its omissions and additions with the Synoptic Gospels' Jesus-material. Several factors may have caused the Fourth Evangelist's omissions and additions to emphasize certain aspects of Jesus. Material that he includes that is not found in the Synoptic Gospels is vast. The FG shares very little of the same material with the Synoptic Gospels in its first twelve chapters (the book of signs). Those few occasions where the FG seems to share the same material with the Synoptic Gospels, it differs significantly from their narrative (see below). Also, Jesus's passion narrative includes material that is not found in the Synoptic Gospels such as Jesus's lengthy Farewell Speech and post-resurrection encounters with his disciples. In the unique bulk of the Fourth Evangelist's Jesus-material, Jesus is painted as God's agent who is focused on his task received from the Father. All narratives direct the readers to recognize that each individual narrative contributes to the portrait of Jesus as divine Messiah who fulfills the will of his patron, the Father, and therefore is the one who provides the life eternal.

Regarding the shared Jesus-material, it becomes evident that the Fourth Evangelist presents Jesus from a perspective that differs from that of the Synoptic Evangelists' presentation. We will look at three narratives that are included in all four Gospels to demonstrate this: (1) the narrative of Jesus feeding five thousand, (2) the Last Supper, and (3) Jesus's arrest

---

6. Cf. Smalley, *John*, 146.

7. Cf. Anderson, *The Riddles of the Fourth Gospel*, 195–218; Smith, *The Fourth Gospel in Four Dimensions*, 81–111.

and crucifixion. In our comparison, we give priority to the Markan account to make the comparison simpler to follow.

The narrative of feeding five thousand with five loaves of bread and two fish is recorded in Matthew 14:13-21; Mark 6:33-44; Luke 9:10-17; and John 6:1-14. The FG's Jesus-portrait differs the following ways from the Markan portrait:

- In the FG, Jesus is found with his disciples and the crowd just following him, whereas in Mark, Jesus is with the crowd feeling compassion towards the people (John 6:3, 5; Mark 6:34).
- In the FG, Jesus tests one of his disciples (Philip) by asking him to provide food for the crowd, whereas in Mark, Jesus responds to the disciples' request to provide food for the people (John 6:5-6; Mark 6:35-36).
- In the FG, Jesus knows why he asks the question from Philip and what he was going to do, whereas, in Mark, it seems like Jesus needs the disciples' reminder that they should think of the people's physical wellbeing as well.
- In the FG, Jesus asks his disciples to gather up the leftovers, whereas in Mark, the disciples do so without Jesus's request (John 6:12; Mark 6:43).

The outline points out that FG's Jesus has control over the situation. He knows the needs of the people and the purpose of his actions. He knows how to respond to the dilemma. In Mark, Jesus is pictured as a passionate teacher of the crowds with no interest to use this moment to test or teach his disciples. On the contrary, in Mark, Jesus's disciples, rather than Jesus himself, are concerned about the need of the people.

At the Last Supper, the Synoptic Gospels include material that is omitted in John. However, all three include the narrative of Judas Iscariot's involvement in Jesus's betrayal. (Luke is more arbitrary at this point than other Gospels, for he does not identify Judas Iscariot as the betrayer; cf. Luke 22:21). Mark notes that Judas Iscariot identified himself as the betrayer by dipping his piece of bread with Jesus in the bowl (Mark 14:20). In the FG, Jesus is the one who points out Judas Iscariot by dipping the morsel and giving it to him (John 13:26). Jesus is actively controlling the situation as he knows what is happening (cf. 13:1, 3).

In the narrative of Jesus's arrest, a similar difference is noticeable as in the narratives of the feeding five thousand and the Last Supper. In

Mark's account (Mark 14:43–50), Judas gives a signal of who Jesus is, one of the disciples uses his sword to fight back, and Jesus criticizes his arresters' method and timing, yet acknowledges its necessity to fulfill the Scriptures. In the FG's narrative (John 18:3–11), Jesus knows what was about to happen (v. 4a); he went to meet his arresters (v. 4b); and he identified himself to them (v.4c). As a consequence of Jesus's "I Am" statement, his arresters fell on the ground, indicating Jesus's superior power and control of the situation. Also, Jesus's voluntary surrender and request for freedom for his disciples demonstrate his control of the situation (v. 8). In this context, Peter's use of his sword is ironic. How would a fisherman's sword skills help against the Roman professional solders (cohort), especially when Jesus has just demonstrated his power and authority over the situation? Jesus's rhetorical question as a part of his response to Peter's foolish act, "the cup which the Father has given Me, am I not drink it?" (v. 11) indicates his deliberate and controlled surrender.

Similarly, in the Passion narrative, Jesus stays in control of the situation all the time. In his *Christobiography*, Keener highlights the following to demonstrate this:

- In John, Jesus himself, rather than Simon, carries Jesus's cross (Mark 15:22; John 19:17).
- John's final recorded cry rings triumphant rather than pitiful (Mark 15:34; John 19:30).
- In John, Jesus remains in control, laying down his own life (10:17–18).[8]

The Fourth Evangelist includes much material in his account that is not found in the Synoptic Gospels, such as Jesus's extensive Judean ministry and the Farewell Speech. These portions of his Gospel portray Jesus inevitably somewhat differently than the other three. This fact, among other differences like chronological disparities, has caused many to wonder if the Fourth Evangelist's Jesus-portrait carries the historical likeness of Jesus. How far can we trust the Fourth Evangelist's account of Jesus to be historical reliable?[9] Is John's picture of Jesus merely the Johannine church's post-Eastern, existential-kerygmatic reflection of Christ? Or can we trust the Fourth Evangelist's portrait to carry the likeness of

---

8. Keener, *Christobiography*, 352.
9. Cf. Smith, *The Fourth Gospel in Four Dimensions*, 134.

## The Fourth Evangelist's Jesus

the historical Jesus of Nazareth, which is colored with his theological agenda?[10]

There is evidence that it was acceptable in antiquity for an author to use historical-biographical material in a flexible way. That flexibility did not require verbatim quotations or chronological accuracy, providing elasticity for an author to put the story into his own words.[11]

Our brief overview has made the point: "Johannine Jesus" is distinct from the "Synoptic Jesus" (if we bundle Matthew, Mark, and Luke together). We have demonstrated this by comparing the four narratives of the events, which occur in all the four Gospels, and showing that Jesus's portrait in the FG is painted to bring forth his power, authority, and knowledge in each situation. This does not however, imply that "Johannine Jesus" is unhistorical or radically other than Jesus in the Synoptic Gospels.

### Names

The protagonist in the FG is called in a variety of ways. The following names or titles are used:

- The Word (1:1, 14)
- *Monogenēs theos/huios* (1:18; 3:16, 18)
- Son of God (1:34, 35, 49; 5:25; 10:36; 11:4, 27; 19:7; 20:3)
- Jesus (too many references to be enumerated; the first occurrence is 1:29)
- Jesus Christ (1:17; 17:3)
- The Son (3:19, 36; 5:19–23, 26)
- Son of Man (1:51; 3:13, 14; 5:27; 6:27; 6:53, 62; 8:28; 9:35; 12:23, 34; 13:31)
- A teacher come from God (3:2)

---

10. Rudolf Bultmann popularized the terms "Christ of Faith" (the view of Jesus by the New Testament authors who portrayed him based on what they believed Jesus was) and "Historical Jesus" (referring to the real man who lived and thus related to the term Jesus of Nazareth). He participated in the "Historical Jesus" debate arguing that we do not need to know who he was as a historical person because one's faith is based on the kerygma.

11. Keener, *Christobiography*, 347–48, 350, 353.

- A prophet (4:19; 9:19; cf. 6:14; 7:40)
- The Messiah/Christ (1:20, 25, 41; 3:28; 4:25, 29; 7:26, 27, 31, 41, 42; 9:22; 10:24; 11:11, 20, 27, 31; 12:34; 20:31)
- King of Israel (1:49; cf. 6:15; 12:13)
- King of the Jews (19:19)
- The Holy One of God (6:69)
- The Lamb of God (1:29, 36)
- The Coming One (12:13)
- The Man (19:5)
- The Sent One of God (3:16–17, 34; 5:30; 7:16–18; 10:36)
- *Egō eimi* (too many references to be enumerated; the first occurrence is 4:26)
- A Paraclete (14:16)
- Rabbouni (20:16)
- The Lord (20:18; 21:7; cf. 6:68)
- My Lord and my God (20:28)

We cannot examine all these names, but we will comment on the following: (1) Jesus, (2) the Son of Man, (3) the Son of God, and (4) *Monogenēs* to see how they (and their usage) contribute to the Fourth Evangelist's portrait of Jesus.

## Jesus

The FG employs the name "Jesus" more frequently than any of the other three Gospels. The name Jesus occurs 237 times in John, whereas only 150 times in Matthew, eighty-one times in Mark, eighty-nine times in Luke.[12] This observation is essential since the Fourth Evangelist's presentation of Jesus starts from above and keeps that slant throughout the Gospel. However, "*Logos*" language that refers to Jesus's heavenly status is dropped after the Prologue and his "earthly" name, Jesus, is applied to him.[13] Although this change takes place early on in the FG's account, the

---

12. Smith, *The Fourth Gospel in Four Dimensions*, 81.

13. Porter correctly notes that the *logos*-language is used several times after the Prologue in the Fourth Gospel, in the sense of Jesus's word (*logos*). The *Logos* became "the

reader who knows the secret reads the account with the understanding that the Prologue gives; Jesus is the *Logos* who became flesh (John 1:14a).[14]

A noticeable characteristic of John's presentation of Jesus is that Jesus is audible. He talks, discusses, teaches, explains, rather than performs miraculous deeds. Jesus has face-to-face conversations with individuals who represent various people groups of different levels of society. He speaks to Galileans, Judeans, and Samaritans. He speaks with men and women, leaders, and ordinary people. He also speaks with his enemies and teaches his followers. Jesus has dialogue even with those who came to arrest him, his accusers, and Pilate himself.

Many of the discourses in which Jesus is engaged are lengthy. His dialogues with a member of a Jewish elite (John 3:1–15) and the Samaritan woman (John 4:4–30) are extensive. He engaged in a long debate with his opponents in chapter 8 (vv. 12–59). His Farewell Speech covers roughly four chapters (John 13:33—17:26). In short, the Fourth Gospel contains lots of Jesus's direct speaking, whereas his miraculous acts are limited to a few.

What is the message of these speeches? The answer depends on with or to whom Jesus is speaking. Jesus's conversation with unbelieving people is characterized by Jesus's revelation of his identity (cf. 3:1–15; 4:5–26; 8:12–59). Sometimes these conversations include forensic aspects as well. The rhetorical purpose is to convince the audience to accept Jesus as the God-sent Messiah. However, the evangelist does not always include Jesus's speech even though it seems reasonable to think that he knew that speech. For example, in chapter 7, Jesus's teaching is not included (7:14); only his few responses to Jews at the temple and his final proclamation are provided (7:37b–38).

When Jesus speaks to his disciples or others who have entrusted themselves to him, he focuses on building their trust in him. His trust-building talk is the most obvious in Jesus's Farewell Speech to his eleven faithful disciples in John 13:33—16:33.

---

public spokesperson or proclaimer of God's word." Porter, *John, His Gospel, and Jesus*, 47. We may add to this that there is an ambiguous *logos*-saying in John 17:17 that can be understood as a reference to Jesus as the incarnated *Logos*.

14. Cf. Myers, *Characterizing Jesus*, 183.

## The Son

The title "the Son" for Jesus is prominent in Johannine literature, occurring not less than eighteen times in the FG, five times in 1 John, and once in 2 John. This title occurs only a few times in the Synoptic Gospels. However, it is not only this title and its frequent appearance in the FG, but also its immediate relation to the Father that is important. In other words, the title implies the Father-Son relationship.[15] Since we have discussed the Son-Father relationship above, we move now to look at two other titles that include "the Son," namely, the Son of Man and the Son of God.

### *The Son of Man*

The Son of Man is Jesus's "favorite" self-designation in the FG (1:51; 3:13, 14; 5:27; 6:27, 53, 62; 8:28; 9:35; 12:23; 13:31). It is used only once by Jesus's audience (12:34). The meaning of "the Son of Man" has caused much gray hair for interpreters. However, it seems that Jesus's immediate audience understood its meaning. Jesus's audience in John 12:34 do not ask what he means by "the Son of Man?" but instead, who is he? Similarly, the healed blind man, in John 9:36, responded to Jesus's question, "Do you believe in the Son of Man?" (9:35), asking, "Who is He, Lord, that I may believe in Him?" In other words, he did not have difficulties understanding the address Jesus uses ("the Son of Man"), he just did not know to whom to apply that designation.

Today's readers may find it is somewhat challenging to grasp what the FG means by it. As a mere phrase, "son of man" in Hebrew and Greek means "human being." This meaning, however, does not make much sense if applied to Jesus's self-designation. Jesus uses "the Son of Man" title in revelatory speeches/statements when he addresses Jews. He uses it mainly in the context where he speaks to unbelieving Jews (members of Israel), like Nathanael (1:51), Nicodemus (3:13–14), "Jews" (5:27; 8:28), multitudes (6:27, 53, 62), and the healed man (9:35). Jesus also uses it when he points towards his glorification and lifting up (e.g., 3:13–14; 12:23; 13:31). C. H. Dodd gives a convincing argumentation of what it means. "The Son of Man," Dodd argues, can be understood as an archetypal Man. However, more than that, "the Son of Man" replaces Israel (cf. John 1:51), which is not "the Jewish nation, but the new humanity, reborn

---

15. Schnackenburg, *The Gospel According to St. John*, 2:172.

in Christ, the community of those who are 'of the truth', and of whom Christ is king."[16] Besides, there is a connection between the Servant of the Lord and the Son of Man (cf. Isa 49). The Servant is lifted up (exalted) and glorified, which is realized in the death of the Son of Man on the cross.[17] Dodd concludes, "Thus the term 'Son of Man' throughout this gospel retains the sense of one who incorporates in Himself the people of God, or humanity in its ideal aspect."[18]

## The Son of God

The title "Son of God," used only a few times in the FG, also poses interpretive difficulties. Various explanations of its meaning and background have been offered. In the ancient world, divination of prominent human beings was not foreign.[19] The Roman emperors could have been addressed with the title "son of God."[20] Jewish usage of the title sprang out from the OT where the title belonged to Israel as well as generally to those who belong to God, especially prominent figures like Moses. Keener points out, however, that "The biggest problem with Hellenistic and most Jewish parallels is that, in extant Gospel tradition, Jesus is not merely *a* son of God, but *the* Son of God, his beloved and unique Son."[21] So, how does the Fourth Evangelist use the phrase "the Son of God?"

The title "Son of God" is used by a variety of characters as well as the narrator. It is used by John the Baptist (1:34), Jesus (5:25; 10:36; 11:4; 19:7), Martha (11:27), Jews (19:7), and the narrator/evangelist (3:18; 20:31), always referring to Jesus. On all these occasions, there seems to be a clear understanding of what the title means and that it means more than a "son of God" in Jewish metaphorical sense. This title is clearly linked to Jesus's identity: John the Baptist confesses at Jesus's baptism that now he knows that this Jesus is the Son of God; Martha similarly confesses that Jesus is Christ, the Son of God; Jesus's opponents, the Jews, used Jesus's self-identification as the Son of God as adequate grounds to request his execution by Roman authorities.

---

16. Dodd, *The Interpretation of the Fourth Gospel*, 246.
17. Dodd, *The Interpretation of the Fourth Gospel*, 244–48.
18. Dodd, *The Interpretation of the Fourth Gospel*, 248.
19. Dodd, *The Interpretation of the Fourth Gospel*, 250.
20. See Keener, *The Gospel of John*, 1:291–94.
21. Keener, *The Gospel of John*, 1:295.

Pilate's reaction when he hears that Jesus has claimed to be the Son of God is revealing. He is afraid and immediately returns to Jesus, asking, "Where are you from?" Pilate links this title to the origin of the person, in this case the origin of Jesus. These examples, including Pilate's reaction, suggest that in the FG, the idea of Jesus being the Son of God is not in line with the ancient idea of a man becoming divine. On the contrary, in the FG, it is the divine *Logos* that becomes a man and carries the identity of God's Son.[22]

We suggest, therefore, that the "Son of God" title, having connotations in Jewish usage of "son of God" terminology, is explicitly used to denote Jesus's status and identity. For Jesus's opponents, that title was a stumbling block, but for those who trusted in him, it was their proclamation of his identity.

## Monogenēs

It is only the FG which refers to Jesus by the Greek word *monogenēs* (only, unique). This term is truly Johannine and is found only in 1 John 4:9 outside the FG. In the FG, it is found in John 1:14 in the phrase *monogenous para patros* (only [one] from [the] Father); in John 1:18 in the phrase *monogenēs theos*;[23] in John 3:16 it appears in the phrase *ton huion ton monogenē* (the Son only); and in John 3:18 in the phrase *tou monogenous huiou tou thou* (of the only Son of God).

*Monogenēs* indicates Jesus's unique, one-of-a-kind status and relationship with the Father. Believers are never called "sons" in the FG but rather "children."[24] Confusion regarding this word's meaning is introduced by the English phrase "only-begotten." "Only-begotten" translation of *monogenēs* finds its roots in church history and especially, as one may expect, in Christology. As noted, the word means "only" or "unique" in the sense of "the only example of its category."[25] However, because of the heretical Christological view concerning the origin of Jesus (*Logos*) as first created being, introduced by Arius (c. 256–336 CE), Jerome translated *monogenēs* with the Latin word *unigenitus* (only-begotten) in the Vulgate. *Unigenitus* was to emphasize the idea of begotten in order to

---

22. Cf. Dodd, *The Interpretation of the Fourth Gospel*, 260.
23. Some mss read *ho monogenēs huios* (the only Son).
24. Helyer, *The Witness of Jesus, Paul and John*, 321.
25. Bauer, *A Greek-English Lexicon*, 529.

counter the Arian claim that Jesus was not begotten but made.[26] Nevertheless, although these later connotations were attached to this word, the Fourth Evangelist uses *monogenēs* "to mark out Jesus uniquely above all earthly and heavenly beings; in its use the present soteriological meaning is more strongly stressed than that of origin."[27]

## Jesus among Other Narrative Characters

We start with two quotations. Stephen Smalley says, "The special contribution which John makes to the understanding of Christ's person concerns the relation between Jesus and God on the other hand, and between Jesus and men on the other."[28] Warren Carter notes, "What the characters do and say, how they interact with other characters, what conflicts they experience, and with whom and over what, are fundamental elements of most plots."[29] We will do what these two quotations advise us to do, namely, study what kind of portrait the Fourth Evangelist paints of Jesus in contrast to other narrative characters.

A prominent feature of Jesus-presentation in the FG is that Jesus is brought into contact with other narrative characters. These interactions are masterfully presented to bring forth Jesus's character, role, and identity. Our selection of narrative characters includes five diverse individuals: John the Baptist, Jesus's mother, Mary, the Samaritan woman, and Pilate.[30]

John the Baptist, called "John" in the FG, stands in the central place at the beginning of the FG. In the Prologue and the following narrative in chapter 1, both the *Logos*/Jesus and John the Baptist are introduced and their leading roles revealed; The *Logos*/Jesus is presented in John 1:1–5, 10–14, 16–18, 29–51 whereas John the Baptist is presented in 1:6–9, 15, 19–28. In these passages, John the Baptist is introduced as God's agent, but not as divine, the Light, the Messiah, Elijah, or the Prophet. He is the one who is subordinate to Jesus. Several comments demonstrate this. First, John the Baptist is introduced as a man with a name, John. He came "only" to witness about the light (1:6–9). Secondly, John testifies

26. Bartels, "μόνος," *NIDNTT*, 2:725.
27. Bartels, "μόνος," *NIDNTT*, 2:725.
28. Smalley, *John*, 210.
29. Carter, *John*, 46.
30. We have left out a discussion of "Jews" (like Nicodemus) as a group of characters as this received detailed attention in the previous chapter.

concerning Jesus that Jesus is higher than him in rank (1:15, 30), whose sandals he is not worthy to untie, a task that belonged to servants (1:27); Jesus was before John the Baptist was, and he is God's Lamb and the Son of God (1:15, 29, 34, 35). Thirdly, John the Baptist is the one who prepares the way for Jesus (the Lord) to arrive (i.e., to start his public ministry) (1:23). Fourthly, John expresses Jesus's superiority in his declaration that he baptizes in the water but Jesus will baptize in the Spirit (1:33). Fifthly, he let his disciples follow Jesus (1:37). John the Baptist is still in the "picture" in the third chapter, where he tells his own disciples how Jesus must increase, whereas as his ministry is winding down, he needs to decrease (3:30). In short, John the Baptist's witness concerning Jesus is centered on his identity and task.

Jesus's mother, Mary, is part of the narrative on two occasions; in the beginning of Jesus's public ministry (2:1–11) and at his cross (19:25–26). Such framing is a typical narrative technique to frame the story. In the first narrative at the wedding in Cana, Mary approaches Jesus for a variety of socio-cultural reasons with a statement, "They have no wine" (v. 3). This statement has the illocutionary meaning of request—requesting Jesus to act a certain way, namely, to fix the problem. What follows has frequently puzzled readers. Jesus's response sounds strange. He addresses his mother saying, "Woman." Secondly, his response suggests that he is not going to act; however, he does act beyond all expectations. Without providing a detailed argumentation, we suggest that Mary's actions are embedded in socio-cultural conventions, but Jesus's actions are embedded his identity and role as God's Messiah. Jesus does not take "orders" from anyone else other than from his patron. Jesus is concerned first of all about his mission, to which he also refers by pointing out that this is not yet "his hour."[31]

Mary appears again at the cross of Jesus (19:25–26) where Jesus commissions her to the care of the Beloved Disciple. There are many readings of this narrative ranging from a socio-cultural literal reading to various symbolic if not allegorical readings.[32] There are a few points we want to make here. This time it is Jesus who addresses his mother (using the same "woman" address as in chapter 2) at his hour. This reveals that Mary did not understand what her earlier request set in motion. It led Jesus to the cross. That was why he did not perform the sign as a response

---

31. See Bennema, *Encountering Jesus*, 69–73.
32. See Bennema, *Encountering Jesus*, 73.

to Mary's request but as a response to his Father's will. Also, this occasion shows that Jesus is aware of his responsibility towards his mother. Finally, there may also be symbolic or spiritual meaning intact. Jesus did not commission his mother to the care of her second oldest son, but to care of his disciple. The new kinship group (community of believers) was not only a community for spiritual but also for physical well-being. In short, in these Jesus's interactions with Mary, Jesus is portrayed as the one whose patron is his Father and not his mother, Mary. Mary made herself a broker between the families of the wedding couple and Jesus. Jesus was a broker between the Father and fallen humankind. Therefore, Jesus was especially concerned about his heavenly task to fulfill his Father's will and not his mother's earthly request.

In chapter 4, Jesus interacts with a Samaritan woman (John 4:1–45) who represents people with whom Jews did not have dealings. The Fourth Evangelist has placed Jesus's conversation with Nicodemus (representing the Jewish elite) and a Samaritan woman back to back to in chapters 3 and 4 to bring out the stark contrast between these two individuals and whom they represent. Their contrast is not, however, our interest here. Instead, we want to see how the Fourth Evangelist uses Jesus's encounter with the Samaritan woman to add characteristics to his portrait of Jesus.

Cornelis Bennema notes that Jesus "seems to be under a divine imperative: he *had to go* through Samaria (4:4). He crosses geographical, ethnic, religious, social and gender barriers to meet this complex character—a Samaritan, a woman and a social outcast."[33] Thus, Jesus's encounter with the Samaritan woman reveals much of who Jesus is. As the conversation develops, the Samaritan woman gradually learns more about Jesus (whose name she does not know). The Fourth Evangelist portrays Jesus as one who is in control and above the situation—he knows things about the woman's life, whereas the Samaritan woman does not know the identity of the one speaking to her. Jesus has the living water that can fulfill one's life, whereas the woman had only an empty pitcher to draw water from the well. In the beginning of the encounter, Jesus requires a drink from the woman who can help him. Nevertheless, at the end of the story the situation is turned around; Jesus is the one who can provide the woman with the living water that she desperately needs. At the end of the day, she has learned that this Jewish man is the Messiah.

---

33. Bennema, *Encountering Jesus*, 87.

In short, Jesus is portrayed as the one who is in control and who knows people and the Father. He seeks to do his Father's will, and in the process of doing so, in this case, he crosses over many people-made boundaries. He is not to please people but God who sent him to take "away the sin of the world."

The last narrative character we discuss is Pilate (John 18:28—19:22). He is a Roman official who wields power and represents the most significant world power of the time. The closer reading of the narrative reveals that Pilate acted according to his own agenda, mocking both Jesus and the Jews. Jesus's encounter with him shows that, whereas Pilate was seeking his own well-being, Jesus was not seeking his own well-being but rather his Father's will. Jesus also corrects Pilate's misunderstanding that he holds the power to do whatever he wants with him—to free or to crucify him. Jesus informs Pilate who has power and who is guilty of a greater sin. In short, the Fourth Evangelist portrays Jesus once again as one who is in control as he stays faithful to the will of the Father.

These examples of the portraits of Jesus in the FG lead us to conclude that the Fourth Evangelist's Jesus is portrayed as somewhat stronger, more "superhuman" than is done in the Synoptic Gospels. Jesus is a less vulnerable individual in the FG than in the Synoptics. This, according to Thomas Dowell, indicates that the Fourth Evangelist's motive to present high Christology is a response to non-believing Jewish arguments based on the Synoptic Gospels' portrait of Jesus as "more" human and a perhaps weaker figure who can thus be ignored.[34]

## Jesus as a New Temple

Scholars have suggested that the FG contains replacement Christology. Jesus replaces or fulfills various feasts. Also, it is argued that Jesus is the new Torah. The Prologue's statement, "For the Law was given through Moses; grace and truth were realized through Jesus Christ" (John 1:17; cf. 1:45; 7:23) among other texts has led to that conclusion. Keener convincingly argues that the FG presents the *Logos* as the Torah. This idea is also seen later in the Gospel when Jesus points out that if the opposing Jews do not accept him, they reject the Torah (John 5:45–47). It is important to note that Jesus was not against the Torah. Torah was God's revelation

---

34. Dowell, "Why John Rewrote the Synoptics," 453, 454.

also for him. Jesus as the new Torah fulfilled the Law rather than disregarded it.[35]

Also, the Fourth Evangelist presents Jesus as a new temple who replace the tabernacle/temple and its cult. By the time of writing the FG, the Jerusalem Temple had already been destroyed. We consider Jesus's replacement of the temple and its cult, including the historical post-temple era, as a significant Christological motif in the FG.[36]

Below, we will identify the key texts in the FG, which bring Jesus-as-a-new-temple understanding to the readers' attention. Then we study Jesus's attitude towards the existing temple and the Jewish response to post-temple reality. Finally, we will investigate replacement Christology in the FG where Jesus is offered as the solution to the lack of the Jerusalem Temple.

## Temple and Israel

The Jerusalem Temple, and its predecessor, the Tabernacle were essential places of worship for Israelites. Not only was the existence of the Jerusalem Temple colorful, its centrality in YHWH worship is undeniable. There are various reasons for its vivid history. God himself designed the Tabernacle, requesting Moses to build it according to a God-given plan (Exod 25:9; 40:2–11). The Tabernacle was a holy place where YHWH's presence dwelt and where Israel approached YHWH by observing the God-given instructions of various sacrifices. However, the Tabernacle's time was over when the Israelites reached the Promised Land, and a desire to build a more magnificent place for YHWH worship was born. Although God did not command the Israelites to build the temple, he gave his approval.

The First Temple was built by king Solomon (968 BCE). It was an important place for Israel since God's name rested there (1 Kgs 8:27–28). The temple and its location were important (Deut 12:5, 11, 21; 14:24–25). The temple was, among other things, "a unifier of the Jewish people" and "the place where God is available to the human being."[37] Jews viewed it as "the center of the world, and the specified spot where

---

35. Attridge, "The Temple and Jesus," 1:360–63.
36. Cf. Ostenstand, *Patterns of Redemption in the Fourth Gospel*, xxi.
37. Schiffman, "The Importance of the Temple," 76–77.

heaven meets earth . . . the only official site for worship and sacrifice according to the Pentateuch."[38]

The First Temple was laid in ruins during the Babylonian exile. Zerubbabel built the so-called Second Temple (515 BCE) when Israel returned from Babylon to Judea and Jerusalem. Later, when Antiochus Epiphanes desecrated the temple, it caused turmoil and rebellion among Jews. The Maccabean revolt ended successfully with the re-dedication of the temple and altar (Hanukkah), bringing extraordinary joy to Jews. The Second Temple was replaced by the so-called Herodian Temple (37 BCE—70 CE). The Herodian Temple was the one that was standing during the time of Jesus. It was destroyed during the second unsuccessful Jewish revolt in 68–70 CE.

Jesus and the first believers (the church) were a part of Israel—a part of the temple worship community. Several passages in the Gospels and Acts indicate the early believers' positive attitude toward the temple. Jesus ministered in the temple and went up to the temple, as did Peter, John, and Paul. Their positive attitude toward the temple itself does not mean, however, that they would have been fully satisfied with the temple cult. There were also other groups who did not share the same view of the temple cult as mainline Judaism. Samaritans had their temple for worship on Mount Gerizim. The Essenes (or Qumran community) did not accept the Jerusalem Temple's worship and its sacrifices because they held that the priesthood was corrupt if not evil. Similar disapproval is recognized in Jesus's words and actions when he cleanses the temple during the Passover feast. Jesus did this, however, to honor the temple as his Father's House.[39] In other words, Jesus was not *against* the temple, but rather *for* proper usage of the temple.

## Jesus as a New Temple

Regardless of Jesus's passion towards the temple, the FG also portrays Jesus as the one who fulfills and replaces the temple and its cult. There are convincing arguments that the tabernacle, as well as the temple, are types; Jesus is their antitype. A proponent of this view is Paul M. Hoskins, on whose observations we lean in this regard. Hoskins emphasizes the following features of typology.

38. Charlesworth, "Jesus and the Temple," 148.
39. Charlesworth, "Jesus and the Temple," 178–80.

[T]he antitype fulfills significant patterns and predictions associated in the Old Testament with the type. This accounts for noticeable points of correspondence or similarity between them. Second, as the goal and fulfillment to which the imperfect type pointed, the antitype goes beyond or surpasses the patterns and predictions associated with the type. As a result, some noticeable dissimilarities exist between the type and the antitype. Third, the first two points lead to the conclusion that the New Testament antitype also fills the place of or replaces the Old Testament type.[40]

Using a typological reading, Hoskins argues that Jesus is not only the replacement but also the fulfillment of the temple. There are several other studies on this topic as well which use various sets of texts.[41] We have chosen the following passages for our study: John 1:14, 51; 2:13–22; 4:20–26; 9:30–38; 14:1–6. All these texts, except the latter two, are usually referred in studies of the topic.

## John 1:14

Our attention in John 1:14 is directed especially towards two ideas: (1) that the incarnated *Logos* "dwelt among us" and (2) his "glory." The verb "dwell" (*skēnō*), is a rare word in the NT, found only here and in the book of Revelation. Two nouns from the same root, *skēnos* and *skēnōma*, mean "tent." John 1:14 is not just indicating what the incarnated *Logos* did, namely "dwelt" among people, but also the way in which he was dwelling, namely "tenting." Tenting is connected to the idea of his "temporary" stay on earth. It can also be connected, and correctly so, to the Tabernacle (the "tent," cf. Exod 33:7). The Septuagint translates "the Tabernacle" with "tent" (*skēnē*). John 1:14 bridges the tabernacle, where God's presence was experienced, and the incarnated *Logos*, in whom God's presence is available. The incarnated *Logos* replaced or fulfilled the tabernacle that used to stand in the midst of Israel.

It is also possible that "tent" which is a metaphorical word for human body in the NT, points toward the idea of Jesus's body as the temple, that is, the place where God dwells.[42] This supports the reading that Je-

---

40. Hoskins, *Jesus as the Fulfillment of the Temple*, 22.
41. See Köstenberger, *A Theology of John's Gospel and Letters*, 423–24.
42. Koester, *Dwelling of God*, 102.

sus's body is a new tabernacle as "God's dwelling place among his people takes on a new form, a human body" (cf. below John 2:13–22).[43]

Also, "glory" in John 1:14 is linked to the tabernacle and temple. As God's glory filled the tabernacle, the incarnated *Logos* was locus of God's glory, explicitly disclosed in his suffering.

## John 1:51

"Truly, truly, I say to you, you will see the heavens opened and the angels of God ascending and descending on the Son of Man" (John 1:51) is the second half of Jesus's response to Nathanael's conclusion, "You are the Son of God; You are the King of Israel" (1:49). Although Jesus is engaged in conversation with Nathanael, which is also demonstrated in the narrator's introductory phrase, "And He [Jesus] said to him" (v. 51a), Jesus's response is not addressed to Nathanael alone. Jesus uses the second person plural "you" in his response. The plural "you" may refer to all Israelites (cf. 1:47). Jesus alludes to Jacob's Bethel experience, the vision of ladder and angels. He also quotes directly the phrase, "angels of God were ascending and descending," from Genesis 28:12. In addition, Jesus's "true Israelite" address connects Nathanael to Jacob, whose name was changed to Israel.

The typological reading of 1:51 (Jacob's experience as a type and Jesus's proclamation as an antitype) suggests the following. First, God's angels ascending and descending in the ladder vision symbolize communication between heaven and earth, which is now realized in Jesus. Second, Jacob's Bethel is now Jesus, who is the new place of God's communication.[44] Finally, the Son of Man as God's means for revelation and as God's revelation among men surpasses (i.e., is greater than)[45] Jacob's experience. These correspondences relate to the tabernacle and temple motif in the FG since Jesus as a locus of God's revelation surpasses all other previous means and places of God's revelation, including the

---

43. Hoskins, *Jesus as the Fulfillment of the Temple*, 118.

44. See Hoskins, *Jesus as the Fulfillment of the Temple*, 130–33, for discussion how to read the Hebrew text in Genesis 28:12, namely, whether the angels descended and ascended "on it" (i.e., ladder) or "on him" (i.e., Jacob).

45. Cf. Keener, *The Gospel of John*, 1:488.

tabernacle and the temple. Hoskins concludes, "he [Jesus] is a suitable replacement for these [Bethel, tabernacle, and temple] holy places."[46]

### John 2:13–22

In the second half of chapter 2, Jesus is in Jerusalem for the first time.[47] He cleanses the temple from all merchandize that was being bought and sold, probably inside the temple walls. There are many interesting questions regarding this event, but here we only discuss Jesus's response to the Jews' question, "What sign do You show us as your authority for doing these things?" (2:18), and the narrator's comments that are directly related to Jesus's action.

Several points relate directly to the replacement motif. First, the narrator notes that the disciples "remembered" Psalm 69:9. This citation points out that king David's zeal for the temple prefigures Christ's zeal for the temple.[48] Here, Jesus's zeal for the temple probably works in two ways. It demonstrates that he is not against the physical temple. It is indeed his Father's house. But on the other hand, it also points towards his cross. His body is the new temple of God that leads to a new reality where his people will be a new temple on earth (the locus in which God's Spirit resides, cf. John 14:16—16:15; 20:19–22) after his glorification.

Secondly, the Jews' request for a sign is interesting because the cleansing of the temple already was a sign of Jesus's zeal for his Father's house. Nevertheless, Jesus promises the other sign, namely that his body (*naos*) will be re-built in three days after its destruction. Jesus's choice of the word "temple" as a reference to his body is a proclamation of a new reality. He is the new temple that provides the point of contact between heaven and earth, between YHWH and his people. The sign of that reality is that the new temple will be destroyed but will be raised again in three days. The narrator gives commentary on Jesus's words explaining their meaning, which were understood only after his resurrection. There is a good reason to think that the evangelist, writing after the destruction

---

46. Hoskins, *Jesus as the Fulfillment of the Temple*, 135. Cf. Keener, *The Gospel of John*, 1:489–90.

47. We suggest that this is not chronologically the first Passover which Jesus spends in Jerusalem during his public ministry. Instead, this seems to be his last Passover in Jerusalem just prior to his crucifixion. See Part Three below.

48. Hoskins, *Jesus as the Fulfillment of the Temple*, 111.

of the Jerusalem Temple, deliberately included this incidence into his account, promoting the centrality of Jesus's importance and role.

### John 4:20–26

Jesus's conversation with a Samaritan woman includes a conversation about the place of worship. The Samaritan woman refers to the historical site of the Samaritan Temple on Mount Gerizim. That temple was destroyed by John Hyrcanus in 129 BCE and was still lying in ruins. The mountain was an important place as it was the God-chosen place for the proclamation of blessing (cf. Deut 11:29; 27:12). The Samaritan woman did not have the opportunity to go to the Jerusalem Temple to worship because she was from Samaria. Therefore, she might have thought that if Jesus was the prophet, as she believed at this point of conversation, perhaps Jesus could give her the solution of where to worship God. Jesus gives the solution: worship that pleases God does not need to take place in one particular location, including the Jerusalem Temple and Mount Gerizim in Samaria, but is a worship that is performed "in spirit and in truth" (John 4:23–24). Since "God is spirit," God can be worshiped anytime and anywhere. It is God alone who can "source" a human to worship this manner.[49] In the FG, it is emphasized that it is Jesus who makes the Spirit available for people through his glorification. Therefore, Jesus's teaching about worship includes a proclamation of his role. No-one can satisfactorily worship God without God's Messiah Jesus—the new temple.

### John 9:30–38

Jesus's healing of the man born blind has not received much attention in FG's temple replacement motif. However, there are a few significant elements in the narrative that suggest Jesus's role as a new temple.

The healing incident takes place in immediate proximity of the temple, and its aftermath takes place at the temple. The man's condition seems to be linked in Jewish thinking to some kind of sinful action, most likely his parents' sin before his birth (John 9:2, 34).[50] As a healed person, he enters the temple before the Pharisees (9:13; later in the narrative called Jews cf. 9:18). At the end of the hearing, he is, however, thrown

---

49. Hoskins, *Jesus as the Fulfillment of the Temple*, 141.
50. Brown, *The Gospel According to John*, 1:371.

out of the temple. After meeting again with Jesus, he puts his faith in him and *worships* him (9:38). In short, the man born blind finds the place of YHWH worship in Jesus.

There is another angle in this story that fits with the replacement-fulfillment motif. In Jewish thought, only the worship of righteous, Torah-observant persons, pleases God. "Cause and result" theology is explicitly emphasized also in this narrative (9:31). Jews were allowed to think that God's righteousness was demonstrated in the blind man's condition since sin had caused his condition. The Jewish notion of God's righteousness could lead one even to praise God for the man's condition; God has judged sin which is explicit now in this man's condition. However, Jesus demonstrates that this kind of Jewish notion of God is incorrect. God is merciful, and Jesus, performing the deed of the Father, heals the man born blind.

The healing was undeniable. Thus, the Pharisees/Jews turned against Jesus because he performed the miracle on the Sabbath day. This was a clear indicator for them that Jesus was not from God, but a sinner. The healed man, a Jew himself and acquainted with Jewish theological notions, recognized the contradiction. How can the prayers of a sinful man be heard by God, particularly the prayer to heal a man born blind? He concludes that this man, Jesus, must come from God. In short, the healed man defeats his interrogators using their own theology. He becomes an object lesson to unbelieving Jews that now true worshipers of God are those who believe in Jesus. The old covenant worship in the temple has reached its end, and new covenant worship in Jesus has dawned. Those who do not accept Jesus as a new locus of worship, remain unknown to God, and their worship is a mere religious action.

## John 14:1–6

Jesus's Farewell Speech to his faithful disciples is also connected to the replacement-fulfillment motif. The key text regarding the replacement-fulfillment, John 14:1–6, includes two items that require careful reading.[51] First, the phrase "many dwelling places" (*monai pollai*) communicates availability. The word "many" (*pollai*), in the FG's soteriological context, is best understood in terms of universality (cf. John 1:29). The first word,

---

51. See Hoskins's discussion of scholarly arguments for and against our view; Hoskins, *Jesus as the Fulfillment of the Temple*, 12–18.

*monai* is translated in several ways in modern English translations. It is translated "dwelling places" (NASB, NET), "rooms" (ESV, NIV) and "mansions" (ASV, KJV).

The idea of "mansions" as a large, stately house comes from Latin *mansio*. This Latin translation is perhaps inspired by Origen's understanding of *monai* as stations on the way to God (cf. Gnosticism). Latin *mansio* means a "stopping place," but Middle English "mansion" means a permanent dwelling place.[52] For this reason, English translations that use the word "mansions" cannot be used to support the view that Jesus is speaking here about fancy heavenly homes that his followers will occupy one day. This is not what the evangelist meant.

The translation of *monai* as "rooms" is probably inspired by the building style and layout of the city of Rome at the time. "Rooms" translation may also give the impression that Jesus is speaking here about heaven as the final destination.

However, the most convincing interpretation of *monai* (dwelling places) is the one that derives its meaning from the cognate verb *menō* (to dwell, to remain). The verb *menō* conveys the idea of a permanent relationship in the FG (cf. John 15:4–10). The permanent relationship is explicit in Jesus's words in his same speech, "My Father will love him [who loves Jesus], and We will come to him and make Our abode [*monai*] with him" (John 14:23b).

The other phrase, "My Father's house" is often understood as the heaven where Jesus goes to prepare the place and then when everything is ready, he will call his people there. This reading, however, is not convincing since Jesus proclaims in the same theological context that he is the only way to the Father (John 14:6). But Jesus does not mean that we come to the Father only when we die. Instead, people's coming to the Father is possible now through Jesus. Keeping this in mind, "My Father's house" seems to refer to Jesus as the new temple (cf. John 2:19). Since Jesus is the new temple that was about to be built in three days (John 2:19), then God's permanent relationship with his people is going to be made possible in Jesus. Jesus's "going to prepare the place" refers to his cross and resurrection. It is noticeable that Jesus already had a permanent relationship with his Father. Now he was about to make that possible for others through his suffering. Therefore, Jesus appropriately proclaims that he

---

52. See NET notes (John 14:2).

is the way, the truth, and the life, and that nobody comes to the Father except through him (John 14:6).

We conclude with a quotation from Keener, in which he brings together the idea of Jesus as a new temple and the OT's promises of God's permanent dwelling among his people.

> [I]n the Fourth Gospel the eschatological temple is clearly in Jesus himself. Since the temple would naturally be viewed as a dwelling of the deity and the hope of Israel was God's covenant-dwelling among them (Rev 21:3, 22), the point of the text [John 14:2] would not have been difficult to grasp. In Scripture, God had promised to dwell among his covenant people (Lev 26:12; Ezek 37:26–28); in the new covenant, God would put his laws in their hearts (Jer 31:33).[53]

## Post-Temple Judaism

The historical-religious situation in Jewish life at the time of the Fourth Evangelist's composition of the FG should also be given due attention. It gives insight why Jesus as the fulfillment-replacement of the temple is such a prominent motif in the FG.

Jewish life was greatly affected by the Jewish wars in 66–70 CE and the Bar Kokhba revolt in 132–35 CE. The results of these wars were devastating. Instead of past military success (the Maccabean revolt in 167–60 BCE), the Jews were utterly defeated. The effect of the first defeat was especially shocking; Jews lost Jerusalem and the Jerusalem Temple. "The event called into question Israel's status as the chosen and protected people of God, and thus provoked 'a profound and far-reaching crisis in their inner and spiritual existence.'"[54] Jewish religious life had to re-organize itself because the central and unifying institution, the Jerusalem Temple, was no longer standing. On the other hand, various Jewish sects ceased to exist. This did not mean, however, that Judaism would have become a unified religion. That happened to some degree and in more systematic ways over a period of time when orthodox Judaism was developed.[55]

---

53. Keener, *The Gospel of John*, 2:936.
54. Motyer, *Your Father the Devil?*, 77.
55. Motyer argues that diversity continued in Judaism after the first Jewish war until the second war (132–35 CE), after which "rabbinic orthodoxy" became an authentic and unifying voice of Judaism. Motyer, *Your Father the Devil?*, 75–77.

After 70 CE, the defeated Jews experienced significant "trauma." This is understandable since "for all Jews, the Temple stood at the place where God had caused His presence to dwell, the place to which all prayers were turned, the place where a God who could not be contained in the universe He had created could somehow be found waiting for His people."[56] Therefore, various activities were invented to fill the gap that the temple's non-existence created. Lawrence Schiffman notes, "rabbinic Judaism as a whole, after the destruction of the Second Temple, would see Torah study and prayer and the Jewish home as a symbolic replacement for the Temple. This symbolism is represented in so many rituals: lighting the Sabbath candles is like lighting the Menorah, and putting the challah bread on the table beforehand is like setting the bread of the showbread table."[57]

The Fourth Evangelist wrote in this context. His message was that God's Messiah, Jesus of Nazareth, replaced the temple. The resurrected Jesus is the center of worship in whom one, Jews and Gentiles, can find God's presence. The FG's message is that there is no need to imitate the Jewish feasts nor the temple cult since Jesus has fulfilled and replaced them all. Jesus is where God's presence dwells, the name in which one is to pray in order to be heard, and the one in whom the entire world would find life eternal (cf. John 1:29; 14:13).

## Concluding Remarks

In this chapter, we have observed various topics regarding the Fourth Evangelist's portrait of Jesus. Based on our study we can suggest the following. First, the FG's Jesus is on two journeys simultaneously. He is on the earthly journey from incarnation to the fulfillment of the work of the cross and on the heavenly journey from the Father to back the Father via fulfillment of being God's Lamb. Since Jesus is on his Father's mission, he always remains in control and focused during his earthly journey. He performs the deeds and speaks the words of the Father as a Jewish man along the way toward the climax and turning point of the narrative, the cross. Secondly, Jesus is portrayed as an audible rabbi rather than as a miracle worker. This might have been the Fourth Evangelist's deliberate choice as he wrote in the context where rabbinic Judaism was forming. Thirdly, Jesus is presented as the fulfillment-replacement of the temple.

---

56. Schiffman, "The Importance of the Temple," 93.
57. Schiffman, "The Importance of the Temple," 85.

He is the new locus of God's presence, the place where prayers are heard, and the center of YHWH worship. This aspect of the Fourth Evangelist's portrait of Jesus is also seen in his words and deeds at Jewish feasts as mentioned in Chapter Two.

We are confident to suggest that Jesus's portrait in the FG is affected not only by the accounts of the evangelist and eyewitnesses, but by the historical context in general and the Jewish "trauma" following the destruction of Jerusalem and the Jerusalem Temple in particular. Israel, as a scattered nation, was seeking the way forward. It formed a theology of what it meant to be God's chosen people and the religious expression thereof in a new and unexpected situation. Early Christianity, since the time of the apostle Paul, communicated the message about the fulfillment of God's promises in Jesus. In the 70 CE post-war context, the Fourth Evangelist has found a new leverage to produce s persuasive gospel account.

## Suggestions for Further Reading

Anderson, Paul N. *The Fourth Gospel and the Quest for Jesus: Modern Foundations Reconsidered*. London: T&T Clark, 2007.

Charlesworth, James H. (ed). *Jesus and Temple: Textual and Archaeological Explorations*. Minneapolis: Fortress, 2014. Pp. 75–86, 145–82, 213–38.

Hoskins, Paul M. *Jesus as the Fulfillment of the Temple in the Gospel of John*. Bucks: Paternoster, 2006.

Smith, D. Moody. *The Fourth Gospel in Four Dimensions: Judaism and Jesus, the Gospels and Scripture*. South Carolina: University of South Carolina Press, 2008. Pp. 47–143.

CHAPTER 12

# The Fourth Gospel among First Three

THE FG'S RELATION TO the Synoptic Gospels has generated many studies and various conclusions.[1] It is also perhaps "the oldest historical-critical problem in the history of the church."[2] The Fourth Evangelist's knowledge and usage of the Synoptic Gospels have been viewed differently in different periods in the history of Johannine scholarship. Robert Fortna and Tom Thatcher outline the history of that discussion as follows:

> Early in the twentieth century, most scholars believed that the Fourth Evangelist . . . had drawn much of his material from the Synoptic Gospels . . . by mid-century, the consensus had moved toward the notion that F[ourth] E[vangelist] either did not know about the Synoptics or did not care to use them if he did . . . [B]y the mid-1970s the tide began to turn once again . . . as C. K. Barrett and Franz Neirynck, who argued that certain parallels between FG and the Synoptics can only be explained under the theory that F[ourth] E[vangelist] borrowed material from those works. Today, there is no solid consensus on the sources F[ourth] E[vanglist] used to compose his gospel.[3]

It is easily noticeable that the Synoptic Gospels are similar to each other. They share the same stories and use similar language. However, the Fourth Evangelist's account is drastically different. Even when the Fourth Evangelist records seemingly the same story as the Synoptics, it

---

1. The most recent is North, *What John Knew and What John Wrote*.
2. Smith, *The Fourth Gospel in Four Dimensions*, 166.
3. Fortna and Thatcher, *Jesus in Johannine Traditions*, 113.

usually differs greatly from their account(s) in vocabulary, point of view, and sometimes even in timing. For example, the story when Jesus fed the five thousand with five loaves of bread and two fish (John 6:1–15) has narrative features which are missing or different from the Synoptic versions of the same event (see above). Or, the story about Jesus cleansing the Jerusalem Temple differs not only in its literary presentation but also in its chronological occurrence. These narratives are examples of three apparent differences between the FG and the Synoptic Gospels: limited literary agreements, theological usage of the narrative, and chronological differences.

Below we will discuss the issue of limited literary agreements between the Synoptic Gospels and the FG. This discussion inevitably includes the Fourth Evangelist's sources and whether he used one or more Synoptic Gospels as his source. Then we will conduct a brief study on the FG's genre and theology. In that section, we will also point out the chronological concerns, but that issue will be discussed more in detail below (Chapter 15). Finally, in this chapter, we will outline the most common suggestions for a solution to the question, "What is the relationship between the Synoptic Gospels and the Gospel of John?"

## Limited Literary Agreements

We will look at three examples of limited literary agreements. First, we will look at the story shared by the Synoptic Evangelist and the Fourth Evangelist, but which shows limited literary agreement. Secondly, we will look at the situation where the Fourth Evangelist and the Synoptics use the same vocabulary, but in different ways or on different occasions. Finally, we give an example of a story in the FG that does not occur in the Synoptic Gospels.

### The Same Story—Different Presentation

Each evangelist includes a narrative that describes events and discourses at the table of the Last Supper. Despite many similarities, there are significant differences. The Fourth Evangelist omits the bulk of material found in the Synoptics' accounts and adds a significant amount of material that is not found in them. The most apparent differences are the FG's omission of the Last Supper meal and the inclusion of Jesus's long Farewell Speech not found in the Synoptic Gospels.

The Fourth Evangelist seems to emphasize the theological significance of Jesus's passion rather than the event itself as he leaves out the preparation narrative of the Last Supper (cf. Luke 22:7–13), the meal itself (cf. Luke 22:14–20), and the dispute among the disciples around the Supper table (cf. Luke 22:24–27). The Fourth Evangelist brings forth the love (loyalty) motif throughout the Last Supper narrative (John 13:1, 34–35; 14:15; 15:12–17; cf. 15:18—16:4; 17:23–26). Jesus demonstrates his love (loyalty) by washing his disciples' feet and by moving towards the cross. He urges his disciples to model their love according to the love that he has shown to them. As an example of disloyalty stands Judas Iscariot, who leaves Jesus and the rest of the disciples. Another significant motif in the FG's Last Supper narrative is its emphasis on the disciples' post-resurrection life. Jesus's promises his presence in the form of the Spirit-Paraclete.

It is noteworthy that the FG does not include the breaking the bread narrative or even its theological significance. There is nothing at all regarding Jesus instituting the Eucharist. The Fourth Evangelist is not concentrating on the new covenant as the Synoptic evangelists are, but rather, as noted above, on the new commandment—the love that the disciples should demonstrate.

The Fourth Evangelist gives much space to footwashing, which is not found in the Synoptic Gospels. The footwashing is part of Jesus's teaching regarding being a servant of others that rests on the "love" motif. The "servant" teaching is not entirely missing from Luke's account as Jesus refers to it in Luke 22:26–27, but that theme is not developed and not taught by using the object lesson of footwashing.

In summary, although each evangelist includes the Last Supper narrative in his Gospel accounts, there are significant differences between the Synoptic Gospels and the FG. The Synoptic Gospels, as one can expect, share a much tighter literary presentation. Other examples of these same limited literary agreements are seen in the FG's different narrative of Jesus's baptism, cleansing the Jerusalem Temple, the resurrection narrative, and how Jesus deals with Peter after his denial.

## Uniquely Employed Different or the Same Vocabulary

All evangelists use the phrase "kingdom of God." It is most often found in Luke (thirty-one times), Mark (fourteen times) and a few times in Matthew (five times). The First Evangelist's synonym for the kingdom of God, namely, the "kingdom of Heaven," occurs thirty times in his account. The Fourth Evangelist does not use the "kingdom of heaven" and limits the "kingdom of God" vocabulary to one discourse where the phrase is used twice. That is when Jesus teaches Nicodemus how one can enter (or see) the kingdom of God (John 3:3, 5).

Mark's Gospel gives a hint that Jesus might have been using "the kingdom of God" and "eternal life" phrases interchangeably, and that this is behind Jesus's usage of "eternal life" phrase in the FG.[4] Jesus in Mark 10:24 is speaking about entering the kingdom of God, and a few verses later, in 10:30, he is talking about the future blessings in terms of "eternal life." Blomberg suggests that the Fourth Evangelist might have chosen to follow "eternal life" vocabulary because he "is contextualizing the Gospel for a Graeco-Roman world that frequently discussed the nature of life after death but was unfamiliar with the uniquely Jewish forms of theocracy."[5] If Blomberg's conclusion is correct, it is quite reasonable for the Fourth Evangelist to use "the kingdom of God" vocabulary when Jesus is having a conversation with a Jewish aristocrat in John chapter 3, but "eternal life" in all other places.

Another example is the "Son of Man" sayings. These sayings are found in all four Gospels, Jesus being the speaker. Moreover, it is found in the same unique format: the Greek in the Synoptics and the FG (except on one occasion, John. 5:27) reads *ho huios tou anthrōpou* (the son of the man) using the article twice.[6] However, "*none* of John's 'Son of Man' sayings find a parallel in the Synoptics."[7] In this case the same vocabulary is employed but such a way that still demonstrate limited literary agreement between the Synoptic Gospels and the FG.

---

4. Cf. Smith, *Fourth Gospel in Four Dimensions*, 170.
5. Blomberg, *The Historical Reliability of John's Gospel*, 50.
6. Wink, "'The Son of Man' in the Gospel of John," 117.
7. Wink, "'Son of Man' in the Gospel of John," 117.

## Narratives Not Found in The Synoptics

The FG has several narratives not found in the Synoptics. For example, Jesus's dealing with the first disciples and Nathanael, Jesus's presence in the weddings at Cana, and Jesus's encounters with Nicodemus and the Samaritan woman are genuinely Johannine. The list goes on and on. The most extended single narrative not found in the Synoptics is Jesus's Farewell Speech.

Every Gospel includes a narrative of Jesus's time with his disciples just before his cross. The Fourth Evangelist is the only one who includes Jesus's lengthy and "formal" Farewell Discourse. He gives a significant space (one-third of his Gospel, chs. 13–19) to twenty-four hours of Jesus's passion. Jesus's speech (13:33—17:26) in that section receives noticeable attention. Although the Synoptic Gospels include some of the Last Supper events, John surpasses them in a great deal, including information not found in the Synoptics.

These examples have demonstrated the limited literary agreement between these two bodies of Gospel writings. The relationship questions are not answered only by looking at this aspect of evidence. Blomberg reminds that "the only way one can confidently declare a literary relationship between two documents without explicit external or internal statements about the author's procedure is when exact verbal parallels in the language of two texts recur."[8] However, since this does not happen, studies on the FG's relation to the Synoptics have taken directions beyond mere literary agreements. Thus, we will turn next to look at FG's genre, theology, and chronology.

## Question of Genre, Theology, and Chronology

Genre, theology, and chronology are components that one should pay attention to while tackling the question of the FG's relationship with the Synoptic Gospels. If one attempts to establish an argument for FG's dependence on or independence from the Synoptic Gospels, then these three areas need to be considered.

---

8. Blomberg, *The Historical Reliability of John's Gospel*, 46.

## Genre

The FG is cast into a historical-narrative genre. Today's scholarship, however, has further defined its genre as a biography. Several literary features in the FG share similarities with ancient bibliographies. The FG tells the story of the protagonist, Jesus, concentrating on his significance. The author carries this out by focusing on Jesus's deeds and teachings that are crucial to build the protagonist's portrait. It was not necessary to include one's childhood in ancient *bioi* as it did not (or it was not considered to) contribute to the description, who the person was, and the person's main contribution, teaching, or influence. Also, the FG's size and structure fit the first-century biographies.[9]

Characterization, which is a part of the ancient biographies, occurs in various ways in the FG. The Fourth Evangelist characterizes his protagonist right in the beginning of his account. He begins before the beginning revealing his protagonist's divine identity. The Synoptic Gospels argue differently for Jesus's identity in their opening chapters. Matthew and Luke include sections on Jesus's ancestry and birth. Mark builds Jesus's characterization by referring the Scriptures.

The ancient *bioi* also included the idea of purpose rather than mere information about that protagonist's life. The purpose could have been to praise the person, give an example to others to follow, preserve the character's memory, or even to fulfil polemical purposes. The Fourth Evangelist has the goal to persuade his readers to accept the protagonist as a God-sent agent for eternal life.

In short, there are several similarities between the FG and ancient biographies. That is the case also with other canonical Gospels. The Fourth Evangelist, however, has used "all" the freedom that the genre gives him.[10] Thus even though the genre is the same in all canonical Gospels, the FG differs significantly from the Synoptics' presentations.[11]

Who first wrote with the gospel genre that shares similarities with the ancient biography? Although several other non-canonical works carry the name "gospel," they do not share features with the gospel genre used by the canonical Gospel authors. Some of those works are not preserved well enough to determine their literary text type. Some are known to us only through the early church Fathers who quoted them

---

9. Culpepper, *The Gospel and Letter of John*, 65–66. Cf. Carter, *John*, 9–12.
10. Keener, *Christobiography*, 346–50; see also 303–27.
11. Blomberg, *The Historical Reliability of John's Gospel*, 58.

in their writings. That does not give adequate ground to determine their genre. Blomberg notes that "What little does exist may suggest that these were simply amalgamations of material from the canonical Gospels with some additions and alterations."[12] Neither "gospels" that are a part of Nag Hammadi library nor the well-known Gospel of Thomas share the same genre with the four Gospels. They are a mere collection of sayings or Gnostic writings that alter the NT Gospels' content and presentation of that content. They do not fit the same genre as the Gospels in the NT. There are still other "gospels" that are fictional attempts to bridge the gap in Jesus's life not told elsewhere. Such gospels, like the Gospels of Peter, Nicodemus, and Bartholomew, differ in genre from the known four Gospels.[13] The Johannine scholarship is quite united that the gospel genre is an invention of the NT evangelists.

Thus, if such a genre is not found outside of the four canonical Gospels, it is reasonable to think that the Fourth Evangelist employs the genre of the previously written Gospels. It would be difficult to believe that he re-invented the gospel-*bios* genre not knowing that it already existed. Although there is no consensus among scholars which one of the Synoptic writings the Fourth Evangelist might have known, it is agreed that he did not deliberately or accidentally create the gospel genre. We can concur with Moody Smith, "the view that John must have been dependent on the Synoptics—at least for its genre—gets a friendly reception."[14] A rather more hesitant conclusion comes from many other Johannine scholars, who say that John is closer to Matthew, Mark, and Luke more than any other writings regarding the genre question.[15]

## Theology

A comparative study of theology in the Synoptics and the FG would be an immense task. Here we can but scratch the surface of this topic. We will do this by looking at the FG's ecclesiology, Christology, and pneumatology. There is no lack of these theologies in the Synoptic Gospels, but they are presented somewhat differently in the FG.

---

12. Blomberg, *The Historical Reliability of John's Gospel*, 58.
13. Blomberg, *The Historical Reliability of John's Gospel*, 58–59.
14. Smith, *The Fourth Gospel in Four Dimensions*, 154.
15. Dunn, "Let John Be John," 338–39.

## Ecclesiology

The FG's ecclesiology is a prominent topic even though it does not use the word *ekklēsia*, which many other NT authors, including the First Evangelist, use. English translations render it "church" when "Christian assembly" is denoted. Matthew is the only evangelist who employs the term *ekklēsia* (Matt 16:18; 18:17) in his Gospel. Luke does not use the word *ekklēsia* in his Gospel but uses it frequently in his Acts. Luke might have adopted the term from Paul. The word applied to Christian community was not a technical term to refer to the church during the first years of the early church. It is also used to denote a pagan assembly (cf. Acts 19:32). Even the Fourth Evangelist, writing decades later, does not use the term *ekklēsia*, which is somewhat surprising since other NT writings had been around already for some time.

Nevertheless, there are narratives in the FG which point towards a believing community. Jesus's Farewell Speech is the most obvious one. Jesus instructed his faithful disciples how they will move on in the presence of the Spirit: they will be the powered, authorized, and privileged people of the Spirit who have access to Jesus through the Spirit (cf. John 20:21–23). In the Spirit's presence, they have access to spiritual realities (God) that are not available to others outside of the believing Spirit-community.

In the Synoptic Gospels, similar activity of the Spirit among the church is suggested as in the FG when Jesus comforts his disciples not to worry in advance what to say before the authorities (Matt 10:19; Mark 13:11; Luke 12:11–12). Yet, the theme of the Spirit's presence in *ekklēsia* is not developed as far as it is in the FG, Luke being an exception. Luke, at the end of his Gospel, brings in the motif of the church's witness that resonates with the FG. But even Luke's account is not as detailed as the Fourth Evangelist's presentation is in this topic. Matthew in his *ekklēsia* passages, on the other hand, concentrates on foundational issues related to the church's existence (Matt 16:18) and purity (Matt 17:19). The FG presents these topics as well, but mainly in pneumatologically terms.

## Christology

As for the FG's Christology, it introduces differences to the Synoptic Gospel's Christology. At the outset, it needs to be noted, however, that despite the different presentation of Jesus, the FG does not contradict but rather contributes to the Synoptic Gospel's Christology. Jesus is the

Son of God and Savior who came from the Father, fulfilling the OT promises. He lived among people and performed miraculous acts. He taught about righteous living and the kingdom of God, suffered at the hands of his opponents, was executed on the cross with the help of Roman authorities, was buried, resurrected, and appeared alive to many after his resurrection.

The FG's Christology differs from the Synoptic Gospels' presentation most radically in its perspective on how Jesus is presented (see Chapter 11 above). Whereas the Synoptic writers begin with the earthly story of Jesus's incarnation (Matthew and Luke), or his public ministry (Mark), the Fourth Evangelist starts with Jesus's heavenly divine state. The high Christology is so apparent in the FG that some have suggested that the FG represents radically modified Christology, which does not have much to do with the historical person Jesus of Nazareth. Although some shaping of the Christology has inevitably happened among the Johannine church community (as we can perhaps notice in our understanding of Jesus today), this does not make the FG's Christology unreliable compared to the Synoptics. For example, Paul, who wrote prior to the Fourth Evangelist, wrote a "high" Christology which has rarely received the same criticism as the FG's Christology has. Also, the Synoptic Gospel's Christology cannot be categorized as "low" Christology despite their different starting point. The point we want to make here is that the FG's Christology has a different perspective to the Synoptics' Christology. The FG emphasizes more visibly Jesus's divine identity, his undivided unity with the Father, and his authority than the Synoptic Gospels do.

### *Pneumatology*

Pneumatology is another theological topic that is very present in the FG (see Chapter 7 above). The Synoptic Gospels also mention the Holy Spirit several times. All the Synoptic Gospels mention the Holy Spirit in the narratives of Jesus's birth story, his baptism, Jesus's wilderness experience, Jesus's teaching about the sin against the Holy Spirit, and Jesus's passion narratives. In addition to these narratives, individual Synoptic authors mention the Holy Spirit in various other narratives.

As we compare this with the FG's presentation of the Spirit, we note that the Fourth Evangelist omits some of the Synoptic narratives. He does not include Jesus's birth story, his wilderness experience, and teaching about the sin against the Holy Spirit. A few other individual passages about the Holy Spirit found in the Synoptic Gospels are not found in the FG. Nevertheless, John is rich in other places regarding the Holy Spirit. Once again, Jesus's Farewell Speech is rich in pneumatology. Also, an account of Jesus's appearance to his disciples after his resurrection includes a significant Spirit-passage (John 20:19–22) not found in the Synoptics.

In summary, the FG omits and adds Spirit-passages to his account compared to the Synoptics' testimony. The Fourth Evangelist's pneumatology is heavily slanted towards how the Spirit testifies about one's identity. Jesus's identity as the Son of God was approved by the Spirit's coming on Jesus at the time of his baptism (John 1:32–34) and upon the disciples at the time of Jesus's post-resurrection appearance (John 29:22).

## Chronology

Here we make only a few comments on the FG's chronology. Its narrative chronology agrees in most parts with the Synoptics' narratives even though there are some differences (see Chapter 15 below). C. K. Barrett has argued that chronological similarity, especially between John and Mark, proves that John knew Mark's account. Barrett lists the following passages, which are found in the same chronological order in both Gospels:

1. The work and witness of the Baptist
2. Departure to Galilee
3. Feeding the multitude
4. Walking on the lake
5. Peter's confession
6. The departure to Jerusalem
7. The entry and the anointing (transposed in John)
8. The Last Supper with predictions of betrayal and denial
9. The arrest
10. The passion and resurrection[16]

---

16. Barrett, *The Gospel According to St. John*, 43–45.

This observation, however, does not function as a strong argument for the Fourth Evangelist's dependence on Mark or other Synoptic Gospels. These events might be narrated in this order because these events simply took place in this order. Leon Morris comments on Barrett's observation and points out that "What seems very clear to many who have examined the evidence closely is that the kind of things that is common to John and the Synoptists is precisely the kind that one would anticipate finding in oral tradition."[17] Thus, the FG's chronological agreement in the area of the grand events with the Synoptic Gospels does not prove that the Fourth Evangelist used the Synoptics narrative as a source for his Gospel. What the similar chronological order does tell is that the FG is a record of the same Jesus events as recorded by the Synoptic evangelists.

## What Kind of Source were the Synoptic Gospels for the Fourth Evangelist?

As far as our study is concerned, we have noticed several similarities and differences between the Synoptics and the FG without being able to answer with certainty the problematic question: Did John know the Synoptic Gospels, and if he did, how did he use them? Below we will look at this issue.

The above question is related to the dates of writing of the canonical Gospels. If one holds the traditional late date theory (as we have) for FG's publication, namely, that it was written towards the end of the first century (in Ephesus), it is reasonable to think that the FG's author knew at least some of the Synoptic traditions. Especially if the author was the apostle John and if he lived in Ephesus serving the church there, it is arguable that he must have been acquainted with one or more of the Synoptic Gospels. However, if that is not the case, then one cannot use the "John-must-have-known-the-Synoptic-Gospel(s)" argumentation. If the FG was written earlier, prior to 70 CE, then the evangelist's possibility to know and use the Synoptic writings is drastically reduced, and one is directed to look at the similarities in terms of shared source theory. Or, if one holds that the FG is early second-century work, one may assume that the Synoptic tradition was known to those responsible for this account, but their motive to write a different Gospel might have been drastically different (cf. developed theology theories). Nevertheless, the question

---

17. Morris, *The Gospel According to John*, 45.

remains, how did the author of the Fourth Gospel use the Synoptic Gospel(s) if he knew at least one of them? Beside there is the question which one of the Synoptic Gospels did John know or use if he knew that tradition? This question has received several conclusions. Most common is that the Fourth Evangelist knew at least Mark's Gospel. Also, the earlier view that John did not know Matthew is now brought into question.

Based on the above discussion, it seems that John knew one or even all the Synoptic Gospels,[18] but that he deliberately deviated from them using other sources as well and thus producing a different Gospel. Whether he was using sources that were also used by the Synoptic evangelists remains unanswered beyond doubt. However, we are confident to say that the Fourth Evangelist used sources which were not used by the Synoptic authors. One primary source, we think, is his own eyewitness story.[19]

## Suggested Solution for Relationship between the Synoptics and the Fourth Gospel

The discussion above has suggested that there is a relationship between the first three Gospels and the Fourth Gospel. However, the exact nature of that relationship is not clear. Stanley Porter summarizes various theories in this regard and categorizes them as follows:

1. Restricted dependence;
2. Flexible dependence;
3. Semi-independence; and
4. Full independence.

Restricted dependence theory is that John's primary source was the Synoptic texts, perhaps Mark's Gospel. Flexible dependence theory claims that all the Gospel accounts use a common source available to all the authors. Semi-independence theory argues that John used a variety of oral and written sources, some of which were also used by the Synoptic writers. Full independence theory argues that John used a variety of sources, which are not, however, used by the Synoptic Gospels.[20] Below

---

18. Cf. "Leuven School's" argument that the Fourth Evangelist knew all the Synoptic Gospels. Cf. Dowell, "Why John Rewrote the Synoptics," 457.

19. Cf. Keener, *Christobiograhpy*, 402–3.

20. Porter, *John, His Gospel and Jesus*, 68–69.

we will outline some recent theories which we have labeled according to these four categories.

### Shared Oral Jesus Tradition ("Flexible Dependence")

This view is based on two central tenets. First, it is believed that before the Gospels were written in the form that we have them today, the gospel tradition was circulated in oral form for quite a long time. However, this does not exclude the possibility that some of that material was written down, as the "oral" culture did not cease overnight but overlapped with "written" culture for quite some time. Secondly, it is held (more or less firmly) that the Fourth Evangelist based his Gospel on his teaching and preaching material.[21] In short, the view is that there was an oral tradition that was used by the Synoptic writers and the Fourth Evangelist used and modified it independently from the Synoptics.

C. H. Dodd is one of the advocates of this view. Dodd summarizes his arguments for the pre-canonical oral tradition, including the following points:[22]

- The Fourth Gospel shows contact with an original Aramaic tradition.
- Some features in the pre-canonical Johannine tradition appear to point to a Jewish (Jewish-Christian) setting.
- There are indications, which point to a particular geographical and chronological setting for the tradition. The author appears to have been well informed about the topography of Jerusalem and southern Palestine but less well informed, perhaps, about the north.
- The forms of oral tradition, both in narrative and in teaching, which form criticism recognizes in the Synoptics reappear in John.

### Theological Development
### ("Restricted Development" and "Full Independence")

James Dunn observes that the relationship between the Synoptics and the FG is not merely a literary or historical question. It is also a theological

21. Tacher, "Introduction," 2–3.
22. These points are adopted from Dodd, *Historical Tradition in the Fourth Gospel*, 424–32.

one.²³ This question is the most essential aspect of the issue at stake, Dunn argues. Theological differences have led some scholars, such as Rudolf Bultmann and Helmut Koester, to look at Gnosticism rather than Synoptics sources as a possible source for the Fourth Evangelist's presentation, so arguing the FG's independence. These arguments have, however, mostly lost ground in modern Johannine scholarship.

Dunn thinks that theological differences between the Synoptic Gospels and the FG can be understood in terms of development. He asserts that if the difference between these two cannot be explained by discontinuity, then continuity has to be explained in terms of development.²⁴ The earliest view was not that there were four canonical Gospels but that there was one gospel according to (*kata*) four authors.²⁵ This implies the idea of unity. The Gospel was Jesus's passion narrative with an extended introduction. Dunn argues that Mark's Gospel set this standard up, which was then followed by the others, the author of the FG included.

The development that one sees in the FG, especially concerning its presentation of Jesus, is not the author's invention but is a continuation of the development that had already started in the Synoptic Gospels.²⁶ For example, "John's portrayal of Jesus' divine sonship as already preexisting in heaven can be seen as a continuation of the trend in the birth narratives of Matthew and Luke to push Jesus' sonship back to his beginning."²⁷

Dunn seems to suggest that the FG is independent in terms of its theological development. Yet, its starting point shares the same sources and the same genre with the Synoptic tradition, thus not being fully independent.

### Interlocking Relationship ("Semi-Independence")

Some scholars like D. A. Carson and Craig Blomberg think that the nature of relationship between the FG and the Synoptic Gospels is that of *interlocking* connection. This view holds that the Fourth Evangelist knew the Synoptic Gospels (at least to some extent) as he wrote the Gospel account intertwined with them.²⁸ The interlocking connection does not,

23. Dunn, "John and the Synoptics," 301.
24. Dunn, "John and the Synoptics," 305.
25. Dunn, "John and the Synoptics," 307.
26. Dunn, "John and the Synoptics," 305.
27. Dunn, "John and the Synoptics," 305.
28. Blomberg, *The Historical Reliability of John's Gospel*, 53.

however, view the situation only from the evangelist's relation to the Synoptics but also the Synoptics' relation to John. In other words, the Synoptic Gospels also explain or reinforce the FG.

This view leads interpreters to start with similarities between the individual Gospel accounts and move from there to analyze differences. Differences are, if possible, viewed as merely a different way of presenting the same matter. For example, Carson notices that "Whatever is made of the 'messianic secret' motif in Mark, the obvious parallel is the 'misunderstanding' theme in John."[29] Furthermore, it is not Mark but the Fourth Evangelist who gives an explicit explanation of why Jesus kept this secret. He did it because people had a wrong understanding of messiahship as they thought Messiah would be a political deliverer. This is explicitly noticed in John 6:14–15.

There is also considerable amount of material that is not shared, material which the Fourth Evangelist omits and material not found in the Synoptics. The interlocking relationship does not take the FG's "additions" as supplements, thus indicating that the Fourth Evangelist did not try to make an incomplete gospel (more) complete. Interlocking means that every Gospel account is complete and makes sense and argues well on its own. However, reading them together helps one to get a fuller picture of the Jesus event. An example of this phenomenon is the fact that the Fourth Evangelist reports Jesus's Judean ministry extensively, but the Synoptic authors concentrate on his Galilean ministry.[30]

Interlocking also does not mean that the Fourth Evangelist had some "difficulties" with certain portions of the Synoptic Gospels' account, and that therefore, he chose to emphasize other aspects of Jesus's ministry to avoid those difficulties. Yet, Blomberg points out that, "John provides help to clarify enigmas in the Synoptics on the assumption that he has access to historical information."[31] The interlocking connection assumes that John was at ease with the Synoptic traditions in terms of their content, but decided not to follow the same tradition perhaps due to the historical situation in which he wrote. Neither does the interlocking connection argue that the Fourth Evangelist tried to harmonize his story with the Synoptic one.[32]

29. Carson, *The Gospel According to John*, 52.

30. For more examples, see Carson, *The Gospel According to John*, 52–54. See also Leon Morris, *Studies in the Fourth Gospel*, 40–63.

31. Blomberg, *The Historical Reliability of the John's Gospel*, 53.

32. Carson, *The Gospel According to John*, 55.

## Fourth Evangelist's "Academic Freedom" ("Semi-Independence")

The Fourth Evangelist used the freedom that biography and gospel genres allowed him to exercise to produce a different gospel account for his own purposes. Johannine scholars have correctly noticed that we should give room for "John" to be "John" and not let the Synoptic tradition "dictate" how to read him. Keener concludes that "John tells these stories freely without direct dependence on the Synoptics, whether we think that his source or sources are pre- or post-Synoptic."[33]

When the Fourth Evangelist's writing style and usage of his sources (as far as we know what they were) are concerned, we notice that he took the liberty to use them differently than the Synoptic authors. Carson points out that "When we see how free John is when citing or alluding to the Old Testament, we perceive that if he adopted a similar practice when citing or alluding to other written works it would be exceedingly difficult to reconstruct any part of them from the Gospel he has written."[34] It seems that whatever sources the Fourth Evangelist used, he made them his own in such a way that it is even hard to recognize which sources he used.[35] He rewrote them and intertwined them with his own (eyewitness) story. Part of the reason for such a use of the sources and for emphatic employment of the material not used (or known) to the Synoptic writers is perhaps partially due to the historical and thus cultural-religious context of writing. We need to keep in mind that Gospel authors wrote for the audience in a setting that asked certain kinds of questions from the Christian community. In short, in the words of Carson, "John wrote his own book."[36]

## Replacement of Synoptic Gospels ("Full Independence")

Suggestions for the FG's and the Synoptic Gospels' relation also include the idea of replacement. Obviously, this view holds that John knew at least to some extent the Synoptic Gospel(s), but for one reason or another did not agree with their presentation or did not hold them sufficient and thus wrote his version of the Jesus-event. This view goes beyond the idea of

---

33. Keener, *The Gospel of John*, 1:42.
34. Carson, *The Gospel According to John*, 51.
35. See Keener, *The Gospel of John*, 1:41.
36. Carson, *The Gospel According to John*, 51.

development (see above). The reason for the Fourth Evangelist's version might have been due to the historical situation as the Synoptic Gospels would not have been adequate for the readership of John's days. This is what Thomas Dowell points out. He notices that John must have had a valid motive to make so many changes to the Synoptic Gospels. He argues that the best motive for him might have been the fact that he saw a need for a different Gospel account. The historical context created that need as the Synoptic account was challenged and perhaps was viewed as insufficient in the Johannine world. His response to the challenge was his rewritten account that would answer better to the contemporary challenges.[37]

In addition, there is a suggestion that the Fourth Evangelist's circle was esoteric and so distinctive, especially regarding their view on Jesus, that the Fourth Evangelist wrote a new Gospel account to reflect his circle's views. In other words, this view pushes the Synoptic Gospels to the margin regarding them as a less complete view of Jesus from the Johannine community's point of view.

The replacement theories have not received much support in modern scholarship. Although being different, the FG is not seen to militate against other Gospel accounts or Christian communities. Nevertheless, one cannot ignore the importance of the historical situation in which the Synoptics and the FG were produced. The Gospel accounts are not neutral academic treaties but rather persuasive writings in a particular historical context addressing a specific intended readership. That has naturally influenced their content as well.

## Concluding Remarks

In this chapter, we have discussed and outlined various views of the FG's possible relation with the Synoptic Gospels. The questions "Did John know the Synoptic tradition?", "Did he use them if he knew them?", and "If he used them, how did he use them?" have been key questions in our investigation. We have pointed out the similarities and differences between these two bodies of Gospel writings. The following points suggest a framework for discussing the nature and link between the FG and the Synoptics.

- Although there is a limited literary agreement between the FG and the Synoptic Gospels, those agreements suggest the FG's partial

37. Dowell, "Why John Rewrote the Synoptics," 457.

usage or knowledge of the Synoptics and/or the same sources than Synoptic authors have used. In other words, the Fourth Evangelist did not write a completely independent account with no connection to the other Gospels.

- The same genre that the FG shares with the Synoptics points towards the same conclusion as above; the Fourth Evangelist was aware of the "gospel" genre and thus previously authored Gospels. It is not reasonable to think that he "re-invented" that literary genre again.
- The chronology of all major events in all four Gospels is lined up similarly with a few minor exceptions. A similar chronology cannot be merely an accident. This suggests that all four evangelists indeed have recorded the same Jesus event and may have used the same oral, written, and eyewitness traditions.
- The Gospels' focus (protagonist Jesus of Nazareth) and theology (Jesus as God's suffering Messiah) correspond with each other even though they are presented and approached differently. Differences in their narratives are perhaps introduced because of authorial intentions and/or circumstantial differences.
- Limited literary connectedness suggests that the Fourth Evangelist probably avoided repetition, that is, what is already said in the Synoptic Gospels.
- We cannot know if he had any of the Synoptic texts in front of him while he was composing his account. It might be so that he also relied on his memory—a memory that clustered the Synoptics, other possible oral and written sources, and the author's own experience. The other possibility is that the Fourth Evangelist forced himself not to quote the Synoptic text(s) verbatim although he had them at hand while writing. These two possibilities are only guesses and cannot be proved beyond doubt. We can say with confidence that the Fourth Evangelist is unique and different from the Synoptic Gospels, which contributes to rather than contradicts them. It is the gospel according to the Fourth Evangelist.

Based on the evidence, it is reasonable to conclude that the Fourth Evangelist was not an independent writer in the sense that he would not have shared other Christian Gospel writings to some extent, even though he relied on other sources as well, including, as we think, his own eyewitness experiences. Thus, it is reasonable to say that the view that the Fourth Evangelist did not know other canonical Gospels is hardly correct. Neither are we convinced that the Synoptic Gospels (or one of them—perhaps Mark) was the primary source for the author. There are too many features and narratives in the FG that do not flow out from the Synoptic tradition. If the Fourth Evangelist used the Synoptic tradition or their sources, he must have deliberately decided not to use much of their material.

## Suggestions for Further Reading

Dowell, Thomas M. "Why John Rewrote the Synoptics." In *John and the Synonptics*, edited by Adelbert Denaux, 453–57. Leuven: Leuven University Press, 1992.

Keener, Craig S. *Christobiography: Memory, History, and the Reliability of the Gospels*. Grand Rapids: Eerdmans, 2020. Pp. 346–64.

North, Wendy E. S. *What John Knew and What John Wrote: A Study in John and the Synoptics*. Interpreting Johannine Literature. Minneapolis: Fortress Academic, 2020.

CHAPTER 13

# The Fourth Gospel and Revelation

JOHANNINE LITERATURE INCLUDES THE Fourth Gospel, the three epistles of John, and the book of Revelation (the Apocalypse). As their names suggest, they represent three different genres. Therefore, we can expect that they differ from each other. Yet the FG and 1 John are perhaps the closest books in their content and expression in the NT canon. However, the FG and Revelation seem to be as far from each other as two writings can be. Saint Dionysius the Great (c. 200—265 CE), a bishop of Alexandria, argued that "The Apocalypse is utterly different from, and foreign to, these writings (i.e. the Fourth Gospel and 1 John); it has not connexion, no affinity, in any way with them; it scarcely, so to speak, has even a syllable in common with them."[1]

The scholarship is divided on whether Johannine writings came to us from the same pen or community. Some scholars have concluded that not even the FG and the epistles proceeded from the same author.[2] Others argue to the contrary with the view that the same person or community authored them.[3] Today Johannine scholarship is hesitant to claim authorship of Johannine literature with any certainty. Raymond Brown points out that even the tradition that has labeled all three epistles as authored by John cannot prove their common authorship, whether they are

---

1. Quoted from Morris, *Revelation*, 29.
2. E.g., C. K. Barrett, Rudolf Bultmann, C. H. Dodd, and Rudolf Schnackenburg.
3. E.g., Karen H. Jobes, L. Howard Marshall, John R. W. Stott, Max Turner, and B. F. Westcott.

related to the FG, or in which order the epistles might have been written.[4] However, in his commentary on John's epistles, Brown works with the theory that all three epistles of John came from the same author.[5] In this chapter, as we examine the relationship between the FG and Revelation, we will work with the hypothesis that the author of 1–3 John is the same as the author of the FG.

Our purpose here is to introduce similarities between the FG and Revelation. This approach is necessary to demonstrate that they are not complete strangers to each other as sometimes suggested.

As noted above, Johannine epistles, especially 1 John, are close to the FG.[6] The case is very different when the book of Revelation is compared with the FG or any other NT books.[7] Revelation as an apocalyptic writing—strange and challenging—stands alone among NT writings. Leon Morris describes Revelation saying, "It is full of strange symbolism. There are curious beasts with unusual numbers of heads and horns. There are extraordinary phenomena, like the turning of one-third of the sea into blood (8:8), which are impossible to envisage . . . For many Revelation remains a closed book."[8] Does this already rule out the same authorship or any close relationship with the FG? We do not think so. However, there must be a legitimate motive or reason why Revelation is so different. Some attribute the differences to the author's unique situation: he is in exile and prophesying through the Spirit.[9] Below we do not develop those suggested causes for different writing. Instead, we will look at the historical, literary, and theological aspects of Revelation to notice similarities between the FG and Revelation. These three aspects point towards many connecting points with the FG even though dissimilarities are apparent.

---

4. Brown, *The Epistles of John*, 14.

5. Brown, *The Epistles of John*, 19.

6. For a chart for similarities between the FG and John's epistles, see Jobes, *1, 2, 3 John*, 25–27.

7. Smalley, *1, 2, 3 John*, xxii.

8. Morris, *Revelation*, 17.

9. Cf. Morris, *Revelation*, 30–31.

## Historical Considerations

### Dates and Places of Writings

The question of the date of writing is an inevitable question when we tackle the common authorship issue. We start with the traditional view that the Fourth Evangelist wrote his Gospel in Ephesus towards the end of the first century. This time and place of writing create fewer problems than other suggestions (see above).

The author of Revelation, John, was on Patmos when he saw the visions, but he neither mentioned when he saw them nor when he wrote the vision down. It is assumed, however, that he wrote the vision down shortly after he saw it (Rev 1:11). Hiding the time of writing and of the vision is typical of apocalyptic literature. John Christopher Thomas points out that "it appears that the text [of Revelation] may intend to conceal rather than reveal the date of the document's composition."[10] OT prophetical books are the opposite. They are specific about when prophets received messages to be delivered (e.g., Isa 1:1; Jer 1:2; Ezek 1:2). The importance of the date in prophetic books suggests that the message was more time sensitive than perhaps it is in apocalyptic literature.

Despite the lack of internal textual evidence for the time of writing, there are two well-argued options. The first one is during the time of Nero's reign or shortly after between 64–70 CE. The second option is that it was written during the reign of Domitian between 81–96 CE. During the reign of these Roman emperors, Christians experienced persecution. Nero's persecution occurred after the fire in the city of Rome; Domitian persecution took place in Asia Minor. The third and more recent suggestion combines these two views arguing that John saw the visions during Nero's reign, but he wrote them down later during the Domitian reign.[11]

Internal textual evidence seems to fit both the major theories for the time of writing. However, the early external evidence seems to favor the view that John wrote the document during the reign of Domitian towards the end of the first century. Supporters of this view include Justin Martyr, Papias, Clement of Alexandria, and Irenaeus.

As far as dates of the writing of the FG and Revelation go, we must learn to live with possibilities and probabilities rather than set in stone

---

10. Thomas, *The Apocalypse*, 39.
11. Thomas, *The Apocalypse*, 30, 38.

conclusions. We work with the hypothesis that the FG and Revelation were published in written form towards the end of the first century.[12]

The place of writing of Revelation was Patmos, an island located southwest from Ephesus on the Mediterranean Sea, not that far from Ephesus. It is reasonable to think that wherever John was before his arrest, he might have resided not far from Patmos. Therefore, Ephesus or its surrounding areas is a good candidate for his location before his Patmos experience. Also, the names of the seven churches, and the order (i.e., towns as they were located on the post-service road) in which they are presented in chapters 2–3, suggest John's familiarity with the area.

## Authorship: Which John?

If the sketch above for the date of writings is acceptable, then the same authorship for the FG and Revelation is arguable. However, dating both documents to the end of the first century gives rise to another question. How can two works from the same period, and most likely from the same region, written perhaps for the same readership, be so diverse? We will look at these in the ensuing section.

The FG does not name its author (none of the Gospels do) and neither does 1 John; however, 2 and 3 John name their author, calling him "the elder." Revelation names its author, calling him "John" (Rev 1:1, 9, 11) without any further information except that he is a "bond-servant" of Christ (Rev 1:1) and that he was sentenced to Patmos (1:9). Therefore, it is reasonable to think that John, the author, was a well-known figure to the document's recipients. Perhaps he was an elderly leader of the community (cf. Rev. 1:9) who uses that title in 2 and 3 John. Whether this John is the same as the apostle John the son of Zebedee who wrote the FG, as we have argued, is not impossible. But the question whether he actually is the same John that authored Revelation is still matter of debate.[13] It is also good to note that although apocalyptic literature is often pseudonymous, "it is highly improbable that 'John' is a pseudonym."[14]

---

12. The FG content was probably circulated first in the oral form, but that is not the case with Revelation. Revelation, even though based on the vision John saw, was a written document right from the beginning.

13 Cf. Thomas, *The Apocalypse*, 49, thinks that a son of Zebedee was not the author of Revelation, whereas Keener, *The Gospel of John*, 1:138–39, thinks that it is not impossible that a son of Zebedee was the author of the both works.

14. Beale, *The Book of Revelation*, 37.

## The Fourth Gospel and Revelation

Patmos was known as a prison island where Rome sent troublemakers to isolate them from the rest of Roman society. The reason for John's presence there, according to his own words, is "because of the word of God and the testimony of Jesus" (Rev 1:9). Whatever that statement might exactly mean, it suggests that the reason for his sentence was related to his faith. Nevertheless, his faith without any "punishable" actions would not have perhaps been enough to send him to exile. Punishment only because one was called a Christian was possible perhaps a little bit later in Bithynia-Pontus under Pliny's rule. Therefore, it is logical to think that he was sentenced to Patmos because he was in some kind of leadership position in the church and thus a well-known figure. We can imagine that the FG and its message preached might have something to do with John's sentence.

Regarding his "testimony" and "actions" that caused his imprisonment, we can imagine the following. Ephesus was one of the leading commercial cities with 250,000 inhabitants with significant religious influence. The temple of Artemis was there (Acts 19:23–41). Also, Emperor-worship was common in the Roman Empire and was prevalent during the reign of Domitian.[15] In Ephesus, a temple was built for the Roman emperor Domitian so that people could practice the Emperor Cult, including incense burning rituals. The temple was only a few steps away from the Curetes Street, one of the main streets in the city.

John, perhaps being a leading figure in the church in that city, can be envisioned to be under constant surveillance. Pious Jews and Roman citizens could have effortlessly noticed whether he participated in one of the Roman practices, emperor worship, from which Jews were exempt. Inhabitants of the city were expected to step into that small temple dedicated to Emperor Domitian, take a pinch of incense, throw it on the fire, and say *"Caesar kurios"* (Caesar is lord). This act was much more than a mere Roman custom. It functioned as a kind of testimony about one's loyalty to Rome. It was also a statement of belief in Caesar's divinized status. If one did not practice this, it was understood as rebellion against or disloyalty towards Rome and Caesar. Rome was keen to ensure citizens' full commitment to the Empire and its purposes to ensure peace in the Empire. Negligence in the loyalty test was a statement interpreted to indicate disloyalty to Rome that may cause unrest. The reason for John's refusal to participate in emperor worship, as we can assume, was not a

---

15. Morris, *Revelation*, 35.

lack of respect toward the emperor, but rather an indication of his complete loyalty to Christ.[16] For him, there was only one Lord, Jesus Christ. He even ends his Revelation with these words, "The grace of the Lord Jesus be with all. Amen" (Rev. 22:21; cf. 4:11 where worship before the throne in heaven is described).

Neglect to participate in emperor worship might have caused pious Jews to persecute their fellow Jews who confessed Jesus as Messiah. Pious Jews could do that by reporting to Roman authorities that Christian Jews were not Jews and therefore, they should not be exempted from Emperor worship (cf. Rev 2:9). It is difficult to think that pious Jews were serving Roman interests here. Instead, they sought their own interest to remove Christians from society as they were a "threat" to their theology and synagogues. They had used Roman power before to reach the goals of their agenda (cf. John 19:6, 14–15).

We notice that the "persecution" motif is not absent from the FG either. We will say more about that below, but here we want to point out Jesus's Farewell Speech in which he instructs his disciples that the world is going to hate them because of Jesus's name (John 15:18–21). The world's hate comes in the form of excommunication from the synagogue and even in the form of killing (John 16:2). It is significant that in the FG and Revelation the persecution that is said to come from Jewish sources is spoken of in terms of "this world." The FG is clear that there is only one Lord, namely Jesus, also called Lamb. The FG's message can be considered a blow to emperor worship. Therefore, it is not difficult to envision that the content of the FG in its oral or written form might, among others, have contributed to John's punishment on Patmos island.

Based on this sketch, it is technically possible to think that the same John authored both Revelation and the FG. However, this matter has so many historical gaps and a lack of internal textual confirmation that we cannot be dogmatic about it. These books may or may not come from the same John. Nevertheless, both came from the authoritative source within the community to whom they were written.

## Historical circumstances

When the book of Revelation and the FG were written, the church's historical circumstances were similar in some respect. While being

---

16. Johnson, *Discipleship on the Edge*, 24.

## The Fourth Gospel and Revelation

punished and exiled for his "rebellion" against Rome, John writes down his vision for seven churches.[17] The circular letter's point is to encourage these churches to be faithful to Jesus under present circumstances without giving up their faith in Jesus even then when they faced martyrdom (Rev 2:10, 26; 3:5, 11–12, 21; 12:11; cf. John 16:2, 33). Its author also urges believers to believe in Jesus alone without compromising their faith amidst the worship of other gods or faith systems (Rev 2:14–15; cf. John 14:1). The FG's tone is also encouraging recipients to stay faithful to Jesus (cf. John 14:1–6; 15:1–17; 20:30–31).

A significant element in Revelation's encouragement is the fact that Christ has won the unseen battle. Revelation reveals, as Darrell Johnson puts it, that "the things are *not only as they seem*."[18] In other words, there is a reality that goes beyond the human's inherent capabilities to observe. It shows that there is an unseen world, and in that world, there is the throne in heaven which is occupied by almighty God, who was, is, and will come, the one who is alpha and omega (Rev 1:8; 4:1–2). The Lamb, who has already won the battle, resides in heaven (Rev 5:6). Therefore, what is happening on earth, under self-claimed authorities, is under the authority of the Lamb. The struggling churches in Asia Minor received the message of encouragement: stay faithful to the Lamb until the end; the church is the victorious messianic Israel because of the victory the Lamb has brought.[19]

This sketch fits the overall presentation of the FG much closer than that of the Synoptic Gospels. Jesus is presented as one who comes from "behind the heavenly curtains" (cf. John 1:1–5). He continually refers his relationship to the one who sent him, performing and speaking his Father's deeds and words. Jesus reveals that he goes back to the Father from whence he came (16:5). He is the one who is the source of God's revelation (1:51). Also, Jesus points out plainly that his followers will suffer for his name's sake (15:18–21). In addition, the FG reminds the church that the reality goes beyond the physical world, and that those who trust in Jesus face difficulties in this world. However, they should remain faithful in the present life since Jesus has already won (cf. John 15:1–11). A similar description of pressure on the church may suggest that these two works

---

17. Bauckham, *The Theology of the Book of Revelation*, 2.
18. Johnson, *Discipleship on the Edge*, 19.
19. Mangina, "God, Israel, and Ecclesia," 94.

address the church during the same era and that they do not necessarily require one to argue for different authorship.

Richard Cassidy argues that the Fourth Evangelist's purpose in writing the Gospel was that "John was concerned to present elements and themes that were significant for Christians facing Roman imperial claims and for any who faced Roman persecution."[20] One obvious imperial claim was the status of Caesar. Cassidy shows how the Fourth Evangelist systematically presents Jesus's sovereign status from the Prologue on to argue that it is not the ruler of the present Roman Empire, but Jesus, who is the Savior of the World, Lord, and God.[21] It is not an accident that the FG gives much space to Jesus's hearing before Pilate. Pilate, who thinks that he has unlimited power to do whatever he wishes with Jesus, represents Rome (John 19:10). But Jesus reveals to Pilate that his power does not come from Rome but from above (19:11).

The book of Revelation reveals the same power structure. The beast together with all his associates persecutes believing communities, but the faithful ones have already won even though the present situation does not demonstrate this. The faithful church is worshiping the Lamb in front of his throne.

In addition, the FG and Revelation take a Jewish slant to present God and his purpose to save those who are faithful to him. We have argued the FG's Jewishness above. Similarly, in Revelation imagery and language is Jewish. Revelation includes several quotations and allusions to the OT. Occasionally, the language also is anti-Jewish like in the FG (e.g., "a synagogue of Satan" in Rev 2:9).[22] In particular, the temple motif in Revelation that is expressed with "new heavenly temple" language is noticeable (e.g., Rev 21:22). The temple motif links the Revelation to the FG and their post-temple context.

## Literary Considerations

Literary questions include topics like genre and vocabulary. What kind of relationship do Revelation's literary features suggest with the FG?

---

20. Cassidy, *John's Gospel in New Perspective*, 80.
21. Cassidy, *John's Gospel in New Perspective*, 29–39.
22. Cf. Beale, *The Book of Revelation*, 77–79.

## Genre

Revelation is often referred to as a "revelation" which is interpreted as a prophecy and which includes seven mini letters to seven churches. This is not, however, an accurate description of what Revelation is. Revelation is from beginning to end a letter (Rev 1:11).[23] After it was written, it circulated among all the seven churches mentioned in chapters 2–3. Thus, all the churches read the same text, the entire book, not only the part that was addressing them. Revelation also starts and ends like a letter (Rev 1:4; 22:21). Nevertheless, it differs from other NT epistles.

It is also a prophecy. Prophecy should not be understood merely as a prediction of the future. If a prophecy is thus understood, which is unfortunately often the case, Revelation is read from chapter 4 onwards as a description of the future events, often referring to the future event from the reader's own time onwards.[24] Prophecy, in the case of Revelation, as also the OT prophetical books, is better understood as God's message via his messenger. The message may, like in Revelation, include future events, but that does not mean that the present situation is not addressed. On the contrary, the present is vital even though the future judgment and restoration (salvation) is also a part of the prophecy. In the case of Revelation, the slant is how the church can cope with the present life difficulties. Revelation "*seeks to set the present in light of the invisible realities of the future.*"[25]

Finally, Revelation is also an apocalypse. Apocalyptic writings flourished between 200 BCE–200 CE. The term does not refer to the contemporary idea of future chaotic events usually related to the collapse of the universe. Apocalypse, which means "uncovering" (revelation), is its own genre. What is characteristically distinctive of this genre is that it employs symbolism and imagery. This presents certain challenges for readers who are distant from the context of the writing. As apocalyptic (revelatory) literature, Revelation has specific literary features known to us also in a few OT apocalyptic writings (Daniel, Ezekiel, and Zechariah, as well as parts of Isaiah) and extra-biblical Jewish (Ezra, 2 Baruch, and 2 Enoch) or other apocalyptic works from that era. Rebecca Skaggs and Priscilla Benham list typical literary features of apocalyptic literature as

---

23. Bauckham, *The Theology of the Book of Revelation*, 1–17.

24. Concise explanation for common four ways of reading Revelation, see Morris, *Revelation*, 18–20; Beale, *The Book of Revelation*, 44–49.

25. Johnson, *Discipleship on the Edge*, 26.

"symbolic utterances, visions, blessings, wisdom sayings, sacred sayings, and paraenetic teaching."[26]

Revelation is a kind of combination of these three distinct genres: epistle, prophecy and apocalypse. Beale says, "The apocalyptic-prophetic nature of Revelation can be defined as God's revelatory interpretation (through visions and auditions) of his mysterious counsel about past, present, and future redemptive-eschatological history, and how the nature and operation of heaven relate to this."[27] According to Carson, Moo, and Morris, Revelation is, "a prophecy cast in an apocalyptic mold and written down in a letter form."[28]

Revelation's different genre explains its unique style of writing.[29] The genre of the FG, although it is gospel, is also historical narrative that fits well with the genre of ancient biography. Both Revelation and the FG are written in accordance with their genres. Due to different genres their vocabulary and expressions are distinctively different. However, despite their different genres, both include many similar aspects in their description of reality. For example, both include material that deals with the present and the future eschatology as well as the unseen reality. In the case of the FG, present eschatology is demonstrated by the Fourth Evangelist's encouragement to keep on believing in Jesus as Son of God in spite of his recipients' oppressed life circumstances (cf. John 15:18—16:4a). The promised presence of Jesus in the form of Spirit-Paraclete is another example of "unseen" reality (John 14:16–18). The question remains, however, whether one author can produce two such different works by using two different genres relatively close to each other in time? Arguments can go both ways.

## Vocabulary

The vocabulary of Revelation is different, even unusual, compared to other NT writings. Timothy Jenny has conducted a statistical study on Revelation's vocabulary, which indicated that Revelation "consists of 911 different words (lemmas) of which 128 are unique to that book within

---

26. Skaggs and Benham, *Revelation*, 2.
27. Beale, *Revelation*, 38.
28. Carson et al., *An Introduction to the New Testament*, 479.
29. Cf. Keener, *The Gospel of John*, 1:128.

NA²⁷."³⁰ He further notices that Revelation's vocabulary shares the least similarity with the rest of the NT corpus, but has more unusual words in common with the Septuagint, the Pseudepigrapha, and the Apocryphal Apocalypses.³¹ This statistic does not promise many similarities between the FG's and Revelation's vocabulary. Elisabeth Schüssler Fiorenza has noted that the FG's "keywords" are not found in Revelation, yet they share eight words that are not found elsewhere in the NT.³²

Keener, however, points out various similarities in their vocabulary and style, yet also reminds us of that the writings' different focus, genre, and situation anticipates different language and style of writing.³³ For this reason even the shared vocabulary may have different connotations. The following four significant words in the FG that occur frequently in Revelation are:

- "Witness" (Rev 1:2, 5, 9; 3:14; 6:9; 11:3, 7; 12:11; 15:5; 19:10; 20:4).
- "Word" (Rev 3:10; 6:9; 17:17; 20:4).
- "Works" (Rev 2:2, 5–6, 9, 22–23, 26; 3:1–2, 8, 15; 15:3; 16:11; 18:6; 20:12–13; 22:12).
- "Glory" (Rev 4:9, 11; 5:12; 11:13; 14:17; 15:4; 19:7; 21:24; see also 15:8; 21:11, 23).

In addition to these words, Keener notes that Revelation's similarity with the FG can be tracked to some sayings which go behind the Synoptic Gospels' Jesus tradition. He points out that "'After these things' serves a literary function in each (Rev 4:1; 7:9; 15:5; 18:1; 19:1; cf. 7:1; 20:3; John 5:1; 6:1; 7:1). The normal expression 'come and see' in John 1:39 and 46 may find apocalyptic expression in Rev 4:1; 11:12; 17:1; 21:9. Similar metaphors (such as the OT linkage of bridegroom with joy, Rev 18:23; John 3:29) appear."³⁴

Also, different perspectives in these writings, like different eschatological point of views, bring differences to their vocabulary. Although both books are heavy in eschatology, the FG's eschatology is mainly realized eschatology. In other words, future blessing is already realized in

---

30. Jenney, "The Vocabulary and Phraseology of Revelation," 250.

31. Jenney, "The Vocabulary and Phraseology of Revelation," 255.

32. Schüssler Fiorenza, *The Book of Revelation*, 93–94.

33. Keener, *The Gospel of John*, 1:128. The following presentation follows Keener, pp. 1:128–32.

34. Keener, *The Gospel of John*, 1:129.

Jesus. The Revelation's eschatology includes both realized and future eschatology, but its distinctive slant is that present struggles are going to be exchanged to a perfect peace and blessedness. Jesus is already conquered the Satan, but the faithful ones will fully reach that victory only in the future by remaining faithful to Jesus. This has probably influenced how the word "sign" is used in these writings. Both works use the word, but they use it quite differently. The FG emphasizes signs of grace, the grace that is available now in Jesus, whereas Revelation stresses signs of judgement, which point towards future reality.[35] Yet the concept of "sign" is strongly present in both works always pointing towards greater authority than that of the authority of Jerusalem or Rome. Similarly, Moses's signs before Pharaoh pointed to greater powers, namely, to God.

## Theological Considerations

Both writings are theological and share many of the same theological topics. As we can imagine, some of that is expected since these writings belong to NT canon. However, due to their different literary genre and historical orientation, one could also expect drastic differences in their theologies. We have chosen to outline four prominent theological areas (pneumatology, eschatology, Christology, and trinitarian theology) to demonstrate that their theology agrees closely with each other.

### Pneumatology

Are there indicators that the Johannine church was comfortable with the idea of having a "new" revelation of Christ?[36] If Jesus was the ultimate revelation of God (cf. John 1:18), how could they dare to receive Revelation that went beyond what they had previously learned about him through the FG? This question would require much more to answer comprehensively than is possible here. We will take up only the community's pneumatological aspect to imagine how they responded when they received John's Revelation.

The FG presents the Spirit as active in the believing community (cf. John 16:13–15). Therefore, it is reasonable to think that recipient churches also believed in the active work of the Spirit among them. In

---

35. Cf. Keener, *The Gospel of John*, 1:130.
36. Rev 1:1 *Apokaluphis Iēsou Xristou*.

his monograph *The Anointed Community*, Gary Burge argues that the Johannine community was charismatic, one in which Spirit experience was Jesus-experience.[37] In addition, the author of the Gospel adds comments that suggest that Jesus's teaching about the Spirit-Paraclete in his Farewell Speech was realized after the Spirit was given. The Spirit's work is realized, for example, in John 2:22 (cf. 3:11; 12:48; 21:24) where Spirit-Paraclete's "reminding" and "teaching" is implicitly referred to. Also, the Spirit-Paraclete is told to reveal Jesus's words (cf. John 16:14–15). Revelation is Jesus's revelation that is communicated through the Spirit (Rev 1:1, 10; 4:2). Therefore, John's Spirit experience was also Jesus-experience. There is no reason why the Johannine community's theology, based on the FG, would not have accepted Revelation. Arguably, the Johannine community might have even expected something like this concrete work of the Spirit taking place among them.

The Spirit also has a significant role not only in communicating the Revelation but also in its message.[38] The Spirit in Revelation, as in the FG, is presented as divine, truthful, and powerful. Another similarity is that the Spirit is working in the world because of Jesus's death and resurrection. Bauckham explains, "it could be said that the seven Spirits as the divine power released into the whole world by the victory of Christ's sacrifice are the power of divine truth: the power of the church's faithful witness to the truth of God and his righteousness against the idolatries and injustices on the world under the sway of the beast."[39] The FG presents the Spirit the same way. Jesus points out that the Spirit's coming requires his going back to the Father (John 16:4b–12, cf. 7:37–39); the Spirit comes on his disciples but witnesses to the entire world (John 14; 16–17; 15:26); and the Spirit is the Spirit of truth (John 14:17; 16:13). Also, in both writings, the Spirit is described as God's life-giving Spirit (Rev 11:11; John 20:22) and locus of true worship (Rev 1:10; John 4:24).

Yet there are some obvious differences as well. John links the Spirit to Zechariah 4:1–14, calling him "the seven Spirits" (Rev 1:4; 3:1; 4:5; 5:6).[40] The Spirit is not called the seven Spirits in the FG. Neither is Paraclete, a term for the Spirit in the FG, mentioned in Revelation. Nevertheless, because the language in Revelation is symbolic, "the seven

---

37. Burge, *The Anointed Community*, xvii.
38. See Thomas, "The Spirit in the Book of Revelation," 254–64.
39. Bauckham, *The Theology of the Book of Revelation*, 114.
40. Cf. Macchia, "The Spirit of the Lamb," 214–15.

Spirit" expression should not be a concern for readers, especially because various similarities in pneumatology are also found between the FG and Revelation. Numbers play a significant symbolic role in apocalyptic writings and in the case of Revelation the number seven describes completeness. The number seven is used throughout Revelation, not only attached to the Spirit, to describe completeness.[41]

## Eschatology

The FG and Revelation share similarities in their eschatology but their eschatologies have different emphases. Both include "realized" and "future" eschatology. The FG emphasizes "realized" eschatology. Believers in Jesus were already moved from darkness into the light and from death to life (John 5:24; cf. 3:36). The heavenly blessings were already now at hand. The "future" eschatology is present but overshadowed by "realized" eschatology. That has caused critical scholarship to suggest that future eschatology in the FG was added later to bring the FG on the same page with the Synoptic Gospels in which eschatology is geared toward the future events. There is no evidence for such an edition of the FG where "future" eschatology would be completely absent, and therefore the suggestion that "future" eschatology is a later addition remains hypothetical.

The eschatological emphasis is different in Revelation. Believers, who have an ear to hear what the Spirit says, are urged to hold on because the final judgment of the wicked and salvation of righteous are not yet fully unfolded (cf. Rev 2:7). Suffering Christians will have a glorious day of salvation from present difficulties when the one who sits on the throne acts.[42] The message of Revelation is oriented to the future and therefore its eschatology can be described by many as a "future" eschatology. Nevertheless, "realized" eschatology is not absent from it. Revelation's eschatology is "realized" because the Lamb has already won the battle.[43] Revelation presents the present-day reality not only in terms of persecution

---

41. Seven churches (1:4, 11), golden lampstands (1:2), stars (1:16, 29; 2:1), lamps (4:5), seals (5:1; 6:1), horns (5:6), eyes (5:6), angels (8:2, 6; 15:1, 6, 7, 8; 17:1; 21:9), trumpets (8:2, 6), peals of thunder (10:3, 4), thousand people (11:13), heads (12:3; 13:1; 17:3, 7, 9), diadems (12:3), plagues (15:1, 6, 8; 21:9), bowls (15:7; 16:1; 17:1; 21:9), mountains (17:9), and kings (17:10, 11).

42. Cf. Elwell and Yarbrough, *Encountering the New Testament*, 382–84. Cf. Bauckham, *The Theology of the Book of Revelation*, 162.

43. Keener, *The Gospel of John*, 1:131.

but also in terms of the heavenly realities. In short, Revelation does not miss "realized" eschatology. On the contrary, Christ's victorious work is the bedrock on which the future eschatology is built.

We suggest that eschatological orientation is linked to the historical context and purpose of these writings. Therefore, they have different eschatological emphases, yet including both present and future eschatology. We may imagine that the author might have produced a two-volume work like Luke did. Keener points out that "as Luke parallels Jesus and the church in Luke-Acts, we could argue (if so inclined) that John emphasizes the continuity of experience between Jesus in the Gospel and the prophetic community in Revelation, emphasizing realized eschatology in the former and future eschatology in the latter."[44]

## Christology

Christology is a substantial theological theme that needs to be considered as well. The Fourth Evangelist sets out his Christology by describing Christ as eternal and divine *Logos*. The following chapters (2—12) establish his role and identity in various ways among people with whom *Logos* incarnate lived. Then the rest of the Gospel, namely, the book of Passion (chs. 13—20) is the narrative of the meaning and significance of Jesus's death and resurrection (cf. 20:19–23). Also, the Fourth Evangelist uses various names for Jesus which are unique and, except for a few, are not found in Revelation. One of the prominent names used for Jesus in both books is "Lamb" (twenty-eight times in Revelation). Revelation describes Jesus as the Lamb who has been slain (Rev. 4:6) and yet is living and victorious. This Lamb receives worship and is depicted as powerful and one who has authority that no one else has. For example, he has the authority to open the scroll that is in the hand of the one who sits on the throne (God). This picture fits well with that of the FG. At the beginning of Jesus's ministry, John the Baptist calls Jesus by the name "the Lamb of God" (John 1:29, 35). This description may have many connections to the OT, just like many other names used for Christ in Revelation (e.g., Lion of Judah and Root of David; Rev 4:5). Nevertheless, this title for Jesus is not found in the NT outside of the Johannine literature. The Lamb in

---

44. Luke and John's difference would be that Luke intended to write a two-volume work right in the beginning, whereas John's "two-volume work" was not a pre-meditated plan. Keener, *The Gospel of John*, 1:132.

the FG and in Revelation is revealed as the divine, sacrificed, and now living. He is God's means of victory and salvation. In short, the Lamb's life, sacrificial death, and resurrection is narrated in the FG, on which Revelation builds up its message.

## Trinitarian Theology

Both writings present trinitarian theology. The FG is utterly trinitarian. Jesus is sent by the Father to do the Father's work in the presence of the Spirit. Jesus reveals to his disciples that he and the Father would send the Spirit. Jesus sends the disciples to the world as the Father sent Jesus. Both Jesus and the church function in the Spirit's presence. Similar trinitarian theology is present in Revelation. An example of trinitarian theology in Revelation is the vision that Jesus showed to John which came from God and was communicated by the Spirit. Bauckham points out that "Revelation has the most developed trinitarian theology in the New Testament, with the possible exception of the Gospel of John."[45]

It is somewhat surprising that these two books, so different in style, genre, and vocabulary, are so unified in their theology. Whether that proves the same authorship is another question, but the theological similarities surely support rather than disapprove the idea.

## Concluding Remarks

Our point in this chapter has been to make students of the FG aware that although the FG and Revelation are different, they share many similarities. Therefore, we have purposefully emphasized similarities in their historical, literary, and theological aspects, which are sometimes overshadowed by the emphasis on differences. The similarities do not prove that they have the same author or even that they sprang from the same community, but they suggest the possibility of that view. Although a critical scholarly world holds that these works cannot and do not come from the same author, it is good to keep in mind that that view also demands evidence.

Our reconstruction of the historical situation has led us to think that it is possible, although not proved, that John's Patmos imprisonment was partially caused by the publication of the FG or by his preaching its

---

45. Bauckham, *The Theology of the Book of Revelation*, 164.

message in pre-literary form.[46] If so, it is not difficult to imagine that both works are attached to the same community (if not to the same author). Also, if the FG's content (in its oral or written form) caused John's arrest (supported by his behavior to skip the emperor worship), that could have been the reason why the FG's circulation was slow in the beginning in Asia Minor and why it soon found its way to a safer location in Fayum or Oxyrhnchus (Egypt).[47] This hypothesis cannot be developed further here, but it is a worthwhile topic of research.

It has also been demonstrated in this chapter that the FG and Revelation represent their historical-contextual backdrop against which they should be read to understand their messages. The FG is a Jewish work with a close relation to the OT and Jewish thought. Therefore, its message and narrative must be read against the Jewish background. Revelation, however, reflects the world of and life in the Roman Empire at the end of the first century.[48] Yet, Revelation uses utterly OT images to convey its message. Therefore, it is connected to the FG's presentation and the believing community's present *sitz im leben*.

For this reason, we suggest that we can approach the FG and Revelation as a twofold work that focuses on the same divine and spiritual matters. The first part (the Gospel) gives the foundation and understanding of how God's salvation plan is fulfilled in Jesus and how it relates to the past revelation (i.e., OT). The second part (Revelation) instructs how the church would navigate in the present world as the world exercises its political, economic, and spiritual powers. Does this sound like Luke's two-volume work, Luke-Acts?

## Suggestions for Further Reading

Bauckham, Richard. *The Theology of the Book of Revelation.* Cambridge: Cambridge University Press, 1993.

Beale, G. K. *The Book of Revelation: A Commentary on the Greek Text.* Grand Rapids: Eerdmans, 1999. Pp. 1–43, 76–99, 171–77.

Keener, Craig S. *The Gospel of John.* Vol. 1. Peabody: Hendrickson, 2003. Pp. 126–39.

---

46. Comfort, *Early Manuscripts & Modern Translations*, 3.
47. Comfort, *Early Manuscripts & Modern Translations*, 55–56.
48. Thompson, "Reading What Is Written in the Book of Life," 155.

CHAPTER 14

# Chapter 21

*An Annexure?*

THE FG'S FINAL CHAPTER consists of two narratives and final comments about the composition and testimony of the Gospel account's truthfulness. The first narrative, Peter's and his companion's unsuccessful fishing trip on the Sea of Galilee and Jesus's intervention to produce a large catch is recorded in John 21:1–14. The second narrative, Jesus's encounter with Peter and its aftermath, follows in John 21:15–23. These two narratives are much discussed and preached passages, especially the latter. Casual readers may not have problems with these narratives or even the final comments. However, a closer examination elicits challenges, which can be summarized by the following two questions. Is chapter 21 an original part of the FG? Furthermore, how does chapter 21's content fit and contribute to the FG's purpose? These questions are justifiable since the evangelist has brought the Gospel to its climactic close at the end of chapter 20, or so it seems.

Both questions are addressed in modern commentaries. The question of the originality of chapter 21 has been studied and debated in scholarly forums for the last hundred years![1] The first question is especially of interest to those scholars who approach the chapter in a historical-critical manner (i.e., diachronically). In contrast, the second question is of interest to those scholars who approach the text synchronically (i.e., in a narrative-critical manner).

---

1. Porter, *John, His Gospel, and Jesus*, 225.

## Chapter 21: To Belong or Not to Belong?

A first-time reader (cf. reader-response criticism) arriving at the climactic end of chapter 20 that includes Thomas's confession (vv. 28–29) and the summary statement (vv. 30–31), indeed feels that this is a proper closing for the Gospel. Thomas's confession "My Lord and my God!" and Jesus's response, "Blessed are they who did not see, and *yet* believed," capture the ideal reader's response to the FG's persuasion. The evangelist's purpose is that his readers would entrust their lives to Jesus as their Lord and God, even without having seen him. The author's rhetorical purpose is explicitly summarized in his statement in 20:30–31.

The harmonious and climactic ending, however, is disturbed when the FG moves on somewhat abruptly, picking up yet another narrative.[2] The highly spiritual and theological moment created by the very last verses at the end of chapter 20 is "flattened" by a fishing story, and a further narrative of Jesus's encounter with Peter. The locale of the events in chapter 20 is Jerusalem, but in chapter 21 it is Galilee. Why does the narration pick up again after the purpose statement? The purpose statement would have been a perfect and forceful (rhetorical) ending for the entire Gospel. The Gospel has plentiful material that argues for the point captured so well in the last two words in John 20 (see Part One above). We should not wonder why hard questions are asked regarding chapter 21's status and role in the FG.[3]

For sound reasons, the question is raised if chapter 21 is an original part of the FG or a later addition. Various descriptions for the nature of chapter 21 have been suggested. Such descriptions include appendix, archive of excess, inclusion, second conclusion/ending, postscript, supplement, final farewell, and epilogue. Suggested descriptions are motivated by the chapter's relation to the body of the Gospel, whereas others are motivated by its content. We will not engage in the discussion of which of the terms best describes chapter 21. We call it an epilogue, as this term describes well its place and function in the FG.[4]

---

2. Cf. Carson, *The Gospel of John*, 666.
3. See Brodie, *The Gospel According to John*, 574.
4. The term "epilogue" fits the best the last two verses of chapter 21, or as Jo-Ann Brant argues, the last two sections (vv. 17–23 and 24–25). She defines "epilogue" as, "additional narration at the end of a story that serves to bring closure to a work by having the narrator address the audience directly and reveal the fates of the characters." Brant, *John*, 278.

At this point of discussion, it is necessary to note that all manuscripts of the FG that we have at hand include chapter 21. We have good reason to accept that there are no undiscovered manuscripts that would not include chapter 21. It has always been part of the published FG. This fact can be used in two different ways; it can be used as an argument for the view that chapter 21 was added to the end of the Gospel very shortly after its composition, perhaps by someone else other than the evangelist. Alternatively, it can be used to argue that chapter 21 was always part of the original Gospel, perhaps written by the same author as chapters 1–20.

Below, we have tried to categorize the various scholarly views.

- Chapter 21 belongs to the original Gospel design and was written by the evangelist (E. Ruckstuhl, R. Mahoney, A. Schlatter, W. Bauer, J. B. Lightfoot, Hoskyns, C. Blomberg, D. A. Carson, and C. Keener).

- Chapter 21 belongs to the published Gospel but was written by a redactor (or belongs to a different tradition than chapters 1—20), added shortly after chapters 1—20 were composed, perhaps after the death of the Beloved Disciple (S. Smalley, M. Boismard, R. Bultmann, R. E. Brown, Schnackenburg, C. K. Barrett, and G. Beasley-Murray, B. F. Westcott, H. Ridderbos, D. Moody Smith, M. Davies, B. Witherington, J. J. Kanagaraj).

- Chapter 21:1–23 belongs to the original Gospel, but 21:24–25 was added later by someone other than the evangelist (e.g., L. Morris, F. F. Bruce, M. C. Tenney).

It should be kept in mind that the generalized categories above do not do full justice to nuanced theories. Scholars attached to these categories may argue more nuanced views than our presentation allows us to explain. Also, some scholars are hesitant to argue for only one specific view. The difficulty of this issue is also demonstrated by the fact that some scholars have changed their view over the course of their research.[5]

Regardless of our presentation's generalizations, it gives a bird-eye view of the issue. The categories also demonstrate how tricky the question is and how divided the Johannine scholarship is on this issue. In the eighties, George Beasley-Murray summarized the situation saying, "In the estimate of the majority of NT scholars, chap. 21 is an addendum in the Gospel, whether it be described as an appendix, a postscript, or an epilogue, and whether it be put to the account of the Evangelist or a later

---

5. See Brown, *The Gospel According to John*, 2:1079.

editor of the Johannine school."[6] The situation has shifted today. Several Johannine scholars argue that chapter 21 is an original part of the FG and comes from the same pen as the first 20 chapters. We turn now to present arguments from both camps. Scholars have pointed out vocabulary, structure, and thematic (dis)unity as key areas on which they have built their views. We will discuss these below.

## Vocabulary

It is noticeable that the vocabulary in chapter 21 is different from chapters 1–20. Rudolf Bultmann and C. K. Barrett have presented lists of the words that are unique to chapter 21.[7] Below is the combination of their findings following Stanley Porter's presentation.[8]

- Fish [*halieuein*] (v. 3)
- Early [*prōia*] (v. 4)
- Beach [*aigialos*] (v. 4)
- Fish [*prosphagion*] (v. 5)
- Be able [*ischu*] (v. 6)
- Fishing net [*diktuon*] (vv. 6, 8)
- Fish [*ichthus*] (vv. 6, 8, 11)
- Outer garment [*ependutēs*] (v. 7)
- Naked [*gumnos*] (v. 7)
- Far [*makran*] (v. 8)
- Cubit [*pēchus*] (v. 8)
- Drag [*surō*] (v. 8)
- Get out [*apobainō*] (v. 9)
- Eat [*aristaō*] (v. 12)
- Dare [*tolmaō*] (v. 12)

6. Beasley-Murray, *John*, 395.

7. See original lists: Bultmann, *The Gospel of John*, 700–701; Barrett, *The Gospel According to St. John*, 576. We have not chosen to give the original lists for their technical nature and usage of Greek.

8. The list is adopted from Porter, *John, His Gospel, and Jesus*, 230. We present the words in the order they occur in the chapter 21.

- Ask [*exetazō*] (v. 12)
- Third [*triton*] (vv. 14, 17)
- Lamb [*arnion*] (v. 15)
- Feed [*boskō*] (v. 15)
- Tend sheep [*poimainō*] (v. 16)
- Sheep [*probation*] (v. 16)
- Younger [*neōteros*] (v. 18)
- Age [*gērasgō*] (v. 18)
- Stretch out [*ekteinō*] (v. 18)
- Fasten [*zōnnumi*] (v. 18)
- Turn around [*epistreph*] (v. 20)
- Think [*oiomai*] (v. 25)

The list of unique words is quite impressive—no wonder some scholars have raised the question of the authenticity of chapter 21 based on its vocabulary. For example, it is interesting that chapter 21 employs three different words for "fish;" none of which was used earlier in the FG (cf. John 6:9, 11).

Counter-arguments point out that the vocabulary in chapter 21 is linked to the subject matter and the author's style. In other words, the reason for the unique vocabulary is not that another author other than the evangelist held the pen. Instead the reason for unique vocabulary is the content that has required the evangelist to use vocabulary that differs from his earlier chapters.[9] D. A. Carson, who makes the same observation as we have just made, notes that "A few words and constructions, however, cannot be dismissed so easily: *e.g.*, in v. 12, the verb 'to ask' is *exetazō*, rather than the expected *erōtaō*; in v. 5 the disciples are addressed as *paidia* rather than the *teknia* used in 1:12; and so forth."[10] Nevertheless, Carson continues saying that the Fourth Evangelist has "a penchant for synonyms," and that the word *paidia* not found from the FG as a direct address is frequently used in 1 John.[11] It is true that the Fourth Evangelist's style throughout his Gospel is to use synonyms (e.g.,

---

9. Cf. Bruce, *The Gospel of John*, 398.

10. Carson, *The Gospel According to John*, 665.

11. Carson, *The Gospel According to John*, 665; cf. Porter, *John, His Gospel, and Jesus*, 230–32.

## Chapter 21

The Spirit, the Holy Spirit, the Spirit of t/Truth, the Paraclete). Therefore, the use of different words in chapter 21 than in the rest of the Gospel, and the use of synonyms in chapter 21 are not surprising literary features for the Fourth Evangelist.

We can summarize this by saying that there is undeniable evidence of unique vocabulary in chapter 21, which Johannine scholars have interpreted differently. Some scholars emphasize disunity and discontinuity between chapters 1—20 and 21. Other scholars emphasize unity and continuity and see the same creative author's pen in chapter 21 as elsewhere in the FG.

### Structure and Thematic (Dis)Unity

We have pointed out above that the ending of the FG demands some answers to the structure. It sounds as if chapter 21 is an afterthought and, therefore, was added to the Gospel's initially planned structure. For example, Rudolf Bultmann argues that chapter 21 is a postscript. He points out that "*Ch[apter] 21 is not a unity*" [his emphasis] and continues to argue for this view as follows:

> It [i.e., chapter 21's narrative portion] is divided into the two sections vv. 1–14 and vv. 15–23, which cannot originally have belonged together. The analysis shows that vv. 1–14 were originally an independent Easter story, which reported an appearance of Jesus to a group of disciples at the Galilean Lake, and that it was due to an editor that the beloved disciple and Peter were assigned a particular role. Throughout this editing however that story has become a kind of introduction to vv. 15–23, where Peter and the beloved disciple are chief persons and where the other disciples, though still present, are completely ignored.[12]

Bultmann also is quite firm in his view that the described author, "the beloved disciple," had died (John 21:23), and therefore, "It is perfectly plain that the Gospel as we have it was edited and provided with the supplementary chapter after his death. For the fiction that the author himself puts himself forward here as identical with the Beloved disciple, and at the same time wishes to attest his own death is quite unbelievable."[13] Bultmann's view represents perhaps the strongest arguments against the thematic and

---

12. Bultmann, *The Gospel of John*, 702.
13. Bultmann, *The Gospel of John*, 702.

structural unity of chapter 21. However, as already noticed above, today we have several voices in Johannine scholarship that argue otherwise.

There are arguments that FG's ending includes more than one stage. Tomas Brodie argues for an ending that consists of a larger unit (19:16b—20:25), including a threefold conclusion (19:35–37; 20:30–31; 21:24–25), in which chapter 21 functions "as a culmination which synthesizes the gospel's many strands."[14] Richard Bauckham argues for a two-stage ending. He points out that John 20:30–31 is a first stage of the FG's overall ending; John 21:24–25 is the second ending that envelopes the Epilogue and its narrative.[15] In other words, the two-stage ending frames the narrative in chapter 21:1–23, separating it from the body of the Gospel and marks it as an epilogue.

The overall structure of the FG, if we follow Bauckham's conclusion, therefore, includes three distinctive and identified sections: The Prologue, the body, and the Epilogue.[16] The Prologue points out what was before Jesus's earthly event, the body of the Gospel narrates the event of Jesus's mission, and the Epilogue foresees the post-history of that event.[17] Also, the content of the Epilogue forms an *inclusio* between the beginning and end. In the Prologue, John the Baptist is a witness to the light (Jesus) who came after him. In the Epilogue, the disciples (20:30) and the Beloved Disciple (21:24) are witnesses to Jesus. Witness to Jesus in both cases contributes to the evangelist's goal that his readers would believe.

There are several other arguments, according to Bauckham, which point out the two-stage ending structure. Both endings (20:30–31; 21:24–25) include the same or similar components. Both mention what is written and that much of the available material has been left out from the account. In other words, both endings testify to more available material which could have been included, but the author has been selective. Both endings include the eyewitness role of the disciples to record Jesus's deeds. The first conclusion calls them "signs," whereas the second one calls them "things." The first ending emphasizes the disciples' role, whereas the second conclusion emphasizes the Beloved Disciple's role.[18]

---

14. Brodie, *The Gospel According to John*, 575. See also pp. 543–96.

15. Bauckham, *Jesus and the Eyewitnesses*, 364–65.

16. This structure of FG's structure is an accepted view among Johannine Scholars today. Bauckham's two ending view argues convincingly for this structure as well.

17. Bauckham, *Jesus and the Eyewitnesses*, 364.

18. Bauckham, *Jesus and the Eyewitnesses*, 365–66.

Chapter 21

Finally, there is also a link between the two stages, or more precisely, between the narratives that precede both endings. Thomas's confession and Jesus's response to him (John 20:28-29) points towards those readers of the Gospel who would put their trust in Jesus even without having had the opportunity to see him. The narrative in John 21:1-23 includes the message of the church's mission; the church is to reach out to people to bring them the life (John 21:1-14), and to take care of people who have entered into the kingdom/church (John 21:15-19). This task lasts until this life is lived or until the Lord returns (John 21:20-23).[19]

Not only those readily available points from the structure and design, but also more complicated numerical evidence, according to Bauckham, support stylistic homogeneity of the FG, including chapter 21. Bauckham notices that "New Testament scholars have rarely taken seriously the use of numerical techniques of literary composition by New Testament authors, but the evidence is mounting that such techniques were used in biblical and related literature."[20] Regardless of hesitation among NT scholars, Bauckham believes that several numerical details are originally designed features.[21] He points out quite a few numerical features to prove the eligibility of this method. The Prologue has 496 syllables, which is a "triangular" number (i.e., 496 is the triangle of thirty-one; the sum of the numbers from 1 to 31)[22] and a "perfect" number (i.e., 496 is equal to the sum of its divisors). The numerical value (cf. gematria) of the Prologue's keyword *monogenēs* (only/unique [Son]) (John 1:14, 18) is 496. "The length of the prologue has clearly been designed to relate to its christological content and climax"[23] Bauckham concludes. The second example is similar to the previous one. The section John 1:19—2:11 has 1550 syllables. The numerical value of *ho christos* (the Christ), which

---

19. Bauckham, *Jesus and the Eyewitness*, 364-69.

20. Bauckham, *The Testimony of the Beloved Disciple*, 274.

21. Scholars who are hesitant to accept gematria or other suggested numerical interpretations of chapter 21 include Carson, *The Gospel According to John*, 672-73; Keener, *The Gospel of John*, 2:1231-33; Thompson, *John*, 437-39.

22. Perhaps the most readily noticeable biblical example of a triangular number is 666 in Revelation 13:18. See Brodie, *The Gospel According to John*, 587, for a simple explanation of "triangular" number.

23. Gematria is Jewish hermeneutical practice "involving the calculation of the numerical value of a word written in Hebrew or Greek letters. In Hebrew and Greek, the letters of the alphabet also serve as numerals, and so every word has a numerical value, which is the sum of the numerical values of its letters." Bauckham, *The Testimony of the Beloved Disciple*, 275-77.

occurs a few times in this section, is 1550. Jesus's prayer that he addresses to his Father in John 17:1b–26 has 486 words, which is the numerical value of *patēr* (Father). The final example Bauckham points out is the word "Jesus" in Hebrew and the phrase "the lamb of God" (John 1:29, 35–36). The numerical value of both is 391. Therefore, John the Baptist may have interpreted the Hebrew name of Jesus by using the Jewish hermeneutical system gematria.[24]

Bauckham notes the following regarding gematria.

> Gematria was a well-known practice that took such popular forms as the graffito found in Pompeii: "I love the girl whose number is 545." Triangular and perfect numbers were known to everyone with a little education and were widely regarded as significant numbers. Furthermore, such NT writers as the authors of Revelation and the Fourth Gospel certainly considered their literary productions as something very like the Jewish Scriptures, and they were familiar with the learned exegetical techniques employed in the exegesis of those Scriptures, involving such numerical techniques as gematria and counting the words of sections of text.[25]

The question is, how the numerical values of the words and numbers of words or syllabuses relate to chapter 21? We will turn back to Bauckham's observations.[26]

The Prologue and Epilogue do not only balance the FG, but their numerical values also point toward deliberate design. The Prologue, as already mentioned, consists of 496 syllables, whereas the Epilogue has 496 words. Contrary to the Prologue, the Epilogue does not have any significant words which would have a value of 496. Another numerical relation is found between the two concluding paragraphs. Both John 20:30–31 and 21:24–25 have 43 words.[27] Despite these exciting observations, the primary attention is given to number 153, which is the number of fish that disciples brought to the shore after obeying Jesus's command to fish one more time after an unsuccessful night of fishing (John 21:4–6). We will follow Bauckham's lead of a study of the number 153 without

---

24. The outline in this paragraph is based on Bauckham, *The Testimony of the Beloved Disciple*, 275–77.

25. Bauckham, *The Testimony of the Beloved Disciple*, 284.

26. The following presentation is based on Bauckham, *The Testimony of the Beloved Disciple*, 274–84, without constant referencing.

27. Bauckham, *Jesus and the Eyewitness*, 365.

## Chapter 21

commenting on other possible significances related to this extraordinary catch or the number 153.

The number 153 is a triangular number of 17. Since it is a significant number, it may have drowned ancient readers' attention to look deeper for its significance. It seems that 153, in this case, is related to Ezekiel 47 as well as the first ending in John 20:30–31. Ezekiel 47:10 has two Hebrew names, Gedi and Eglaim, with numerical values of 17 and 153. Thus, an ancient reader might have made this connection, especially because the passage in Ezekiel 47 is about the stream of water that flows from the new temple to the Dead Sea, turning it into fresh water. When this happens, people may fish at its shores from the spring of Gedi to the spring of Eglaim (Ezek 47:10). Carson argues against this interpretation, noting that the readers of the FG did not know Hebrew well enough to make the use of gematria applied to Hebrew words since even elementary Hebrew words in the FG are transliterated into Greek for its first readers' convenience.[28] Despite Carson's fair critique, Bauckham's argument may carry some significance, mostly because of the subject matter in Ezekiel 47, which relates not only to chapter 21 but also to other passages in John, namely, John 7:37–39 and 19:34.

Bauckham also sees that the number 153 is related to John 20:30–31. The keywords in the first conclusion are "sign," "believe," "Christ," and "life." They all occur a last time in that first ending. The word "sign" occurs 17 times in the entire Gospel, and thus is related to a triangle number 153, the triangle being number 17. When the occurrences of the rest of the keywords (believe 98, Christ 19, and life 36) are summed up, we get to number 153. Bauckham concludes, "So the number 17 and its 'triangle' 153 are written into the whole Gospel in the form of those words statistics and are implicit in 20:30–31."[29]

We may conclude, saying that there are several arguments, some more explicit than others, that support the view that chapter 21 fits the structure and design of the FG. It is difficult to think, if Bauckham's argumentation from the numerical structure is acceptable, that anyone else other than the author of chapters 1—20 would have been able to design such a structure for the Epilogue. Bauckham points out that "The fact that many of the stylistic features are inconspicuous and not imitable

---

28. Carson, *The Gospel According to John*, 673.
29. Bauckham, *The Testimony of the Beloved Disciple*, 281.

proves that this homogeneity reflects not the sociolect of a Johannine group, but the idiolect of a single author."[30]

## Content of Chapter 21

Chapter 21 comes as a surprise after the climactic narrative of Jesus's resurrection and his appearance to his disciples. How does the content of the third manifestation of the resurrected Jesus relate to the rest of the Gospel? Or does it?

The fishing narrative (20:2–14) has been interpreted various ways, including an allegorized explanation of number 153, the unbroken fishing net, Peter's dress, the number of disciples who went fishing, and the right side of the boat.[31] Allegorical reading tends to concentrate on small details, not paying attention to a broader narrative context and content. Historical-literal interpretations have not paid much attention to the features mentioned earlier in the narrative. On the contrary, the focus has been on the presentation of Peter and the Beloved Disciple in that chapter. Historical-critical readings have the propensity to read chapter 21 as an independent unit, concentrating on source-critical questions. Historical-critical readings view the chapter as a later addition, which does not have a genuine relationship with the rest of the Gospel. Instead, chapter 21 is viewed as connected to the community's historical situation and perhaps a "dilemma" created by Beloved Disciple's death.[32] The plot-sensitive narrative-theological interpretation of the text reads the narrative in its theological context. In this case, the context of chapter 21 is the entire Gospel.[33] Narrative-theological reading also creates the possibility to read the narrative to include symbolic significance, the literary feature that is present throughout the FG. Craig Koester, among several other commentators, has noticed the value of the symbolic meaning of

---

30. Bauckham, *The Testimony of the Beloved Disciple*, 273.

31. Representatives of allegorical readings are Augustine, Cyril of Alexandria, and Rupert of Deutz. Augustine took the number to indicate the Trinity; Cyril thought the number pointed out the fullness of Gentiles, the remnant of Israel, and the Trinity. Rupert explained that the number 100 represents the married, 50 the widows, and 3 the virgins. See Beasley-Murray, *John*, 402.

32. The view held by Rudolf Bultmann.

33. Among the scholars who applied literary-critical features to chapter 21 was Minear, "The Original Functions of John 21," 85–98. See Brant, *John*, 278.

the fishing narrative.³⁴ When this way of reading is applied, chapter 21's thematic-theological connection to the rest of the Gospel is more readily recognized than using, say, historical-critical methodology.

## John 21:1–14

Chapter 21 starts with an introductory note, "After these things Jesus manifested Himself again" (21:1). The same opening phrase, "After these things," is used several times in the FG. Those other occurrences of the phrase indicate a new scene in the Gospel narrative (cf. 3:22; 5:1, 14; 6:1; 7:1) as it does here. In 21:1, however, the narrative flow is not that obvious because of what follows. Peter goes fishing (21:3). Even casual readers raise their eyebrows, asking, "What is going on with Peter?" Peter's decision to go fishing is sometimes interpreted as an act of a backslider who has forgotten Jesus's call and returns to his old life, taking several other disciples with him.³⁵ However, this might not be the correct understanding as Frederick Bruner was reminded by a Sunday school attendee who pointed out that "even apostles have to eat, and that other apostles worked for their lives" as well!³⁶ In the narrative, Jesus is not concerned about finding Peter and other disciples fishing. Instead, he uses their unsuccessful fishing trip as an object lesson, which leads to Jesus's encounter with Peter in 21:15–17. That encounter is not related to Peter's decision to go fishing, although some have suggested that.³⁷ Peter's leadership and decision to go fishing are in line with his characterization elsewhere in the FG, that is, his "tendency towards impulsive speech or action."³⁸

When we do not read guilt into Peter's decision to go fishing, then chapter 21 can be read in a way that puts readers into an excellent position to connect chapter 21's narratives to the entire Gospel. In other words, these narratives are not isolated stories that have their own storyline and climax. They are not disconnected from the rest of the Gospel even though the two endings (20:30–31 and 21:24–25) bracket the narrative

---

34. Koester, *Symbolism in the Fourth Gospel*, 134–36.
35. Bruner, *The Gospel of John*, 1207.
36. Bruner, *The Gospel of John*, 1207. So also Beasley-Murray, *John*, 399.
37. Jesus's question to Peter, "Do you love Me more than these?" is suggested to relate Peter's fishing equipment and profession or even fish. Grammatically this is quite possible, but the narrative and its structure points elsewhere. It is much more convincing to read "these" to refer to other disciples. See Keener, *The Gospel of John*, 2:1236.
38. Tenney, *John*, 197.

structurally. Like other narratives in the FG, which can stand alone, these two narratives in chapter 21 are connected to the overall theological and spiritual purpose of the entire Gospel. We suggest that the content of the narratives in chapter 21 points towards the view that they are not an afterthought and independent, but a well-designed part of the Gospel's ending.

As he has done so many other times in the FG, Jesus gives a spiritual and theological lesson that he builds on a life situation. This list includes wine (ch. 2), wind (ch. 3), water (ch. 4), healing (ch. 5), five loaves of bread and two fish (ch. 6), various festival rituals (ch. 7–8), sheep (ch. 10) and the vine (ch. 15). This time Jesus uses fish and fishing as an object lesson. It seems to be the Fourth Evangelist's style not to include an explicit explanation of the analogy between the event and its spiritual and theological significance. He leaves that to readers to discover through heuristic moments, which are highly memorable. Koester and others have suggested that the object lesson Jesus gives this time is about the church's obedient mission in the future. Jey Kanagaraj thinks that "the large catch of fish may symbolize the ingathering of many new converts from all nations through the disciples' ministry. The gospel net will never break, no matter how many converts it catches."[39] Although we may not buy that highly symbolized reading, it is a widely accepted view among the Johannine scholars that the catch represents the church's mission after Jesus's ascension.

It has been suggested that one of the themes that the first narrative teaches is obedience. Obedience, which is an inevitable part of the church's mission, is presented in the disciples' response to Jesus's request to cast the net on the right side of the boat. Even though the FG does not depict Peter or other disciples as fishermen, that information is readily available in the Synoptic Gospels (Matt 4:18; Mark 1:16–18; Luke 5:2–11). Among these seven disciples, at least Peter and two other disciples were fishermen by trade.[40] Therefore, their fishing, we may propose, was not recreational. For professional fishers, unsuccessful fishing trips must have been frustrating (cf. Luke 5:4–5). Jesus's request to fish from the right side of the boat just one hundred yards away from the shore was odd. It is suggested that it was more natural to fish from the boat's left side because a steering oar was on the right side.[41] Whether it was more difficult to fish

---

39. Kanagaraj, *John*, 208.
40. Neyrey, *The Gospel of John*, 333.
41. Keener, *The Gospel of John*, 2:1228.

from the right side of the boat or not, Jesus's request does not make much sense to professional fishers. Nevertheless, they obeyed the "order." Although they obeyed Jesus's request, they may have responded more from frustration than from obedience since they had not yet recognized (they had not seen) that the one who requested them to cast the net was their Lord.[42] That happened only after the catch (21:6–7). Therefore, we cannot be entirely sure if the narrative emphasizes obedience to the resurrected Lord. However, Brodie makes a valuable observation that may support the view that the obedience motif cannot be ignored. He points out that these disciples do not "see" Jesus in this narrative. The narrative does not employ "seeing" language at all. According to Brodie, this creates a bridge between "the not-seeing motif in 20:29" and this narrative. He concludes that the narrative "tells of a time when interaction with Jesus will occur at another level."[43]

Although the obedience motif might well be part of the narrative, we suggest that the main focus in John 21:2–14 is on the fact that disciples (i.e., the church) cannot accomplish anything without Jesus's presence.[44] Jesus is the broker who provides access to the patron's resources.[45] What takes place in John 21:2–14 reminds readers of a few other narratives. First, in John 6 Jesus feeds five thousand people with five loaves of bread and two fish.[46] Similarly, in John 21 Jesus had already prepared the breakfast for his disciples before they hauled 153 fish onto the shore. Also, the great catch speaks to the same end; Jesus provides when even skilled people are unable to achieve the desired results. In John 15:5, Jesus reminds his disciples that they are unable to do anything apart from him.

Therefore, symbolically the disciples' fishing trip teaches the spiritual truth. It is an object lesson. The disciples' efforts to catch fish were a waste of time despite their skills and experience. Only when Jesus appeared on the shore did the great catch take place. Other parts of Jesus's Farewell Speech also point in the same direction. Jesus ensures that, in his presence, the disciples would be able to function in the world without compromising their faith, to perform even greater things than they had seen him perform prior to his crucifixion and experience peace in

---

42. Cf. Brant, *John*, 281.

43. In short, the church will engage in God's mission without seeing Jesus. Brodie, *The Gospel According to John*, 575.

44. Cf. Brodie, *The Gospel According to John*, 579–82.

45. Neyrey, *The Gospel of John*, 337.

46. Cf. Brodie, *The Gospel According to John*, 358.

his presence (cf. John 14:15–18, 27–28; 16:5–8; 17:13–21). In short, the fishing narrative symbolically speaks about the mission in which the disciples will be engaged in the world. They are called to be involved in the task of the gospel after Jesus has departed to the Father. That mission can be accomplished only in Jesus's presence, whereby he has promised to be available to them through the Spirit.[47]

The number 153 (number of fish) has generated various interpretations. Several are linked to the church's task to evangelize (see above). It has been suggested by H. Kruse and others that a gematrical interpretation of 153 signifies "the children of God" and "the church of love." The numerical value of these phrases in Hebrew is 153. Therefore, this interpretation speaks about the church and its mission to bring in the children of God.[48] Also, it is suggested that there were 153 different kinds of fish known to people at that time. This interpretation implies that the future church will consist of all kinds of people. These suggestions remain vague, however. A naturalistic interpretation suggests that fishers usually want to know their catch's size, especially if it is extraordinarily large. In this case, the fishermen counted the fish. Also, fishers need to count the fish if they are to share them among themselves. The number 153 continues to be a tough nut to be cracked by those who think that it contains a spiritual or theological significance.

## John 21:15–23

It is sometimes argued that John 21:15–23 is disconnected from the narrative that precedes it. One of the arguments for this view is that there is a shift from "fish" to "sheep/lamb"[49] and from the group of disciples to only two disciples, namely Peter and the Beloved Disciple, who is not even mentioned in the preceding narrative. Raymond Brown comments on the former argument saying, "the fish symbolism, while well suited to the theme of a Christian mission in [John 21:] 1–14, could scarcely have been adapted to the theme of the care of the faithful, which is the central

---

47. Hoskyns has argued that the FG's closing includes the mission of the disciples. See Brown, *The Gospel According to John*, 2:1078, 1084.

48. Beasley-Murray, *John*, 403.

49. Brown, *The Gospel According to John*, 2:1084.

idea in the threefold command of [vv.] 15–17 ... One can catch fish, but fishermen do not take care of fish the way shepherds take care of sheep."[50]

The latter argument that there is no unity because the narrative's focus shifts from the group of disciples to two disciples is not convincing either. The Fourth Evangelist makes a similar shift from the group of disciples to Peter and the Beloved Disciple in the passion narrative (John 18:1–27). In chapter 18, as well as in chapter 21, both Peter and the Beloved Disciple have a significant narrative role to play. Besides, Jesus's teaching in John 15—17 is in the backdrop of Peter's denial narrated in John 18. Thus, the narrative's development from general to specific (from group to individuals) in John 21:1–23 is not strange for the FG as the evangelist has done this before. Neither is the narrative design that brackets 21:2–13 (cf. "this is the third time;" 21:1, 14) from the following narrative (21:15–23) an indicator which proves discontinuity between these two narratives.[51] Although it brackets the fishing narrative, it also appropriately draws attention to the second part in which Simon Peter and the Beloved Disciple are the main characters. Raymond Brown says that "one cannot establish with certainty the original unity of 1–14 and 15–17 [15–23], but the arguments in favor of it seem more persuasive than the arguments against it."[52]

Interpreters have argued for two interpretations of Jesus's initial question to Peter, "do you love Me more than these?" (21:15). First, this is understood as Jesus's way of asking Peter if he loved him more than fish (or fishing).[53] If that is the meaning of Jesus's question, then Jesus is not asking about the quality of Peter's love, but instead about the object of Peter's love. This way of reading makes the preceding narrative (20:1–14) function as an introductory narrative to the main point found in 21:15–23. Chapter 21's unity is also then underlined. This reading, though grammatically possible, has not received much support. In addition, if a comparison of Peter's love is between Jesus and the fish/fishing, then it suggests that Peter not only backslid when denying Jesus but also when he went fishing. However, if that is the case, why did the Fourth Evangelist give so much attention to Peter's second error, not his first

50. Brown, *The Gospel According to John*, 2:1084.
51. See Brant, *John*, 279.
52. Brown, *The Gospel According to John*, 2:1084.
53. Keener, *The Gospel of John*, 2:1236, says that "To love Jesus more 'than these' may refer to loving him [Jesus] more than the fellow disciples, but probably refers to loving him more than the fish."

one when he denied knowing Jesus and belonging to his group? Due to grammatical ambiguity and narrative possibility, some have suggested that Jesus's question may carry a double meaning. In other words, Jesus is asking Peter if he loved him more than anything else.

The most common way of reading Jesus's words "more than these" in his initial question to Peter is to compare Peter's love, that is, the quality of his love, to that of the rest of the disciples.[54] Even though not all disciples were present at this time,[55] Jesus is referring to Peter's declaration of his boastful love towards Jesus. Peter claimed that he would never leave Jesus even though everyone else would desert him (Matt 26:31–35; Mark 14:27–31). The FG, however, does not record Peter's boastful love towards Jesus in that fashion. It records Peter's boastful love declaration in John 13:37 when Peter claims, "Lord, why can I not follow You right now? I will lay down my life for You." Thus, if we read Jesus's words "more than these" as a reference to other disciples, we have two narratives in chapter 21 built on the information the Synoptic Gospels. In the Synoptic Gospels, Peter is presented as a fisherman and boasting disciple who compared his quality of love to that of the other disciples.

The word "love" in the present context has also given rise to a variety of interpretations. The Greek words for "love" employed in the conversation are *agapē* and *philos* in their verbal forms, *agapaō* and *phileō*, respectively. The standard lexical meaning of *agapaō* is understood in the NT context as a self-sacrificial love.[56] Nevertheless, the word has a range of meanings, having nuances that overlap with *phileō*. *Phileō*, the most general word for "love" in Greek, indicates "a general attraction towards a person or thing. In the foreground stands the meaning of love for one's relatives and friends . . . , but the whole area of fondness is also included with gods, men and things as possible objects."[57] It is suggested that in the NT *philos* love signifies brotherly love whereas *agapē* love denotes the highest type of love with which God loves people self-sacrificially (cf.

---

54. Cf. Harris, *John*, 343.

55. There were seven disciples present. Number seven is the number of completeness. Therefore, this may be symbolically interpreted to refer to the future church. It might not be an accident that twelve disciples who are linked to twelve tribes of Israel (cf. Luke 22:30) is changed to seven disciples after Jesus's glorification in John 21 where the future work of the church is communicated.

56. Günther and Link, "Love," NIDNTT 2:538.

57. Günther and Link, "Love," NIDNTT 2:538.

John 3:16).[58] The following table demonstrates how Jesus and Peter use *agapē* and *philos* "love" words in their conversation.

|  | Jesus | Peter |
| --- | --- | --- |
| First round 21:15 | do you *agapas* me more than these? | I *philō* you. |
| Second round 21:16 | do you *agapas* me? | I *philō* you. |
| Third round 21:17 | do you *phileis* me? [repeated by the narrator: "Do you *phileis* me?"] | I *philō* you. |

Table 14.1

Several comments need to be made. Quite recently, David Shepherd has proposed, we would say, a radical reading of John 21:15–17 that seems to play down Peter's status. He argues that Peter, by using *philos* instead of *agapē*, demonstrates that he does not grasp Jesus's love and what it means to love Jesus as Jesus requires Peter to love him. Peter remains, Shepherd argues, partial in his understanding and, therefore, in his relationship with Jesus. This reading inevitably elevates the Beloved Disciple's status as the ideal disciple above and beyond what Peter was able to demonstrate and to be. Shepherd's interpretation requires one to put much weight on Jesus's and Peter's usage of two love words and categorizes them into lower (*philos*) and higher (*agapē*) types of love. As far as we are aware, this interpretation has not received much support.[59]

The opposite is the popular view among Johannine scholars, namely, that the two love verbs do not have significance in this context as both love words carry the same meaning and are exchangeable.[60] It is argued, therefore, that use of synonymous verbs here is just another example of the typical style of the evangelist as he uses synonyms in his Gospel

---

58. Differentiation between *agapaō* and *phileō* is reflected in NIV translation where *agapaō* was translated as "truly love" and *phileō* as "love." This distinction is not present in the latest version of NIV (2011), following today's scholarly opinion that such a distinction is not in the picture in John 21:15–17.

59. Shepherd, "'Do You Love me?,'" 777–92.

60. Keener, *The Gospel of John*, 2:1236.

generally and in chapter 21 particularly. A strong argument to support this view is his interchangeable use of both "love" words elsewhere in his Gospel. The evangelist describes God's love not only with *agapē* kind of love but also as *philos*-love (John 5:20; 16:27; cf. 14:31). Further, if the conversation took place in Aramaic, such a differentiation between *philos* and *agapē* types of love might not have been possible, since those categories belongs to Greek semiotics and are not clearly present in Aramaic. The case is the same with the Hebrew.[61] Therefore, it is argued that it is the evangelist, who, writing in Greek, is given the linguistic possibility to use two different "love" words. The question remains: Is the evangelist using them just for stylistic reasons or for the hermeneutical key that helps readers grasp the conversation's tone and meaning?

A third way of understanding the usage of love words in this dialogue is that Peter, although loving Jesus, indicates that he cannot return Jesus's love with the same kind of love. Marianne Thompson, who does not agree with this reading, says,

> While Peter answers affirmatively ('Yes Lord'), he uses verb *phileō*, showing that he is not capable of or cannot commit to the level of love that Jesus himself has manifested . . . because Peter cannot rise to Jesus' level, Jesus condescends to Peter's level. Peter grieves that, in this third query, Jesus has lowered his expectations to account for Peter's failure to render what Jesus asks."[62]

Interpreting the conversation this way requires giving distinctive meanings to the two love words as portraying two different love-types and thus focusing on the quality of love to which Peter is ready to commit.[63]

We suggest that even though *agapē* and *philos* can be used interchangeably, as demonstrated elsewhere in the FG,[64] it needs to be taken into account that these words are employed in this conversation rhetorically. They do not, however, carry the full rhetorical power and the conversation's significance. Other rhetorical elements include the number of Jesus's queries, which reminds the readers of Peter's triple denial (John

---

61. Günther, "φιλέω" NIDNTT 2:547–51.

62. Thompson, *John*, 442.

63. Thompson, *John*, 443.

64. See Thompson, *John*, 442. It is also notable that the use of words "sheep" and "lamb" in the same conversation have not received so much attention in interpretations to point to different objects of Peter's future task. Instead, they are usually treated as the evangelist's stylistic choice. See also Brant, *John*, 283.

18:15–18, 25–27) as well as of Peter's boastful claim of the love he bore Jesus prior to his arrest (John 13:37). All these rhetorical elements, together with Peter's usage of the *philos* word and his final emphatic response, bring forth the sensory-aesthetic texture of the conversation (i.e., feelings and emotions).[65] Therefore, Peter, now emotionally exhausted, has reached the end of the conversation as transparent as he possibly could become. He confesses his love three times towards Jesus without any hint of boasting. That might be very well the reason why he always uses *phileō* instead of *agapaō*. Peter also points out, as in the other two instances, that Jesus knows that he loves him, but this time he adds the emphasis to it, "Lord, you know all things" (21:17).[66] The Greek verb Peter always uses for "know" in his responses to Jesus is *oida* (vv. 15–17), except in the very last time in v. 17 where he repeats the statement using the verb *ginōskō*. Merrill C. Tenney points out that *oida* "implies the intellectual knowledge of a fact," but *ginōskō* "denotes knowledge gained through experience."[67] If we can distinguish between these two verbs in this context, as Tenney has suggested, it demonstrates how transparent Peter is with Jesus. Jesus knows Peter's quality of love by experience. Peter does not need to give any arguments or further reassurance.

Without going into more detail, we conclude that Peter seems to surrender here to the Lord the way that could be paraphrased by the following: "Jesus, you *know* my heart, you know that I love you, but I cannot say that I love you more than others do. Your love towards me is greater than my love towards you." Reading the conversation in this way implies that the conversation does not only re-direct Peter's focus to the ministry Jesus had called him to earlier but also includes Peter's confession necessary for re-establishing his relation to the Lord and other fellow believers.[68] As such a person, Peter is charged to be a shepherd of God's people till the end of his life (cf. John 10:1–18; John 21:18–19). That indicates Jesus's acceptance of Peter's confession.

The aftermath of the Jesus-Peter conversation in vv. 18–23 picks up two topics: (1) Peter's life-long service and (2) reminders of what the focus in Peter's life is. Both these are in interaction with the vv. 15–17. First, Peter's love toward Jesus and his ministry as a shepherd will last the rest

---

65. See Robbins, *Exploring the Texture of the Texts*, 29–37.
66. See Brant, *John*, 284.
67. Tenney, *John*, 202.
68. Cf. Torrance and Torrance, *The Gospel According to St John*, 218.

of his life. Jesus reminds Peter that his main task in life is to follow Jesus (21:19). When Peter began to compare the Beloved Disciple and Jesus's words to him regarding the end of his life, Jesus again reminds Peter that his main task is to follow Jesus rather than others (21:22). This is a profound instruction to Peter to stay focused on his relationship with Jesus, but it also functions as an *inclusio*. In the beginning of the FG, in the narrative where the first individuals were coming to Jesus, he instructs Philip with these same words "Follow Me" (John 1:43). The evangelist invites all his readers to follow Jesus.

The Beloved Disciple is brought into the picture by Peter's comments about him. We argue that it is difficult to read any ideas of the Beloved Disciple's superiority over Peter in this. Peter will glorify God, says the narrator (21:19). This comment is not ill-motivated. Instead, it is said respectfully and admiringly. The point seems to be elsewhere. Everyone's primary concern is to safeguard his/her stand before Jesus as they serve him. Although life treats Jesus's servants differently, that is not the focus of his people to observe and measure. The attention is on the relationship between them and Jesus.

It is much debated if the final section in chapter 21, the second ending (John 21:24–25), belongs to the original author or to a later editor/redactor. We have discussed this matter in Chapter Eight, so we will not address the point again in detail. We only note that it is not impossible to consider these last verses as belonging to the original author of the FG. Howard Jackson, who argues convincingly that chapter 21 belongs to the original Gospel points out that the change from "we" (v. 24) to "I" (v. 25) does not "necessary imply a change of subject, still less a redactional addition . . . The shift to the first person singular in verse 25 is explicable on the grounds of a shift from the one subgenre to the other, from the solemn, formal posture demanded of the documentary subscription being followed as a model in verse 24a to the more informal, familiar tone, characteristic of the epistolary postscript, evident in verse 25."[69]

## Concluding Remarks

Does chapter 21 belong to the FG? Yes, it does. Is it the original part of the Gospel? Most likely, it is. Did the evangelist write the last few verses?

---

69. Jackson, "Ancient Self-Referential Conventions," 8. See also Bauckham, *Jesus and the Eyewitnesses*, 380.

It is possible (even probable), but it cannot be proved beyond doubt. We suggest that based on the pieces of evidence from historical, literary, and thematic aspects, chapter 21 should be read as a genuine and meaningful "second ending" of the FG. It is also important to note that a typical reader reads chapter 21 as an integral part of the FG without asking historical-critical questions. "We read the text before us synchronically, that is, as coherent in itself," Robert Fortna reminds.[70]

Chapter 21 contains two narratives that have received a variety of treatments. We have suggested that they are not separated historically or thematically from each other and relate closely to the rest of the content of the FG. Readers do not need to support this view by the most radical symbolical, numerical, or allegorical readings to see that connection. Yet, there are many gaps, especially in the historical level of the events, which we cannot currently be solved. The existing historical gaps may not be significant for the readers who read the text synchronically. Historical details were not so crucial to the evangelist either, as he did not include that information into his account.

It seems that the Fourth Evangelist has included the second ending (ch. 21) in order to point towards the time after Jesus's ascension. God's people—now the people of the Spirit (cf. John 20:19–23), his church—would have Jesus's presence and thus would be successful in spreading the Gospel (cf. 21:1–14). They need to stay connected to Jesus (i.e., love him) and have unity (i.e., love Jesus without comparing their love with that of others) in order to shepherd God's people (cf. 21:15–17). Finally, they need to keep on following Jesus until they reach the end of their days in this life (cf. 21:18–23).

## Suggestions for Further Reading

Bauckham, Richard. *The Testimony of the Beloved Disciple: Narrative, History, and Theology in the Gospel of John*. Grand Rapids: Baker Academic, 2007. Pp. 271–84.

Brown, Raymond E. *The Gospel According to John XIII–XXI: Introduction, Translation, and Notes*. Vol. 2. AB. New York: Doubleday, 1970. Pp. 1066–1130.

---

70. Fortna, "Diachronic/Synchronic Reading John 21 and Luke 5," 397.

Culpepper, R. Alan. "John 21:24–25: The Johannine *Sphragis*." In *John, Jesus, and History, Volume 2: Aspects of Historicity in the Fourth Gospel*, edited by Paul N. Anderson et al., 349–64. Atlanta: Society of Biblical Literature, 2009.

Keener, Craig, S. *The Gospel of John*. Vol. 2. Peabody: Hendrickson, 2003. Pp. 2:1219–42.

Morris, Leon. *The Gospel According to John*. Revised ed. NICNT. Grand Rapids: Eerdmans, 1995. Pp. 757–77.

— PART THREE —

# Interpretations of the Fourth Gospel

CHAPTER 15

# Questions Every Reader of the Fourth Gospel Faces

IN THE PREVIOUS CHAPTERS, we have discussed various topics that relate to this chapter's title. We will not repeat what we have already said, but instead, we will introduce other questions and issues faced by today's readers of the FG. This chapter is not a comprehensive presentation of these issues but rather an outline of various kinds of questions that the text brings to the reader. The topics we have chosen to present here are from hermeneutical, literary, and theological areas.

## Reading with Three Dimensions

Every Gospel account could be read with three dimensions in mind. Each parameter of these three dimensions introduces the reader to a different set of questions to tackle. These parameters are the vertical, the horizontal, and the contextual. The vertical parameter is the FG's narrative from the beginning to the end. The horizontal parameter refers to the fact that we have three other canonical Gospels which relate the same Jesus event.[1] The contextual parameter refers to the contexts of the author and the historical events that the author recorded. Reading context forms another context.[2] These parameters are especially significant in the case of the FG because it is further removed in time from the events it records

---

1. See Klein et al., *Introduction to Biblical Interpretation*, 403–6.
2. Davies, *Rhetoric and Reference*, 44.

than the Synoptics, and its presentation of the Jesus event and its unique persuasive style of writing also differs from the Synoptic Gospels. Below we will explain these parameters (except the reading context what will be discussed in the last chapter of this volume) and what kinds of hermeneutical questions they may bring to the reader.

## Reading Vertically

Vertical reading refers to a fundamental hermeneutical rule that the text must be read entirely, from the beginning to the end, within its terms. The vertical reading is the first parameter in the three dimensions. Readers start with the text. The text leads them to the subject matter and directs them to the slant from which that subject is presented. In the case of the FG, it means that the FG must be read within its own theological, chronological, and rhetorical terms. The parts of the FG must be interpreted in the context of the entire Gospel (cf. hermeneutical circle). This means that even when a reader finds the FG's presentation different (even incompatible with) to the other three Gospel accounts, they do not try to harmonize the FG's text with them. We must let the Fourth Evangelist be the Fourth Evangelist and not Matthew, Mark, Luke, or any other NT author. Vertical reading is necessary before one moves on to interpret smaller sections or systematize the text's theology.

The vertical reading of the FG is especially significant because the FG differs so radically from the Synoptic Gospels. The danger is that readers may keep on their Synoptic "lenses" when they arrive at the FG and therefore approach it as if they were reading a Synoptic Gospel. When this happens, the first question readers may ask is why does the FG differ from the Synoptics? That is not, however, the first question that should be asked. The questions readers should ask first are the questions about the FG's content, style, and purpose.

For example, the FG presents prominent roles for John the Baptist and Moses. The Fourth Evangelist compares and contrasts them with Jesus. The evangelist does not play down the roles of Moses and John the Baptist or their significance. His slant shows how they were part of God's plan to reveal his promised ultimate broker. Moses and John the Baptist are present in the Synoptic Gospels, but they function differently in those narratives. We could describe Moses and John the Baptist's presence in the Synoptic Gospels as more neutral concerning Jesus's role and status, whereas in the FG, they are sharply contrasted to Jesus albeit in favorable terms. Other examples would include the usage of the phrase "eternal life" with all its cognates, rather than the terminology of the "kingdom of God/Heaven."

## Reading Horizontally

Horizontal reading of the text is not a new practice. It has been practiced in a variety of ways. The well-known apparatus, called the *Hexapla*, edited by Origen (184–253 CE), placed OT Hebrew and various Greek texts, including Greek transliteration, side by side for easy textual comparison. The English Hexapla (1841) follows the same idea where six early English translations of the NT are placed in columns side by side.[3] The idea of Hexapla is present when the (Synoptic) Gospels are placed side by side in columns for "horizontal" (parallel) reading. Sometimes this kind of comparison of the Gospels is motivated by attempts to harmonize the gospel account. As early as around 160 CE, Tatian produced a harmonized Gospel text, the *Diatessaron*. In the case of the Synoptic Gospels, the comparison is often motivated by the desire to understand the textual and historical relationship between the Gospels of Matthew, Mark, and Luke.

We suggest that the horizontal reading of the FG with all other canonical Gospels is a meaningful and even necessary exercise even though its purpose is not harmonizing the FG with the Synoptic ones.[4] This is a fruitful way to read the FG even though it shares only eight-to-nine percent of the material with the Synoptic Gospels. Taking notice of how a small portion of the FG's material is found in the Synoptic Gospels is already an outcome of horizontal reading. Reading the FG together with the Synoptic Gospels helps readers further recognize the FG's uniqueness and paint a larger portrait of Jesus's earthly life.

## Reading Contextually

The distinctive dimension in the FG is a contextual one. Every Gospel has two contexts (or time zones). The first context refers to the setting in

---

3. The English Hexapla presents the following early English translations of the NT: Wycliffe (1380), Tyndale (1534), Cranmer (1539), Geneva, (1557), Rheims (1582), and Authorised version (1611).

4. See Fee and Stuart, *How to Read the Bible*, 132–53.

which the events that are recorded took place, the context in which Jesus spoke and acted. The second context refers to the context in which the text was produced and in which its first readers lived. Although all the Gospels were written a few decades after Jesus's life, the FG was written most likely several decades later than the Synoptic Gospels. Therefore, the FG was also written cultural-ideologically in a different locale than the Synoptic Gospels. The FG's writing context addressed the Johannine community and their beliefs differently from the way the Synoptic Gospels' writing contexts addressed the believing communities at that time. Thus, it has become quite common to hold that the Johannine world's historical context caused the writer of the FG to write a different Gospel. This understanding is exhibited clearly in past theories, which argues that the FG was a Hellenized Gospel. Today, the FG is understood to be Jewish rather than Hellenistic, but its uniqueness is still argued to be influenced by its context of writing.

In his *History and Theology in the Fourth Gospel* (1968), J. Louis Martyn argues that the FG is a two-level drama, namely, Jesus's story and the story of the Johannine community. This means, Martyn argues, that the FG is as much a story of the believing community in the context of writing as it is the story of Jesus. Whether one agrees with Martyn's conclusion or not, his study is a benchmark work to remind us how the context of the Fourth Evangelist and his community are not disconnected from what is in the text. The historical context's influence on the content and style certainly carries some weight, but it would be a mistake to explain all differences on contextual grounds.

The point we want to make here is this: the readers of the FG must keep in mind contextual dimensions, which include two quite different historical contexts: the contexts of the Jesus-event and the recording of those events. These historical contexts are not readily available for readers through the text. Therefore, so-called background studies are required.

## Chronology and Timing

The chronology of the FG differs from the Synoptic Gospels. As we have noted, the earlier view that the Synoptic Tradition is more trustworthy in terms of history and chronology has been challenged. D. Moody Smith has argued that the FG follows the order of the actual events more closely than the Synoptic Gospels. We will not enter that discussion here to argue which Gospel tradition is more accurate historically. Our purpose is to notice chronological differences between these two traditions and what it might mean for readers as they interpret the FG. We draw the readers' attention to this matter by demonstrating it with a few examples.

## Cleansing the Jerusalem Temple

The most well-known example of a chronological difference between the FG and the Synoptic Gospels is perhaps Jesus's cleansing of the Jerusalem Temple. The Synoptic Gospels place it at the end of the Gospel narrative just before Jesus's crucifixion (Matt 21:12–12; Mark 11:15–18; Luke 19:45–47), whereas the FG places it at the beginning of Jesus's public ministry (John 2:13–22). The Fourth Evangelist seems to arrange his material theologically rather than historically at this point. It is hard to believe, we think, that the Synoptic Gospels would have deviated from the event's timing at the end of Jesus's ministry just before his crucifixion, or that there were two temple cleansings, one in the beginning and the other at the end of Jesus's public ministry.

To look at the FG's presentation of the temple cleansing, we note the following. John 2:12 summarizes what happened after Jesus had performed his first sign at Cana. Jesus and his companion went to Capernaum and stayed there. John 2:12 is, therefore, a chronological marker. In the next v. 13, the evangelist picks up the Passover in Jerusalem, which Jesus attended. The evangelist gives again a chronological maker telling that Passover was near. There is quite a jump from Capernaum to Jerusalem, from the wedding to the Passover. Readers may read this without asking any tough questions of chronology. However, those who stop here to contemplate what they have just read may ask the question to what "The Passover of the Jews was near" is referring. Is it referring to the time when Jesus was in Capernaum (v. 12), or does it refer to Jesus's going to Jerusalem? In other words, is the evangelist pointing out that Jesus went to Jerusalem just prior to the Passover? If the answer to this is "yes," the Fourth Evangelist hints that he does not follow chronological order here. He has inserted an event that chronologically belongs to Jesus's later life. Nevertheless, for his theological and rhetorical purposes, he brought together the beginning of Jesus's public ministry and the end of it, pointing out his destination as a new temple (2:13–22) and the new way of purification (2:1–11). It needs to be kept in mind, however, that the FG is not entirely off the chronological map of this event. The Fourth Evangelist attaches Jesus's temple cleansing to the final Passover as the Synoptic evangelists do. It is just that the Fourth Evangelist brings it to the beginning of Jesus's public ministry and first sign to show what is going to be the end of his ministry and final sign (i.e., the cross).

Chronological issues continue in the next chapter. If Jesus was in Jerusalem in 2:13—3:21, why then does the evangelist give a chronological marker in 3:22 saying, "After these things Jesus and His disciples came into the land of Judea." They were already in the land of Judea, weren't they? Why then this chronological marker, including geographical location? Keener gives two possible solutions: "Jesus came into Judea (3:22), which either refers to 'Judea outside of Jerusalem' . . . or implies that the author refers to a point after that of 3:1–21, with an unmentioned elapse of time and return to Galilee."[5] However, it is not impossible to argue that 3:22 picks up chronology again, where 2:12 left the readers. The Passover narrative and the following discourse (2:13—3:21), which has most likely taken place during the last Passover, is inserted here. Therefore, "After this" in 2:12 and "After these things" in 3:22 would frame the Passover narrative from the narrative's chronology. John 3:22 moves back to the baptism motif and Jesus's first disciple narrative (John 1:29–51), which are also elements in John 3:22–36.

## Farewell Discourse

At the end of John 14:31 in the first part of his Farewell Speech, Jesus says, "Get up, let us go from here." However, Jesus's Farewell Speech continues for still two more chapters (chs. 15—16), including a long prayer in chapter 17. In John 18:1 the narrator informs the audience, "When Jesus had spoken these words, He went forth with His disciples over the ravine of the Kidron." This may not seem to be a chronological dilemma for all readers. It is possible to think that Jesus indeed left the room where he was with his disciples and walked through Jerusalem and to the nearby temple where he also prayed (ch. 17). After the prayer, he crossed the Kidron valley to the garden where he spent a short time before his arrest. This is an acceptable interpretation when the text is read narratively.

The historical-critical scholars have suggested that there have been two Farewell Speech traditions and that the Fourth Evangelist has

---

5. Keener, *The Gospel of John*, 1:576.

included both in his account. Therefore, John 13:33—14:31 follows one tradition whereas John 15:1—17:26 follows the other.

There might still be another way of looking at this chronological issue. If we read the text narrative-theologically, the statement in 14:31 may not point only to the time of action when Jesus leaves the room and begins his journey towards the garden. It may also function as Jesus's statement of obedience. The words that Jesus had just spoken, namely, that he does not have anything to do with the ruler of this world (14:30), points out that his words, "Let us go from here," demonstrate his full engagement in obeying his Father's commands to face the cross. In other words, the ruler of this world has nothing in him (John 14:29–31). Jesus stays obedient to the Father and faces the cross.

## Final Passover Events

Another chronological issue is found in the Fourth Evangelist's presentation of the last supper and Jesus's crucifixion. The difference does not become evident without a comparison of the FG with the Synoptic Gospels (horizontal reading), which offers a slightly different chronology of these events. In Mark 14:12, the last supper that Jesus had with his disciples is depicted as a Jewish Passover meal. That "pushes" Jesus's crucifixion and burial to after the Passover (Mark 15:1–47). In the FG, the meal Jesus had with his disciples was not a Passover meal. It took place before the Passover (John 13:1–32). Jesus's crucifixion in the FG is aligned with the slaughter of the Passover lambs in the Jerusalem Temple (John 19:14). For that reason, Jesus's Jewish accusers did not enter Pilate's quarters to keep themselves ceremonially clean to celebrate the Passover meal later that day. We do not see "Jews" at Jesus's cross testifying to his death except his closest followers, including Jesus's mother and a few other women (John 19:25b–27). Jesus's death in the FG, therefore, takes place before the Passover. He is hanging on the cross while Jews are celebrating the Passover meal.

It is suggested that the FG follows the Judean method of counting days that was used by the Sadducees. In contrast, the Synoptic Gospels follow the Galilean method that is followed by Jesus's disciples and the Pharisees. These two methods are said to differ in the manner in which they consider the start of a new day.[6] All scholars do not share this at-

---

6. Hoehner, "Chronological Aspects," 241–46; Smalley, *1, 2, 3 John*, 24–25.

tempt of harmonization.[7] Keener suggests something entirely different, namely, that John's Passover chronology should be read symbolically.[8]

It is reasonable to think that the Fourth Evangelist, as a persuasive communicator, presents Jesus's passion the way that suited his theological (especially christological) purposes the best. By lining up the chronology of Jesus's passion narrative with the Jewish Passover celebration, the Fourth Evangelist explicitly demonstrates that Jesus is the Lamb of God. He brings life and freedom as did that first Passover lamb in Egypt and the ensuing memorial celebrations foretold this. When Jesus was hanging on the cross, dying as God's perfect Lamb, the Jews participated in the slaughter of the temple lamb. When they were reflecting on the first Passover meal in Egypt, Jesus shed his blood to be available to people to receive protection from death. We join the scholars who think that "John certainly had theological reasons to place the death of God's lamb (John 1:29) on Passover (19:36)."[9]

These few examples of the FG's chronological landscape have proved the point we want to make. Although the Fourth Evangelist has placed events in chronological order, he occasionally has organized his material thematically to bring forth theological points and rhetorical force. Furthermore, he narrates the events occasionally in such a way that supports his theological goal. We disagree with the voices who argue that the FG is theological rather than historical. That would be an overstatement. The Fourth Evangelist is historical in his account, but he also has the theological agenda which he pushes through by using the flexibility that the chosen literary genre offers.

## Narrator as Interpreter

The FG contains direct and indirect discourses. They are understood to be the author's editions of the original discourses reflecting their content rather than being verbatim repetitions.[10] The narrator enters these discourses by explaining them to readers, a typical feature in the narrative genre. The narrator not only explains discourse material, but he also knows more than readers do and even more than the narrative characters

---

7. Anderson, *The Riddles of the Fourth Gospel*, 51.
8. Keener, *The Gospel of John*, 2:1100.
9. Keener, *The Gospel of John*, 2:1101.
10. Keener, *The Gospel of John*, 1:68–69.

know. The narrator is like a superhuman who helps readers to grasp obscure dialogue or events. Therefore, he is not just the one who tells the story but he also interprets it and steers the readers' thinking. He is an interpreter par excellence.

The narrator's role as an interpreter is seen in various places. In John 2:21–22 the narrator explains that Jesus was not speaking of the Jerusalem Temple but rather of his own body. None of the narrative characters besides Jesus himself, who is the speaker, understood this. The narrator reveals the correct interpretation of Jesus's words. In John 7:39, the narrator expounds Jesus's proclamation, revealing that Jesus "spoke of the Spirit, whom those who believed in Him were to receive; for the Spirit was not yet *given*, because Jesus was not yet glorified." In John 21:19, the narrator knows that Jesus's words to Peter indicate how he is going to die and glorify God.

In John 3, we have an example of the narrator's skills to move from direct discourse to commentary sections in such a way that readers may not even notice the shift. What happens then is that readers who enter the commentary section assume that they are still reading the character's speech, but actually they are reading the narrator's explanation and commentary.

John 3:16 is perhaps the most well-known single verse of the entire NT.[11] It is called the mini-gospel and is often introduced by a phrase, "Jesus said." Red-letter Bibles, where all Jesus's words are printed in red, have often supported that reading.[12] Recently that reading has been challenged. It is argued that John 3:16 and the following verses are the narrator's commentary. A similar situation, it seems, is found in the end of chapter 3. Here it is argued that the narrator starts his commentary in such a way that readers assume that it is John the Baptist who is speaking, but actually it is the narrator who further explains and develops the theme that John the Baptist points out in vv. 27–30. Below we present the traditional reading and a new proposal of John 3:10–36.

---

11. Brant, *John*, 19, notes that "John 3:16 is the most-quoted passage in Scripture. The popularity of John 3:16 has led to a peculiar phenomenon. The phrase John 3:16, or simply the numbers 3:16, written on a sign, a lapel pin, a T-shirt, or a bumper sticker has come to signify a confession of faith."

12. The NIV (2011) Red-letter version drops the red letters at 3:16. See also how quotation marks are used in various English translations in John 3.

Traditional Reading:

| Narrator | Jesus | John the Baptist | Baptist's Disciples |
|---|---|---|---|
| 10a | | | |
| | 10b–21 | | |
| 22–26a | | | |
| | | | 26b |
| 27a | | | |
| | | 27b–36 | |

Table 15.1

New Proposal:

| Narrator | Jesus | John the Baptist | Baptist's Disciples |
|---|---|---|---|
| 10a | | | |
| | 10b–15 | | |
| 16–21 | | | |
| 22–26a | | | |
| | | | 26b |
| 27a | | | |
| | | 27b–30 | |
| 31–36 | | | |

Table 15.2

The two main differences between the traditional reading and the new proposal are that John 3:16-21 is the narrator's commentary that follows Jesus's and Nicodemus's dialogue (esp. vv. 14-15),[13] and that John 3:31-36 is not John the Baptist's words but the narrator's commentary on John the Baptist's statement (vv. 27b-30).[14]

The new proposal may be correct: John 3:16-21 and 3:31-36 may belong to the narrator's commentary rather than Jesus's and John the Baptist's speeches, respectively. It is also worth noting that John 3:16-21 and 3:31-36 are similar in content. Both commentary sections elevate Jesus's role and superiority.

Some readers may find it somewhat shocking that John 3:16 does not belong to Jesus but rather to the narrator. This concern, however, is unnecessary. If one holds a high view of biblical authority, taking the entire Bible as God's Word, the fact that the narrator rather than Jesus testifies to the truth should not reduce its significance. John 3:16 is still the authoritative and truthful testimony about God and his Christ.

## Authorial Omissions and Scribal Additions

The readers cannot escape the fact that the FG is sometimes obscure because the evangelist has omitted information that would have been benefitted today's readers. The reasons for omissions might be that he wanted to draw attention to something other than the information he omits. In other words, omissions are used rhetorically. Another reason is that today's readers do not share the same cultural and historical context with the author and his first readers. The information that might have been readily available to them is unknown to us. Thus, historical, literary-rhetorical, and socio-scientific studies are recommended for today's readers of the FG to obtain a better understanding of the text.

Regarding rhetorical omissions, we note that a basic hermeneutical principle, namely, that we read what is written and do not try to read what is not written, needs to be qualified. Readers should also pay attention to what is not written, but without filling the "blanks" by using their imagination—imagination colored by the readers' ideological context. On the contrary, in cases where omission is motivated by rhetorical reasons, readers need to ask strategic questions from the text to see possible

---

13. Klink, *John*, 189-91; Cf. Brodie, *The Gospel According to John*, 195.
14. Klink, *John*, 212-13.

reasons for omissions. An excellent example of this is found in an omission of the name of the Jewish feast in John 5:1 (see Chapter 2 above). It is not mentioned, we argue, because the evangelist wants to draw his readers' attention to the fact that the day was the Sabbath when the healing miracle took place. The Sabbath day is used rhetorically to bring forth the narrative's point.

We will now turn to examine the omitted narratives. Readers have wondered for a long time why the Fourth Evangelist omits such essential events as Jesus's baptism, the Last Supper (actual event), and Jesus's ascension?[15] As far as Jesus's baptism and the Last Supper is concerned, the evangelist is explicit that they took place. He narrates what happened "around" these events, so indicating that they were known to him. He records John the Baptist's proclamation about Jesus after he had baptized Jesus (John 1:28–34). The evangelist also relates what took place just prior to and after the Last Supper (John 13:1—17:26). The narrative after Jesus's resurrection is not that revealing regarding Jesus's ascension.

Since the evangelist does not record Jesus's baptism and the Lord's Supper, interpreters have turned to "water" and "eating/drinking" texts in the FG to find reasons for those events' absence. That has led some scholars to a sacramental reading of "water" and "eating/drinking" passages. Therefore, Jesus's words to Nicodemus, "unless one is born of water and the Spirit he cannot enter into the kingdom of God" (John 3:5), are taken as a reference to water baptism practiced by the church. Brown comments that "there can be little doubt that the Christian readers of John would have interpreted vs. 5, 'being begotten of water and Spirit,' as a reference to Christian Baptism; and so we have a secondary level of sacramental reference."[16] John 6:53–58, where Jesus calls his audience to eat his flesh and drink his blood, is taken as a reference to the Eucharist.[17] Sacramental reading, however, whether correct or not, does not fully explain why the Fourth Evangelist omits narratives of Jesus's baptism and the constitution of the Eucharist.[18]

The absence of ascension in the FG has not stopped interpreters from suggesting that Jesus's ascension is hidden but found in the last

---

15. Other narratives like Jesus's temptation in the wilderness, the transfiguration, and Gethsemane's prayer are also missing.

16. Brown, *The Gospel According to John*, 1:141–42. For a different interpretation, see Aker, "John," 55–56.

17. See Brown, *The Gospel According to John*, 1:272–80.

18. Cf. Smalley, *John*, 128–30.

two chapters. Some have suggested that it took place between Jesus's encounter with Mary and Thomas. This interpretation is based on the observation that Jesus denied Mary's attempt to touch him ("Stop clinging to Me"; 20:17), the reason being that Jesus was not yet ascended to the Father. Later, in the same chapter, Jesus calls Thomas to reach out and touch him ("Reach here with your finger"; 20:27). Therefore, it is argued that Jesus ascended to the Father between these two occasions and made a post-ascension appearance to the disciples, including Thomas in 20:27. Another suggestion is that Jesus's ascension happened somewhere between chapters 20 and 21. For this reason, Jesus's appearance to seven disciples (church?) at the shore of the Sea of Tiberias was a post-ascension appearance.

These suggestions, as logical as they might be, have not received much support. The fact is: The Fourth Evangelist does not record Jesus's ascension as Luke does (Luke 24:50–53). He does not even give the context in which the ascension took place as Matthew does (Matt 28:16–20).

What should we do about these omissions? Can we find the answer to the question of why the Fourth Evangelist omitted them? Our modest suggestions for an answer to these questions are the following. First, we should not try to find them from the text if they are not there. Secondly, we should read these narratives around these un-mentioned events to see if the Fourth Evangelist wants to draw his readers' attention to something else. In the case of Jesus's water baptism, it seems that the evangelist concentrates Jesus's identity revelation through the testimony of John the Baptist. In the case of the Last Supper, the evangelist seems to emphasize servanthood, loyalty, and the future life of the believing community. In the case of the ascension, the evangelist seems to emphasize the community that is about to live and function as the representative of Jesus's earthly being. Finally, it is reasonable to think that the Fourth Evangelist likely being aware of the Synoptic tradition, perhaps did not feel it necessary to include these narratives because these accounts were readily available in the other Gospels known to his intended readers.

There are also additions to the FG's original text. These additions cause textual critical questions. The two most prominent passages that are later additions are found in John 5:3b–4 and 7:53—8:11.

The first one (John 5:3b–4), "*waiting for the moving of the waters; for an angel of the Lord went down at certain seasons into the pool and stirred up the water; whoever then first, after the stirring up of the water, stepped in was made well from whatever disease with which he was afflicted*" is a later scribal addition to explain the text. The evangelist had omitted the popular understanding of the pool water's healing power, which the later scribe has felt to be an essential piece of information. By adding it to the text, the later scribe hoped to help readers to understand the phrase "the water is stirred up" found in v. 7. Early manuscripts do not include this text, whereas the Byzantine text form includes it. The German Bible Society's editing committee of UBS[4] notes that v. 4 is a gloss. The reasons for that conclusion include the fact that it is not found in the earliest and best manuscript witnesses; there are several Greek manuscripts showing that the words are spurious; it includes words which are not Johannine and not found from elsewhere in the NT, and it has "rather wide diversity of variant forms in which the verse was transmitted."[19] That portion is left out from English translations such as ESV, NET, and NIV, but is included, for example, in KJV, NASB, and RSV.

The story of a woman caught in adultery (John 7:53—8:11) is also a later addition to the FG. It is not included in the earliest Greek manuscripts, including P[66] and P[75]. The narrative appears the first time in the Greek manuscript Bezae (D) in the fifth century but is not found in other Greek manuscripts until the ninth century. The first church father to comment on the passage was Euthymius Zigabenus in the twelfth century. He pointed out that accurate manuscripts do not contain it. The story of the woman caught in adultery is also found in various places in later manuscripts. It is sometimes found after Luke 21:38, at the end of the FG, and after John 7:52.

Internal evidence such as the story's unique vocabulary, a large number of variant readings, and its lack of fit to the narrative flow are pointed out as arguments against the story's belonging to the original FG.[20] Today, the majority of the Johannine scholars view it inauthentic for the Fourth Evangelist.[21] Nevertheless, it is probable that the story has a long oral tradition and made its way into the later Greek manuscripts and various early NT translations sometime after the Gospels were published.

The question that these scribal additions raise is: what should readers do with them? To answer this question from a textual point of view is not difficult. They do not belong to the original Gospel. Since they are part of the several modern English translations, having historical value,

---

19. Metzger, *A Textual Commentary*, 179.

20. Comfort, *Early Manuscripts and Modern Translations*, 115–16; see also Metzger, *A Textual Commentary*, 187–89.

21. Keener, *The Gospel of John*, 1:735.

and likely coming from oral tradition, should they be read as if they came from the evangelist? The case with John 5:3b–4 is especially tricky because a casual reader may understand the addition in a way that is contrary to the scribe's intention. The addition is to explain the people's popular view regarding the water's healing power, not a divine revelation about God's special treatment of the water in order to heal any sick who reached the water first. This is not to say that the popular view of the water's healing capacity was merely people's own imagination. The site served after Jesus's time as a pagan healing shrine, which might also be the source for the scribal addition.[22] We suggest that John 5 should be read without the addition first, and then learn how the added text informs the text and its interpretation.

The case with 7:58—8:11 is somewhat different. It does not belong to the context of the narrative, the Feast of Tabernacles. It is its own unit, which does not seem to contradict the portrait of Jesus painted by the four evangelists.[23] We suggest a careful reading of it. We should not base any distinctive teaching on this portion of the text alone. Surely, we cannot come up with a definite conclusion of what Jesus wrote on the ground to satisfy human curiosity. All suggestions given are guesses at best. The story may, however, have an illustrative capacity. It contains many fascinating features that we cannot comment on here but are available in standard scholarly commentaries.[24]

## Future Now and Later

Christian thought tends to view eschatology (last things) exclusively as a future reality. The basic tenets of this kind of future eschatology resonate with the first-century Jewish understanding of eschatology as the final end-of-the-age event when God will judge good and evil.[25] The FG, however, depicts eschatology differently. There are two different kinds of eschatologies: realized (present) eschatology and futuristic (future) eschatology. The FG is not the first ancient writing that describes

22. See Keener, *The Gospel of John*, 1:637–38.
23. Keener, *The Gospel of John*, 1:736.
24. Concise comments on the passage is found in Brown, *The Gospel According to John*, 1:335–38; Carson, *The Gospel According to John*, 333–37; Keener, *The Gospel of John*, 1:736–38.
25. Helyer, *The Witness of Jesus, Paul and John*, 345.

eschatology in terms of present reality and not only as of the future events at the end-time. It is found elsewhere in the NT (especially in Ephesians and Colossians) and the Dead Sea Scrolls. Both eschatological aspects co-existed in the early Christian thought and the Qumran community.[26]

Realized eschatology refers to those actualities that belong to the time after this life but are already accessible. NT testifies how Christ had brought the church eschatological hope. Jesus had already brought the church, through his death and resurrection, eternal blessing, including benefits of the future. Futuristic eschatology, on the other hand, refers to those events which are going to take place at eschaton or the individual's departure from this age.

It has become common to refer to the NT's eschatological landscape with the phrase "already—not yet."[27] The figure below presents this idea.

| This Age: | _____Christ's 1st Advent_____ Christ's 2nd Advent |
| --- | --- |
| | *"Already – Not Yet"* |
| Age to Come: | Christ's 1st Advent_____Christ's 2nd Advent_____ |

**Figure 15.5**

"Already—not yet" is the period between Christ's two advents, during which many eschatological realities are already realized but not yet fully fleshed out. This age ceases after Christ's second coming. The age to come, which began at the first advent of Christ, will be fully fleshed out at his second coming. When "this age" fades away, the "age to come" emerges, and futuristic eschatology ceases as it becomes fully realized.

The FG is unique in that it presents eschatology mainly in terms of the realized eschatology. Realized eschatology is readily seen in the fact that those who put their trust in Jesus already live in the reality of their future status. John 5:24 presents present reality in clearly identified terms.[28] Below, the verse is presented in a grammatical outline. We have added the emphasis.

---

26. Keener, *The Gospel of John*, 1:322.
27. See Fee and Stuart, *How to Read the Bible*, 149–53.
28. Other passages where realized eschatology can be seen are in the FG are: John 1:33; 3:18, 34; 4:21–24; 5:28; 6:47, 63; 10:10; 12:23, 27; 13:1; 15:3; 16:32; 17:1.

> Truly, truly,
> I say to you,
>> he who hears My word,
>> and
>> believes Him who sent Me,
>>> *has eternal life,*
>>> and
>>> *does not come into judgment,*
>>> but
>>> *has passed out of death into life.*

The last three statements require commenting on. The phrase, "has eternal life" (*exei zōēn aiōnion*), is present active indicative which indicates continuous action in the present. Therefore, the message is that the one who hears and believes is having eternal life at the present moment. Eternal life is not therefore something that one has to wait for; something that takes only place later on when one moves beyond "this time." Secondly, the phrase, "does not come into judgment" (*eis kristin ouk erxetai*), is also in the present indicative. Therefore, one who hears and believes is not approaching judgment. This idea can be expressed in English, like the NASB translates it, in the present tense as a statement of fact. Finally, the phrase, "has passed out of death into life" (metabebēken ek tou thanatou eis tēn *zōēn*), is rendered in the perfect active indicative. The perfect tense in Greek denotes a past action that has effect at the time of speaking.[29] In this present case, the one who hears and believes, and therefore is living eternal life without judgment waiting for him/her, has passed already out of death and entered eternal life. "Passing out of death into life" takes place when one comes to faith in Jesus. It does not happen sometime later in the future. It is realized in the present moment.

Realized eschatology is also expressed in the following verse, "an hour is coming and now is" (John 5:25; cf. 4:23). This phrase, as well as other passages where eschatology is spoken as a present reality,[30] confirms that the evangelist has not reduced eschatology only to the present. Keener notes that "There can be no dispute that John emphasizes realized eschatology. What is more is [sic] dispute is whether John does so to the exclusion or near exclusion of future eschatology."[31]

---

29. Robertson, *A Grammar of the Greek New Testament*, 893.
30. See John 3:36; 12:31–32.
31. Keener, *The Gospel of John*, 1:321.

The tendency of futuristic eschatology's exclusion from the FG is seen in Bultmann's existential interpretation of 5:24. He says the life that the evangelist refers to here "is that authenticity of existence, granted in the illumination which proceeds from man's ultimate understanding of himself."[32] This reading does not require the existence of futuristic eschatology. Bultmann further argues that future eschatology is added to the FG by a later redactor to harmonize the FG with the church's eschatological view.[33] However, it is more convincing to take both aspects of the eschatology as the original. We do not have textual evidence that future eschatology was once absent from the FG. We can hold that the Fourth Evangelist's realized eschatology is built upon his futuristic eschatology, rather than the evangelist's existential understanding of himself. Klink investigates this from another slant. He criticizes the either-or view, noting that "proponents of both views [realized and future eschatology] have a tendency to speak past the other." Klink argues that "for John the promise of a future eschatology is the best argument for the reality of a present eschatology. The present state of the 'eternal life' Jesus gives need not deny its future implications or reality, just as future reality need not deny its present implications."[34] We agree with Klink, whose point argues against Bultmann's view.

The FG presents an eschatology which is indisputably futuristic while maintaining its present implications. The popular Christian view of eschatology as a future "escape" from the present evil is not the eschatological view of the FG. The FG does not emphasize so much the "end" than it emphasizes the "beginning" and "present."[35] This point of view is explicitly presented in Jesus's prayer in the end of his Farewell Speech in 17:18–19. Jesus is not praying that his disciples would escape one day from the world, but rather that as he sends them into the world, they would be protected and sanctified. Yet, the beginning and present project towards the future as well.

---

32. Bultmann, *The Gospel of John*, 258.
33. Bultmann, *Theology of the New Testament*, 2:39.
34. Klink, *John*, 288; see also Hagner, *The New Testament*, 288.
35. See Ernst Käsemann, *The Testament of Jesus*, 15–16.

## Concluding Remarks

This chapter has presented several questions that readers encounter in the FG. To note these topics is important as they affect readers' hermeneutical approach and understanding of the text. Three dimensions of the text, chronology and the evangelist's arrangement of his material, the narrator's role, omissions and later additions, and eschatological landscape are all aspects that are critical and need to be noted by the interpreter of the FG. These items arise from the text and from the fact that the reader is dealing with an ancient text written two thousand years before our time. Many other issues and features that would belong to this chapter's category are found in the Part One and Part Two in this volume.

## Suggestions for Further Reading

Anderson, Paul N. *The Riddles of the Fourth Gospel: An Introduction to John*. Minneapolis: Fortress, 2011. Pp. 175–244.

Davies, Margaret. *Rhetoric and Reference in the Fourth Gospel*. JSNTS 69. Sheffield: Sheffield Academic Press, 1992. Pp. 22–66, 112–14.

Fee, Gordon D., and Douglas Stuart. *How to Read the Bible for All Its Worth*, 4th ed. Grand Rapids: Zondervan, 2014. Pp. 132–53.

CHAPTER 16

# A Very Short History of Interpretation

AN ATTEMPT TO PRESENT a brief history of interpretation is a difficult task, particularly for two reasons. First, the history of biblical interpretation is so complex that every attempt to outline it risks oversimplification. Our attempt does not avoid this risk. The second difficulty, which is related to the first one, is that such an account can hardly do justice to biblical interpretation's rich history and present complexity. Biblical interpretation has taken many turns and has been influenced by events, people, and movements "outside" of the text itself.[1] For this reason, the topic we are dealing with is not only the history of interpretation but also the history of interpreters. Despite these challenges, we have chosen to outline the major trends in the history of biblical interpretation. The purpose of this sketch is to paint a big picture of the past which prepares us to move forward and present various interpretative approaches in the current Johannine scholarship in the following last three chapters in this volume.

We will divide the history of interpretation into three eras: (1) pre-modern (i.e., Patristic and Middle Ages), (2) modern (i.e., from the age of Enlightenment forward), and (3) post-modern (i.e., from the Second World War to the present). These historical eras of interpretation roughly correspond with three significant approaches to biblical interpretation, namely, (1) theological, (2) historical, and (3) literary.[2]

---

1. Lategan, "Current Issues in the Hermeneutical Debate," 1.
2. Brodie, *The Gospel According to John*, 3–10.

## Interpretation during the Pre-Modern Era

The term "pre-modern" refers to the lengthy era before the seventeenth and eighteenth centuries which mark the start of the so-called modern era. Pre-modern thinking and interpretation were neither uncritical nor uninfluenced by philosophy, but interpreters were attached to the church and the church's authority—at least until the Reformation. During pre-modern times, large theological opuses were produced, including biblical commentaries. Well-known contributors include Origen, Augustine, Tertullian, Thomas Aquinas, Martin Luther, and John Calvin, to mention but a few.

During the pre-modern era, biblical texts were approached in various ways, yet the hermeneutical landscape was not so multi-fractured as it became after the Enlightenment. At the end of the pre-modern era, the Reformation did not reform only the church but also hermeneutics. The most drastic changes were made by reformers who shook off the church's authority from their interpretation and conclusions. The authority to determine the meaning of the Bible had previously belonged to the church, its traditions and dogmas. The new hermeneutical approach at the end of the pre-modern times changed hermeneutics, but it did not bring about the complete separation between interpretation and the church. The Bible was still the book that belonged exclusively to the church.

Regarding methodologies during the pre-modern era, the church sought the hermeneutical system that served its purposes. The three major approaches were typological, allegorical, and literal readings. The earliest way of reading was typological reading that was mainly a Christological reading of the OT. "[T]ypology is a condition of understanding within which the older text represents more than simply its subject . . . typological interpretation is more hermeneutical than exegetical because it is less concerned with learning what the ancient text *says* than with understanding *how they are to be taken* in the light of later texts (the New Testament documents) that the Fathers recognized to be works of interpretation as well as scriptural texts in their own right."[3]

The allegorical reading, springing from two influential individuals of the School of Alexandria, Clement of Alexandria (150–215 CE) and Origen (185–254 CE), was a common reading mode until the Age of Reason. It won the hermeneutical battle against literal reading and became a preferred approach to the biblical text for centuries. It was practiced

---

3. Yarchin, *History of Biblical Interpretation*, xiv–xv.

side by side with the literal reading even then when the literal meaning and its value was noticed like in the work of St. Augustine's *De Doctrina Christiana* (397–426 CE). The allegorical reading was not static. It went through various evolutions throughout the centuries.

Allegorical reading was not an acceptable for everyone. In the areas where the Jewish Synagogue influenced the church, the literal meaning of the Scriptures was preferred.[4] The literal reading was urged by the so-called Antiochian school. Theodore of Mopsuestia (350–428 CE) and John Chrysostom (347–407 CE), among other Antiochians, insisted that even though the Bible has higher and deeper meaning than a mere literal or historical one, its meaning is firmly based on the letter.[5] Although a literal reading of the Scriptures was marginalized during the Middle Age, it was not completely forgotten. It was picked up again, perhaps the most recognizable example in the works of Martin Luther in the early 1500s.

There were two major movements towards the end of the pre-modern era, which changed interpretation and prepared the way for more radical change that was about to emerge when the world moved from pre-modern to modern times. These two movements were Scholasticism and the Reformation. We may describe these movements' contributions to interpretation, respectively, as (1) a move from allegorical-spiritual reading toward literal reading and as (2) a return to the reading that provides spiritual nourishment to people. A literal reading of the Bible became preferred in early monastic schools and universities where theologians were the newer generation of interpreters who adopted the Aristotelian view of nature. However, the allegorical reading still lived on in pulpits of the church.[6]

The other significant change, the Reformation, also did not happen overnight, although the day when Martin Luther nailed his ninety-five theses on the door of the Wittenberg church, October 31, 1517, is referred to as the day of Reformation. The Reformation was a process that included various theologians who began to bring new nuances to the reading of the Bible even before Luther's contribution. One such a person was a humanist, Desiderius Erasmus (1466–1536 CE). Now the Bible was not read as a proof text for the church's theology and dogma, but rather Bible reading was seen as an interaction between the reader and the text

---

4. Grant, *A Short History of the Interpretation*, 63.

5. Grant, *A Short History of the Interpretation*, 66.

6. Grant, *A Short History of the Interpretation*, 84–87. See also Hernando, *Dictionary of Hermeneutics*, 56–57.

## A Very Short History of Interpretation

that had transformational power over the reader.[7] The Reformers took these ideas and developed them further, concluding that the Scriptures stand alone and thus are the sole foundation for faith and theology.[8] Also, the Reformers called for a reading that would provide readers with spiritual nourishment, not the "dry" literalism of scholastic reading.

What was the FG's place in the hermeneutical landscape during the pre-modern era? Throughout the long pre-modern period, the FG enjoyed a special place among the Gospels. It had the highest place of honor in the church, especially in the early period of the pre-modern era as it was known to be authored by one of the closest disciples of Jesus. Also, its Christological statements were very valuable during the early controversies within the church. The FG enjoyed this position until a skeptical study of the FG began in European universities at the rise of the Age of Reason. The catalyst to bring the FG down from its elevated position was the young David F. Strauss. In his *The Life of Christ* (1835), Strauss argued that the FG is unhistorical and, therefore, untrustworthy, at least historically.[9]

The text of the FG was also a suitable text for allegorical interpretation since its historical references were understood to yield to its symbolic language and theological agenda. Clement of Alexandria (150–215 CE) claimed that "Last of all, John, perceiving that the bodily facts had been made plain in the gospel, being urged by his friends, and inspired by the Spirit, composed a spiritual gospel."[10] Heretical movements' usage of the FG also testifies to its suitability for the allegorical and "spiritual" approach. Early gnostic writers, Heracleon and Montanus used it. Montanus, for example, "claimed to be the coming Paraclete or Comforter described in John 14–16."[11]

From the Early Church Fathers until the Reformers, the hermeneutical landscape led the church to read the FG allegorically, seeking proof in the text for the church's theological standpoints. An example of Origen's allegorical reading of John 2:6 is a good example. His interpretation demonstrates that the goal was to find out the text's theological/spiritual meaning through allegorical interpretation. Origen writes:

---

7. Jasper, *A Short Introduction to Hermeneutics*, 52.
8. Grant, *A Short History of the Interpretation*, 92.
9. Burge, *Interpreting the Gospel of John*, 16–19.
10. *Hist. eccl.* 4.14.7.
11. Burge, *Interpreting the Gospel of John*, 16.

> [W]e must certainly not forget that there are some passages of scripture in which this that we call the body, that is, the logical and literal meaning, is not found, as we shall show in what follows; and there are places where those meanings which we have called the soul and the spirit are alone to be looked for. I believe that this fact is indicated in the gospels, when six waterpots are said "to be set there for the purifying of the Jews, containing two or three firkins apiece" (John 2:6). Here, as I said, the language of the gospel seems to allude to those who are said by the apostle to be Jews "inwardly" (Rom 2:29), and to mean that these are purified through the word of scripture, by receiving in some cases "two firkins," that is, by accepting the soul meaning and the spiritual meaning in accordance with what we said above, and in other cases three firkins, when the reading also retains for the edification of the hearers a bodily meaning, namely the literal one. And six waterpots are approximately mentioned in allusion to those who are being purified while living in the world. For we read that this world and all that is in it were finished in six days, which is a perfect number.[12]

The FG's treatment in the hands of the Reformers changed. They moved away from an allegorical reading and called for a more literal reading. A literal interpretation, reading the text in its historical meaning, was argued to represent the author's intent.

To summarize what we have covered so far, we can say that the biblical text, during the pre-modern times until the Reformation, was read to find theological support for the church's orthodoxy and orthopraxy. David Jasper summarizes it as follows:

> Increasingly in the Middle Ages . . . the theology and the theological speculation of the church tended to be separated from the processes of biblical interpretation, and *sacra scriptura* became merely the proof of the truth of *sacra doctrina*. Any textual divergence from the sacred doctrines of the church was liable to the consigned to the flames as heretical. To read was largely a matter of following order and remaining faithful to the tradition handed down.[13]

In retrospect, the interpretations in the pre-modern era mainly followed the pre-formulated dogmas and theological positions. The "interpreters" had a tendency, even a mandate, to use the text as a proof text

---

12. Quoted in Yarchin, *History of Biblical Interpretation*, 47.
13. Jasper, *A Short Introduction to Hermeneutics*, 46.

for the pre-decided dogmatic position. The biblical text was like the buttresses in architecture, which were planned to support, for example, the large church building from lateral forces. They were necessary to keep the building standing. However, the Reformation brought a change where the text was still read for theology, but the theology found from the text in the reformed minds of interpreters was not any longer dictated by the church.

## Interpretation during the Modern Era

Anthony Thiselton points out that "There have been two great paradigm shifts in NT interpretation. The first, in the eighteenth century and later, was toward a single preoccupation with historical method, and the second, in the late twentieth century, has been toward a methodological pluralism."[14] If the pre-modern area was a golden era for the allegorical method, the modern era became a golden era for the historical-critical method. Various advances in Western society during the seventeen and eighteen centuries changed how researchers "read" the past.

At the outset, it needs to be mentioned that study of historical aspects of the ancient text, even in a critical manner, is not synonymous with the historical-critical method that is applied to such a research. Biblical hermeneutics (i.e., hermeneutics that is applied to biblical text) may include historical research that is conducted in various ways. The historical-critical method is a particular way of doing such a study that was developed during and after the seventeenth and eighteenth centuries. This will be explained further below.

The modern period was marked by development in humanism and science. New scientific findings were discovered, and new theories were accepted. These findings were received enthusiastically and applied to various disciplines, including hermeneutics. Philosophy, which was now placed over faith in the enterprise to define the truth, broadly shaped biblical interpretation. That was seen in two significant shifts in hermeneutics. First, before modern times exegesis and theology were treated as one, but now, exegesis became separated from theology. Secondly, before the modern era, faith and reason were treated as a unit and in harmony. Harmony between these two was reached by submitting reason to faith. However, the modern era began to elevate human reason. The reason was given independent authority to determine the truth. Faith was given

14. Thiselton, "New Testament Interpretation," 10.

a role only in one's devotion. Immanuel Kant (1724–1804 CE) declared that enlightenment is "man's emergence from immaturity. It is man learning to think for himself without relying on the authority of the church, the Bible, or the state to tell him what to do."[15] Figuratively speaking, theology was forced to divorce from the faith and biblical interpretation and was re-married, perhaps against its own will, to philosophy. Human reason was now on the driver's seat, and faith and ecclesiastic authority were placed in the back seat, if not in the trunk of the car. David Jasper points out that this change already began to emerge in the great Reformers' work. Although they did not mean it, their hermeneutical approach opened the door to anthropocentric reading that introduced subjectivism, giving more authority to the mind of the individual reader.[16]

The fact that contributed to the shift from faith and the church's authority to reason and freedom of the dogmas was the development of academy. Jasper writes, "In the eighteenth century, hermeneutics and the interpretation of the Bible finally moved largely away from the church and readers whose purpose was pious or religious, to find its focus in the academy and university and it readers whose purpose was essentially academic."[17] In academia, students of the Scriptures eagerly applied the methodologies of the day within the framework of a new understanding of human capacity to understand and know, including the sense of freedom from previous authorities.

Gradually new discoveries in sciences and even in mathematics (cf. Isaac Newton) influenced biblical interpretation. Hope and trust were placed in scientific methodologies and the logic of induction and deduction, with such force, that they were now applied to disciplines outside of traditional sciences, including historical research and hermeneutics. There was a hope that all findings are objective without subjective elements. This was translated to biblical interpretation as well. What inevitably followed was that the text's claims of, for example, miraculous events were placed under the scientific method's microscope. They were now interpreted in the framework of new scientific findings that were marked by natural laws (e.g., new understanding of universe). The interpretations were judged right or wrong based on what is possible and impossible according to the newly discovered universe and its laws, which were

---

15. Brown, "Immanuel Kant," 599.
16. Jasper, *A Short Introduction to Hermeneutics*, 62.
17. Jasper, *A Short Introduction to Hermeneutics*, 70.

## A Very Short History of Interpretation

discovered by the power of the human. The scientific world view eventually became a standard measuring stick for what is true or possible and what is untrue and impossible.

The Enlightenment brought a strong sense how unscientific people had viewed existence previously and how enlightened people now understood and explained it. Biblical texts were approached with that view in mind, and therefore, the Bible was read as a product of pre-scientific authors who lacked the knowledge of today's scientific readers. That kind of reading mode led interpreters to concentrate on the text's history and an authorial pre-scientific worldview. It was thought that modern readers understand the world better than biblical authors and therefore, can explain the text in a way that was suitable for the scientific world. Schleiermacher, during the Age of Romanticism, concluded that contemporary readers should and can understand the biblical text better than its author.[18]

Ernst Troeltsch's theory of historical research serves as an example of how scientific methodology was applied to historical research. His theses influenced the mode of historical research of the Bible as well. He developed three principles to evaluate the historical account.

1. His *principle of criticism* sets the mode for historical research. It says that no historical documents can be accepted as authoritative; the modern critic must weigh all past claims. At most, we can arrive at a greater or lesser probability concerning the past, never a certainty.

2. *The principle of analogy* is the key to the past. Events of the past must all be analogous to what is possible today.

3. *The principle of causality* is the principle of cause and result. This means that history is a closed continuum of events, in which every event has an antecedent immanent cause, and there is no divine intervention (miracle) in history.[19]

It is evident how Troeltsch's principles gave authority to human reason and experience, which were attached to the scientific mindset that has captured the spirit of the Enlightenment. In short, questions of the theological meaning of the text were largely replayed by the question: "What really happened?" The purpose was to re-create the "true" historical story. Oeming puts this in the following words, "Rationalism and Enlightenment contribute a critical scepticism towards miracles and the

---

18. Jasper, *A Short Introduction to Hermeneutics*, 85.
19. Hernando, *Dictionary of Hermeneutics*, 24.

doctrine of inspiration; from their time on, the Bible could no longer be seen as a work of God, fallen from heaven, but rather as a very earthly product of human creativity."[20]

Nevertheless, a mere historical-critical reading received some critique. Johannine scholar, Raymond E. Brown tells that "when he was about to embark on his Anchor Bible commentary on John, W. R. Albright, his prestigious mentor and editor, counseled him to write a work which would deal with history rather than theology. Brown replied that in view of the way in which the Gospel begin [In the beginning was the Word and the Word was with God . . . ], it would be difficult to write a commentary which did not deal with theology."[21] Therefore, even though Brown wrote a commentary of the day which paid attention to historical issues, he wrote a work that concentrated on theology.

The historical-critical method generated other approaches as well, such as the socio-scientific approach. It began by asking a new set of questions, not only about Jesus-events but about the historical life of the believing community. The socio-scientific studies produced views of the Johannine community as a more or less esoteric Christian group.

The historical-critical method of interpretation is still practiced even though it has lost its place as *the* approach.[22] Several influential works written on the FG, published after the modern period, between 1940s to 1970s, are influenced by the historical-critical reading mode. These commentaries and studies are still much in use and make a valuable contribution to Johannine scholarship, although today's Johannine scholars no longer share some of their conclusions. These commentators include Rudolf Bultmann, Raymond E. Brown, C. K. Barrett, C. H. Dodd, and Rudolf Schnackenburg. One needs to keep in mind that historical study is a natural aspect of biblical hermeneutics. We are indeed dealing with the ancient text which was born in a different world than our own. The importance of this fact is demonstrated by various background studies, the latest written by N. T. Wright and Michael F. Bird.[23] However, a historical study of the background of the NT is something other than the historical-critical methodology that has a distinctive philosophical underpinning, as we have pointed out above.

---

20. Oeming, *Contemporary Biblical Hermeneutics*, 31.
21. Brodie, *The Gospel According to John*, 5.
22. Oeming, *Contemporary Biblical Hermeneutics*, 31.
23. Wright and Bird, *New Testament in Its World*.

## Interpretation in Post-Modern Times

The shift that has taken place most recently is the move from the diachronic reading to the synchronic reading of the text. The text is read as readers find it in front of them (synchronic reading). The questions related to the historical context of writing, textual-critical questions, and previous interpretations (diachronic reading) are not the reader's interest.[24] Many recent approaches have turned toward the synchronic study of the biblical text. However, it should be noted that this shift did not take place overnight, and that various scholars have pushed back to insist that diachronic reading is still valuable if not necessary. For that reason, there are several kinds of combinations of synchronic and diachronic readings today.

The post-modern era, which started roughly around the Second World War, has introduced a change to hermeneutics that has resulted in various interpretative applications. Post-modernism brought an attitudinal shift in human thinking that once again touched concepts like truth and objectivity. Now the truth becomes local and plural, and subjectivism is celebrated over objectivity. All meta-narratives and universal truth claims are denied in principle.[25] Needless to say, these post-modern trends have had an impact on biblical interpretation. Now the biblical text was viewed more subjectively than before.

Figure 16.1

But the focus was not on the entire process of communication. More specifically, the emphasis was not on the realities behind the text. In other words, the emphasis was not on the *author*/text like previously, but rather on the text/*reader*. It is the reader and the readers' interaction with the text that was now highlighted in the meaning formulation.

The author of the text and other historical questions that lie behind the text are no longer the interest of interpretation, not even necessary, and sometimes considered to be beyond readers' reach. In other words, it

---

24. Ashton, "John and the Johannine Literature," 260.
25. Rosenau, *Post-Modernism and Social Sciences*.

is argued that today's readers are not able to re-construct authorial intention, and that it is not even desirable. The text is seen as an independent closed entity that is "freed" from its author. The underpinning assumption is that when one reads the text, its author is not there to answer the reader's questions, and so the author cannot clarify the text's intended meaning. Therefore, readers are left alone with the autonomous text, which is now read and re-read in the readers' ever-changing context. Readers formulate (or create) the meaning of the text as they read. This kind of reading has moved far from, for example, the earlier appeal of Schleiermacher's (1768–1834 CE) psychological reading that calls readers to empathize with the author.[26] Therefore, the post-modern chain of the written communication process looks more like this:

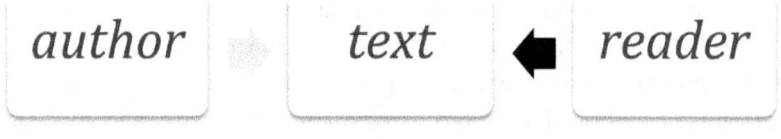

Figure 16.2

An interpretational mode that argues that the meaning formulation takes place between the text and the reader is not exclusively the post-modern invention. Like Calvin, the Reformers insisted that the Scriptures do not need any external proof since the Bible interprets itself. "There is nothing outside of the text," says Jasper concerning the Reformers' thought; he suggests that "postmodern, literary theory has come to the same conclusion . . . though there God is left out of the equation and the text becomes *self*-authenticating."[27] In short, the post-modern hermeneutical tendency is to empower the reader over the text and certainly over the author.[28]

In the most radical form, the post-modern reading mode could be described using an image of a "sandbox." The text is like a sandbox. Some kids play in the sandbox; after they have finished their play, they leave behind formations in the sand. The next kid comes along and re-imagines the play, continuing it by using his/her imagination. That kid develops

26. Oeming, *Contemporary Biblical Hermeneutics*, 16.
27. Jasper, *A Short Introduction to Hermeneutics*, 61.
28. Bartholomew, *Introducing Biblical Hermeneutics*, 118.

the previous play making it entirely his/her own. The first kid's "original" play may or may not carry over to the new play. It is up to the second kid how much he/she takes from the previous play into the new play. The earlier kids are not around to assist him/her with the original idea of the play, its plot, purpose, characters, and the rest. Similarly, the author who produced the text is no longer present to assist the reader. The reader enters the text, re-imagines it, and makes the text to his/her own.

B. C. Lategan explains the recent shifts in biblical interpretation in the following:

> Historical period, which actually coincides with the beginnings of New Testament research as a scholarly enterprise, was dominated by questions of origins: sources, authorship, *autographa*, reconstruction. From these interests developed the formidable tool of the historical-critical method . . . The first real 'paradigm switch' occurred with the advent of structuralism and its emphasis on the auto-semantic nature of texts. The text itself becomes the focal point . . . The most striking feature of recent developments in the field of hermeneutics is without doubt the massive movement toward the right-hand sector of our diagram [i.e., see above our communication model] . . . The unifying factor is the interest in the final phase of the communication process. The focus is on the relationship text—reader, in the realization that reading is far from merely a passive acceptance of the message, but a very productive activity.[29]

The first Johannine scholar who applied literary, narrative-critical interpretation to the FG, and thus "text-reader" mode of reading is R. Alan Culpepper.[30] In his *Anatomy of the Fourth Gospel*, Culpepper lays down a narrative-critical reading model where the narrative text becomes independent from the historical questions. He claims, "The gospel [of John] as it stands rather than its sources, historical back-ground, or themes is the subject of this study."[31] As it stands, the text creates the text world, which is then accepted or rejected by the reader. However, the narrator of the story, who is both part of the text and its commentator, explains the narrative, which he hopes to be adopted by the reader. This way of reading the biblical text becomes "literally" true and thus does not answer directly to whether it is "historically" true. In fact, what is argued

---

29. Lategan, "Current Issues in the Hermeneutical Debate," 3–4.
30. Porter and Fay, *The Gospel of John in Modern Interpretation*, 37.
31. Culpepper, *Anatomy of the Fourth Gospel*, 5.

is that the truth is not only historical in nature. The truth is revealed in other ways as well. Narrative, whether historical or fictional, can carry forth the truth. The point is that readers can find the meaning of the text and truth in interaction with the text without going "behind" (i.e., historical-critical questions) the text. Even though Culpepper's literary reading is not the only new application, it serves as an example of the shift that has been introduced in the most recent times. The new approach shakes off the historical-critical mantel and concentrates more on the readers and their dealings with the text.

## Concluding Remarks

Our brief sketch of the history of biblical interpretation has shown how the biblical text, including the FG, has been treated in various ways over the centuries. The FG has been a particular "battle ground" in the history of the interpretation. The "battle" is embedded in the FG's theology and historicity. The FG's unique exhibition of the Jesus event and its theological presentation have caused interpreters to ask numerous questions from the text and to develop various approaches to it.

The nature of the FG has been argued to be theological rather than historical, but never the other way around. After a gradual recognition of the FG, it enjoyed an elevated status in the early church, partially due to its historical reliability that was attached to its apostolic authorship. Its historical credibility was not questioned even though it became treated as a "spiritual gospel." During the time of the Enlightenment and after, some scholars argued that it is not historically reliable. Because the FG differs from the Synoptic Gospels, it was suggested that it is a mythical and Hellenized Gospel which has not much to do with the historical person, Jesus. More recent scholarship has argued the opposite, namely, that the FG is historically reliable and should not be placed in an inferior position to the Synoptic Gospels. Currently, the scholarly climate holds that the FG is historical and theological in its own style. Nevertheless, the "tension" between these two views is still occasionally felt.

The Johannine scholarship has been periodically interested in either historical or theological aspects of the FG. Several factors have influenced its interpretation, like the philosophical climate and methodology of the day. During the early years, its theology was the readers' interest, whereas allegorical methodology was preferred. The rise of the Enlightenment and during the following decades, historical questions rather than theological ones were the interest of Johannine scholars. This is somewhat ironic because, during that same period, the FG was argued to be historically unreliable, but historical realities behind the "unhistorical" text were scrutinized. The rise of the post-modern times and new methodologies, especially literary criticism, opened the door to concentrate again on the text and its theology. Therefore, the latest development can be described as a U-turn back to the FG's text and message and away from a mere historical study of the text's development. That resonates more closely with the FG's earlier pre-modern reading, although methodology has changed radically since then.

Post-modern times have still introduced another kind of reading model that authorizes the reader to re-imagine the text. In these models, the reader is powered over the author and the text. It is perhaps too early to say where reader-response and its variant reading models are going to lead. However, before we leave this chapter, we note that today hermeneutical approaches and methodologies are plentiful, reflecting "elements from every era of its history."[32] This is true to the FG's interpretation as well.

## Suggestions for Further Reading

Burge, Gary M. *Interpreting the Gospel of John*. Grand Rapids: Baker Books, 1992. Pp. 15–36.

McKim, Donald, ed. *Historical Handbook of Major Biblical Interpreters*. Downers Grove: InterVarsity, 1998. Pp. 1–16, 75–84, 123–52, 257–80, 403–22, 541–47.

Porter, Stanley E., and Ron C. Fay, eds. *The Gospel of John in Modern Interpretation*. Grand Rapids: Kregel Academic, 2018.

Yarchin, William. *History of Biblical Interpretation: A Reader*. Peabody: Hendrickson, 2004. Pp. xi–xxx.

---

32. Yarchin, *History of Biblical Interpretation*, xxx.

## CHAPTER 17

# The Fourth Gospel as a Window

THERE ARE MANY WAYS to analyze and categorize the methodologies applied to the interpretation of the Bible. Below we will follow Krieger's "glass" analogy that is further developed by Patrick Counet.[1] These remaining three chapters will employ a "glass" analogy to demonstrate various methodologies applied to the FG since the 1950s.

Krieger introduced the terms "window" and "mirror" to describe how interpreters handle the biblical text.[2] Text-as-a-window uses the text as a gateway (i.e., a window) to see the other side of the text in order to reconstruct historical realities behind the text. Such a reading is diachronic. The text and the reader are not the focus of such a reading. Counet explains, "The subject which uses the text is of no importance in this model and the text itself is only a means."[3] The assumption is that the historical context has shaped the text and, therefore, also unfolds its meaning. Issues like why the text was written, who wrote it, under what circumstances was it written, and within what kind of social system the writing took place, become essential to determine the meaning in the window reading. The window reading may disconnect the reader from the text's transforming capacity since it asks only certain kinds of questions from the text, namely those questions that help readers deal with

---

1. Counet, *John, a Postmodern Gospel*.
2. See Culpepper, *Anatomy of the Fourth Gospel*, 3–4.
3. Counet, *John, a Postmodern Gospel*, 108.

the historical past before and during which the text was written.[4] Perhaps an appropriate analogy would be "window shopping." The window is a necessary separation between the observer and items observed, but it is not the focus of the event that we call "window shopping."

The text-as-a-mirror reading, that is, synchronic reading of the text, is quite the opposite. It places meaning formulation between the reader and the text. The meaning is thus produced "this side" of the text. Counet puts it this way, "The subject [the reader] is the starting point and the ultimate end. It recognizes his/her situation in the text, feels challenged by it or resists it so that it can enter into debate with the text, can listen to it or reject it."[5] In other words, mirror reading is a reader-response model "in which pragmatics and the role of the subject are central."[6] The author's intention is not considered in the reader-response criticism since the reader, who stands in responsive relation to the text, forms the text's meaning.

A third reading model is the "ornamental glass" model.[7] This model, which resonates somewhat with the "mirror" reading, focuses on the text, including the implied author, the narrator, the narratee, the characters, and the implied reader. It visualizes, as the word "ornament" suggests, the figures, colors, and other artistic parts of the text. "The text is seen as a self-sufficient phenomenon, a world unto itself in which one can wander around, which one can admire, but upon which one cannot exert any influence because ultimately one is outside it."[8] As we can notice from its description, the "ornamental glass" reading is also "mirror" reading in the sense that the meaning formulation takes place this side of the text, between the text and the reader, rather than behind the text. Narrative criticism falls into this category. It takes the text as a play and the reader as a spectator of that play.

Inevitably, there is a certain degree of one-sidedness in all of these three reading models outlined above. Therefore, other models of reading have been introduced. The fourth model we will introduce in the last chapter of this book is a synthetical (integrated) reading model called the "stained glass" reading. It is a synthesis of the mirror, window, and

---

4. Cf. Thiselton, *Interpreting God and the Postmodern Self*, 66.
5. Counet, *John, a Postmodern Gospel*, 110.
6. Counet, *John, a Postmodern Gospel*, 110.
7. Counet, *John, a Postmodern Gospel*, 109.
8. Counet, *John, a Postmodern Gospel*, 109.

ornamental class readings. W. R. Tate maintains that the author, the reader, and the text has to be taken into account in the proper interpretation and that the locus of the meaning is found in the interplay between these three.[9] The "stained glass" reading model tries to accomplish this kind of integrated reading. The metaphor 'stained glass' describes the fact that the reader sees behind the text, the text, and him/herself as the stained glass also reflects the reader.

In the present chapter, we will introduce Johannine scholars and their interpretations who represent "window" interpretations. We have selected Rudolf Bultmann, J. Louis Martyn, Raymond E. Brown, Bruce J. Malina, and Richard L Rohrbaugh to represent the window reading model in this chapter. Other well-known scholars who also apply mainly window reading in their study on the FG include Robert Kysar, C. H. Dodd, C. K. Barrett, and Rudolf Schnackenburg. Bultmann and Martyn have produced highly influential historical-critical works on the FG. Brown's two-volume commentary, which is still a benchmark work, represents the historical-critical era of commentary writings. Brown's historical-critical approach to the background of the Johannine writings, which he presents as a separate study from his commentary, is distinctive and deserves a few comments in this chapter. In our list, the last-mentioned two scholars, Malina and Rohrbaugh, represent a new way of using the text as a "window." They work socio-scientifically, reconstructing the social matrix of the text's community. In the remaining final two chapters of this book, we will introduce "mirror," "ornamental class," and "stained class" readings of the FG. A word of warning is in order: the reader needs to understand that these metaphors are not absolute, and they are used here mainly as helpful catchwords that represent these approaches.

## Rudolf Bultmann: History-of-Religions Reading

In his *The Gospel of John: A Commentary* (1971 English translation; original German work published in 1964), Rudolf Bultmann uses a "window" (diachronic) approach to the text. More specifically, he interprets the FG using a historical-critical methodology.[10] The starting point of the historical-critical method is a belief that the religion has to be understood

---

9. Thiselton, "New Testament Interpretation," 28.

10. See also Bultmann, *Theology of New Testament*. This work was first published in two volumes in 1951 and 1955, respectively.

## The Fourth Gospel as a Window 323

and interpreted in its own context where it was born.[11] The task the interpreter has, therefore, is to reconstruct that historical world. Bultmann reconstructs the context of Johannine Christianity, applying the history-of-religions approach. He concludes that Hellenistic and Gnostic ideas influenced the composition of the FG. For him, Johannine dualistic symbolism indicates that the Fourth Evangelist used Gnostic ideas in his presentation of the gospel.

Bultmann is known by his five programs that rise from his reconstructed view of Johannine context and the historical-critical interpretation informed by the history-of-religions approach. These programs include (1) demythologization, (2) *kerygmatic* gospel, (3) form criticism, (4) ecclesiastical redactor, and (5) source theory. We will sketch these below.

For Bultmann, the NT represents the pre-scientific period when its authors did not have access to modern scientific knowledge. In the NT times, people were imagining reality as a three-story-world (heaven above, this world, and hell below). Therefore, the biblical text had to be stripped of its mythical clothing, "not to eliminate myth but to interpret it."[12] Demythologizing is not to be done by denying the author's existential experience with the events described in the text through myths but by reinterpreting myths to modern scientific readers so that the core meaning of the text can be existentially available. This program includes stripping the text of its mythological clothing. This process is called demythologization. Bultmann's demythologization project went deep and wide and included core Christological events such as "theological dogmas of the virgin birth, incarnation, atonement, resurrection and ascension."[13]

Bultmann finds an example of demythologization in the FG. He argues that the evangelist's *Logos* figure is not found from the OT or directly from Judaism or any Israelite thoughts. There is a connection, though, between Judaic Wisdom myth and the Johannine Prologue. Judaic Wisdom myth, according to Bultmann, does not originate from the OT but pagan mythology. "Israelite Wisdom poetry took over the myth and demythologized it. The Wisdom myth is, however, only a variant on the *Revealer-myth*, which is developed in Hellenistic and Gnostic literature; and the kinship of the Johannine Prologue to the Judaic Wisdom speculation is due to the fact that both go back to the same tradition for their

---

11. Bray, *Biblical Interpretation*, 221.
12. Fergusson, "Rudolf Bultmann," 454.
13. Fergusson, "Rudolf Bultmann," 454.

source."[14] This example points out one of the results of window reading; the reconstruction of history leads the interpreter (in this case, Bultmann) to make claims about the author's sources (redactor). What follows is that the created understanding of the sources informs the reading.

Bultmann also argues that the FG's theology is *kerygmatic* theology, which concentrates on the proclamation of the message(r) (Christ) rather than historical facts (Jesus of Nazareth). This means that the proclaimed message is the core and basis of one's faith. James Hernando explains what happens when kerygma takes place over the historical value of Jesus event. "Even though historical-critical studies are necessary, their results are irrelevant with respect to faith because *kerygma* calls one to make an existential choice about Christ."[15] Therefore, although Bultmann took part in the historical Jesus dialogue, the historical Jesus was not essential for him. The Christian proclamation, like the FG, is the message about the Christ of Faith (proclaimed by the apostles), which is the basis of faith. Historical research into the person Jesus of Nazareth can be conducted, and as such, it is interesting, but it is not needed for faith.

The form criticism that Herman Gunkel had applied to the OT was picked up by Bultmann. He applied it to the Synoptic Gospels and the FG as well. The purpose of form criticism for Bultmann was to categorize and analyze the biblical material and its history before its literary form and determine how early Christian communities shaped the oral material. Bultmann applied form-critical analysis to the Synoptic Gospels, which led him to conclude that the FG is not historically accurate. He assumes that the Johannine community is behind the text and that the community's *Sitz im Leben* and theology have dramatically influenced the product. The community was influenced significantly by Gnostic ideas and Hellenistic writings. Bultmann argues that the author takes "over traditions that have come from outside Christianity, and carries out his redactional reconstructions on a much grander scale than the Synoptists."[16] In short, Bultmann's window reading of the text uses reconstructed history behind the text as a hermeneutical key to interpret the FG.

Bultmann also argued that an ecclesiastical redactor modified the text prior to its current form. There is no author as such for Bultmann, but a redactor who edited and re-organized the text. The redactor's activity is

---

14. Bultmann, *The Gospel of John*, 22–23.
15. Hernando, *Dictionary of Hermeneutics*, 60–61.
16. Bultmann, *The Gospel of John*, 5.

demonstrated in his commentary on the FG. Bultmann presents what he thinks is more plausible original order of the text. For example, he places chapter 6 before chapter 5 in order to make John 6:1 read smoothly. He also thinks that chapter 18 should be read immediately after chapter 14 to make 14:31 a meaningful chronological marker.[17] The ecclesiastical redactor also had an agenda to bring forth some doctrines practiced in his time, such as sacraments. Bultmann argues that this is seen, for example, in the Gospel's "water" motif, especially as attached to salvation passages, which are a later ecclesiastical redactor's additions to the original text.

Finally, Bultmann is also known for his source theory. He argued that all evangelists used various sources and that the Fourth Evangelist was no exception. According to Bultmann, there are two distinct parts in the FG, namely stories and sayings, which both have their own "source history." The FG's stories are coming from the written "Signs Gospel," which is based on two other written sources, namely "Signs Source" and "Passion Source." These two sources grew from an oral Jesus tradition. The other part of the FG, "Sayings," comes from a written Gnostic "saying source."[18]

Bultmann's source theory suggests that he finds early Gnosticism a suitable context in which the FG was written. This understanding also appears in his commentary on the FG. For example, his comments on the Spirit Paraclete. He says, "The most probable explanation, therefore, may be taken to be that the figure of the . . . [*paraklētos*], which the Evangelist found in his source, is this Gnostic figure of the 'helper.'"[19] According to Bultmann, the "other Paraclete" (John 14:16) also comes from Gnostic ideas. He thinks that the idea of the successor came from the Pseudeo-Clementines and the Mandean Literature, rather than the Hebrew Scriptures.[20]

These few examples from Rudolf Bultmann exhibit the nature of interpretative affairs during the twentieth century. His focus was primarily on the history lying behind the text and on scientific methods which were greatly influenced by modern philosophy, especially Hegelian existentialism, through the influence of Bultmann's colleague at Marburg, Martin Heidegger.

17. Bultmann, *The Gospel of John*, 10–11.
18. Thatcher, Introduction, 4.
19. Bultmann, *The Gospel of John*, 572.
20. Bultmann, *The Gospel of John*, 567.

## J. Louis Martyn: Two Level Story of the Fourth Gospel

Like Bultmann's commentary on the FG, J. Louis Martyn's study on the FG entitled *History and Theology in the Fourth Gospel*,[21] first published in 1968, has been and continues to be an influential work in Johannine scholarship. Martyn begins with a note that readers often read the FG as if Jesus's sayings are readily understood without paying attention to the ancient setting in which it was written. The reason for such a reading is that the FG seems to encourage readers to do that. Jesus's proclamations sound like timeless, universal statements. In his own words, "Some of the Johannine Jesus' words seem to be so free of any first-century Palestinian provincialism that we chisel them into the walls of our university libraries, from Chicago to Freiburg, implying that they are philosophical aphorisms, immediately understood in every enlightened age: 'You shall know the truth, and the truth shall make you free.'"[22] According to Martyn, that kind of reading does not tackle the crucial issue of what took place in the past, in which context the text took shape, and what the author was reflecting on in the text.

The leading question for Martyn is how the Johannine community reflects itself in the FG. In other words, how much history of the community is inserted in the text. This phenomenon is, in fact, present with every NT writing. Therefore, an interpreter's task is to find out how the NT authors balanced the tradition and current issues in their believing community at the time of writing, Martyn argues. None of the NT authors "merely repeats the tradition. Everyone hears it in his own present and the means in his own way; everyone shapes it, bends it, makes selections from among its riches, even adds to it."[23] According to Martyn, this reality calls readers of the FG to "make every effort to take up temporary residence in the Johannine community."[24] By saying this, Martyn suggests that the FG readers must first reconstruct the Johannine community and its context within which it functioned then and there. By doing that, a reader becomes a more competent interpreter of the text and is better positioned to understand how the community might have shaped the historical tradition.

---

21. Martyn, *History and Theology in the Fourth Gospel*.
22. Martyn, *History and Theology in the Fourth Gospel*, 27.
23. Martyn, *History and Theology in the Fourth Gospel*, 30.
24. Martyn, *History and Theology in the Fourth Gospel*, 29.

For this reason, Martyn pays attention to the gap between the historical Jesus-tradition and the Johannine community's life situation. He argues that the Fourth Evangelist shaped the historical tradition so that the story of Jesus also became the story of the evangelist's community. Martyn claims that the FG is, therefore, a *two-level drama*; the Johannine community tells the story of itself through Jesus's story.

Martyn concentrates on the narrative of the man born blind (John 9) as a key "drama" for his study. Along the way, he compares the FG with the Synoptic tradition to identify traditional material and the Fourth Evangelist's reflection. Martyn says that John 9 is a "dramatic expansion of the miracle story" that is recorded in the beginning of the chapter, vv. 1–7. The expansion demonstrated the Johannine church's struggle and interaction with the Jews who represent the synagogue. He finds support for this in the Eighteen Benedictions,[25] especially its twelfth benediction, the Benediction Against Heretics. The benediction was used in the synagogue to identify heretics, like Christians, who are "blotted out of the Book of Life."[26] Martyn expands John 9:22 based on his view of the historical setting of the FG, suggesting that it could read something like as follows:

> The parents feared the Jewish authorities, for the latter had already enacted a means whereby followers of Jesus could be detected among synagogue worshipers. From Jamnia had come the official wording of the *Shemoneh Esre*, including the reworded Benediction Against Heretics. Henceforth anyone arousing suspicion could be put to a public test.[27]

Martyn tries to demonstrate how the Fourth Evangelist moves between two historical realms, Jesus and the author's realms. Jesus healed the man, after which the synagogue authorities engaged in debate with the man. That leads to the healed man's excommunication from the synagogue. Such an excommunication was more severe than a mere denial of his access to the place of worship. This story is, however, also a story of the Johannine community, which lived in a world of re-worded Eighteen Benedictions. Martyn arrives at the conclusion that "[i]n the two-level

---

25. The Eighteen Benedictions are a collection of Jewish prayers expected to be prayed every morning, afternoon, and evening. During the first century, many of these benedictions were incorporated into the Synagogue service.

26. Martyn, *History and Theology in the Fourth Gospel*, 63.

27. Martyn, *History and Theology in the Fourth Gospel*, 65.

drama of John 9, the man born blind plays not only the part of a Jew in Jerusalem healed by Jesus of Nazareth, but also the part of Jews known to John who have become members of the separated church because of their messianic faith and because of the awesome Benediction."[28]

When this reading is applied to other parts of the Gospel, like to the Spirit-Paraclete passages, Martyn holds that it is the Paraclete in whom Jesus comes back to the disciples as the Son of Man, who is simultaneously in heaven and on earth. Thus, it is, in fact, *"precisely the Paraclete who creates the two-level drama."*[29]

Before we leave Martyn's window reading, we quote him once more. This quotation captures well the ethos of his theory and hermeneutical approach.

> Theologically the boldest step we have seen John take is the "doubling" of Jesus with the figures of Christian witnesses in his community. Since we are acquainted with Luke's second volume in which a part of the postresurrection history of the church is narrated, it strikes us that John could have narrated the history of his own church in a direct and straightforward manner. Instead, we find him presenting a two-level drama in which it is not an apostle but rather Jesus himself who ministers to Jews known to John as men who have suffered the fate of excommunication from the synagogue. Jesus also acts the part of the Jewish-Christian preacher who is subjected to arrest and trial as a beguiler. Jesus engages in the debates which John's church has with the Jewish community regarding his own identity as the Mosaic Messiah.[30]

Martyn's thesis has had a long and profound effect on the Johannine scholarship, which is still alive.[31] However, it has also received criticism.[32] We suggest that students of the FG need to pay attention to Jesus-event and its context and the context in which the FG retold that event. For this reason, Martyn't work might become a valuable read even though one may disagree with its conclusions.

---

28. Martyn, *History and Theology in the Fourth Gospel*, 66.
29. Martyn, *History and Theology in the Fourth Gospel*, 140.
30. Martyn, *History and Theology in the Fourth Gospel*, 124.
31. See, for example, Smith, *The Fourth Gospel in Four Dimensions*.
32. Cf. Bauckham, *Testimony of the Beloved Disciple*, 116–17.

## Raymond E. Brown: History of the Johannine Community

Raymond E. Brown authored an influential two-volume commentary on the FG. It is still a much-used work and considered one of the benchmark commentaries on the FG.[33] Even though his commentary was written when several historical-critical works on the FG were produced, Brown does not concentrate on mere historical-critical issues. Brown is much interested in the message and theology of the FG. His *The Community of Beloved Disciple* presents Brown's "window" reading at its best.[34]

In his *The Community of Beloved Disciple*, Brown studies the history of the Johannine writings, aiming to reconstruct and present the history of the Johannine community within which the texts (Gospel and the Letters) were born and developed. Brown's purpose may sound much the same as what Martyn was doing in his monograph, but it there are differences. Martyn was keen to find out how the Johannine author molded the traditional material of Jesus. In contrast, Brown seeks to understand what kind of community Johannine community was and how that community changed. Brown identified four distinctive phases of the Johannine community, namely (1) before the Gospel was written, (2) the time when the Gospel was written, (3) the time when the epistles were written, and (4) after the epistles.[35]

Even though Brown's and Martyn's goals were different, Brown adopted Martyn's thesis, which was published just a few years before (see above). He also follows, yet re-shapes, Wellhausen's and Bultmann's view that the Gospels primarily tells the story of the community and only secondarily, the story of Jesus. Brown explains his approach to the following:

> *Primarily*, the Gospels tell us how an evangelist conceived of and presented Jesus to a Christian community in the last third of the first century, a presentation that indirectly gives us an insight into that community's life at the time when the Gospel was written. *Secondarily*, through source analysis, the

---

33. Brown, *The Gospel According to John*. Other works with similar status include, Schnackenburg, *The Gospel According to John*; C. K. Barrett, *The Gospel According to St. John*.

34. Brown, *The Community of the Beloved Disciple*.

35. In his appendix 1, entitled "Recent Reconstructions of Johannine Community History," Brown offers a valuable outline of various theories of Johannine community that were developed up to his date of writing. Brown, *The Community of the Beloved Disciple*, 171–82.

Gospels reveal something about the pre-Gospel history of the evangelist's Christological views; indirectly, they also reveal something about the community's history earlier in the century, especially if the sources the evangelist used had already been part of the community's heritage. *Thirdly*, the Gospels offer limited means for reconstruction the ministry and message of the historical Jesus.[36]

After laboring with the FG and reconstructing the Johannine community, Brown argues the following regarding the history of the Johannine community: Before the FG was written, new groups of believers, whether Jews of an anti-temple bias or Gentiles, were brought into the original Johannine group causing a new development in the community's theology and views. Not only new groups but also the community's geographical location influenced this development. During the second phase, the community's move from Palestine to Diaspora contributed to the change in the community's view regarding "the Jews" and the Greeks and thus bringing universalistic thoughts into its theology. That was the time when the FG was authored. It was this time when part of the community, namely Jewish Christians with low Christological view, were considered as people of unbelief. Phase three, at the time of the epistles, brings more significant division within the community resulting the split into "the adherents of the author of the epistles" and "the secessionists." This division developed further in the fourth phase when the second-century "Johannine" communities continued to polarize; "the adherents of the author of the epistles" joined to the church, but "the secessionists" moved on in the road to Gnosticism.[37]

This reconstruction is developed using the text as a "window" to the other side of the text in order to see the history of the community in which such text might have been born and developed. Although Brown's, as well as Martyn's, conclusions are still referred to in Johannine scholarship, they remain hypothetical at their best.

---

36. Brown, *The Community of the Beloved Disciple*, 17.

37. See the chart "The History of the Johannine community" in Brown, *The Community of the Beloved Disciple*, 166–67. See also Jipp, "Raymond E. Brown and the Fourth Gospel," 175–76.

## Bruce J. Malina and Richard L. Rohrbaugh: Socio-Scientific Reading

Bruce J. Malina and Richard L. Rohrbaugh are members of Context Group, a society of biblical scholars approaching the text from the point of view of the social-sciences.[38] Malina and Rohrbaugh are pioneers of reading the FG social-scientifically. They co-authored a socio-scientific commentary in 1998. However, Wayne Meeks and his famous 1972 essay "The Man from Heaven in Johannine Sectarianism," was the first attempt to apply socio-scientific insights to the FG.

This approach is another kind of example of the "window" reading. It does not attempt to reconstruct the author or his community. Instead, its goal is to understand the society in which the community and the writing (communication) took place. However, the goal is not to reconstruct society but the usage of reconstructed society and its social system as a hermeneutical key to reading the meaning of the text. In other words, the attempt here is to expose the meaning of the text by reading it in its historical-sociological fabric of relationships. This reading method takes the reader behind the text to reconstruct the social world and then interpret the text from that standpoint.

Malina and Rohrbaugh correctly note that the meaning of any text is derived from its social system. The Bible translators have recognized this fact as well. "Translation... becomes an act of cross-cultural transfer where the translator must be both cultural as well as bilingual," Dietmar Neufeld says and continues, "Translations of the Bible that fail to take into account the problem of social distance will suffer from ethnocentric and theological myopia."[39] The focus on social life at the time of writing is necessary to understand how its first recipients understood the written communication. The assumption is that the communication derives its meaning *from* and *in* its own social context, not from another context(s). Therefore, this model emphasizes the importance of a social gap as the most fundamental one of all gaps which must be bridged. "[R]eading is a social act," they claim.[40] The socio-scientific reading guards the modern reader from reading the text merely through his/her contemporary social experience.

---

38. See essays by the Context Group in Pilch, *Social Scientific Models*.
39. Neufeld, *The Social Sciences and Biblical Translation*, 4.
40. Manila and Rohrbaugh, *Social-Science Commentary*, 16.

The socio-scientific commentary aims to bring the readers as close as possible to the first-century Mediterranean society's social system within which the evangelist's community operated. Malina and Rohrbaugh maintain that the Johannine community is an anti-society because "John's society" differs from the society around it, resisting it and attempting consciously to change it.[41] If adequate understanding of the social system of the anti-society is reached, then incorrect recontextualization can be avoided.[42] For example, when the readers have learned to read the FG's language as the community's anti-language, they have learned to read the Johannine community and surrounding competing groups like "world" and "Judeans." In short, Malina and Rohrbough insist that "John's group and the story that held it together make sense only in the Judean society in which it originated. Thus, when removed from the society in which it directly and immediately made sense, the Gospel of John quickly loses its original meanings."[43]

An anti-society develops anti-language to maintain the inner solidarity of that society. It also identifies the anti-society, resocializing its members and function as a defense mechanism against the wider society. For example, slang words, such as "road dog" (close friend) and "old bird" (mother), are often well-defined anti-language words in certain anti-societies.[44] In these examples, the words are *relexicalized*. In other words, the reality is referred by the word that is not usually used to refer to that reality. Malina and Rohrbaugh point out that in the FG, this is demonstrated in "John's selection of words to refer to the realm of God: *spirit, above, life, light, not of the/this world, freedom, truth, love*."[45] The other way of constructing anti-language is to *overlexicalize*. Overlexicalization takes place when several different words or expressions are used for one thing. For example, "John speaks of *believing into Jesus, following* him, *abiding in* him, *loving* him, *keeping* his word, *receiving* him, *having* him, or *seeing* him"[46] but means one and the same action.

Social-science reading attempts to go one step further than historical-critical methods. The text's background questions are not yet

---

41. Malina and Rohrbaugh, *Social-Science Commentary*, 7.
42. Malina and Rohrbaugh, *Social-Science Commentary*, 11.
43. Malina and Rohrbaugh, *Social-Science Commentary*, 11.
44. For more examples, see Malina and Rohrbaugh, *Socio-Science Commentary*, 7–8.
45. Malina and Rohrbaugh, *Socio-Science Commentary*, 4.
46. Malina and Rohrbaugh, *Socio-Science Commentary*, 5.

# The Fourth Gospel as a Window

answered for the social-scientific reader when "what" questions are answered. The reader has to understand the behavior models of people in the context of writing as well. Therefore, "why" and "how" questions (e.g., questions regarding the people's behavior in the society) have to be asked and answered as well. It is this area where the social-scientific approach has contributed to NT scholarship and continues to do so.

Before we leave this chapter, we offer one example of a social-scientific "window" reading from Malina and Rohrbaugh's commentary. Our example comes from their interpretation of John 7:1-9. In this passage, Jesus is having a conversation with his unbelieving brothers regarding Jesus's public appearance and the feast of *Sukkoth* festivities in Jerusalem.[47] Here are the main points from Malina and Rohrbaugh:[48]

- *Iudaios* in 7:1 should not be taken as "Jews" but rather "Judeans" to bring vivid contrast between Judeans and Galileans and how these two groups treated Jesus. Judeans are told to seek to kill Jesus (7:1). This theme continues throughout the present section (John chs. 7 and 8), demonstrating how Judeans rejected Jesus.

- Honor-shame is an underpinning sociological concept in this passage. As an honor of a person was determined by public opinion, a person wanted to guard his/her image, not letting the public know anything that might not match his/her public image and thus lowers his/her honor status. This behavior is called "information control."

- "Information control" leads to secrecy. A person wants to hide certain things from the public that might be known only by his/her in-group.

- According to Malina and Rohrbaugh, in John 7:1-9, honor-shame and secrecy (information control) are in play. The public has not yet understood who Jesus is. People had not yet accepted his role as Christ. If he went publicly to Jerusalem to reveal his secrets, especially from where he came from and where he is going, that would not have been understood, which would have affected his public honor status. Therefore, it was not yet his "hour" to do so. On the other hand, his in-group (disciples/Johannine anti-society) knew more than the public (out-group). For example, Jesus in his farewell

---

47. The following section is based on Malina and Rohrbaugh, *Socio-Science Commentary*, 139-45.

48. See further Malina and Rohrbaugh, *Social-Science Commentary*, 139-45.

speech (chs. 13—17), informs his in-group, but that information is kept secret from the out-group.

- The socio-scientific reading of John 7:1–9 leads Malina and Rohrbaugh to interpret Jesus's response to his brothers and his later actions in terms of "lying" (or "truth" telling) in a collectivist culture. In a collectivist culture, one's self was defined privately and by in-group. Thus, what a person was privately was expected from him/her also in-group. Lying (to think one thing and say another) would be keeping the truth from his/her in-group. However, hiding the truth from the out-group would not be "lying" (to think one thing and say another). That would be an honorable act if that would protect the truth known only to the person's in-group. Thus, when Jesus tells one thing to his brothers, who represent the out-group, but yet acts contrary to his words, it is an honorable act of protecting the truth (knowledge) only for his in-group members. Malina and Rohrbaugh conclude, "In so doing, he [Jesus] shows himself to be an honorable person who knows with whom the truth is properly to be shared."[49]

By this example from Malina's and Rohrbaugh's social-science "window" reading, we can see how sociological categories have entered into the exegetical process, guiding it and influencing the text's exposition. The question is: How much should the socio-scientific findings and their application to the FG's historical setting direct one's interpretation?

## Concluding Remarks

In this chapter, we have outlined four "window" readings applied to the FG. There are several ways how the text is used as a window to go behind the text. These examples have demonstrated that reading the FG as a window is supplemented by other like philosophical, historical, or socio-scientific studies.

In the above-sketched works, the scholars' point has not been, however, to gain mere historical information. They have tried to understand the text employing the window reading model. These scholars also examine the text's theology or some aspect of the FG's theology (e.g., Brown, whose aim is to understand Johannine ecclesiology). In that process, the

---

49. Malina and Rohrbaugh, *Social-Science Commentary*, 145.

historical matters have become a hermeneutical key for them. The reconstruction of the community, society, and other historical matters are applied to the text. This creates a circular argumentation in some cases. The text is used to reconstruct the past, and that reconstruction is then used as an interpretative key. Therefore, the question is how much reconstructed historical setting can steer the interpretation.

## Suggestions for Further Reading

Brown, Raymond E. *The Community of the Beloved Disciple: The Life, Loves, and Hates of an Individual Church in New Testament Times.* New York, Paulist, 1979.

Bultmann, Rudolf. *The Gospel of John: A Commentary.* Translated by G. R. Beasley-Murray. Philadelphia: Westminster, 1971.

Malina, Bruce J., and Richard L. Rohrbaugh. *Social-Science Commentary on the Gospel of John.* Minneapolis: Fortress, 1998.

Martyn, J. Louis. *History and Theology in the Fourth Gospel*, 3rd ed. NTL. Louisville: Westminster John Knox, 2003.

Porter, Stanley E., and Ron C. Fay, eds. *The Gospel of John in Modern Interpretation.* Grand Rapids: Kregel Academic, 2018. Pp. 119–39, 173–96.

CHAPTER 18

# The Fourth Gospel as Mirror and Ornamental Glass

"THE TWENTIETH CENTURY HAS seen a growing fascination with the Bible 'as literature', with an accompanying persistent sense of theological unease, apart from the obvious recognition that it is a collection of 'literary' texts having, in common with other literature, narratives, poems, epistles and so on."[1] Reading the Bible as literature has advanced mirror and ornamental glass readings which emphasize the role of the text and the readers' interaction with the text in the process of the text's meaning formulation.

The new interest in the Bible as literature is not, however, a twentieth century invention. Friedrich Schleiermacher's (1768–1834 CE) hermeneutical claims paved the road for text-immanent readings in which the focus of interest was the text rather than its pre-history. The text, as it was found in the front of the reader, is all that the reader needed (Schleiermacher's psychological interpretation) if its linguistic, grammatical, and syntactical structures are carefully observed (grammatical interpretation). Schleiermacher also paved the road for a new attitude, which is found in reader-response reading models, by claiming that the interpreter's task is to know the text better than its author.[2] This is a flight away from the earlier necessity to find authorial intention. "To know the text better than its author" thesis is possible if one holds a

---

1. Jasper, "Literary Reading of the Bible," 21. For an example of "Bible as literature" studies in the FG, see Stibbe, *The Gospel of John as Literature*.

2. Jasper, *Short Introduction to Hermeneutics*, 85.

view that the original author does not determine the meaning of the text, but that it is today's reader who does.

The mirror and ornamental glass reading methods are synchronic ones. A shift from diachronic to synchronic readings was caused by the people's negative attitudes towards scientific positivism.[3] Since then, the synchronic reading of the Bible has grown to be a major approach. This is especially clearly seen in interpreters' approach to the narrative material of the Scripture, like the Gospels and Acts. Mark W. G. Stibbe sketches the history of that shift in biblical scholarship in the following:

> Until the late 1970s, the traditional methods for the study of the gospels and Acts were form criticism, source criticism, historical criticism, tradition history, redaction criticism, and textual criticism . . . traditional methods of interpretation were more concerned with what lay behind NT narratives than with their form and their literary, artistic features . . . A change began to occur most noticeably in the 1980s, when two books were published on *Mark as Story* (Rhoads and Michie, 1982; Best, 1983); one on *Matthew as Story* (Kingsbury, 1986), and on *The Narrative Unity of Luke—Acts* (Tannehill, 1986), and one on the *Anatomy of the Fourth Gospel* (Culpepper, 1983). Each of these works, and a number of lesser-known books and articles . . . took up the challenge of looking at the final form of the gospels and Acts in order to highlight those narrative dynamics which traditional methods had neglected.[4]

To summarize, the new interest in the Bible as literature caused the Gospels to become a subject of reading using literary methodologies that are applied to other narratives, even fiction literature. The inevitable outcome of this was that the status of the Bible as a sacred text was diminished, and its literary character was emphasized. Now the text, rather than the text's historical context, receives the attention.[5]

Several methods focus on the text and the reader. In his *Contemporary Biblical Hermeneutics: An Introduction*, Manfred Oeming outlines the following linguistic-structuralist methods:

- New literary criticism
- Canonical interpretation

---

3. Brueggemann, *Texts under Negotiation*, 2.
4. Stibbe, *John as Storyteller*, 5.
5. Barton (ed), *The Cambridge Companion to Biblical Interpretation*, 10.

Part Three: Interpretations of the Fourth Gospel

- Speech-act and word-act
- The history of effect
- Psychological exegesis
- Symbolic exegesis
- Bibliodrama
- Liberation theology and exegesis
- Feminist exegesis[6]

Below we are going to introduce two examples of synchronic readings of the FG. The first example, narrative-critical reading, is a much-used method whereas the other, speech-act theory, is not used as frequently, at least not yet.

## R. Alan Culpepper: Narrative-Critical Reading

R. Alan Culpepper's ground breaking work, *The Anatomy of the Fourth Gospel: A Study in Literary Design*, is categorized as a "mirror" reading, as he also labels it, but it can also be viewed as an "ornamental glass" reading of the text.[7] To clarify, Culpepper's reading is an "ornamental glass" reading in the sense that it takes the text as it is before the reader and lets the text's design direct the reading and the reader. The narrative of the FG is read as its own closed narrative world, which may or may not be historically accurate. But, Culpepper's reading is also a "mirror" reading in the sense that the readers, looking at the art of the text, formulate the meaning between the text and themselves without consulting the author.[8] In that process, the readers do not see only the text, but also a reflection of themselves in the text. They respond to the text either accepting or rejecting it. The reader is left alone with the text to generate the meaning this side of the text with the help and lead of the narrative.

Culpepper believes that narrative criticism that was originally developed for study of fiction is a suitable methodology for a study of sacred texts like the FG.[9] An assumption is that the narrative, whether fictional

---

6. Oeming, *Contemporary Biblical Hermeneutics*.

7. See other examples of narrative reading: Tolmie, *Jesus' Farewell to the Disciples*; Tovey, *Narrative Art and Act*.

8. Fay, "R. Alan Culpepper," 214.

9. Culpepper, *Anatomy of the Fourth Gospel*, 6, 9, 10.

or historical, sacred or not, has ability to "move" its readers according to the will of the implied author. The implied author is found from the text. He/she is "the sum of the choices reflected in the writing of the narrative, choices of the use of settings, irony, characterization, the handling of time, suspense, distance, and all the problematics and potential of narrative writing which must be dealt with in one way or another."[10] In other words, the real fresh and blood author has inserted something of him/herself into the text by his/her choices of content, style, and so forth, but obviously has not included an exhaustive portrait of him/herself in it. In spite of the incomplete picture of the author, the text tells us something about the author. That "something" is called the "implied author." The real reader of the text reads the text the way the implied author tells it.[11]

Culpepper's reading of the FG seeks neither the historical author nor the Johannine community, nor even the historical Jesus of Nazareth. This is not to say, however, that historical realities are completely ignored. Questions like the time of writing and culture of that time are considered in order to read the words within that cultural setting rather than in the reader's setting. Yet, narrative-critical reading concentrates on the meaning of the narrative world rather than re-constructing the historical world in which the writing took place. The story, not its pre-history, is read and studied.

Culpepper's narrative critical reading is based on Seymour Chatman's theory of narrative text.[12] In that theory, the text is viewed more than a mere text on the surface. The text includes the implied author, narrator, narratee, story, story time, characters, setting, explicit and implicit commentary, and implied reader. In short, by viewing the text that way, the text becomes "alive." Only the real author and real reader are left outside of the text. Here is the simplified figure of the communication process that is the focus of narrative-critical reading:

---

10. Culpepper, *Anatomy of the Fourth Gospel*, 6–7.

11. To read the Gospel of John from implied reader's point of view, see Staley, *The Print's First Kiss*.

12. Culpepper, *Anatomy of the Fourth Gospel*, 6.

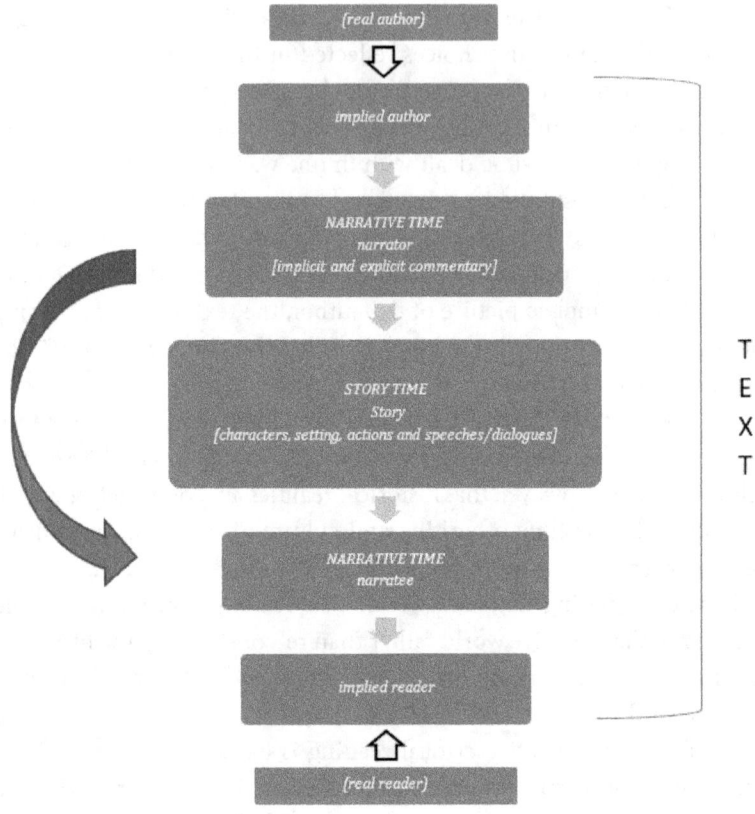

Figure 18.1

Even though the text is the sole interest of a narrative critical reading, Culpepper does not discard the historicity of the text altogether. He defines parameters within which historicity can function, namely, for bridging the gap between our world and the world in which the story was told. But understanding, he insists, does not come through reconstruction of the *Sitz im Leben* of the writing, but through the dynamic between the narrative and the reader. An outcome is that "Readers dance with the [implied] author whether they want to or not, and in the process they adopt his perspective on the story."[13]

Narrative critical reading has received criticism because of its capacity to ignore biblical narrative, like the FG, as historical. If the narrative

13. Culpepper, *Anatomy of the Fourth Gospel*, 233.

reading of John does not take into account historical realities, the narrative, although a very persuasive one, may only stay on the level of fiction.[14] Culpepper claims, however, that narrative analysis that concentrates solely on the text opens the text to the reader and exposes the anatomy of the FG, revealing "what the gospel is and what gives it its power as a narrative."[15]

Regarding the author and narrator, he says the following:

> In this story of history interpreted by faith, the narrator leads the reader to view each character and event from his point of view. Although the implied author and the real author may be distinguished from the narrator in theory, in John the narrator is the voice of the author and the vocal expression of the choices and perspective of the implied author. One of the ways the gospel achieves its powerful effects is through the role of this narrator, who is omniscient winsomely intrusive, and entirely reliable.[16]

Characters also play a special role in the overall anatomy of this Gospel. Characters are not merely there to make the narrative vivid. They are employed to contribute to the narrator's point of view. Characters are "sharply defined by their response to Jesus, by the measure of their ability to believe, and by their progress toward or away from the perspective of the narrator."[17] Various characters represent different responses to Jesus. Based on their response their status is indicated. For example, the Beloved Disciple is the ideal character whose response to Jesus demonstrates the authentic faith. It is this character's response to Jesus that is supposed to convince the reader to respond in the same way.

Towards the overall picture of the world of the FG and the way it should be understood (read), Culpepper suggests that the FG challenges today's reader to accept the narrative world as presented in the Fourth Evangelist's account (which should not be read as a "literally" true story). That narrative world is presentation of how the world really is and interacts with the reader's existential world within which he reads the narrative. The task is not to seek historicity of the story, but to let these two worlds, namely, the narrative and the reader's world, interact. With Culpepper's own words,

14. Cf. Carson, *The Gospel According to John*, 65–66.
15. Culpepper, *Anatomy of the Fourth Gospel*, 231.
16. Culpepper, *Anatomy of the Fourth Gospel*, 232.
17. Culpepper, *Anatomy of the Fourth Gospel*, 232.

> When the gospel is viewed as a mirror, though of course not a mirror in which we see only ourselves, its meaning can be found on this side of it, that is, between text and reader, in the experience of reading the text, and belief in the gospel can mean openness to the way it calls readers to interact with it, which life, and with their own world ... When once again we learn to read the gospel, we will be able to deal with the relationship between our world and its world "above" rather than the relationship between the evangelist's world and Jesus' world, or their world and our world. The, when the horizons of our world and the world of the narrative merge, we will have heard the gospel, the story will have fulfilled its purpose, and the truth to which it points can once again abide in its readers.[18]

An example of Culpepper's reading of FG is in order. From the following quotations, it becomes obvious how the narrative's design, its characters, dialogues and actions lead the reading. Culpepper says the following regarding John 4 in relation to the plot development in the FG:

> In John 4 there is again little opposition to Jesus. The chapter opens with an allusion to the threat posed by the Pharisees (4:1, 3). There is a proleptic reference to Jesus' rejection in 4:44 (cf. 1:11), but the rest of the chapter is positive. Jesus is making more disciples than John (4:1). The Samaritan woman hails him as the Christ, and many in her village say he is "the savior of the world" (4:29, 39–42). He is received in Galilee (4:45) and brings an official to faith by means of his second sign (4:46–54). There is therefore no more than token opposition in the first four chapters and a foreshadowing of more to come. These chapters have a powerful "primacy effect," that is, they firmly establish the reader's first impression of Jesus' identity and mission. The reader is led to accept the evangelist's view of Jesus before the antithetical point of view is given more than passing reference. It is hardly possible after these chapters for the reader to be persuaded by another view of Jesus.[19]

Before we leave Culpepper's narrative critical reading of the FG, it is necessary to point out another narrative-critical approach, namely, narrative structural exegesis. Structuralism is a blanket term under which various application are found. The common feature of structuralism is that "the structural methods assume a linguistic paradigm, that is, that

---

18. Culpepper, *Anatomy of the Fourth Gospel*, 236–37.
19. Culpepper, *Anatomy of the Fourth Gospel*, 91.

# The Fourth Gospel as Mirror and Ornamental Glass

expression in language is to be taken as a fundamental category and not as an access to something else, e.g., history."[20] Perhaps the most useful structural method for narratives is the study of narrative structures by applying an *actantial* model.[21] The actantial model, first introduced by Vladimir Propp, can be utilized as a supplementary method to narrative-critical reading. It is based on the belief that narratives, no matter which kind of narratives we are referring to, have a so-called deep structure. This structure is like a "grammar" of the narrative that authors of narratives follow consciously or unconsciously. The actantial model is the following:

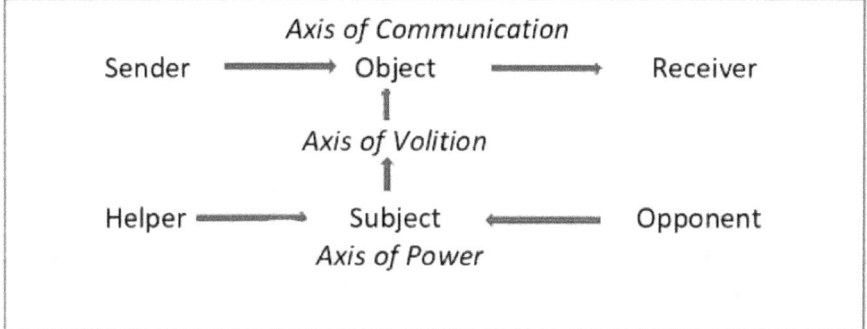

**Figure 18.2**

The axis of communication, the "sender" is the originator of the action and determines what the "receiver" needs. The "object" is what is, or what is meant to be, communicated. The "receiver" is the one who is intended to receive the "sender's" communication and thus gains something that the "receiver" did not previously have. The axis of volition is the plot of the narrative. The axis of power demonstrates which components in the narrative support the "subject" to move towards the "object" and components which are obstacles for the "subject" to accept the "object." When the actantial model is applied to John 4:1–26, we may arrive at the following narrative structure:

---

20. Patte, *What is Structural Exegesis?*, 1.

21. See Patte, *What is Structural Exegesis?*, 35–52; Provan, *The Reformation*, 517–47; Routledge, *Old Testament Theology*, 47–50.

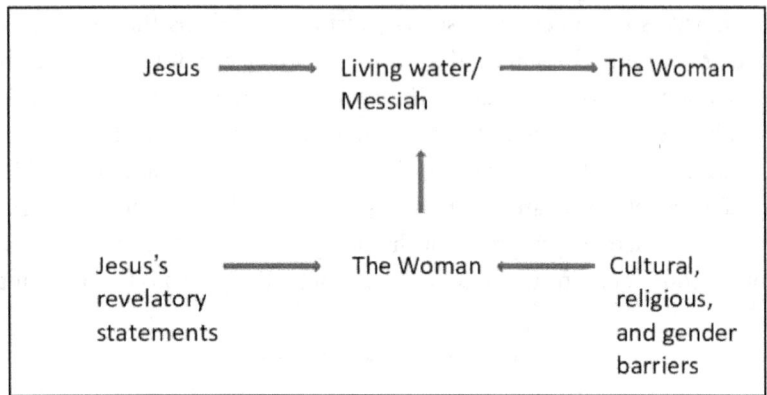

**Figure 18.3**

The study of narrative structure is helpful at least for two fronts. First, it forces the readers to seek the opening and ending of the narrative, in other words, to study the entire narrative unit. Secondly, it demands the readers to find out the plot that includes who is the originator of that which is communicated to whom and what the power struggles are in that narrative. In order to do that, the narrative is studied in its own terms in detail.[22]

## J. Eugene Botha: Speech-Act Reading

The speech-act theory has not received as much attention in Johannine studies as narrative-criticism. But because of its promising results, we will introduce it here as a "text" focused reading model. It was introduced by J. L. Austin in his 1955 William James Lectures and later in his book, *How to Do Things with Words*, published in 1962.[23] The speech-act theory applied to the written text seeks certain kinds of qualities in the literary communication, especially those qualities that cause characters in the narrative or recipients of that communication to act, that is, to do something.

The fundamental observation of the speech-act theory is that words can do things. When this is translated to the reading process, interpreters become interested in not only what the text says but also, and foremost,

---

22. For more detailed presentation of that model, see Patte, *What is Structural Exegesis?*, 42–51.

23. See the second edition: Austin, *How to Do Things with Words*.

what it does. Therefore, as the name of the theory suggests, readers using the speech-act theory, do not only concentrate on sentences of the text to find out whether they are true or false, but pay attention to utterances to see what the words might do in the life of narrative characters as well as in the readers of the narrative. J. Eugene Botha writes, "Sentences are the object of the study of formal grammar and also of semantics, where they are perceived as abstract and syntactical structures . . . Speech acts are much more related to the pragmatics of language usage—that is, utterances made in a specific context have a specific 'force', not necessarily related to the form of the utterance, but certainly distinguishable from it."[24]

The speech-act theory takes the narrative-critical reading mode into account and therefore builds upon it. Thus, characters' utterances in the narrative should not be read in isolation. The speech-act reading works only if utterances are read in the larger context of the narrative in which they are found. Botha explains further, "For example, in an [sic] context where a person has expressed the fact that s/he is hungry, the utterance 'I have bread' can be construed as an offer to provide food, rather than a mere assertion that the speaker has access to bread. It is thus important to know who is speaking, in what manner, under which circumstances, to whom and why."[25] Another example of this is the statement, "It is Sunday." This sentence points out the day of the week (if it is a truthful statement). But it *also* may have another meaning in a certain context. It may mean, "Let's go to the church!" It becomes obvious that the speaker does not just say those words but performs an utterance that makes a recipient react on it.

In the above example, the utterance "It is Sunday" is a so-called *locutionary* act of the speaker, that is, actual words in proper syntax and grammar. This act is not, however, the focus of speech-act theory. What is more important and to which the locutionary act leads are so-called *illocutionary* and *perlocutionary* acts. An illocutionary act can be defined as what the speaker hopes to accomplish by performing a locutionary act. Therefore, the speaker uses implicature to communicate. A perlocutionary act is what the recipient does or how he/she reacts. In the above example, "It is Sunday" is not meant to be taken as mere information about the day of the week. The speaker's illocutionary act is to communicate what always happens on Sundays. Therefore, a statement becomes

---

24. Botha, *Jesus and the Samaritan Woman*, 64.
25. Botha, "Speech Act Theory," 278.

an encouragement or even a command, "Let's go to church!" A perlocutionary act is how the listener acts upon the locutionary act, accepting or denying the illocutionary force.

Botha compares and contrasts speech-act reading with other previous attempts to understand Jesus's abrupt request to the Samaritan woman in John 4:16, "Go, call your husband and come here." According to Botha, previous interpretations miss something as they do not explain the sudden change of topic or interpret it as a mere need to point out to the Samaritan woman her sinfulness.[26] Botha argues that Jesus's request to the Samaritan woman to fetch her husband is not that abrupt after all. In the beginning of the narrative the Samaritan woman is superior to Jesus who needs water that Samaritan woman can provide. But as the narrative improves, "the relationship between him [Jesus] and the woman has been changing from two strangers meeting at a well, to that of an individual person holding authority over the other."[27] This is recognized in 4:15 where the woman requests Jesus's "water."[28] In that new power structure where Jesus is in a superior/authoritative position, he can make the request. Botha explains, "This is the reason why the woman does not question Jesus' right to give a command, but merely responds and explains why she is unable to do so."[29] Jesus's word, therefore, has a force to make the woman to act, which is also reflected in her response in 4:17. "Her utterance has the illocutionary force of a constative, asserting something, in this case denying that she has a husband. The perlocution or intended perlocution could explain her inability to comply with the imperative of Jesus."[30]

The above example has demonstrated how the speech-act theory works in the narrative level. Yet, it also works in the other level between implied author and implied reader. Botha argues that several earlier commentators have concentrated on what is happening only between the author and the reader. For this reason, he claims that speech-act theory is necessary to complement other readings. In the case of John 4:16, he writes, "The implied readers ... are intended to pick up that there is misunderstanding on the woman's side and that a change of topic has become

26. See Botha, "Speech Act Theory," 284; Botha, "John 4.16," 181–82.
27. Botha, "Speech Act Theory," 287.
28. Botha, "John 4.16," 188.
29. Botha, "Speech Act Theory," 287.
30. Botha, "Speech Act Theory," 287.

necessary. They [previous commentators] mostly interpret the abrupt change (anachronistically) in the light of what followed (Jesus showing that he is omniscient and divine and so on) and not in terms of the utterance itself and its intended perlocution."[31] When the utterance is read following the speech-act theory, it leads readers to ask necessary questions about the "gaps" that needs to be filled. This example has demonstrated that the gap is found in the utterance when read in the holistic narrative context. Jesus's utterance demands the woman's action, which she willingly does, as Jesus has claimed a higher position on the ladder of authority and is now above the woman's authority status in her eyes. The informed reader knows that Jesus is superior, but in the narrative world of the Samaritan woman, she does not know that and therefore the implied author leads the reader to see that from the point of view of the woman.

The following examples demonstrate another aspect of the speech-act theory. The speech-act theory works on two levels, namely between the narrative characters (in John 4, between Jesus and the Samaritan woman) and between the implied author and implied reader. We offer below a few of Botha's interpretations as examples how he applies the speech-act reading model to John 4 considering both levels. This time we do not rehearse the narrative context in relation to these utterances. We assume that the readers are aware of the basic story line of the dialogue between Jesus and the Samaritan woman.[32]

- John 4:7b: "Jesus said to her, 'Give Me a drink.'"
    - Form: imperative
    - Type of illocution: request
    - Perlocution: The character Jesus opens the conversation and induces the woman to furnish water. The author wants the readers to understand that Jesus is acting contra the accepted norms. The author wants the readers to recall the intertext of betrothal scenes. The author wants to induce in the readers an evaluative attitude.

---

31. Botha, "Speech Act Theory," 287.
32. The following examples are adopted word for word (except the biblical statements which are taken from NASB instead of the Greek New Testament text of NA27) from Botha, *Jesus and the Samaritan Woman*, 121–22.

- John 4:8: "For His disciples had gone away into the city to buy food."
  - Form: statement
  - Type of illocution: constative
  - Perlocution: The author wants the readers to understand why Jesus is alone; delaying tactic to allow information to sink in, thus increasing suspense. The fact that Jesus and the woman are alone also problematizes the situation further.
- John 4:9a: "Therefore the Samaritan woman said to Him, 'How is it that You, being a Jew, ask me for a drink since I am a Samaritan woman?'"
  - Form: question
  - Type of illocution: constative (disputative)
  - Perlocution: The woman wants to get Jesus to desist in his socio-culturally unacceptable conduct. The author wants the readers to have positive feelings toward the woman and react negatively towards the conduct of Jesus.
- John 4:9b: "For Jews have no dealings with Samaritans."
  - Form: statement
  - Type of illocution: constative (confirmative)
  - Perlocution: The author wants the readers to accept the position of the woman that Jesus is wrong. The readers are to take an evaluative stance.

These few examples show the purpose of the speech-act reading: to see how the text communicates beyond the mere grammar and syntax, evoking the reader's feelings, actions, and understanding, and so getting the point of view of the text (implied author). This is also to show that the author did this intentionally. In other words, the author wanted to move the reader in a certain way. Yet now it is the text that conveys this intention as the reader is having the conversation with the text.

Botha, in his 2007 article, "Speech Act Theory and Biblical Interpretation," acknowledges various ways how the speech-act theory can be applied to the NT interpretation.[33] He notes, "On the one hand there is an

---

33. Botha, "Speech Act Theory," 274–94.

approach which deals with each speech act in detail and the [sic] there is an approach where the focus is more on the overall perlocutionary effect of a text."[34]

## Concluding Remarks

In this chapter, we have outlined two reading models applied to the FG which concentrate on the text and meaning formulation between the text and the reader. Narrative-critical reading, as Culpepper's groundbreaking work demonstrates, concentrates on the narrative design that is supported by various narrative features such as characters, their worlds, and actions. The plot is sought by framing the narrative properly determining its beginning, middle, and ending, and examining how the narrative's problem is solved. In the case of John 4, Culpepper does not only study the individual narrative of the Samaritan woman, but also notices how chapter 4 is a part of the "introductory" chapters in which Jesus's role and status is built before the FG enters into a new "climate" marked by controversy between Jesus and "Jews."

The speech-act reading pays attention to utterances and seeks to find out what those utterances accomplish. In the case of John 4, Botha concentrates on seeing how various statements and requests move the characters to act in a certain way, namely, to accept Jesus's status as greater than the woman's, which causes the woman to react to Jesus's words in a certain way. Narrative-critical and speech-act reading models, therefore, are distinctively different, but still share the same ethos as they work with the reader's side of the text and can complement each other.

There are benefits in both readings. The narrative-critical reading is helpful for readers to see the narrative holistically. Occasionally readers may have tendency to read only a small portion of the narrative, which is not arguably a unit. The application that follows such a reading may not be the one that can be supported by the larger narrative context. For example, in the case of John 5, the reader may concentrate on the healing story that is in the beginning of that chapter, ignoring the aftermath of the healing which is actually the main portion of the story.[35] Even further,

---

34. Botha, "Speech Act Theory," 274. For advanced study on speech-act theory, consult Thiselton, *New Horizons on Hermeneutics*. See also Thiselton, *Thiselton on Hermeneutics*.

35. Cf. Attridge, "Argumentation in John 5," 190.

the reader may also miss the understanding how John 5 is a part of the entire Gospel narrative. The narrative-critical reading seeks the opening-middle-closing of the story and reads the text unit's meaning based on the entire narrative. The structural exegetical actantial model is helpful in this aspect of narrative critical reading as well.

The speech-act reading brings a different benefit. It helps readers to move from the mere cognitive field to the empirical and psychological field of interpretation. The readers' energy is not expended on the question whether the statements are true or false, but on the question of what the text accomplishes and how it does it. The question like, "What does the speaker accomplish by saying this?" goes further than mere understanding of sentences in the text in their grammatical or historical sense.

The speech-act reading also moves beyond the "text world" to the world of the reader by informing the reader how the implied reader is expected to re-act narrative characters' utterances. Therefore, the questions that speech-act reading bring to the narrative characters is somewhat different than what it brings to the readers. The readers are informed, and thus know more than the characters in the narrative. Therefore, speech-act reading further informs readers how the narrative (protagonist) accomplishes its purpose through the utterances. This is clearly observed in Jesus's abrupt change of topic in John 4:16. The readers understand that Jesus's sudden change of topic is not disconnected from the entire discourse and Jesus's purpose, but is a vital part of the conversation and is possible because the previous utterances have changed Jesus's status in relation to the woman's status paving the way for Jesus's request.

## Suggestions for Further Reading

Culpepper, R. Alan. *The Anatomy of the Fourth Gospel: A Study in Literary Design*. Philadelphia: Fortress, 1983.

Fay, Ron C. "R. Alan Culpepper and the Literary Approach to John's Gospel. In *The Gospel of John in Modern Interpretation*, edited by Stanley E. Porter and Ron C. Fay. Grand Rapids: Kregel, 2018. Pp. 211–35.

Patte, Daniel. *What is Structural Exegesis?* NTSer. Philadelphia: Fortress, 1976. Pp. 35–52.

Thiselton, Anthony C. *New Horizons in Hermeneutics: The Theory and Practice of Transforming Biblical Reading.* Grand Rapids: Zondervan, 1992. Pp. 283-90, 358-67.

———. *Thiselton on Hermeneutics: Collected Works with New Essays.* Grand Rapids: Eerdmans, 2006, Pp. 51-149.

CHAPTER 19

# The Fourth Gospel as Stained Class
*Text as Lived, Living, and Livable*

RECENTLY, THERE HAVE BEEN several attempts to develop integrated reading methods.[1] W. Randolph Tate, quoted by Thiselton, points out that there is "the need for a multi-angled or integrated set of methods since 'text-centered methods tend to treat the text as literary artifacts,' 'reader-centered methods' encourage 'interaction between the reader and the text . . . in a dialogue.' But in addition to asking 'what actually takes place' when a text is read, an interpreter needs to ask about the situation of the writer who produces the text: 'the locus of meaning is not to be found exclusively in . . . any two of the worlds, but in the interplay between all three worlds.'"[2] An integrated reading that follows Tate's argument and considers all three worlds in the interpretation process can be described as the "stained glass" reading, using Counet's glass images.

If you had a stained sheet of glass in your hand, you would see the stained glass, but you also would see through it. The view behind the stained glass is not that clear but perhaps you could recognize some shapes, forms, and items that are the other side of the stained glass. Also, since the glass is stained, it reflects back to you, and therefore, you would see a reflection of yourself. The "stained glass" reading, therefore, is not the "window" reading that works mainly behind the text. It is not the "ornamental glass" reading that only works with the world that the text

1. Thiselton, "New Testament Interpretation," 27–31.
2. Thiselton, "New Testament Interpretation," 28.

creates. It is not a mere "mirror reading" that emphasizes what happens between the text and the reader.³

Integrated reading is then best categorized as the "stained glass" reading that works with all three worlds: historical, textual, and readers' worlds. It recognizes that meaning effects are found not in one place but from all of these places. When the reader is acquainted with the text's meaning effect that arises from these three worlds, the reader is in a good position to understand that text holistically. Therefore, it is necessary to take all these worlds as part of interpretation to arrive at the text's best possible meaning. The subtitle of this chapter points towards this idea as well. The text and its meaning were once lived, the text still lives in the text-world, and it can be lived again to some extend by today's reader.

In recent years, there have been studies that argue for a comprehensive reading model that goes beyond mere window (diachronic) or mirror (synchronic) readings. For example, Martin De Boer has observed that Culpepper, who critiqued historical criticism, is actually trying to reconstruct the "intended reader" at the end of his *Anatomy of the Fourth Gospel*. This proves, De Boer argues, that historical questions cannot be completely avoided, and they should not be avoided even in a synchronic reading of the FG.⁴ The same can be said about window readings. It is almost impossible to ignore the text and see only what is on the other side of it. The text is not a transparent "window glass" which does not affect one's view of what one is trying to observe on the other side of it. Actually, the text is a compulsory medium that leads the reader to see behind the text. Therefore, a "stained glass" reading is an attempt at an integrated reading that takes into account the text's historical context, the text itself, and the reader of the text. Below we introduce a few applications of this kind of reading to the FG.

## Mark W. G. Stibbe: Text, Context, and Pre-text

At the beginning of the 1990s, Mark W. G. Stibbe presented his critique of two extreme phenomena in biblical hermeneutics: (1) "the recent

---

3. In the end of 1990s, John Ashton observed that diachronic (window readings) and synchronic (mirror readings) methods "are rarely combined, though why this should be so is something of a mystery, since the possibilities of dialectic enrichment are, one would have thought, fairly obvious." Ashton, "John and the Johannine Literature," 260.

4. Motyer, "Method in Fourth Gospel Studies," 28.

anti-historical bias of text-immanent, literary analysis of biblical texts" and (2) "the largely anti-aesthetic bias of traditional, historical-critical methods."[5] He argued for a more comprehensive reading model, which considers three "texts," namely, text, context, and pre-text. This kind of reading means that an interpreter should study "the surface level of the narrative, the social context of the narrative, and the historical reference sources and tradition of the narrative."[6] Even though he works narrative-critically, his reading moves beyond narrowly applied narrative critical readings. Narrative-critical reading can be extended to include historical categories, Stibbe argues. In other words, the model that is narrative-critical should study not only literary aspects of the text such as form and style but also historical aspects of the narrative, such as its context and pre-text.[7]

Thus, Stibbe's integrated reading model includes synchronic and diachronic orientations. His synchronic orientation is divided into two facets: (1) analysis of John's text (John as narrative Christology), and (2) analysis of John's text (John and its narrative genre). Similarly, diachronic orientation is divided into two: (1) analysis of John's context (John as community narrative), and (2) analysis of John's pre-text (John as narrative history).[8] The diachronic aspects are added to the narrative-critical model to bring "behind the text" realities to the meaning formulation process. In Stibbe's presentation, it is neither the text nor the reader alone, but also the author as "masterful storyteller" (to use Stibbe's words) who receives the attention.

Stibbe applies this reading to the FG chapters 18—19. Below we outline a few key points of his interpretation. First, Stibbe outlines the narrative, its characters, and point of view, concluding that the narrative's chronology is inseparable from narrative Christology.[9] For the Fourth Evangelist, Jesus's role as a paschal lamb, and especially this role in the passion narrative, is overruling factor so much so that chronology yields to the "lamb Christology." He also points out that the main character contrast is found between Jesus and Peter, not between Jesus and Judas Iscariot or Jesus and "Jews." Peter is holding a role in the center stage in the FG with Jesus; his role in the narrative is not to demonstrate an

---

5. Stibbe, *John as Storyteller*, 1
6. Stibbe, *John as Storyteller*, 1.
7. Stibbe, *John as Storyteller*, 197.
8. Stibbe, *John as Storyteller*, 13.
9. Stibbe, *John as Storyteller*, 115.

ideal Jesus's follower, but instead it is brought into sharp contrast to Jesus. That contrast between Jesus and Peter is skillfully presented in the passion story. Jesus goes forward at the garden identifying himself twice with "I AM" (*ego eimi*) to the Roman soldiers and the officers from the chief priests and the Pharisees (John 18:5, 8). Peter, on the other hand, denies Jesus twice, saying, "I am not" (*ouk eimi*) Jesus's disciple (John 18:17, 25). When Jesus is being interrogated before the Jewish authorities inside the house, Peter is standing outside the house. Jesus speaks the truth, whereas Peter speaks untruth (John 18:15–38). Jesus is assaulted during the interrogation, whereas Peter assaults a servant of the high priest who asks about his relation to Jesus.[10] When the trial moves from the high priest's quarter to Pilate's praetorium, the evangelist skillfully continues to use the trial motif where Pilate and Jews, outside of praetorium, and Pilate and Jesus, inside of praetorium, "become progressively more confrontational."[11]

Secondly, regarding the narrative genre, Stibbe argues that Jesus's passion narrative (indeed the entire Gospel) is not an ancient comedy. Instead, Stibbe argues that all the gospel narratives are best characterized as tragedy.[12] Even though the evangelist did not purposefully copy, perhaps did not even know, other Greco-Roman authors who wrote using the tragedy genre, Stibbe argues that the evangelist did so unconsciously. The evangelist treated the Jewish themes employing Greek techniques, in this case, Greek tragedy genre. As an historian, he had only a few models to choose from: romance, tragedy, comedy, and satire. He "chose" tragedy, Stibbe argues. He further points out that, "The reason why John's gospel therefore appears to us as tragedy is that John the storyteller, like Thucydides, lived in a culture in which the tragic form was deeply embedded. When John narrated his tradition, something inevitably tragic emerged in his story of the killing of the King."[13] To see the narrative from that perspective has naturally influenced how the story is understood. So Stibbe reads the FG as a tragedy where the creator of all is killed. Nevertheless, he is resurrected, but again, those who were instrumental in his execution, namely Pilate and Jews, are denied insight, whereas Peter and Thomas are brought back to him. Stibbe thinks that "John's story is a tragic

---

10. Stibbe, *John as Storyteller*, 97.
11. Stibbe, *John as Storyteller*, 113.
12. Stibbe, *John as Storyteller*, 129.
13. Stibbe, *John as Storyteller*, 137.

performance."[14] Stibbe's work goes beyond narrative structural categories to study historical realities and their possible influence on the author.

Thirdly, Stibbe looks into the text's sociological aspects that move his integrated reading model towards the diachronic approach. He does this by first analyzing the language of the narrative and then applying the findings' plausible sociological function in the community's life situation.[15] He is especially interested in seeing how the language "operates as an index of the community's value-system," whether reflecting, establishing, or correcting it.[16] Stibbe sees that the doorkeeper/sheepfold and family motifs play a meaningful part in the sociological aspects, making the Beloved Disciple the doorkeeper like the Good Shepherd himself was (John 18:1–27). Whereas Peter denies Jesus, the Beloved Disciples remains faithful. In John 19:25–27, "Jesus creates a new family of faith by adopting the BD [Beloved Disciple, who, according to Stibbe, is Lazarus] as his true successor on earth."[17] The consequence of this is that the church becomes a family of faith.

Finally, Stibbe looks at narrative-historical factors attempting to "explore the journey from narrative history through narrative source to narrative gospel."[18] He presupposes that FG's passion narrative is independent of the Synoptics. The passion story that the FG is following might have been in touch very early with pre-Synoptic stories and thus share some similarities. According to Stibbe, the Beloved Disciple (i.e., Lazarus) is the source for the passion story, who also was an eyewitness of these events.[19]

Stibbe concludes that the FG, as the study on John 18—19 has shown, is the masterpiece of a storyteller. His narrative-critical reading does not "murder" the author nor give power to historical-critical aspects.[20] Even though it is called "narrative critical," his reading model attempts to read the narrative in a more holistic manner, integrating diachronic aspects into the synchronic approach. Yet, his integrated reading model does not give a clearly defined role for the reader.

14. Stibbe, *John as Storyteller*, 138.
15. Stibbe, *John as Storyteller*, 148,
16. Stibbe, *John as Storyteller*, 149–50.
17. Stibbe, *John as Storyteller*, 153, 163.
18. Stibbe, *John as Storyteller*, 168.
19. Stibbe, *John as Storyteller*, 179–87.
20. Stibbe, *John as Storyteller*, 198.

## Stephen Motyer: Context, Co-text, and Text

In his monograph entitled, *Your Father the Devil?: A New Approach to John and "the Jews,"* Stephen Motyer develops his application of the "stained glass" reading. We outline his method first and then give examples of his interpretation.

Motyer, like Stibbe, argues for a need of integrated synchronic and diachronic reading of the biblical text. He claims that a holistic hermeneutical approach is possible which focuses not only on the text (mirror reading) or the text as a mere gateway to the historical events behind the text (window reading) but combines these two into a meaningful whole. The reader's world is left to receive lesser attention than, for example, in the socio-rhetorical integrated reading model that we will introduce below. Motyer uses the catchwords *context, co-text* and *text* to sketch his approach.[21]

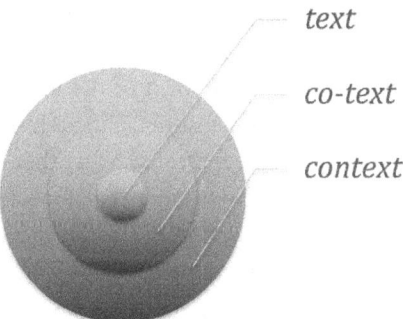

**Figure 19.1**

Readers start with the text but move towards the outer circle, keeping the text, however, always in the front of their eyes as a source and reference. Thus, even though the contexts and co-texts are studied before the detailed exegetical study of the text, the text is the reader's main interest and medium for other meaning effects found in the contexts and co-texts. When the sense of the context of the text is gained, readers turn their interest back to the co-texts and the text for more detailed study. Finally, readers re-read the text with the gained background knowledge that guides them in the process of interpretation and helps them to understand the text from the point of view of its author and intended readers.

---

21. Motyer, *Your Father the Devil?*, 32.

To put this in Motyer's words, the first step is to find out what the text tells about the social setting of the people's lives in the narrative. This step is combined with "appropriate external indicators."[22] The second step goes outside of the text to find out in which kind of context the text seems to sit the most comfortably. Motyer reminds us that this step has to be holistic and general to avoid some earlier "errors" to relate the background to only one seemingly fitting historical phenomenon, *such as the Birkat ha-minim* (curse on the heretics). Finally, the reader returns "back to the text and re-reads it against the background now more fully delineated."[23]

Motyer's purpose is to understand "Jews" in chapter 8 of the FG. He looks first for internal "points of sensitivity"[24] in the FG. He does that by examining seven topics: (1) The temple and festivals, (2) the law, (3) revelation and apocalyptic, (4) Judea and "the Jews," (5) the creation of faith, (6) the signs, and (7) Johannine language and argumentation.[25] He concludes that the context in which the FG was read was post-temple times (after 70 CE), and that the work was mainly evangelistic, addressing Judean Jews who have felt the impact of the temple destruction the most. It was Jesus whom the evangelist presents to his readers as the one who has replaced the temple in its full sense.[26] In other words, the Fourth Evangelist communicates that the trauma that Jews felt because of the destruction of the temple and cessation of the sacrifices can be solved by accepting Jesus. One's faith in him supersedes the temple worship in the fullest sense.

Next, Motyer moves on to study external evidence of Jews and Judaism after the destruction of the temple. At this point, the purpose is "to clarify the points of reference which enabled the text to be heard as *Gospel* in that world."[27] His conclusions provide the point of view against which the text is re-read. The first one is that Judaism, according to Motyer, was not unified after the destruction of the temple. Instead, it continued to have multiple trends within itself including the Pharisees. It was later in

---

22. Motyer, *Your Father the Devil?*, 33.
23. Motyer, *Your Father the Devil?*, 33.
24. This phrase is used by James Dunn "to describe those features of the Gospel which seem to engage with issues or needs in its environment." Motyer, *Your Father the Devil?*, 35.
25. For the full study and argumentation, see Motyer, *Your Father the Devil?*, 36–73.
26. Motyer, *Your Father the Devil?*, 73.
27. Motyer, *Your Father the Devil?*, 74.

132–35 CE, after the Bar Kokhba revolt, when rabbinic orthodoxy became the dominant form of Judaism.[28] Secondly, Motyer argues that evidence shows that Judaism was not strengthened by the temple destruction but weakened. Jews were "traumatized" by not having the Jerusalem Temple. Its destruction brought "shame" to them as their God could not protect the temple. It is into this situation that "the Fourth Gospel speaks a message of hope and salvation."[29] The new temple, Jesus, is the locale in which his people have access to the Father.

Finally, Motyer turns to work with the text (John 8) with this general understanding of the life setting within which he believes the first readers read and understood the text. He does this in three stages. First, he studies literary and rhetorical structures of 5:1—12:50 and then 7:1—8:59. After these two steps, he concentrates on the passage (8:31–59) that is the main narrative text he exegetes. Motyer's concluding remarks are as follows:

> Our discussion has shown that, far from being heard as insulting and denigrating, this passage would have served as a powerful appeal to Jews in the later first century to believe in Jesus the Christ. Its rhetoric coheres with other examples from the period and earlier, which show that "you are of your father the devil" would not have been heard as a designation of Jewish ontology, but as a severe *warning* about the real nature of a certain course of action (executing Jesus). Hearing such a warning, the late first-century reader must decide what attitude she will take to the Christ-faith, which is quite possible being vigorously canvassed and debated in her environment.[30]

This conclusion, Motyer argues, fits the background that was painted earlier before the exegetical study. This might sound like a circular argumentation. Namely that the interpreter first recreates the background for the text and then interprets the text against that created background making it fit to that. Motyer's attempt is not ill-motivated. To the contrary, his model is correctly based on the view that we can know something (perhaps never everything) concrete from the historical background of biblical text, which we should incorporate in meaningful ways in our endeavor of interpretation.

---

28. Motyer, *Your Father the Devil?*, 75, 103.
29. Motyer, *Your Father the Devil?*, 104.
30. Motyer, *Your Father the Devil?*, 209.

## Vernon K. Robbins and Jerome H. Neyrey: Socio-Rhetorical Reading

Before this chapter is complete, we introduce socio-rhetorical criticism that continues to receive attention among biblical scholars. Socio-rhetorical criticism, perhaps better than the above sketched reading models, can be described as a "stained glass" reading. The expression "socio-rhetorical" means that this method pays attention to socio-scientific aspects both in the events' historical context and in the narrative. Further, it suggests that the text is persuasive (rhetorical) communication. The persuasion can be recognized in the narrative among the characters, and at the reading moment as the narrative persuades the reader to accept the author's point of view. Vernon K. Robbins developed his model of the socio-rhetorical criticism in the 1990s. He has not, however, applied it to the FG.[31] Ten years later, Jerome H. Neyrey wrote a commentary on the FG using a socio-rhetorical approach. Before we outline Neyrey's reading of the FG, we will present Robbins's model of the socio-rhetorical criticism that differs from Neyrey's application of this approach.

Robbins developed a comprehensive and integrated method that pays attention to the text (narrative), historical context, and present context in which the narrative is read.[32] The text is the starting point and gets the readers' attention throughout the reading process. Therefore, the narrative is approached narrative-critically, but in a way that does not ignore historical realities like a mere ornamental glass/mirror application of narrative-critical reading tends to do. The way Robbins reaches his ambitious goal is to study what he calls textures of the text. The textures he has introduced are (1) inner texture, (2) intertexture, (3) social and cultural texture, (4) ideological texture, and (5) sacred texture. These textures bring three "dimensions" to the process of interpretation, as it will be shown below in figure 19.2. Those dimensions are (1) historical, (2) present, and (3) text immanent. The goal of textures' examination is to identify meaning effects that can be utilized to bring forth the narrative's meaning.[33]

---

31. For a few attempts, see Botha and Tuppurainen, "The Roles of the Spirit," 23–43; Tuppurainen, "The Role(s) of the Spirit-Paraclete."

32. Two of the significant works that explain socio-rhetorical criticism are Robbins, *Exploring the Texture of Texts*; and Robbins, *The Tapestry of Early Christian Discourse*.

33. Tuppurainen, "Reading St. Luke's Narrative as 'Texture.'"

Each texture has its own set of questions. The different sets of questions require the reader to read the text many times. Figuratively speaking, the reader must walk around the text and in the text several times. In that process the reader also explores aspects that go beyond the text, such as historical context, modern commentators who have earlier worked with the same text, and even the reader him/herself. The multiple times of re-reading the text and answering various questions that each text's texture requires, bring the reader to a position where he/she feels the text's persuasion in the current context of reading. Here is the figure of Robbins's socio-rhetorical model of textual communication that demonstrates its nature as "stained glass" reading:[34]

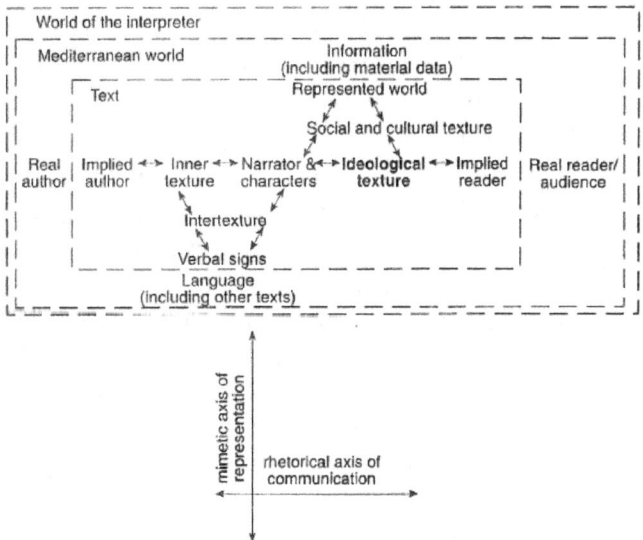

**Figure 19.2**

As the above figure illustrates, the interpreter's approach is to regard the text as a thick tapestry of colorful texture. Inner texture deals with the text's flat surface to see how the words function as tools of rhetorical communication. Intertexture deals with other literary texts

---

34. Robbins, *The Tapestry of Early Christian Discourse*, 21. Figure: Socio-rhetorical model of textual communication. (Reproduced with permission of the Licensor through PLSclear.) Note that this figure does not display the "sacred texture." The sacred texture is, however, explained in Robbins's *Exploring the Texture of Texts*.

(intertextuality) and cultural, social, and historical factors presented as a textualized form in the text. The social and cultural texture is to depict what kind of cultural and social world the text creates. The ideological texture is interested in people. Here the reader examines the author's ideologies, the reader who now reads the text, and the previous readers and how that might have shaped their writings and readings. The sacred texture examines systematically the relationship between the human and divine presented in the text. This outline of the textures is far from the comprehensive explanation of them. Therefore, further consultation of Robbins's works is required. Nevertheless, even our brief sketch of Robbins's socio-rhetorical criticism shows that it is an integrated reading model which includes synchronic and diachronic methods. It is multi-dimensional and multi-disciplinary that seeks not mere information but the message/meaning of the text that has capacity to persuade the present reader. Therefore, the ideal reader is not a mere objective observer of the text but an object of the text's persuasion. The text challenges the reader, demanding his/her reaction.

Neyrey's commentary on the FG claims to be written according to a socio-rhetorical perspective.[35] As mentioned above, however, his reading method does not follow Robbins's socio-rhetorical criticism. Nevertheless, his commentary represents the same idea of reading the FG within its socio-ideological context as Robbins's model does. Also, the Gospel's rhetoric deserves attention, even though Neyrey's study on rhetoric does not reach the reader in the same capacity as Robbins's model where the reader is placed as an object of its persuasion.

In his introduction, Neyrey outlines several components which are vital for socio-rhetorical and narrative readings. Therefore, his introduction differs drastically from many introductions to FG which habitually include historical questions such as authorship, date, and place of writing. Instead of these kind of historical questions, typical for historical-critical studies, Neyrey introduces the author's social location, characters, role and status, language and the strategies of secrecy, insights from the social sciences, and other cultural concepts like gossip network and limited good.[36] Neyrey's program to read the FG agrees with the socio-scientific approach which holds that the meaning of the text can be understood only

---

35. Neyrey, *The Gospel of John*, 1. A similar work, even though it does not carry a socio-rhetorical label, is Brant, *John*. See also Neyrey, *The Gospel of John in Cultural and Rhetorical Perspective*.

36. Neyrey, *The Gospel of John*, 2–27.

in its socio-historical matrix of relationships. That socio-historical matrix, including the rhetoric of the day, is reflected in the narrative world that the text creates. Therefore, the FG's narrative world is central for Neyrey's socio-rhetorical reading similar to that of Robbins's reading model.

Neyrey discusses literary/narrative and socio/rhetorical topics that are evoked by the text in the commentary section. His commentary is an example of the reading that is informed by socio-historical and rhetorical notions. Below we will give a quotation from his commentary to demonstrate this. In his exposition of John 14:13–24, Neyrey uses the first-century Mediterranean patron-broker-client relationship model as a leading socio-cultural concept to extract the meaning from the text. One needs to bear in mind that the brokerage concept is also a rhetorical one. The broker in that society enjoyed a place of power in his relation to his patron's clients that the broker may use rhetorically to achieve his patron's goals. In Neyrey's own words:

> At no time and in no way does Jesus present himself as a patron, but only as the Patron's mediator and broker. He bridges and joins clients and Patron; he is the go-between, or the exclusive "way" to the Father . . . [T]he broker cements his relationship with the patron, the source of all benefaction; in many ways he declares it to be strong and solid . . . (14:10–11). The broker-patron relationship is utterly reliable. Jesus, moreover, brokers the Patron's works (14:1) and words (14:24). Similarly, the Broker facilitates the clients' access to the Patron: They may ask in his name (14:13–14). He, in fact will broker the Paraclete for them (14:16–17, 26). The Broker, moreover, is solicitous for his clients: He warns them of coming crises, exhorting them not to be disturbed (14:1, 28); he tells them prophecies of future hard times for the express purpose of alerting them how to weather those storms successfully (14:29; see also 13:19); and finally, he gives them otherworldly peace (14:27).[37]

This excerpt of Neyrey's socio-rhetorical reading demonstrates how socio-rhetorical categories are employed to inform the reader. However, as noted above, Neyrey's application of socio-rhetorical reading differs from that of Robbins's model in that he does not pay attention to the reader and his/her context of reading the same way as Robbins's model does.

---

37. Neyrey, *The Gospel of John*, 244–45.

## Concluding Remarks

Integrated reading models that we have sketched in this chapter are promising methods to read the FG. The FG is a persuasive work written in the context in which rhetoric was part of the education system and everyday life. The FG is argued to have also a trial motif that fits well with the use of rhetoric.[38] Even without applying the trial motif to the FG, it indeed has Jesus-Jews tension, that can be read as is done by Motyer, as a robust persuasive encouragement for Jews to accept Jesus as the only access to God's kingdom (the eternal life). Stibbe's reading pays attention to Jesus-Peter dynamics. That reading may suggest that the evangelist encourages believing community members to keep on following Jesus.

The historical context is also noticed as an essential component that informs the reader. However, the history-behind-the-text is not the *telos* of the study of the text but rather valuable, even necessary material that helps readers understand the narrative. The sociological gap is taken seriously. The language's meaning is derived from society's social matrix where the language is used. Therefore, the study of Johannine society and the study of the text's sociological outlook are invaluable exercises that are part of an integrated reading of socio-rhetorical criticism.

Perhaps one of the most exciting and important pieces in Robbins's socio-rhetorical model of reading the biblical narrative is that it not only allows but requires the modern readers to examine themselves in relation to the text's persuasion. This self-examination enables readers to become objects of the text's persuasion. In other words, the old scientific "laboratory" reading, where the readers distance themselves from the text for the sake of "objectivity," is not celebrated. Instead, the socio-rhetorical readers are called to react to the text according to the implied author's persuasion. In the case of the FG, that could lead one to join Thomas and confess with him that Jesus is "My Lord and my God" (John 20:28).

## Concluding remarks to Part Three

In this final part of the book, we have outlined the history of interpretation of the Fourth Gospel. The intention here has not been to provide a comprehensive account of the hermeneutical matters in relation to the FG. That would have required much more space. Instead, the purpose is

---

38. See Lincoln, *Truth on Trial*.

to describe how the FG has been handled throughout the history of interpretation, especially the more recent history, and to give a few snapshots of various interpretative approaches applied to the FG.

Today, scholars read the FG by employing various hermeneutical approaches and interpretation methodologies. The plentiful approaches become apparent by looking at the titles, sub-titles, or introductory pages of the recently published commentaries and monographs on the FG. Today's approaches concentrate on issues behind the text, in the text, or this side of the text (reader), or combining one or more of these to a comprehensive whole.

In sum, historical-critical questions are still part of the Johannine scholarship. However, they are no longer the only questions that interest scholars as more text and reader-oriented models have been introduced. The fruit of the newer approaches to the text is not yet fully mature. The most recent wave includes integrated reading models that attempt to combine various approaches to bring forth a more holistic reading. The Johannine scholarship has left still much work undone. We want to invite the readers to study the FG—the Gospel that has blessed everyone who has engaged with it—to advance our understanding of its persuasive message.

## Suggestions for Further Reading

Motyer, Stephen. *Your Father the Devil?: A New Approach to John and "the Jews."* Carlisle: Paternoster, 1997.

Neyrey, Jerome H. *The Gospel of John*. NCBC. Cambridge: Cambridge University Press, 2007.

Robbins, Vernon K. *Exploring the Texture of Texts: A Guide to Socio-Rhetorical Interpretation*. Valley Forge: Trinity International, 1996.

Stibbe, Mark W. G. *John as Storyteller: Narrative Criticism and the Fourth Gospel*. Cambridge: Cambridge University Press, 1994.

# Bibliography

Akala, Adesola J. *The Son-Father Relationship and Christological Symbolism in the Gospel of John*. London: Bloomsbury T&T Clark, 2014.

Aker, Ben C. "John." In *Life in the Spirit New Testament Commentary*, edited by French L. Arrington and Roger Stronstad, 1–118. Grand Rapids: Zondervan, 1999.

Anderson, Paul N. *The Fourth Gospel and the Quest for Jesus: Modern Foundations Reconsidered*. London: T&T Clark, 2007.

———. *The Riddles of the Fourth Gospel: An Introduction to John*. Minneapolis: Fortress, 2011.

Ashton, John. "John and the Johannine Literature: The Woman at the Well." In *The Cambridge Companion to Biblical Interpretation*, edited by John Barton, 259–75. Cambridge: Cambridge University Press, 1998.

———. *Studying John: Approaches to the Fourth Gospel*. Oxford: Clarendon Press, 1994.

———. *Understanding the Fourth Gospel*. Oxford: Clarendon, 1991.

Attridge, Harold W. "Argumentation in John 5." In *Rhetorical Argumentation in Biblical Text*, edited by Andres Eriksson et al., 188–99. ESEC. Harrisburg: Trinity International, 2002.

———. "The Temple and Jesus the High Priest in the New Testament." In *Jesus and Temple: Textual and Archaeological Explorations*, edited by James H. Charlesworth, 213–37. Minneapolis: Fortress, 2014.

Austin, J. L. *How to Do Things with Words*. 2nd ed. Edited by J. O. Urmson and Marina Sbisà. Cambridge: Harvard University Press, 1975.

Balford, Glenn. *A Step-by-Step Introduction to New Testament Greek*. Mattersey: Mattersey Hall, 2005.

———. "Is John's Gospel Antisemitic? With Special Reference to Its Use of the Old Testament." PhD diss., University of Nottingham, 1995.

Ball, David Mark. *"I Am" in John's Gospel*. Sheffield: Sheffield Academic, 1996.

Barrett, C. K. *The Gospel According to St John: An Introduction with Commentary and Notes on the Greek Text*. London: SPCK, 1967.

———. *The Gospel According to St. John: An Introduction with Commentary and Notes on the Greek Text*. 2nd ed. Philadelphia: Westminster, 1978.

———. "John and Judaism." In *Anti-Judaism and the Fourth Gospel*, edited by Reimund Bieringer et al., 231–46. Louisville: Westminster John Knox, 2001.

Bartholomew, Craig G. *Introducing Biblical Hermeneutics: A Comprehensive Framework for Hearing God in Scripture*. Grand Rapids: Baker Academic, 2015.

Barton, John, ed. *The Cambridge Companion to Biblical Interpretation*. Cambridge: Cambridge University Press, 1998.

Bauckham, Richard. *God Crucified: Monotheism & Christology in the New Testament*. Grand Rapids: Eerdmans, 1998.

———. "Holiness of Jesus and His Disciples in the Gospel of John." In *Holiness and Ecclesiology in the New Testament*, edited by Kent E. Brower and Andy Johnson, 95–113. Grand Rapids: Eerdmans, 2007.

———. *Jesus and Eyewitnesses: The Gospels as Eyewitness Testimony*. Grand Rapids: Eerdmans, 2006.

———. "Monotheism and Christology in the Gospel of John." In *Contours of Christology in the New Testament*, edited by Richard N. Longenecker, 148–66. Grand Rapids: Eerdmans, 2005.

———. *The Testimony of the Beloved Disciple: Narrative, History, and Theology in the Gospel of John*. Grand Rapids: Baker Academic, 2007.

———. *The Theology of the Book of Revelation*. Cambridge: Cambridge University Press, 1993.

Bauer, Walter. *A Greek-English Lexicon of the New Testament and Other Early Christian Literature*. Translated and edited by W. F. Arndt and F. W. Gingrich. Chicago: University of Chicago Press, 1957.

Beale, G. K. *The Book of Revelation: A Commentary on the Greek Text*. Grand Rapids: Eerdmans, 1999.

Beasley-Murray, George R. *John*. WBC 36. Waco: Word, 1987.

Bennema, Cornelis. *Encountering Jesus: Character Studies in the Gospel of John*. Milton Keynes: Paternoster, 2009.

———. *The Power of Saving Wisdom: An Investigation of Spirit and Wisdom in Relation to the Soteriology of the Fourth Gospel*. Tübingen: Mohr Siebeck, 2002.

Berg, Robert Alan. "Pneumatology and the History of the Johannine Community: Insights from the Farewell Discourses and the First Epistle." PhD diss., Drew University, 1988.

Bernard, J. H. *A Critical and Exegetical Commentary on the Gospel According to St. John*. ICC. Edinburgh: T&T Clark, 1928.

Betz, Otto. *Der Paraklet: Fürsprecher im Häretischen Spätjuderntum, im Johannes-Evangelium, und in Neu Gefundenen Gnostischischen Schriften*. Leiden: Brill, 1963.

Bieringer, Reimuld, et al. "Wrestling with Johannine Anti-Judaism: A Hermeneutical Framework for the Analysis of the Current Debate." In *Anti-Judaism and the Fourth Gospel*, edited by Reimund Bieringer et al., 3–37. Louisville: Westminster John Knox, 2001.

Blomberg, Craig L. *The Historical Reliability of John's Gospel: Issues and Commentary*. Downers Grove: InterVarsity, 2001.

Boismard, Marie-Émile. *Moses or Jesus: An Essay in Johannine Christology*. Translated by B. T. Viviano. BETL 84a. Leuven: Leuven University Press, 1993.

Borgen, Peder. "The Gospel of John and Hellenism: Some Observations." In *Exploring the Gospel of John: In Honor of D. Moody Smith*, edited by R. Alan Culpepper and C. Clifton Black, 98–123. Louisville: Westminster John Knox, 1996.

Botha, J. Eugene. *Jesus and the Samaritan Woman: A Speech Act Reading of John 4:1–42*. Leiden: Brill, 1991.

———. "John 4.16: A Difficult Text Speech Act Theoretically Revised." In *The Gospel of John as Literature: An Anthology of Twentieth-Century Perspectives*, selected and introduced by Mark W. G. Stibbe. 181–92. Leiden: Brill, 1993.

———. "Speech Act Theory and Biblical Interpretation." *Neot* 41.2 (2007) 274–94.

Botha, J. Eugene, and Riku P. Tuppurainen, "The Roles of the Spirit in John 16:4b–15: An Integrated Reading." *Acta Patristica et Byzantina* 19 (2008) 23–43.

Brant, Jo-Ann A. *John*. PCNT. Grand Rapids: Baker Academic, 2011.

Bray, Gerald. *Biblical Interpretation: Past and Present*. Leicester: InterVarsity, 1996.

Breck, John. *Spirit of Truth: The Holy Spirit in Johannine Tradition*. Vol. 1, *The Origins of Johannine Pneumatology*. Crestwood: St. Vladimir's Seminary Press, 1991.

Brenton, Lancelot. *The Septuagint Version of the Old Testament and Apocrypha with an English Translation*. London: Samuel Bagster and Sons, n.d.

Brodie, Thomas L. *The Gospel According to John: A Literary and Theological Commentary*. Oxford: Oxford University Press, 1993.

Brown, Colin. "Immanuel Kant." In *Evangelical Dictionary of Theology*, edited by Walter A. Elwell. Grand Rapids: Baker, 1984.

———, ed. *New International Dictionary of New Testament Theology*. 4 vols. Grand Rapids: Zondervan, 1975–1985.

Brown, Raymond E. *The Community of the Beloved Disciple: The Life, Loves, and Hates of an Individual Church in New Testament Times*. New York: Paulist, 1979.

———. *The Epistles of John*. AB. New York: Doubleday, 1982.

———. *Gospel According to John: A New Translation with Introduction and Commentary*. 2 vols. AB. New York: Doubleday, 1966–1970.

Brown, Tricia Gates. *Spirit in the Writings of John: Johannine Pneumatology in Social-Scientific Perspective*. JSNTSup 253. London: T&T Clark, 2003.

Bruce, F. F. *The Gospel of John: Introduction, Exposition and Notes*. Grand Rapids: Eerdmans, 1983.

Brueggemann, Walter. *Texts under Negotiation: The Bible and Postmodern Imagination*. Minneapolis: Fortress, 1993.

Bruner, Frederick Dale. *The Gospel of John: A Commentary*. Grand Rapids: Eerdmans, 2012.

Bultmann, Rudolf. *The Gospel of John: A Commentary*. Translated by G. R. Beasley-Murray et al. Philadelphia: Westminster, 1971.

———. *Jesus and the Word*. Translated by Louise Pettibone Smith and Erminie Huntress Lantero. New York: Charles Scriber's Sons, 1958.

———. *Theology of the New Testament*. Vol. 2. Translated by Kendrick Grobel. New York: Charles Scribner's Sons, 1955.

Burer, Michael H. *Divine Sabbath Work*. BBRSup 5. Winona Lake: Eisenbrauns, 2012.

Burge, Gary M. *The Anointed Community: The Holy Spirit in the Johannine Tradition*. Grand Rapids: Eerdmans, 1987.

———. "'I Am' Sayings." In *Dictionary of Jesus and the Gospels*, edited by Joel B. Green and Scott McKnight, 354–56. Downers Grove: InterVarsity, 1992.

———. *Interpreting the Gospel of John*. Grand Rapids: Baker Books, 1992.

———. *Jesus and the Jewish Festivals: Uncover the Ancient Culture, Discover Hidden Meanings*. Grand Rapids: Zondervan, 2012.

Burridge, Richard A. "The Gospels and Acts." In *Handbook of Classical Rhetoric in the Hellenistic Period 330 B.C—A.D. 400*, edited by Stanley E. Porter, 507–32. Leiden: Brill, 1997.

Carson, D. A. "The Function of the Paraclete in John 16:7-11." *JBL* 98 (1979) 547-66.

———. *The Gospel According to John*. Grand Rapids: Eerdmans, 1991.

———. "Understanding Misunderstandings." *TynBul* 33 (1982) 59-91.

Carson, D. A., et al. *An Introduction to the New Testament*. Grand Rapids: Zondervan, 1992.

Carter, Warren. *John: Storyteller, Interpreter, Evangelist*. Peabody: Hendrickson, 2006.

Casey, Maurice. *Is John's Gospel True?* London: Routledge, 1996.

Cassidy, Richard J. *John's Gospel in New Perspective*. Maryknoll: Orbis, 1992.

Charlesworth, James H. "A Critical Comparison of the Dualism in 1QS 3:13—4:26 and the 'Dualism' Contained in the Gospel of John." In *John and the Dead Sea Scrolls*, edited by James H. Charlesworth, 76-106. New York: Crossroad, 1990.

———. "The Gospel of John: Exclusivism Caused by a Social Setting Different from that of Jesus (John 11:54 and 14:6)." In *Anti-Judaism and the Fourth Gospel*, edited by Reimund Bieringer et al., 247-78. Louisville: Westminster John Knox, 2001.

———. "Jesus and the Temple." In *Jesus and Temple: Textual and Archaeological Explorations*, edited by James H. Charlesworth, 145-81. Minneapolis: Fortress, 2014.

———, ed. *Jesus and Temple: Textual and Archaeological Explorations*. Minneapolis: Fortress, 2014.

Coetzee, J. C. "The Gospel According to John: The Theology of John." In *Guide to the New Testament Volume VI: The Gospel of John: Hebrews to Revelation: Introduction and Theology*, edited by A. B. Du Toit, 40-77. Halfway House: NG Kerkboekhandel, 1993.

Collins, J. J. "Powers in Heaven: God, Gods, and Angels in the Dead Sea Scrolls." In *Religion in the Dead Sea Scrolls*, edited by J. J. Collins and R. A. Kugler, 9-28. Grand Rapids: Eerdmans, 2000.

Collins, Raymond F. "Speaking of the Jews: 'Jews' in the Discourse Material of the Fourth Gospel." In *Anti-Judaism and the Fourth Gospel*, edited by Reimund Bieringer et al., 158-75. Louisville: Westminster John Knox, 2001.

Comfort, Philip Wesley. *Early Manuscripts & Modern Translations of the New Testament*. Grand Rapids: Baker Books, 1990.

Counet, Patric Chatelion. *John, a Postmodern Gospel: Introduction to Deconstructive Exegesis Applied to the Fourth Gospel*. Leiden: Brill, 2000.

Cullmann, Oscar. *The Johannine Circle: Its Place in Judaism, among the Disciples of Jesus and in Early Christianity*. London: SCM, 1976.

Culpepper, R. Alan. *Anatomy of the Fourth Gospel: A Study in Literary Design*. Philadelphia: Fortress, 1983.

———. "Anti-Judaism in the Fourth Gospel as a Theological Problem for Christian Interpreters." In *Anti-Judaism and the Fourth Gospel*, edited by Reimund Bieringer et al., 61-82. Louisville: Westminster John Knox, 2001.

———. *The Gospel and Letter of John*. Nashville: Abingdon, 1998.

———. "John 21:24-25: The Johannine *Sphragis*." In *John, Jesus, and History. Volume 2: Aspects of Historicity in the Fourth Gospel*, edited by Paul N. Anderson et al., 349-64. Atlanta: Society of Biblical Literature, 2009.

———. *John, the Son of Zebedee: The Life of a Legend*. Edinburgh: T&T Clark, 2000.

———. "Reading Johannine Irony." In *Exploring the Gospel of John: In Honor of D. Moody Smith*, edited by R. Alan Culpepper and C. Clifton Black, 193-207. Louisville: Westminster John Knox, 1996.

Daise, Michael A. *Feasts in John: Jewish Festivals and Jesus' "Hour" in the Fourth Gospel.* WUNT 2.229. Mohr Siebeck: Tübingen, 2007.

Daly-Denton, M. "The Psalms in John's Gospel." In *The Psalms in the New Testament*, edited by S. Moyise and M. J. J. Menken, 119–37. NTSI. London: T&T Clark International, 2004.

Dana, H. E., and Julius R. Mantey. *A Manual Grammar of the Greek New Testament.* New York: Macmillan, 1957.

Daube, David. *The New Testament and Rabbinic Judaism.* New York: Arno, 1973.

Davies, Margaret. *Rhetoric and Reference in the Fourth Gospel.* JSNTS 69. Sheffield: Sheffield Academic, 1992.

Davies, W. D. "Reflections on Aspects of the Jewish Background of the Gospel of John." In *Exploring the Gospel of John*, edited by R. Alan Culpepper and C. Clifton Black, 43–64. Louisville: Westminster John Knox, 1996.

De Boer, Martinus C. "The Depiction of 'the Jews' in John's Gospel: Matters of Behavior and Identity." In *Anti-Judaism and the Fourth Gospel*, edited by Reimund Bieringer et al., 141–75. Louisville: Westminster John Knox, 2001.

De Jonge, Henk Jan. "'The Jews' in the Gospel of John." In *Anti-Judaism and the Fourth Gospel*, edited by Reimund Bieringer et al., 121–40. Louisville: Westminster John Knox, 2001.

Dennert, Brian C. "Hanukkah and the Testimony of Jesus' Works (John 10:22–39)." *JBL* 132.2 (2013) 431–51.

DeSilva, David, A. *Introducing the Apocrypha: Message, Content, and Significance.* 2nd ed. Grand Rapids: Baker Academic, 2018.

Dodd, C. H. *Historical Tradition in the Fourth Gospel.* Cambridge: Cambridge University Press, 1963.

———. *The Interpretation of the Fourth Gospel.* Cambridge: Cambridge University Press, 1968.

Dowell, Thomas M. "Why John Rewrote the Synoptics." In *John and the Synoptics*, edited by Adelbert Denaux, 452–57. Leuven: Leuven University Press, 1992.

Du Rand, J. A. "The Gospel According to John." In *Guide to the New Testament Volume VI: The Gospel of John; Hebrews to Revelation: Introduction and Theology*, edited by A. B. Du Toit, 1–77. Halfway House: NG Kerkboekhandel, 1993.

Dunn, James D. G. "The Embarrassment of History: Reflections of the Problem of 'Anti-Judaism' in the Fourth Gospel." In *Anti-Judaism and the Fourth Gospel*, edited by Reimund Bieringer et al., 41–60. Louisville: Westminster John Knox, 2001.

———. "John and the Synoptics and a Theological Question." In *Exploring the Gospel of John*, edited by R. Alan Culpepper and C. Clifton Black, 301–13. Louisville: Westminster John Knox, 1996.

———. "Let John Be John—A Gospel for Its Time." In *Das Evangelium und die Evangelien*, edited by Peter Stuhlmacher, 309–40. Tübingen: Mohr Siebeck, 1983. Reprint, Eugene: Wipf and Stock, 2017.

Elwell, Walter A., and Robert W. Yarbrough. *Encountering the New Testament: A Historical and Theological Survey.* Grand Rapids: Baker Academic, 1998.

Epstein, I., ed. *The Babylonian Talmud.* London: Soncino, 1938.

Erickson, Millard J. *The Word Became Flesh: A Contemporary Incarnational Christology.* Grand Rapids: Baker Books, 1991.

Evans, Craig A. *Ancient Texts for New Testament Studies: A Guide to the Background Literature.* Peabody: Hendrickson, 2005.

———. "Evidence of Conflict with the Synagogue in the Johannine Writings." In *John and Judaism: A Contested Relationship in Context*, edited by R. Alan Culpepper and Paul N. Anderson, 135–54. RBS 87. Atlanta: Society of Biblical Literature, 2017.

Fay, Ron C. "R. Alan Culpepper and the Literary Approach to John's Gospel." In *The Gospel of John in Modern Interpretation*, edited by Stanley E. Porter and Ron C. Fay, 211–35. Grand Rapids: Kregel, 2018.

Fee, Gordon D., and Douglas Stuart. *How to Read the Bible for All Its Worth*. 4th ed. Grand Rapids: Zondervan, 2014.

Fergusson, David. "Rudolf Bultmann (1884–1976)." In *Historical Handbook of Major Biblical Interpreters*, edited by Donald K. McKim, 449–56. Downers Grove: InterVarsity, 1998.

Flebbe, Jochen. "Feasts in John." In *Feasts and Festivals*, edited by Christopher Tuckett, 107–24. Contributions to Biblical Exegesis and Theology. Leuven: Peeters, 2009.

Forestell, J. T. "Jesus and the Paraclete in the Gospel of John." In *Word and Spirit: Essays in Honor of David Michael Stanley*, edited by J. Plevnik, 151–97. Toronto: Regis College Press, 1975.

Fortna, Robert T. "Diachronic / Synchronic Reading John 21 and Luke 5." In *John and the Synoptics*, edited by Adelbert Denaux, 387–99. Leuven: Leuven University Press, 1992.

Fortna, Robert T., and Tom Thatcher, eds. *Jesus in Johannine Traditions*. Louisville: Westminster John Knox, 2001.

Franck, Eskil. *Revelation Taught: The Paraclete in the Gospel of John*. CBNTSer 14. Malmö: CWK Gleerup, 1985.

Glasson, T. Francis. *Moses in the Fourth Gospel*. SBT. London: SCM, 1963.

Godet, Frederick Louis. *Commentary on the Gospel of John*. 3rd ed. Funk & Wagnalls Company, 1893. Reprint, Grand Rapids: Zondervan, n.d.

Graham, Daniel W. "Heraclitus." In *Stanford Encyclopedia of Philosophy* (Fall 2019 edition), edited by Edward N. Zalta. Accessed June 13, 2019. https://plato.stanford.edu/entries/heraclitus/.

Grant, Robert M. *A Short History of the Interpretation of the Bible*. With David Tracy. 2nd ed. Minneapolis: Fortress, 1984.

Grayston, K. "The Meaning of *PARAKLĒTOS*." *JSNT* 13 (1981) 67–82.

Hagner, Donald A. *The New Testament: A Historical and Theological Introduction*. Grand Rapids: Baker Academic, 2012.

Hamid-Khani, Saeed. *Revelation and Concealment of Christ: A Theological Inquiry into the Elusive Language of the Fourth Gospel*. Tübingen: Mohr Siebeck, 2000.

Harner, Philip B. *The "I Am" of the Fourth Gospel: A Study in Johannine Usage and Thought*. Philadelphia: Fortress, 1970.

Harris, Elizabeth. *Prologue and Gospel: The Theology of the Fourth Evangelist*. JSNTSup 107. Sheffield: Sheffield Academic, 1994.

Harris, Murray J. *John: Exegetical Guide to the Greek New Testament*. Nashville: B&H Academic, 2015.

———. *Prepositions and Theology in Greek New Testament*. Grand Rapids: Zondervan, 2012.

Harstine, Stan. *Moses as a Character in the Fourth Gospel: A Study of Ancient Reading Techniques*. JNTSup 229. Sheffield: Sheffield Academic, 2002.

Hegel, Martin. "The Prologue of the Gospel of John as the Gateway to Christological Truth." In *The Gospel of John and Christian Theology*, edited by Richard Bauckham and Carl Mosser, 265–94. Grand Rapids: Eerdmans, 2008.

Helyer, Larry R. *The Witness of Jesus, Paul and John: An Exploration in Biblical Theology*. Downers Grove: IVP Academic, 2008.

Hendriksen, William. *Exposition of the Gospel According to John*. Grand Rapids: Baker Book House, 1953.

Hengel, Martin. *The Johannine Question*. Philadelphia: Trinity International, 1989.

———. "The Prologue of the Gospel of John as the Gateway to Christological Truth." In *The Gospel of John and Christian Theology*, edited by Richard Bauckham and Carl Mosser, 265–94. Grand Rapids: Eerdmans, 2008.

Hernando, James D. *Dictionary of Hermeneutics: A Concise Guide to Terms, Names, Methods, and Expressions*. Springfield: Gospel Publishing House, 2005.

Hillar, Marian. "Philo of Alexandria. (c. 20 B.C.E.—40 C.E.)" In *Internet Encyclopedia of Philosophy*. Accessed Sep. 12, 2019. https://www.iep.utm.edu/philo/.

Hoehner, Harold W. "Chronological Aspects of the Life of Christ, Part IV: The Day of Christ's Crucifixion." *BSac* 131 (1974) 241–64.

Holladay, William L., ed. *A Concise Hebrew and Aramaic Lexicon of the Old Testament*. Leiden: Brill, 1988.

Hoskins, Paul M. *Jesus as the Fulfillment of the Temple in the Gospel of John*. Bucks: Paternoster, 2006.

Howard, James M. "The Significance of Minor Characters in the Gospel of John." *BSac* 163 (2002) 63–78.

Jackson, Howard M. "Ancient Self-Referential Conversations and Their Implications for the Authorship and Integrity of the Gospel of John." *JTS* 50 (1999) 1–34.

Jasper, David. *A Short Introduction to Hermeneutics*. Louisville: Westminster John Knox, 2004.

———. "Literary Reading of the Bible." In *The Cambridge Companion to Biblical Interpretation*, edited by John Barton, 21–34. Cambridge: Cambridge University Press, 1998.

Jenney, Timothy P. "The Vocabulary and Phraseology of Revelation." In *But These Are Written . . . : Essays on Johannine Literature in Honor of Professor Benny C. Aker*, edited by Craig S. Keener et al., 247–57. Eugene: Pickwick, 2014.

Jensen, Matthew D. "John Is No Exception: Identifying the Subject of εἰμί and Its Implication." *JBL* 135 (2016) 341–53.

Jipp, Joshua W. "Raymond E. Brown and the Fourth Gospel: Composition and Community." In *The Gospel of John in Modern Interpretation*, edited in Stanley E. Porter and Ron C. Fay 173–96. Grand Rapids: Kregel Academic, 2018.

Jobes, Karen H. *1, 2, 3 John: Zondervan Exegetical Commentary on the New Testament*. Grand Rapids: Zondervan, 2014.

Johnson, Brian D. "The Jewish Feast and Questions of Historicity in John 5–12." In *John, Jesus, and History, Volume 2: Aspects of Historicity in the Fourth Gospel*, edited by Paul N. Anderson et al., 117–29. Atlanta: Society of Biblical Literature, 2009.

Johnson, Darrell W. *Discipleship on the Edge: An Expository Journey through the Book of Revelation*. Vancouver: Regent College, 2004.

Kanagaraj, Jey J. *John*. NCCS. Eugene: Cascade, 2013.

———. *"Mysticism" in the Gospel of John: An Inquiry into Its Background*. JSNTSup 158. Sheffield: Sheffield Academic, 1998.

Kärkkäinen, Veli-Matti. *Christology: A Global Introduction*. Grand Rapids: Baker Academic, 2003.

———. *Pneumatology: The Holy Spirit in Ecumenical, International, and Contextual Perspective*. Grand Rapids: Baker, 2002.

Käsemann, Ernst. *The Testament of Jesus*. Translated by Gerhard Krodel. Philadelphia: Fortress, 1978.

Keener, Craig S. *Acts: An Exegetical Commentary*. Grand Rapids: Baker Academic, 2012.

———. *Bible Background Commentary: New Testament*. Downers Grove: InterVarsity, 1993.

———. *Christobiography: Memory, History, and the Reliability of the Gospels*. Grand Rapids: Eerdmans, 2019.

———. *The Gospel of John: A Commentary*. Peabody: Hendrickson, 2003.

———. *Miracles: The Credibility of the New Testament Accounts*. Grand Rapids: Baker Academic, 2011.

Kim, Dangsoo. "The Paraclete: The Spirit of the Church," *AJPS* 5 (2002) 255–70.

Kittel, Gerhard, and Gerhard Friedrich, eds. *Theological Dictionary of the New Testament*. Translated by Geoffrey W. Bromiley. 10 vols. Grand Rapids: Eerdmans, 1964–1976.

Klein, William W, et al. *Introduction to Biblical Interpretation*. Revised ed. Nashville: Thomas Nelson, 2004.

Klink, Edward W., III. *John*. Zondervan Exegetical Commentary on the New Testament. Grand Rapids: Zondervan, 2016.

Koester, Craig R. *Dwelling of God: Tabernacle in the Old Testament, Intertestamental Jewish Literature and the New Testament*. CBQMS 22. Washington: Catholic Biblical Association of America, 1989.

———. *Symbolism in the Fourth Gospel: Meaning, Mystery, Community*. 2nd ed. Minneapolis: Fortress, 2003.

Köstenberger, Andreas J. "John." In *Commentary on the New Testament Use of the Old Testament*, edited by G. K. Beale and D. A. Carson, 415–512. Grand Rapids: Baker Academic, 2007.

———. *A Theology of John's Gospel and Letters*. Biblical Theology of the New Testament Series. Grand Rapids: Zondervan, 2009.

Kysar, Robert. *John: The Maverick Gospel*. 3rd ed. Louisville: Westminster John Knox, 2007.

Lategan, B. C. "Current Issues in the Hermeneutical Debate." *Neot* 19 (1984) 1–17.

Lee, Dorothy A. *The Symbolic Narratives of the Fourth Gospel: The Interplay of Form and Meaning*. JSNTsup 95. Sheffield: Sheffield Academic, 1994.

Levison, John R. *Filled with the Spirit*. Grand Rapids: Eerdmans, 2009.

Lieu, Judith. "Anti-Judaism, the Jews, and the Worlds of the Fourth Gospel." In *The Gospel of John and Christian Theology*, edited by Richard Bauckham and Carl Mosser, 168–82. Grand Rapids: Eerdmans, 2008.

Lincoln, Andrew L. *Truth on Trial: The Lawsuit Motif in the Fourth Gospel*. Peabody: Hendricksen, 2000.

Loader, William. *Jesus in John's Gospel: Structure and Issues in Johannine Christology*. Grand Rapids: Eerdmans, 2017.

Louw, Johannes P., and Eugene A. Nida. *Greek-English Lexicon of the New Testament Based on Semantic Domains*. New York: United Bible Societies, 1988.

Macchia, Frank D. "The Spirit of the Lamb: A Reflection on the Pneumatology of Revelation." In *But These Are Written . . . : Essays on Johannine Literature in Honor of Professor Benny C. Aker*, edited by Craig S. Keener et al., 214–20. Eugene: Pickwick, 2014.

Malina, Bruce J., and Richard L. Rohrbaugh. *Social-Science Commentary on the Gospel of John*. Minneapolis: Fortress, 1998.

Mangina, Joseph L. "God, Israel, and Ecclesia in the Apocalypse." In *Revelation and the Politics of Apocalyptic Interpretation*, edited by Richard B. Hays and Stefan Alkier, 85–103. Waco: Baylor University Press, 2012.

Manson, William. *Jesus and the Christian*. Greenwood: Attic, 1967.

Martyn, J. Louis. *History and Theology in the Fourth Gospel*. 3rd ed. NTL. Louisville: Westminster John Knox, 2003.

Matera, Frank J. *New Testament Theology: Exploring Diversity and Unity*. Louisville: Westminster John Knox, 2007.

McGrath, James F. *The Only True God: Early Christian Monotheism in Its Jewish Context*. Chicago: University of Illinois Press, 2009.

McHugh, John F. *A Critical and Exegetical Commentary on John 1–4*. ICC. London: T&T Clark, 2009.

McKim, Donald, ed. *Historical Handbook of Major Biblical Interpreters*. Downers Grove: InterVarsity, 1998.

Meeks, Wayne A. "'Am I a Jew?'—Johannine Christianity and Judaism." In *Christianity, Judaism, and Other Greco-Roman Cults: Studies for Morton Smith at Sixty*, edited by Jacob Neusner, 163–86. Leiden: Brill, 1975.

———. "Breaking Away: Three New Testament Pictures of Christianity's Separation from the Jewish Communities." In *"To See Ourselves as Others See Us": Christians, Jews, "Others" in Late Antiquity*, edited by J. Neusner et al., 93–115. Chico: Scholars, 1985.

Menken, Maarten J. J. *Old Testament Quotations in the Fourth Gospel: Studies in Textual Form*. Kampen: Kok Pharos, 1996.

Metzger, Bruce, M. *A Textual Commentary on the Greek New Testament*. 2nd ed. Stuttgart: United Bible Societies, 1994.

Meyer, Paul W. "The Presentation of God in the Fourth Gospel." In *Exploring the Gospel of John: In Honor of D. Moody Smith*, edited by R. Alan Culpepper and C. Clifton Black, 255–73. Louisville: Westminster John Knox, 1996.

Michaels, J. Ramsey. *John*. Good News Commentaries. San Francisco: Harper & Row, 1984.

Minear, Paul S. "The Original Functions of John 21." *JBL* 102 (1983) 85–98.

Morris, Leon. *The Gospel According to John*. Revised ed. NICNT. Grand Rapids: Eerdmans, 1995.

———. *Revelation*. TNTC. Grand Rapids: Eerdmans, 1987.

———. *Studies in the Fourth Gospel*. Exeter: Paternoster, 1969. Reprint, Eugene: Wipf and Stock, 2006.

Motyer, Stephen. "Bridging the Gap: How Might the Fourth Gospel Help Us Cope with the Legacy of Christianity's Exclusive Claim Over Against Judaism?" In *The Gospel of John and Christian Theology*, edited by Richard Bauckham and Carl Mosser, 143–67. Grand Rapids: Eerdmans, 2008.

———. "Method in Fourth Gospel Studies: A Way Out of the Impasse?" *JSNT* 66 (1997) 27–44.

———. *Your Father the Devil? A New Approach to John and "the Jews."* PBTS. Carlisle: Paternoster, 1997.

Mounce, William D. *Basics of Biblical Greek: Grammar.* Grand Rapids: Zondervan, 1993.

Myers, Alicia D. *Characterizing Jesus: A Rhetorical Analysis on the Fourth Gospel's Use of Scripture in Its Presentation of Jesus.* London: T&T Clark, 2012.

Neufeld, Dietmar, ed. *The Social Sciences and Biblical Translation.* Symposium Series 41. Atlanta: Society of Biblical Literature, 2008.

Neusner, Jacob, trans. *The Mishnah: A New Translation.* London: Yale University Press, 1988.

Newman, Barclay M., and Eugene A. Nida. *A Translator's Handbook on the Gospel of John.* London: United Bible Societies, 1980.

Neyrey, Jerome H. *The Gospel of John.* NCBC. Cambridge: Cambridge University Press, 2007.

———. *The Gospel of John in Cultural and Rhetorical Perspective.* Grand Rapids: Eerdmans, 2009.

North, Wendy E. *What John Knew and What John Wrote: A Study in John and the Synoptics.* Interpreting Johannine Literature. Minneapolis: Fortress Academic, 2020.

O'Connell, Jake H. "A Note on Papias's Knowledge of the Fourth Gospel." *JSBL* 129 (2010) 793–94.

O'Day, Gail R. "Miracle Discourse and the Gospel of John." In *Miracle Discourse in the New Testament*, edited by Dane F. Watson, 175–88. Atlanta: Society of Biblical Literature, 2012.

O'Neill, J. C. "The Jews in the Fourth Gospel." *ISB* 18 (1996) 58–74.

Oeming, Manfred. *Contemporary Biblical Hermeneutics: An Introduction.* Translated by Joachim Vette. Vermont: Ashgate, 2006.

Ostenstand, Gunnar H. *Patterns of Redemption in the Fourth Gospel: An Experiment in Structural Analysis.* Studies in the Bible and Early Christianity 38. Lewiston: Edwin Mellern, 1998.

Parsons, Mikeal C. "A Neglected ΕΓΩ ΕΙΜΙ Saying in the Fourth Gospel? Another Look at John 9:9." In *Perspectives on John: Method and Interpretation in the Fourth Gospel*, edited by Robert B. Sloan and Mikeal C. Parsons, 145–80. Lewiston: E. Mellen, 1993.

Patte, Daniel. *What is Structural Exegesis?* NTSer. Philadelphia: Fortress, 1976.

Pilch, John J., ed. *Social Scientific Models for Interpreting the Bible: Essays by the Context Group in Honor of Bruce J. Malina.* Leiden: Brill, 2001.

Pippin, Tina. "'For Fear of the Jews': Lying and Truth-Telling in Translating the Gospel of John." *Semeia* 76 (1996) 81–97.

Porter, Stanley E. *John, His Gospel, and Jesus: In Pursuit of the Johannine Voice.* Grand Rapids: Eerdmans, 2015.

Porter, Stanley E., and Ron C. Fay, eds. *The Gospel of John in Modern Interpretation.* Grand Rapids: Kregel Academic, 2018.

Provan, Iain. *The Reformation and the Right Reading of Scripture.* Waco: Baylor University Press, 2017.

Reinhartz, Adale. "'Jews' and Jews in the Fourth Gospel." In *Anti-Judaism and the Gospel of John*, edited by Reimund Bieringer et al., 213–27. Louisville: Westminster John Knox, 2001.

Ridderbos, Herman. *The Gospel of John: A Theological Commentary.* Translated by John Vriend. Grand Rapids: Eerdmans, 1997.
Robbins, Vernon K. *Exploring the Texture of the Texts: A Guide to Socio-Rhetorical Interpretation.* Valley Forge: Trinity International, 1996.
———. *Tapestry of Early Christian Discourse: Rhetoric, Society and Ideology.* London: Routledge, 1996.
Robertson, A. T. *A Grammar of the Greek New Testament in the Light of Historical Research.* Nashville: Broadman, 1934.
Rosenau, Pauline Marie. *Post-Modernism and Social Sciences: Insights, Inroads, and Intrusions.* Princeton: Princeton University Press, 1992.
Routledge, Robin. *Old Testament Theology: A Thematic Approach.* Nottingham: Apollos, 2008.
Sandmel, S. *Anti-Semitism in the New Testament?* Philadelphia: Fortress, 1978.
Schiffman, Lawrence H. "The Importance of the Temple for Ancient Jews." In *Jesus and Temple: Textual and Archaeological Explorations*, edited by James H. Charlesworth, 75–93. Minneapolis: Fortress, 2014.
Schild, E. "On Exodus iii 14—'I Am That I Am.'" In *Vestus Testamentum* 4 (1954) 296–302.
Schnackenburg, Rudolf. *The Gospel According to St. John.* New York: Seabury, 1968–1980.
Schüssler Fiorenza, Elisabeth. *The Book of Revelation: Justice and Judgment.* Philadelphia: Fortress, 1985.
Shepherd, David. "'Do You Love me?' A Narrative-Critical Reappraisal of ἀγαπάω and φιλέω in John 21:15–17." *JBL* 129 (2010) 777–92.
Sheridan, Ruth. "Issues in the Translation of οἱ Ἰουδαῖοι in the Fourth Gospel." *JBL* 132 (2013) 671–95.
Skaggs, Rebecca, and Priscilla C. Benham. *Revelation.* PCS. Dorset: Deo, 2009.
Smalley, Stephen S. *1, 2, 3 John.* WBC. Waco: Word, 1984.
———. *John: Evangelist and Interpreter.* Exeter: Paternoster, 1983.
Smith, D. Moody. *The Fourth Gospel in Four Dimensions: Judaism and Jesus, the Gospels and Scripture.* South Carolina: University of South Carolina Press, 2008.
———. "Judaism and the Gospel of John." In *Jews and Christians: Exploring the Past, Present, and Future*, edited by James H. Charlesworth, 76–99. New York: Crossroad, 1990.
———. *The Theology of the Gospel of John.* Cambridge: Cambridge University Press, 1995.
Staley, Jeffrey L. *The Print's First Kiss: A Rhetorical Investigation of the Implied Reader in the Fourth Gospel.* Atlanta: Scholars, 1988.
Stauffer, Ethelbert. *Jesus and His Story.* New York: Alfred A. Knopf, 1959.
Stevick, Daniel B. *Jesus and His Own: A Commentary on John 13–17.* Grand Rapids: Eerdmans, 2011.
Stibbe, Mark W. G. *The Gospel of John as Literature: An Anthology of Twentieth-Century Perspectives.* Leiden: Brill, 1993.
———. *John as Storyteller: Narrative Criticism and the Fourth Gospel.* Cambridge: Cambridge University Press, 1992.
Tenney, Merrill C. *John: The Expositor's Bible Commentary with the New International Version.* Grand Rapids: Zondervan, 1995.
———. *John: The Gospel of Belief.* Grand Rapids: Eerdmans, 1997.

Thatcher, Tom. "Introduction." In *Jesus in Johannine Tradition*, edited by Robert T. Fortna and Tom Thatcher, 1–9. Louisville: Westminster John Knox, 2001.

———. "The Riddles of Jesus in the Johannine Dialogues." In *Jesus in Johannine Tradition*, edited by Robert T. Fortna and Tom Thatcher, 263–77. Louisville: Westminster John Knox, 2001.

———. *Why John Wrote a Gospel: Jesus—Memory—History*. Louisville: Westminster John Knox, 2006.

Thiselton, Anthony C. *Interpreting God and the Postmodern Self: On Meaning, Manipulation and Promise*. Grand Rapids: Eerdmans, 1995.

———. *New Horizons in Hermeneutics: The Theory and Practice of Transforming Biblical Reading*. Grand Rapids: Zondervan, 1992.

———. "New Testament Interpretation in Historical Perspective." In *Hearing the New Testament: Strategies for Interpretation*, edited by Joel B. Green, 10–36. Grand Rapids: Eerdmans, 1995.

———. *Thiselton on Hermeneutics: Collected Works with New Essays*. Grand Rapids: Eerdmans, 2006.

Thomas, John Christopher. *The Apocalypse: A Literary and Theological Commentary*. Cleveland: CPT, 2012.

———. "The Spirit in the Book of Revelation: A Narrative Hearing." In *Reading St. Luke's Text and Theology: Pentecostal Voices: Essays in Honor of Professor Roger Stronstad*, edited by Riku P. Tuppurainen, 254–64. Eugene: Pickwick, 2019.

Thompson, Marianne Meye. *John: A Commentary*. NTL. Louisville: Westminster John Knox, 2015.

———. "Reading What Is Written in the Book of Life: Theological Interpretation of the Book of Revelation Today." In *Revelation and the Politics of Apocalyptic Interpretation*, edited by Richard B. Hays and Stefan Alkier, 155–71. Waco: Baylor University Press, 2012.

Tolmie, D. Francois. *Jesus' Farewell to the Disciples: John 13:1—17:26 in Narratological Perspective*. New York: Brill, 1995.

Tomson, Peter J. "'Jews' in the Gospel of John as Compared with the Palestinian Talmud, the Synoptics, and Some New Testament Apocrypha." In *Anti-Judaism and the Fourth Gospel*, edited by Reimund Bieringer et al., 176–212. Louisville: Westminster John Knox, 2001.

Torrance, David W., and Thomas F. Torrance, eds. *The Gospel According to St John 11–21 and the First Epistle of John*. Calvin's Commentaries. Translated by T. H. L. Parker. Grand Rapids: Eerdmans, 1959.

Tovey, Derek. *Narrative Art and Act in the Fourth Gospel*. JSNTSS 151. Sheffield: Sheffield Academic, 1997.

Tuppurainen, Riku P. "Jesus, the Spirit, and the Church: Succession in the Fourth Gospel." *JEPTA* 36 (2016) 42–56.

———. "Reading St. Luke's Narrative as 'Texture': Acts 2:1–4 in the Light of Socio-Rhetorical Criticism." In *Reading St. Luke's Text and Theology: Pentecostal Voices: Essays in Honor of Professor Roger Stronstad*, edited by Riku P. Tuppurainen, 48–60. Eugene: Pickwick, 2019.

———. "The Role(s) of the Spirit-Paraclete in John 16:4b-15: A Socio-Rhetorical Investigation," DTh diss., University of South Africa, 2006.

———. "The Whole World or Not Quite: ΚΟΣΜΟΣ in John 16:8." *Journal of Early Christian History* 1 (2011) 165–84.

Twelftree, Graham H. "Exorcisms in the Fourth Gospel and the Synoptics." In *Jesus in Johannine Tradition*, edited by Robert T. Fortna and Tom Thatcher, 135–53. Louisville: Westminster John Knox, 2001.

Van der Horst, P. W. "The Birkat H-Minim in Recent Research." In *Hellenism-Judaism-Christianity: Essays on Their Interaction*, edited P. W. Van der Horst, 113–24. Leuven: Peeters, 1998.

VanGemeren, Willem A., ed. *New International Dictionary of Old Testament Theology and Exegesis*. 5 vols. Grand Rapids: Zondervan, 1997.

Wahlde, Urban C. von "The Pool of Siloam: The Importance of the New Discoveries for Our Understanding of Ritual Immersion in Late Second Temple Judaism and the Gospel of John." In *John, Jesus, and History. Volume 2: Aspects of Historicity in the Fourth Gospel*, edited by Paul Anderson et al., 155–73. Atlanta: Society of Biblical Literature, 2009.

Wallace, Daniel B. *Greek Grammar Beyond the Basics: An Exegetical Syntax of the New Testament*. Grand Rapids: Zondervan, 1996.

Wayne A. Meeks. *In Search of the Early Christians: Selected Essays*. New Haven: Yale University Press, 2002.

Westcott, B. F. *The Gospel According to St. John: With Introduction and Notes*. London: John Murray, 1896.

Wheaton, Gerry. *The Role of Jewish Feasts in John's Gospel*. SNTS 162. Cambridge: Cambridge University Press, 2015.

Whitenton, Michael R. "The Dissembler of John 3: A Cognitive and Rhetorical Approach to the Characterization of Nicodemus." *JBL* 135 (2016) 141–58.

Wigram, George V. *The Englishman's Greek Concordance of the New Testament*. Peabody: Hendrickson, 1998.

Williams, Catrin H. "'I Am' or 'I Am He'?: Self-Declaratory Pronouncements in the Fourth Gospel and Rabbinic Traditions." In *Jesus in Johannine Tradition*, edited by Robert T. Fortna and Tom Thatcher, 343–52. Louisville: Westminster John Knox, 2001.

Wink, Walter. "'The Son of Man' in the Gospel of John." In *Jesus in Johannine Tradition*, edited by Robert T. Fortna and Tom Thatcher. Louisville: Westminster John Knox, 2001.

Witherington, Ben, III. *John's Wisdom: A Commentary on the Fourth Gospel*. Cambridge: Lutterworth, 1995.

Wolfson, Harry A. "Philo Judaeus." In *Encyclopedia of Philosophy*, 2nd ed, edited by Donald M. Borchert, 7:303–4. Detroit: Thomson Gale, 2006.

Wright, N. T. and Michael F. Bird. *New Testament in Its World: An Introduction to History, Literature, and Theology of the First Christians*. Grand Rapids: Zondervan Academic, 2019.

Yarchin, William. *History of Biblical Interpretation: A Reader*. Peabody: Hendrickson, 2004.

Yee, Gale A. *Jewish Feasts and the Gospel of John*. Eugene: Wipf and Stock, 2007.

www.ingramcontent.com/pod-product-compliance
Lightning Source LLC
Chambersburg PA
CBHW071438300426
44114CB00013B/1484